D0080278

THE
EUROPEAN
RENAISSANCE

1400–1600

ARTS, CULTURE AND SOCIETY IN THE WESTERN WORLD

GENERAL EDITOR: BORIS FORD

This major new series examines the arts and culture of Western civilization within the social, economic and political context of the time. Richly illustrated, each book is structured around a concept of the age as a whole, integrating the different arts into a single analytical portrait of it. Music, literature and drama will be as important to the argument as architecture and the visual arts. The books will give readers their bearings in the cultural landscape via its major landmarks; but, more particularly, they will also examine the artistic activity of the age for what it can tell us of the preoccupations and priorities of the society that produced it.

Now available:

The Enlightenment and the Age of Revolution 1700–1850
JOHN SWEETMAN

Gothic Europe 1200–1450
DEREK PEARSALL

The European Renaissance 1400–1600
ROBIN KIRKPATRICK

THE EUROPEAN RENAISSANCE

1400–1600

ROBIN KIRKPATRICK

Longman

An imprint of **Pearson Education**

Harlow, England · London · New York · Reading, Massachusetts · San Francisco
Toronto · Don Mills, Ontario · Sydney · Tokyo · Singapore · Hong Kong · Seoul
Taipei · Cape Town · Madrid · Mexico City · Amsterdam · Munich · Paris · Milan

PEARSON EDUCATION LIMITED

Head Office:
Edinburgh Gate
Harlow CM20 2JE
Tel: +44 (0)1279 623623
Fax: +44 (0)1279 431059

London Office:
128 Long Acre
London WC2E 9AN
Tel: +44 (0)20 7447 2000
Fax: +44 (0)20 7240 5771

Website: www.history-minds.com

First published in Great Britain in 2002

© Pearson Education 2002

The right of Robin Kirkpatrick to be identified as author
of this Work has been asserted by him in accordance
with the Copyright, Designs and Patents Act 1988.

ISBN 0 582 29444 4 (PPR)
ISBN 0 582 29445 2 (CSD)

British Library Cataloguing-in-Publication Data
A CIP catalogue record for this book can be obtained from the British Library

10 9 8 7 6 5 4 3 2 1

Set in 10/12pt Sabon by Graphicraft Limited, Hong Kong
Produced by Pearson Education Malaysia Sdn Bhd
Printed and bound in Great Britain by Biddles Ltd, *www.biddles.co.uk*

The Publishers' policy is to use paper manufactured from sustainable forests.

TO MY COLLEAGUES AND ALL THOSE I HAVE
TAUGHT IN THE FACULTIES OF MODERN AND
MEDIEVAL LANGUAGES AND ENGLISH AT THE
UNIVERSITY OF CAMBRIDGE

1978–2001

CONTENTS

GENERAL INTRODUCTION

In these days of ever greater specialization, few people who write about the arts venture beyond their particular field, and virtually none dare to stray over the boundary into an adjacent art. This is a serious loss, for the arts in any age are bound to share common ideals and characteristics and they emerge, after all, from the same society even if they address somewhat different audiences. And thus they can illuminate each other, both through their similarities and contrasts.

This series of ten volumes aims to present and study Western civilization as expressed in its arts, including the social and economic soil from which these arts rose and flourished. The scope (but not necessarily the titles) of these volumes is as follows:

The Greek World

The Roman World

Early Medieval Europe (from the late Empire to c.950)

Romanesque Europe (c.950–c.1200)

Gothic Europe (1200–1450)

The European Renaissance (1400–1600)

Baroque Europe (c.1575–c.1750)

The Enlightenment and the Age of Revolution (1700–1850)

The Romantic Age (c.1800–1914)

The Twentieth Century

The series as a whole does not resemble an encyclopedia of the arts, with chapters on the separate arts. Built around a concept of the age and its distinctive civilization, the central argument of each volume is illuminated by a discussion of individual artists and their works, including popular culture; and of how, by looking at their social roles, their conventions and symbolism, and their formal structures, these works of art may best be understood and enjoyed.

Finally, the series provides a social, political and economic context for these works, and examines the artistic activity of the age for what it can tell us of the preoccupations and priorities of the society that produced it.

BORIS FORD

PREFACE

This book has developed over a number of years in response to a number of different questions. Many of these questions originated in early and very stimulating discussions with the General Editor of the series, the late Boris Ford and with Andrew McLennan, both of whom were rightly concerned that this account of the Renaissance should speak of Europe at large and not be too constricted by conventional dates of origin or conclusion. The aim should also be to deal with each of the major arts but to place them in their social and intellectual context.

This generous vision proved to be particularly stimulating for an author whose main concerns had hitherto been Dante and Shakespeare. The study of Dante inclined him to believe that the Renaissance need not be approached in a spirit of undiluted enthusiasm (as if all history were benignly a matter of progress) and also suggested that, from an Italian point of view, the beginnings of the Renaissance era might be dated much earlier than they often are – and certainly earlier than the date as specified, conventionally, in my title. In this regard the present volume follows on from its excellent predecessor in this series, Derek Pearsall's *Gothic Europe 1200–1450* and re-interprets some material – especially from Northern Europe – that has hitherto been regarded as Gothic as being a direct contribution to the development of Renaissance thought and style. A reading of Shakespeare, on the other hand, led to the realization that, while much that is characteristic of the Renaissance is first formed in Italy, the full development of these original impulses is often to be found elsewhere and often to be appreciated best from later points in the conventional period.

Shakespeare's own response to the Renaissance also revealed further grounds for caution in our enthusiasm for the period. For his plays point to much that remains unresolved, conflictual and uncomfortable in a vision that is often supposed to be joyously self-confident. At one point, this book might reasonably have been entitled 'The Tragic Renaissance' – save that Shakespeare's critical view is as well expressed in comedy as in tragedy. The book, however, will have suceeded in its purpose only if it prompts further debate on both general issues and particular texts. Indeed, for reasons that will appear in the Introduction, I am more concerned with questions and with the adjustment of certain emphases in standard positions than with offering any complete survey of all the artists in all the fields under consideration; and I am well aware of the absence of certain important topics, as for example the relation between Islam and the Western World in this period. Each topic that I attempt to deal with deserves – and has usually received elsewhere – book-length treatment in its own right. For general arguments I am indebted to many experts in many fields, and have indicated particular debts in the bibliographies to each chapter. There could at any point have been an endless series of footnotes. It was either all or none.

In pursuing this debate through many countries and over a relatively wide time-span, I have been greatly assisted by my colleagues in the Faculty of Modern and Medieval Languages at Cambridge, to whom this work is dedicated, and especially though not exclusively to Virginia Cox, Liz Guild, George Gomöri, Anthony Close and the members of the Interdisciplinary Seminar on Renaissance Studies. I am grateful to Tiarnan O'Cleirigh for his vital contribution to the discussion of Renaissance music. I am especially grateful to Bill Sherman and Steve Milner for their scrupulous reading of the manuscript and for their many illuminating comments and criticisms. I alone am to blame for the faults that remain. Nor would the excitement that particular texts and examples have stimulated have been as acute as it has been without the constant enthusiasms and constantly changing emphases that emerge in discussion with Cambridge students. Finally, my very warmest thanks are due to the editorial team of Pearson Educational, to Heather McCallum, Emily Pillars and Faith Perkins for their efficiency, clarity of decision and above all their enthusiasm. It has been the utmost pleasure to work with them over the years and a welcome reminder that not all publishers hate books.

LIST OF ILLUSTRATIONS

Figure 1 Raphael, *Baldassare Castiglione*, c.1515, Canvas, 81.9 × 67.3 cm. The Louvre, Paris. With permission from Scala (ref. K88132).

Figure 2 Albrecht Dürer, *The Great Cannon*, 1518, Etching 27.3 × 38.7 cm. This figure is reproduced by kind permission of the Syndics of the Fitzwilliam Museum, Cambridge.

Figure 3 Masaccio, *The Raising of the Son of Theophilus*, c. 1425 (completed by Filippino Lippi), Fresco. Brancacci Chapel, Church of the Carmine, Florence. With permission from Scala (ref. K104993).

Figure 4 Gentile da Fabbriano, *Adoration of the Magi*, 1423, Panel 299.3 × 282 cm. The Ufffizi Gallery, Florence. With permission from Scala (ref. K90133).

Figure 5 Giovanni Antonio Amadeo, *Façade of the Certosa*, Pavia, 1473-first half of the 16th century. With permission from Scala (ref. KS00171).

Figure 6 Androgynous, *Portrait of Francis I*, (detail). Bibliothèque Nationale, Paris.

Figure 7 Leonbattista Alberti, *Terrace to surround a Market place*, from *De Re Aedificatoria. VIII* c.1450 (illustrated from Italian translation, C. Bartoli, 1550). This figure is reproduced by kind permission of the Syndics of the Cambridge University Library.

Figure 8 Luciano Laurana (designer; probably painted by Piero della Francesca), *View of an Ideal City*, late 15th century, Panel, 60.5 × 200.5 cm. Galleria Nazionale delle Marche, Palazzo Ducale, Urbino. With permission from Scala (ref. K69162).

Figure 9 Perugino, *Christ giving the Keys to St Peter*. Fresco Sistine Chapel, Rome. With permission from Scala (ref. K91560).

Figure 10 Medieval Towers of San Gimigniano, Tuscany. With permission from Scala (ref. K69668).

Figure 11 Filippo Brunelleschi, *Ospedale degli Innocent*, begun 1419 and completed mid-15th century. Piazza della SS. Annunziata, Florence. With permission from Scala (ref. K66513).

Figure 12 Filippo Brunelleschi, *The Dome at the Cathedral at Florence*, 1420–1436. With permission from Scala (ref. K26662).

Figure 13 Leonbattista Alberti, *Façade of Santa Maria Novella*, c.1456–70, Florence. With permission from Scala (ref. K76894).

Figure 14 Piero della Francesca, *Profile Portraits of Federigo da Montefeltro and his wife Battista Sforza*, c.1478, Panel, 47 cm × 33 cm. Uffizi Gallery, Florence. With permission from Scala (ref. K119449).

Colour plate section:

NOTES ON THE COVER

Cover Illustration: Isaac Oliver *Unknown Man*. c.1610, vellum on card 55.2 × 43.75 cm. Victoria and Albert Museum (Ham House 379–1948).

This image may be taken to reflect many of the skills and tensions that had spread throughout Europe by the end of the sixteenth century. The artist, Isaac Oliver (1560–1617), son of a Rouen goldsmith, came to London with his family in 1568 as a refugee, fleeing the French Wars of Religion, and worked for a time with Nicholas Hilliard, whose *Art of Limning* skilfully adapts lessons drawn ultimately from Alberti and Dürer to the sophisticated demands of miniaturism. Oliver maintains his own distinctive style, nurtured by an acquaintance particularly with the art of the Low Countries. The unknown subject of this miniature is represented as a lover consumed with but sustained by the fires of passion. With his sad yet questioning eye the lover wears a robe which is looped in the manner of an ancient classical mantle. The inscription, however, reflects the paradoxical sentiments of Petrarchan love-poetry, declaring that the lover will freeze without the sustenance of burning desire: *Alget qui non ardet*.

INTRODUCTION:
RENAISSANCE QUESTIONS

'Renaissance' signifies 'rebirth' and suggests – more resonantly perhaps than any other historical term – that our conversations with the past may be a source of cultural renewal and a vital stimulus to continuing endeavour. In the two centuries dating (approximately) from 1400 to 1600, artists and intellectuals, along with many of their wealthy patrons, developed an ardent interest in the ancient civilizations of Rome and Greece. With this, there began a movement, originating from Italy and extending progressively to the rest of Europe, that cultivated an ever-more precise understanding of classical achievements – in the fields of rhetoric and architecture, the visual arts, literature, philosophy and politics – and subsequently produced an unprecedented wave of modern experimentation.

Over the following centuries, a similar spirit of enthusiastic inquiry has impelled scholars, travellers and intellectual adventurers to return to Italy in the expectation that they will rediscover there the foundations of their own civilization. Most have been impressed by the harmony, order and elegance, of those great civic spaces – Florence, Rome and Venice – that were first opened to view during the fifteenth and sixteenth centuries, and equally by the evidence of intellectual care and artistic energy displayed in libraries and galleries, in brilliant canvases and richly bound books. Many, likewise, have been inclined to see here the beginnings of a modern world in which technological progress confidently enters into alliance with rational inquiry and also nurtures a new delight in the colours, shapes and textures of aesthetic form. Some indeed have supposed that it was in the Renaissance that a characteristically secular mentality first began to reveal itself. On this analysis, the affinity that many intellectuals in the Renaissance sought to establish between their own thinking and that of their classical forebears demonstrates the extent to which one human mind can speak across the centuries directly to another. A universe of universally comprehensible truths was thus opened up, from which even the scientific mentality could derive encouragement.

As will appear, responses such as these – though by now very familiar and certainly in need of qualification – rightly reflect at least one important aspect of the Renaissance mind. For instance, in a justly famous *Oration on the Dignity of Man*, Pico della Mirandola (1469–1533) speaks of man as 'the maker and moulder of his own self', and imagines how God, in creating human nature, determined that self-determination alone should be the defining characteristic of the human race:

> We have set thee, Adam, at the world's centre that thou mayest from thence more easily observe whatever is in the world, so that with freedom of choice and with honour . . . thou mayest fashion thyself in whatever shape thou shalt prefer. Thou shalt have the power to degenerate into the lower forms of life, which are brutish. Thou shalt have the power out of thy soul's judgement to be reborn into the higher forms, which are divine.

In Pico's vision, God has chosen to endow the human being with no specific attribute save that of the free and creative will that individuals are then called to exercise in their temporal lives. Such sentiments justify the recent descriptions of the Renaissance as an age of 'self-fashioning' in which the human person 'constructs' itself according to its own social and political impulsions. And so too do similar attitudes, visible in one form or another in all parts of Europe during the fifteenth and sixteenth centuries. The Spanish humanist Juan Luis Vives (1492–1540) in his *Fable of Humanity* spins a light-hearted version of Pico's words: the pagan Gods are relaxing at a banquet in honour of Juno's birthday: then Jupiter devises a play in which Man, the offspring of the Gods, is the principal actor; Man acts his part in the fable with such brilliance that he wins a place for himself as a deity at the banquet-table. Or else more sombrely, Christopher Marlowe at the end of the sixteenth century bequeaths the legend of Doctor Faustus, whose very appetite for knowledge collides, apparently, with the established order of Hell, Damnation and Divine Judgement. Mankind in this case is not only the fashioner of his own destiny but also an aspiring 'overreacher'.

None of this can fail to make a contribution to the chapters that follow. There is, however, reason at the outset to pause, and to ask how far such opinions represent the most accurate or fruitful reading of the Renaissance achievement.

Consider, for instance, the notion that the period may, unambiguously, be regarded as the beginning of the modern era. This view has a certain rhetorical attraction. Yet it registers far too faintly the extent to which Renaissance thinkers themselves took their inspiration from the past – and in doing so could easily display a mentality as reactionary as it might be progressive. Or suppose that Renaissance culture did in some sense adumbrate our own. This in itself cannot count as an unqualified recommendation. The modern world is not self-evidently a promised land; and when in the early twentieth century Ezra Pound declared that European civilization was an 'old bitch gone in the teeth', he revealed the extent to which modes of thought and expression largely attributable to the Renaissance had in his view become the rotting clichés of the present. (Significantly, Pound along with other modernists, such as T.S. Eliot, preferred to explore anew the work of thirteenth-century poets such as

Dante Alighieri.) Judgements formed in the twentieth century may legitimately be reversed in the twenty-first. Even so, one cannot deny that inventions as character-istic of the Renaissance as, say, linear perspective have been radically called into question by artists such as Picasso and Mondrian.

Specifically, it needs to be recognized that, over the last fifty years, students of the Renaissance have themselves been seeking a radical revision in our understanding of the culture of the period. To some indeed the very notion of the Renaissance – as the description of a precise historical epoch with a definable interest in the celebration of human individuality and the advancement of rational inquiry – is best seen as a cultural myth, developed initially in the nineteenth century by historians such as Jules Michelet and Jacob Burckhardt. There were undoubtedly many Renaissance thinkers who spoke in their own time of a 're-birth' or re-awakening of antiquity. Yet, so far from representing a disinterested assessment of historical data, such terms were devised with polemical intent (as one might speak of 'futurism' or 'postmod-ernism') to articulate a particular programme of intellectual action. Conversely, the term 'Middle Ages' and others like it – such as 'Gothic' – were used by Renaissance thinkers to disparage a period from which, for their own purposes, they wished to distinguish themselves.

To a degree, the nineteenth-century interpretation of Renaissance culture may now be seen as wishful thinking, reflecting conceptions of individuality, reason and progress that are more characteristic of the nineteenth century than of the fifteenth and sixteenth. Nor has it proved possible (or even desirable) to identify any unified and consistent philosophy that could confidently be called 'the Renaissance Philosophy of Man'. On the contrary, it will quickly emerge (in Chapter Two) that, while this was indeed a period of great philosophical inventiveness, much that was most fruitful in Renaissance thought derived from the rejection of any unitary pro-gramme or single-minded commitment to the principles of 'reason', 'individualism' or 'human liberty'. The period made its own contribution to the development of these notions (as did the Middle Ages, the Enlightenment and the Nineteenth Century). At the same time, the Renaissance is also the time at which institutional power and efficient bureaucracies first began to tighten their grip on the lives of particular persons. It was the Renaissance – not the Middle Ages – that obsessively concerned itself with magic and witchcraft, inquisition and persecution: the standard manual for detecting and trying witches – the *Malleus Maleficorum* – was published in the Rhineland during the 1480s; the same decade saw a concerted attempt in both German and Iberian territory to segregate and persecute the Jews.

Then, too, it has become difficult to accept without question that the Renaissance in its intellectual character was radically distinct from preceding centuries. Renais-sance intellectuals were generally opposed to the great manifestations of Christian rationalism that emerged during the thirteenth century in the writings of philosophers such as Albert the Great and St Thomas Aquinas. Yet they owed often an unacknowledged debt to these earlier systems of thought. In any case, the books of ancient Greece and Rome that Renaissance scholars enthusiastically re-discovered had frequently been preserved by the very monks and priests whom some of them affected to despise.

It is correspondingly inaccurate to suppose that the Renaissance was a singlemindedly secular age. The suggestiveness of the word 'humanism' vaguely encourages this supposition. However, when Renaissance thinkers themselves spoke of humanism, their purpose was not to proclaim a new vision of human nature or rebel against the divine but rather to promote a specific form of educational practice and intellectual style. Humanist education will be the subject of Chapter Two. Here, it is enough to note that by the end of the fifteenth century, Pico della Mirandola himself – along with artists such as Botticelli and Michelangelo – had willingly embraced the prophetic teachings of the Dominican Savanarola.

Finally, there is a case (especially in a book entitled *The European Renaissance*) for asking whether the Italy in this period was the only contributor to the advancement of new modes of thought and sensibility. The evidence suggests that it was not. Italian cities provided a very stimulating arena for international debate. But Italy was by no means the only arena. At the fifteenth-century Councils of Constance (in Switzerland) some 18,000 members of the Church assemble; and while their purpose was to debate Church unity, their number included Italian humanists such as Poggio Bracciolini (see below pp. 76–7) and also the German Nicholas of Cusa (see p. 88 *et seq.*) who was arguably the most original thinker of the Renaissance period. So too, attention needs to be given to the contribution made to Renaissance culture by the great Duchy of Burgundy – which, in the fifteenth century, included the Low Countries and stretched almost as far as the Mediterranean. This realm has now slipped from the political map, and also from scholarly consideration. In its time, however, the Duchy supported a culture of the utmost sophistication, particularly, as Chapter Eight will show, in the sphere of music. If Flemish music rather Italian painting were the only remaining evidence of culture in the fifteenth century, the orientation of the Renaissance would be distinctly North to South. Then finally by the end of the sixteenth century France, Spain and belatedly England developed their own versions of the Renaissance enterprise, and advanced – in the works, say, of Montaigne or Shakespeare – far beyond the horizons of the Italian original.

In the chapters that follow, I shall emphasize the extent to which the Renaissance can be regarded as a European and not purely an Italian phenomenon. Similarly, I shall suggest that, in considering the origins and consequences of Renaissance culture, attention needs to be given to the legacy of the so-called Middle Ages and to developments that occurred in the Reformations of the sixteenth century. By way of preparation, I shall offer in the third section of this Introduction a brief outline of the economic and political developments that occurred in Europe between 1400 and 1600. At no point, however, will I suggest that there is any strong causal link between the cultural achievements of the period and their historical context. On the contrary, I shall argue that there is much in Renaissance culture that seeks precisely to transcend the historical sphere or to shelter itself protectively from the immediate impact of historical forces. In section four below, I shall look at some of the myths that the Renaissance spun around itself – many of them enduring into modern interpretations of the period. Throughout, however, my concern will be to look at specific examples of Renaissance art and thought rather than to attempt any general account of the mentality or spirit of the period. It is, after all, through a constantly renewed encounter with specific instances that we now come to know most directly the character of the Renaissance mind and the diversity of achievements that this great culture proved able to generate. Such encounters with text, argument and image will reveal many recognizable and enduring aspects of Renaissance culture but also much that is self-contradictory, disturbing and strange.

It is in this vein – to confirm the suggestions that have so far been made and to prepare in greater detail for later arguments – that one may turn to an instance in which a Renaissance artist himself reviews the achievements of his own culture. This is the *Orlando Furioso* – a poem of some 40,000 lines by the Ferrarese poet Lodovico Ariosto – which may rightly be considered the greatest poem to emerge from the culture of the High Renaissance, and its most enthusiastic and intelligent arbiter.

EUROPE UNITED?

In 1532 – at a point that is usually taken to represent the height of the Renaissance in Italy – Lodovico Ariosto published the final version of his epic-romance, *Orlando Furioso*. Written in celebration of the Este court of Ferrara where Ariosto (1474–1533) was engaged throughout his life as a diplomat, poet and writer of theatrical comedies, the poem itself, as it approaches its conclusion, envisages a scene at a marriage in which the young Cardinal Ippolito d'Este walks in procession amid a throng of artists, astronomers, musicians and philosophers:

Of Poets then, and Philosophers
About him you shall see a worthy band,
To make him know the course of wandr'ng stars,
How heav'n doth move, and why the earth doth stand,
Fine Epigrams, Odes hard to understand:

Or reading of Elegies, or verse of wars,

Or sometime instruments of Musick hearing,

In all his acts a speciall grace appearing.

Here in a single exuberant verse (as translated around 1590 by Sir John Harington, godson of Queen Elizabeth I) Ariosto expresses the delight that many – in his own time and since – have experienced on surveying the diverse spectrum of cultural achievements that had been produced in the Renaissance. In particular, one notes the emphasis upon the 'speciall grace' of the courtier. Harington's own verses may lack the magical play of negatives, superlatives and simple verbs of motion that Ariosto conjures up in his original verse: *né senza somma grazia un passo muove*. Yet Harington's words are sufficient to suggest that the Renaissance in its Italian aspect – to contemporaries as ever since – offered above all else examples of poise, elegance and unemphatic command.

At the same time, in cultivating his own 'speciall grace' Ariosto, at every point in the *Orlando Furioso*, looks back to the origins of his own culture; and, while he invariably acknowledges the benefit he has drawn from the reading of classical texts, he also claims the right to modify and even outdo these originals. In one of its many facets, Ariosto's poem is a war poem. In this, it resembles Homer's *Iliad* and Virgil's *Aeneid*, and constantly alludes to both. Yet the scene of the action is neither Troy nor Rome but rather the ever-varying landscape – still dominated by mysterious woods – of ninth-century Christendom. Seeking to celebrate the origins of the Este dynasty (who descend from a Christian woman-warrior and a converted Muslim), Ariosto sets his poem in the Carolingian period when Europe was threatened by the Islamic invasions that eventually did establish a hold over Spain. The heroes of his story are the knights and paladins of the Emperor Charlemagne who muster from as far afield as the Orkneys and Etna, moved by a vision of a feudal but pan-European unity, to defend the heartland of Europe (which the Italian Ariosto, demonstrating his own pan-European sympathies, locates in Paris). Much as he had learned from the classics, Ariosto here invokes a world that is recognizably Christian, Medieval and chivalric in its lineaments, rejoicing in its geographical solidarity and temporal continuity.

In form as well as in theme, Ariosto transforms the classical legacy. The *Orlando Furioso* is not only an epic but also a romance and, in large measure, a comedy, too. Here, in contrast to Homer and Virgil, the author takes a particular pleasure in complicating the theme of military loyalty by pursuing the countervailing pressures of sexual adventure, fantasy and imaginative suggestion, drawn from Arthurian and Medieval sources. The protagonists are all likely to be endowed with ancestral swords, or magic helmets and rings and to move around Europe on the back of flying horses (or Hippogriffs). For the most part, too, the developing action is dominated by the quests, conflicting loyalties, mental torments and downright absurdities that are aroused by the experience of romantic love. The 'Orlando' of Ariosto's title is the greatest of Charlemagne's champions who first appears in European literature as 'Roland', the doomed hero of the Old French *Chanson de Roland*. In Ariosto's hands, however, he becomes one of the many unrequited lovers of Angelica, the elusive (and Muslim) daughter of the Great Khan of Cathay who, straying through Europe, finally precipitates Orlando into madness by marrying a humble foot-soldier from the Muslim rank-and-file. Tracing this affair through a sustained sequence of interwoven plots Ariosto, eventually, shows how Orlando's senses are restored to him. Yet this restoration only occurs when an English knight, Astolfo – on his Hippogriff – flies to the moon, the *luna* which is the fitting repository of many lunatic minds; having located the phial that contains the wits of Orlando, Astolfo returns to earth, and breaks open the bottle beneath the hero's nose – so that by inhaling its contents, which thus return to his brain, the warrior may once again become a sane and effective member of Charlemagne's entourage.

The title of Ariosto's *Orlando Furioso* carries an allusion to Seneca's stoic *Hercules Furens*; and the Renaissance in self-glorifying mood was always ready to recall that Hercules became a God heroically by virtue of his human effort. However, enough has been said of Ariosto's poem to suggest how far his own vision has travelled from its epic origins. The Renaissance may be a 're-birth' of classical learning; yet there is little in Renaissance culture that could be described merely as neoclassical. In the *Orlando Furioso*, as in most of the works that will be examined later, a knowledge of classical precedent serves as a spur, exciting – often – an interest as much in suppos- edly Medieval antecedents as in the worlds of Rome and Greece, and almost invari- ably contributing – in the sixteenth century – to a celebration of present possibilities. Indeed, in the second century of the Renaissance, works in the modern vernacular, such as Ariosto's, themselves became canonical points of reference, to be admired, challenged and sometimes outdone by their aspiring heirs. Ariosto's own work is suc- ceeded by a long line of imitators and translators. It was from Ariosto that Spenser derived the narrative style of *The Faerie Queen*; and even the sober Milton, in the plan- ning stages of *Paradise Lost*, considered writing his poem in the genre of Arthurian epic-romance. Cervantes's comic romance (see p. 336 *et seq.*) openly acknowledges its debt to Ariosto.

'Imitation' as exemplified by Ariosto, encourages rather than represses originality; and this understanding will prove to be fundamental not only to artistic practice in the Renaissance but also (as will appear in Chapter Two) to the educational pro- grammes that the period favoured. There are, however, at least three other ways in which Ariosto's example may serve – briefly but vividly – to introduce the central characteristics of High Renaissance culture.

The first appears in the view the poem offers of human individuality. There is much in the *Orlando Furioso* that reflects Pico della Mirandola's confidence in the creative power of the human mind. At every point in the narrative, Ariosto asserts his omniscient command over an ever-inventive and ever-changing weave of stories – to the extent that he, rather than Divine Providence, appears to be the ruler of his own fictional world. Yet this implies no brash self-affirmation. Indeed, Ariosto – or his authorial *persona* – repeatedly comments with tolerant good humour on the heroic excesses of warriors and lovers. And the humour is turned just as often against his own authorial self or even the expectations of his courtly audience. Ariosto will teasingly interrupt the action at some extravagant or titillating climax, insisting that other strands of his narrative demand attention, or else that tedium will result from too obsessive an attention to any particular narrative line. The very sanity that he and his audience enjoy – in contrast to the protagonists of the narrative – depends upon a sophisticated, flirtatious yet unassuming ability to maintain a diversity of apparently competing interests. On this view, poise rather than pretension is the defining characteristic of the Renaissance individual.

Poise, too, is a characteristic that defines, in the second place, the communal relationships that the Renaissance characteristically cultivates. For the Renaissance individual would be nothing were he or she not also a citizen or a courtier. So Ariosto constantly represents himself as a courtly performer; and, if the poet glories in anything, it is in the recognition that an intelligent (and aristocratic) audience might bestow upon him, in acknowledgement of his artistry (see canto XLVI). In this regard, Ariosto is entirely in sympathy with the author of one of the most influential books of the Renaissance, Castiglione's *Book of the Courtier*. As will be seen in Chapter One, the culture of the High Renaissance is a court culture; and for Castiglione, the principal attribute of the courtier will be a certain *sprezzatura* – an indefinable skill in courtly activities, a gracefulness in comportment, a nonchalant intelligence that aims ideally not at self-aggrandizement but rather at the greater good of court life itself. There can be no better example of such nonchalance than the delicately controlled virtuosity that Ariosto consistently displays in the forty-six cantos of the *Orlando Furioso*.

Figure 1   Raphael, *Baldassare Castiglione*, c.1515, Canvas, 81.9 × 67.3 cm. The Louvre, Paris. With permission from Scala.

Then finally there is a quality of irony, even of comedy which is a feature not only of the *Orlando Furioso* but also some of the most serious works of philosophy that the Renaissance would produce. Ariosto is no philosopher. Indeed, when he looks back to Dante, the great philosopher–poet of the Middle Ages, he does so with admiring deference yet also with a parodic lilt, implying that the systematic or even logical pursuit of philosophical truth may be no less an impediment to wisdom than the outrageous folly of heroical and amorous warriors. In this respect, he is at one with the many philosophers of the Renaissance who claim to seek wisdom wherever wisdom might be found, and has much in common with Erasmus and Cusanus – who, as will be seen, having learned the Socratic lesson, were always ready to recognize the relativity of their own most ambitious projects.

So far, the picture of Renaissance culture that has emerged from the *Orlando Furioso* corresponds – in its celebration of order, unity, elegance and poise – to that which Burckhardt first delineated in the nineteenth century. Yet this cannot be all. For even within the courtly canvas of the poem itself – where Ariosto contemplates with strange equanimity, insanity, illusion, infidelity in love and death in battle – there are suggestions of a latent disturbance. And how real these are will quickly appear if one turns now from the literary text to its historical context. For the profound irony is that, while the ironist Ariosto may have been writing of a world of Carolingian unity, the Europe of his day was entering a century of particularly violent change.

In 1494 French troops invaded the Italian peninsula, stimulating a counter-thrust from the Imperial descendants of Charlemagne – the Habsburgs of Spain – and thus setting off a series of conflicts that would not be settled until 1559. In the course of these wars, much that had been characteristic of Italian political life in the fifteenth century was challenged or destroyed; and the campaigns themselves were anything but chivalric – involving, often, mercenary troops and advanced military techniques – where infantry supplied with pikes, muskets and artillery wreaked havoc alike on mounted knights and civilian populations. In 1527, five years before the final publication of the *Orlando Furioso*, Rome itself was sacked by Swiss mercenaries in the pay of the Catholic Emperor. The shock of this assault upon the mythic centre of Western civilization is registered in the account offered by the Senecan tragedian and literary theorist Giambattista Cinthio (now remembered mainly for providing the plots of Shakespeare's *Othello* and *Measure for Measure*) who writes:

> No mercy was shown to sex or to person, neither to years or to age, nor to the sacraments or to the religion of our Lord and Redeemer. . . . Children were seen running to the breast of their desolate mothers who twined their own hands in the beards of their assailants, seeking to protect their daughters from the brutality of these cruel men. This served no purpose save to increase their evil appetite. For these villains plucked up the mothers and, flinging them to the earth (O dreadful spectacle) raped their own virgin daughters

Figure 2 Albrecht Dürer, *The Great Cannon*, 1518, Etching 27.3 × 38.7 cm. This etching comes from a period when Dürer was greatly interested in illustrating fortifications and military works. Leonardo and Michelangelo were both actively involved in designing fortifications. The painter David Hockney (in a television discussion of Canaletto) reminds us that the development of perspective is contemporary with the development of gun-sights and the art of artillery. This figure is reproduced by kind permission of the Syndics of the Fitzwilliam Museum, Cambridge.

on top of them . . . slaughtered both mother and daughter before the eyes of their fathers and husbands who were their prisoners.

Suddenly a chasm opens beneath the confident stride of the Renaissance vision. What happens when the creativity, self-fashioning and freedom of mind that Pico celebrates descend – as Pico knew they might – to the brutal ingenuities displayed in such symphonies of rape and murder?

There are many possible answers to this question. A certain fascinated indulgence – such as Cinthio himself displays – is one response and will be registered in the horrors of Senecan tragedy and the taste for decadence displayed by authors such as John Webster and Cyril Tourneur. Another response – as in Calvin's religious vision – is to admit the utter depravity of human nature in the interests of revealing the glory of the divine. But between these two extremes, Ariosto maintains an understanding that may, to some, seem illusory but which defends nonetheless a fragile yet urbane recognition of another more human reality. Ariosto himself knew what the Europe around him was coming to. Throughout the *Orlando Furioso* he records in supposedly prophetic episodes great disasters such as the Battle of Pavia at which in 1525 the French King Francis was taken prisoner by his Spanish enemies 'the flower of French Chivalry lie stricken on the ground' (canto xxxii). He even writes five cantos that depict the treachery and discord that eventually lead to the death of Orlando at Roncevalles. But then he excises these from the definitive text. Nor does he mention that, historically, the young Cardinal Ippolito, the golden youth of the Este wedding, had – as the story goes – put out the eyes of his half-brother on discovering that this brother was his rival in love. Ariosto does, however, whimsically recognize that gunpowder and artillery have utterly changed the character of chivalric warfare. In Canto ix 91 he describes how a cannon – 'the invention of the Devil' – had been sunk in Charlemagne's era, supposedly for ever deep beneath the waves. He knew this was a fiction. In history, the cannon were thunderingly alive. And turning to history one may ask how far these violent realities could be held at bay by the aesthetic harmonies and ironic intelligence that Ariosto's along with many of his contemporaries, so subtly cultivates. Arguably, the poise and coherence of the *Orlando Furioso* are necessary and valuable precisely in offering an alternative to a world in which instability, untruth and brutality are the norm.

HISTORICAL OUTLINES

It is obvious that ever since the Roman Empire, more than a thousand years ago . . . Italy had never enjoyed such prosperity or known so favourable a situation as that in which it found itself so securely at rest in the year of our Christian salvation, 1490.

Then came the invasions:

> French troops began to stir up very great dissension here . . . and Italy suffered for many
> years all those calamities with which miserable mortals are usually afflicted.

These are the words of the historian and close associate of Machiavelli, Francesco Guicciardini (1483–1540); and it is natural enough that the Italian mind should have seen the Franco-Spanish invasions in a tragic light. Yet within a few years of its eventual publication in 1561, Guicciardini's *History of Italy* had been translated into Latin, French, German, Dutch, Spanish and English, testifying not only to the force of Guicciardini's example as a modern historian but also to the significance that Europe at large attached to Italy's tragic suffering. With hindsight, this was the point in history at which feudal orders began to be transformed into nation-states and empires, and where even the cities that in Italy had for centuries challenged feudal overlordship were themselves confronted with forces beyond their power to resist. At the time, these developments seemed to come from the hand of malicious Fortune.

As Guicciardini acknowledges, Italy itself could not be absolved from inviting the disasters that now fell upon it. The series of inter-city alliances that for Guicciardini represented a source of flourishing peace were a flimsy – if subtle – expedient against rivalry between the great political forces of Florence, Milan and Venice, while divisive energies had had already begun to be generated by the ambitions of the Papacy. The Borgia Pope Alexander VI (a Spaniard, whose years of office ran from 1492 to 1503) and his arch-enemy and successor, the warrior Julius II (in office 1503–13) promoted the territorial interests of the Church with a ferocity and guile that ran parallel to the depredations of the invaders. Suddenly much that had been achieved in Italy over the preceding century began to display its inherent fragility.

The fourteenth century had witnessed the Black Death of the 1340s and (even when the plague had receded) a series of bitter winters and failing harvests. Demographic recovery from the Plague was only achieved by mid-1440s. But the growth of commercial, industrial and financial activity in cities from Baltic ports of the Hanseatic League, through Flanders and into Italy itself resulted in the increased prosperity of an international merchant class. It is in these cities that the origins of the Renaissance are to be found; and Chapter One will look more closely at this connection. But in Italy the civic sense, and the humanism associated with it, was especially acute. The myth of ancient Rome inspired in Italian intellectuals an awareness of the principles of civic virtue, while in the fifteenth century the modern cities of Italy were so various in character as to stimulate, along with intense rivalry, an acute political consciousness of the different ideologies to which urban life might give rise. Venice, though a Republic, was also a commercial Empire, foreshadowing, in its domination of the Adriatic, the empires of wider reach that would develop over the next three centuries. Florence, too, was a republic; and its relatively advanced understanding of associational politics was sharpened by decades of resistance to Milan – a despotism pursuing its own vigorously expansionist policy throughout the fourteenth century.

It was this constellation of civic interests – economic, political and intellectual – that was challenged and transfigured in 1494. At this point, indeed, the very success of the fourteenth-century city contributed to its downfall, producing economic resources, know-how and examples of military and political enterprise that were now turned against the walls in which they had first been developed: the French campaigns were funded, to a significant degree, by Italian bankers resident in Lyons. But the political energies that had been gathering in France and Spain throughout the fifteenth century all favoured the development of nation-states rather than city-states. As in the English Wars of the Roses, so in France and Spain, hereditary monarchs had been attempting to resist the centrifugal forces generated by the independent power of magnates and barons, and to transform the last manifestations of feudalism – which had crumbled under the combined effects of the Black Death and the growth of a commercial bourgeoisie – into sovereign entities capable of concerted action in a national or at least a dynastic cause.

This is not the place to examine in any detail the dynastic histories of sixteenth-century Europe. Chapter One will look to the examples of Florence, Urbino, France, Geneva and Rome to estimate the developments in political philosophy that occurred in the period. There is, however, one court – that of the Duchy of Burgundy – that had a far greater influence on the Renaissance scene than has generally been recognized, and certainly illustrates, at a point of nexus, the web of transactions, issues and accidents that unravelled in the course of the sixteenth century, to the advantage and disadvantage of both France and Spain.

Though the Dukes of Burgundy owed family allegiance to the King of France, the powerful diplomacy of Philip le Hardi in conjunction with a series of advantageous marriages ensured that by the mid-fifteenth century Burgundy ruled a great corridor of domains (comparable in area to England measured from Berwick to Barnstaple) running down the eastern line of the French heartland and thus connecting the industrial and commercial cities of Flanders to the shores of the Mediterranean. Map 1 (see p. 14) reveals the extent and north–south orientation of this domain; and it is was along this axis that artists – particularly painters, sculptors, goldsmiths and, above all, musicians – travelled in both directions and exchanged expertise. Burgundy itself was the centre of a particularly abundant artistic culture. Likewise Table 1 emphasizes a network of affiliations centring on Burgundy which brought the Low Countries into relationship with the arterial centre of Europe and prepared for violent redistributions of power on the demise of the Burgundian dynasty itself (see p. 15).

In political terms, the Burgundian Dukedom was, uniquely, a feudal relic, that flourished nonetheless on the benefits of commercial traffic. The Burgundian bloc at

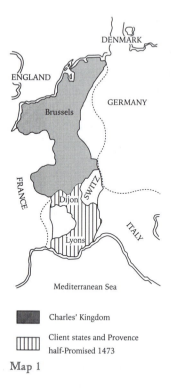

Mediterranean Sea

▬ Charles' Kingdom

▥ Client states and Provence
half-Promised 1473

Map 1

the centre of Europe had presented a real threat to the sovereignty of France. Indeed, a pact between Burgundy and Lancastrian England ensured that the English King Henry VI – in title at least – became King of France (while Burgundy expected to divide the spoils of the French domain and itself become a Kingdom). The thought of what the shape of Europe would have been – partitioned between England and Burgundy – if the pact had held, is enough to indicate how crucial the outcome of Burgundian affairs would be to the shape of modern Europe.

In the event, it was the Swiss who ensured that Europe would not be divided between an Outremer England and a Greater Burgundy. In response to the over-ambitious politics of the Burgundian Duke Charles the Reckless, Swiss pikemen (anticipating their fearsome role in wars to come) ambushed and destroyed the chivalry of Charles's army in the Haute-Savoie; and France, under Joan of Arc, having driven out the English, was able to consolidate its national integrity.

In Spain no less than in France, Burgundian politics acted as a catalyst in an expansion of national interests. In this case, however, the effect did not arise from territorial friction but rather from a wholly unpredictable chain of marriage alliances and infant mortalities (see Table 1 below). On the death of Charles the Bold, the heir to the Burgundian Dukedom was Charles's daughter Maria who had married Maximilian, the Holy Roman Emperor in the year of her father's death in 1467. This union ensured that the Low Countries – as possessions of Burgundy – came under the rule of the Empire. But the son of the Imperial union then married (in 1496) the daughter of Isabella and Ferdinand of Spain. And this union in turn produced Charles V, who not only inherited Spain but also (in 1519 as the Habsburg heir) the Empire, including the Flemish lands appertaining to it.

When in 1494 Charles VIII of France marched into Italy under a national and dynastic banner there seems to have been a certain colour of chivalric adventure to his actions, as well as an aspiration to spiritual heroism. His purport was to re-assert a dynastic claim to Naples. (The city had been part of an Angevin Kingdom in the thirteenth century, but in the fifteenth century had been inherited by the House of Aragon.) Once he had achieved his Neapolitan objective, it was Charles's intention to mount a Crusade to free the Holy Land from Ottoman subjection. Significantly, many of the nobility who might once have contested the sovereignty of the French crown were drawn into this glamorous enterprise.

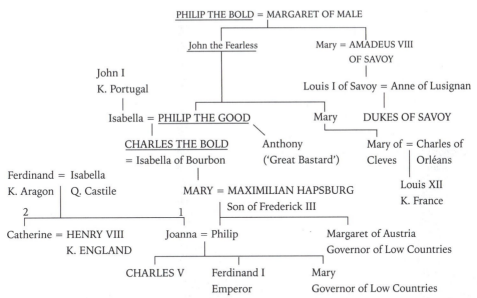

Table 1   The Duchy of Burgundy from the marriage of Philip the Bold to Margaret of Male in 1369, who brought Philip possession of Flanders, Artois, and Rether.

In the Spanish arena, too, hidalgos – the military aristocrats who had once been ranged against Arab-occupied Granada – sought new employment in the Italian wars. However, with the entrance of the Imperial and ultimately Habsburg armies into the fray, it became clear chivalry and spiritual knightliness provided only a thin if very effective cover for the pursuit of strategic purposes. Milan in particular became a bone of strategic contention. Not only was this city the most northerly and most aggressively powerful of the Italian cities, it also occupied (after the Habsburgs succeeded to the Spanish Throne) a crucial position on the land route between the German and Iberian arms of the Empire. Siege-warfare ranged around the city; and the unchivalric reality of the Italian wars revealed its true character. Musketry and artillery became increasingly the weapons of war. And this development too favoured strong and centralized interests: where once a knight had mustered his own horse and trappings, now only kings and emperors could command the resources needed to supply the masses of metal required in an attack. Milan was the capital of a French Government set up by Louis XII that lasted from 1500 to 1521. But in 1526 the city suffered a devastating siege and eventually yielded to Habsburg dominion in 1535. From this point on, most of the other cities of Italy – with the exception of Venice and Rome – were drawn into the Spanish sphere of influence.

To the military implications of this long campaign a further dimension was added in 1517 by the beginning of the Protestant Reformation. The consequences of this movement began to mingle with the aggression of newly national states, including increasingly the ambitions of Tudor England; and the focus of historical (if not of artistic) interest swings decisively away from Italy. In political terms, the Italian cities now began to experience, in a collaborationist posture, something of what it would mean in an overseas possession to be the colonial subject of an Empire; and sixteenth-century Italy witnessed a long process of elegant decline in the erstwhile centres of civic and aristocratic authority. The dominant players, however, also had their difficulties: Spain discovered that Imperial gold could also cause inflation in the home-market; France felt the stirrings of the religious conflict that culminated, under Catherine de' Medici, in the Massacre of St Bartholomew's Day.

It was, in fact, in Germany, Switzerland and, above all, in the Low Countries that political developments in the sixteenth century proved to be at their most creative. In Germany, for instance, a number of local princedoms embraced Protestantism, relishing (as did the English Henry VIII) the revenues they might derive from newly dispossessed monasteries, and simultaneously grasping the opportunity to assert their freedom from the nominal overlordship of the Habsburg Empire. Most German princedoms and electorates in fact remained Catholic. Yet a certain pragmatic accommodation – even tolerance – was achieved in matters of conscience as witnessed by, for instance, the Religious Peace of Augsburg in 1555. As for Switzerland, this was hardly a haven of tolerance. Yet the puritanism developed by Zwingli in Zürich and Calvin in Geneva pointed to a religious conception of the communal life which to many (at the time and since) held out the possibility of radical social reform. Most important of all, the Dutch Republics – fired by Protestantism and by an ancient sense of civic pride, demonstrated – as Italy most certainly did not – the possibilities of resistance to Spanish domination and of progressive constitutional experiment. England, a latecomer to Renaissance culture, benefited in terms of political cohesion from its relative isolation. In economic terms, too, the emphasis had begun to shift from South to North. By the mid-sixteenth century the richest business organization in Europe was not the Florentine Medici – who in the fifteenth century had earned that title as industrialists, merchants and bankers to the Papacy – but rather the Fugger family of Augsburg, who were the paymasters of the Habsburgs and derived a fair proportion of their wealth from copper-mining in Hungary.

In terms, however, of intellectual currency, and particularly in regard to political theory, Italy was still able to provide the analytical apparatus in which to address the changing nature of political and military power. Machiavelli was an Italian.

Niccolò Machiavelli is a figure who will henceforth appear in many guises, as scholar, humanist and the author of brilliant comedies. But in his role as political philosopher, he addressed himself – to quote Sir Francis Bacon's admiring comment – to the question of what men in politics actually do and 'not what they ought to do'. It was Machiavelli who realized that, in response to any such shift of 'Fortune' as the sixteenth century experienced, the fundamental virtue required of a successful ruler was the ability to act, regardless of moral preconception, in the way that decisiveness and political intelligence demanded. Only by doing so could a ruler – on behalf of his subjects – secure the ground on which the aspirations of any civic community to liberty, glory and honour might firmly be defended. Notably – in the light of contemporary conceptions of mercenary warfare – such *virtù* or manliness of behaviour was to be expected of all participants in the realm, as if a soldierly contribution of the militia were itself a form of democratic franchise. However, whether in regard to communal or individuals' actions, Fortune can only be overcome by the ruthless, impetuous and 'manly' actions that for Machiavelli were supremely exemplified in the policies of the unrelenting Pope Julius II: Fortune after all is a woman, says Machiavelli, and only yields to those who treat her with boldness and vigour: 'if she is to be submissive it is necessary to beat and coerce her' (*The Prince*, xxv).

With an irony not at all out of keeping with Ariosto's, Machiavelli calls upon political leaders to bring, when needed, mendacity as well as vigour to battle against delusive Fortune. In Machiavelli's view, the great city-states of the fourteenth century had long been guilty of self-delusion, mouthing words such as 'liberty', 'honour' and 'glory' without any realization of what might be required to defend these principles. But the Franco-Spanish invasions – though marching under the colours of chivalric enterprise and crusading zeal – had demonstrated that any such mealy-mouthedness was dangerously redundant. The time had come when the virtue of highly principled immoralism was the only way to be sure of liberty or honour. Such double-think may have led in part to a misapprehension of Machiavelli's position, to judge from the scandalized and often disingenuous responses of French and Spanish victors. But Machiavelli's thinking – in recognizing power as a reality independent of moral constraint – lies at the heart of modern statecraft. By the end of the sixteenth century a conception of the state had arisen that would have been unimaginable without the invasions of Italy and Machiavelli's searching response to them.

ARTISTIC CONTINUITIES

In the perspective of Renaissance *realpolitik*, one might inquire whether the cultural achievements of the period were anything other than a gauzy illusion drawn gracefully over brutal ambition. This is a Machiavellian question. It reflects the enduring current of analytical scepticism that Machiavelli introduced into European thought; and recent studies of the Renaissance have with good reason brought a Machiavellian eye to bear on some of the central claims of Renaissance civilization.

At the same time, art, learning and passionate devotion to beauty have a reality of their own. Renaissance intellectuals came to realize this; and the evidence is that these aspects of Renaissance culture – and the values they reflect – are at least as enduring as political realism or analytical acumen. It is these that in the view of many still set the standard of what a civilization ought to be. And in the Renaissance itself there were certain quite practical ways in which the arts, the life of the intellect and even the cult of beauty proved more resilient and maintained a greater continuity than any political regime could enjoy.

As has already been suggested, Renaissance culture first developed in the small city-states of Europe. Yet, despite the upheaval of dynastic and religious warfare which largely erased the original ambience of such activity, the arts and intellectual practice flourished and expanded their territorial influence during the sixteenth century, while artists and intellectuals themselves won increasing independence in an international arena. It is true that for the most part such independence was demonstrated by a willingness to accept and profit from the prevailing ethos, whether economic or political: and in practice there was a closer connection at this time than ever since between the arts of the mind and the practice of technology: Leonardo and Michelangelo were both employed by their patrons as military engineers; and many other artists won attention for their skill in, say, bronze casting or their understanding of the mathematics of measurement. Moreover, the development of printing – a crucial factor in the cultural history of the sixteenth century – represented an unprecedented alliance of humanist intellectuals, metallurgists, engineers and designers. Yet increasingly throughout the period we find that figures such as Michelangelo, Erasmus, Titian and the composer Josquin des Prez were able to bargain with the estates of political and ecclesiastical power and all but establish an intellectual estate in their own right. Machiavelli speaks of *virtù*; Renaissance intellectuals – often referred to as *virtuosi* – showed in their own field the energy, resourcefulness and, sometimes, the ruthless cunning that Machiavelli recommended in his.

Travelling on roads that had first been opened up by commerce and later by war and dynastic or national ambition, artists and educators from North and from South were ever more impelled to meet each other in pursuit of interests specific to the advancement of their artistic or educational concerns. In later chapters, we shall see the results of these meetings in, for example, Dürer's response to the Italian science of perspective and Piero's interest in Northern representations of light and landscape. As for literary humanists, they made a profound contribution – which only they could make – to the development of national languages and national myths, and were fêted as cultural heroes for their poetic achievements: Serafino is a case in point (see p. 231). Musicians – mostly Northern in origin though flourishing in Southern courts – derived great benefit from the publication of their work in (extremely sophisticated) print and music for the Renaissance became a dominant symbol of its deepest aspirations.

In this perspective treatises soon began to be written triumphantly proclaiming an age of artistic rebirth and cultural progress. Claims of this sort were made on behalf of all the arts. However, the most influential proved to be those that Giorgio Vasari (1511–74) entered for the figurative arts in his *Lives of the Painters*, written from the vantage-point of the mid-sixteenth century.

If, in a Machiavellian spirit, one sought evidence of how easily in the Renaissance art and power could cohabit, then Vasari's own life would provide it. Known now mainly as the architect of the Uffizi in Florence, Vasari, an artist of some celebrity in his own day, was much involved in devising political imagery for the Medici Dukes of the early Cinquecento. Vasari himself, however, was especially proud of his friendship, as a fellow artist, with Michelangelo; and in the *Lives* he outlines a cultural history that, following its own logic, delivers painting from medieval ignorance, encourages advances in both theoretical understanding and practical application, and finally produces in the form of his stupendous friend, Michelangelo, an individual who could exercise a 'divine' independence from any kind of political or even artistic restraint.

On Vasari's account, the true mission of the artist had been obscured by barbaric ignorance, and equally by the unconcern of primitive Christians who opposed all manifestations of classical achievement and, 'striving to cast out every occasion of sin ruined or demolished all the marvellous statues . . . pictures, mosaics and ornaments representing the false pagan gods' (p. 37). Then 'in 1250 under a subtle influence of the very air in Italy heaven took pity on the talented men who were being born in Tuscany and led them back to pristine forms' (p. 45). At this point – identified with such confident precision – there began a process of technical improvement guided by an attention simultaneously to classical examples and to the details of the natural world: 'our art consists first in the imitation of nature but then . . . in the imitation of the most accomplished artists'. Among the Florentines, Giotto led the way, followed by painters, such as Masaccio, who consciously cultivated a knowledge of classical rules as well as showing an intuitive understanding of the natural world. Then finally, in Michelangelo's work, rules and example prove to have been so thoroughly absorbed that art can effortlessly recreate with its own particular *grazia* the objects first seen in the natural world, or never seen at all. With Michelangelo, artists are restored to the free condition that they enjoyed in (p. 31) Athens and Rome where they were honoured as 'freemen of the city' (p. 28). Indeed, they may now fulfil the exalted mission that God as Creator had first bestowed on them and themselves become creators of their own worlds.

Michelangelo did not wholly dissent from Vasari's view; and one will see shortly how his own sense of divine mission was reflected in his art. As for Vasari himself, it will already be apparent that in a number of ways his historical analysis provides the foundation for the view which first became established in the nineteenth century and which sees the Renaissance primarily as an Italian phenomenon, marching ever onward in the light of classical and clear-eyed reason. One need not deny the validity of this view. Yet it is hardly sufficient to explain the strength and independence that the arts displayed in this period. One is bound rather to insist, against Vasari's Italo-centric (or rather Florentino-centric) triumphalism that the strength and independence of Renaissance art derived from roots that ran deeper in preceding ages than Vasari allows and spread far wider in the receptive field of a Europe-wide sensibility. One must also emphasize that the apparent rationality of the process that Vasari describes cannot be taken to exclude a close engagement with other more disturbing facets of the human spirit. (As will be seen in Chapter Five, the divine art of Michelangelo also articulated a profound spirit of Christian penitence.)

Consider for instance – in regard to temporal range – the two illustrations, Figures 3 and 4. From the Vasarian point of view, there can be no question as to which of these is the more advanced or *rinascimentale*. The Florentine Masaccio (Fig. 3) here places figures in space with a notable understanding of volume, anatomy, facial feature and perspective. The scene indeed includes several portrayals of contemporary Florentine dignitaries, while the composition of the crowd avoids all rigidity in the magnificently free S-shape that runs horizontally through heads and torsos. By comparison Figure 4 pays little attention to coherent narrative space, concentrating rather upon local flourishes of colour and detail and a certain complication of design. Yet the painter – Gentile da Fabbriano, to whom Vasari gives only the briefest of mentions in his *Lives* – was not only an Italian but the almost exact contemporary of Masaccio.

This is enough to suggest that, alongside the classical and Florentine tradition that Vasari favours, there was at least one other tradition that commanded equal – or even greater attention. Gentile's style – with its fluent complication of line and an appetite for chivalric display – may rightly be designated 'International Gothic'. Yet that designation serves at once to call to mind a long-enduring tradition that – preceding the

Figure 3   Masaccio, *The Raising of the Son of Theophilus*, c.1425 (completed by Filippino Lippi), Fresco. Brancacci Chapel, Church of the Carmine, Florence. With permission from Scala.

Figure 4 Gentile da Fabbriano, *Adoration of the Magi*, 1423, Panel 299.3 × 282 cm. The Ufffizi Gallery, Florence. With permission from Scala.

Florentine revolution – went back to an earlier renaissance that occurred during the twelfth century in the arts of Northern Europe. This revival had been centred on Paris and expressed itself in the great wave of architectural experiment, connoisseurship, manuscript illumination, neoplatonic mysticism and love-literature that accompanied the building of the Gothic cathedrals. But the confidence that inspired this movement lay not in the re-discovery of triumphal arches or classical draperies but rather in a devotion to the Blessed Virgin Mary. The realization that God at the Incarnation could enter the human body was itself the inspiration for a proto-humanistic confidence in the possible dignity of any material thing that was receptive to divine illumination. Cathedrals in particular – with their windows admitting a light from beyond – were themselves frequently regarded as architectural equivalents of the physical body of the Blessed Virgin; and the contemplation of her image and character led to a concern with love, grace, delicacy of emotion and depths of joy and suffering which is no less evident in the works of Donatello or even Michelangelo than in the works of anonymous northerners. Indeed, qualities of realistic observation are especially apparent in works of the International Gothic. In short, alongside the interest in volume and monumental dignity that were inspired by classical models, the International Gothic style – which in the Quattrocento was far more widely diffused than its Florentine competitor – satisfied an appetite for detail, dynamic calligraphy and a certain delicacy of emotional apprehension.

There are times when in terms of stylistic taste, International Gothic recalls the arabesques of Islamic art; and a full account of the Renaissance palette would need to look East as well as North, particularly in assessing the art of Venice, with its strong trading relations with the Muslim world (Fig. 5). Vasari, however, turning now to questions of geographic range, can scarcely extend his sympathies even to Venice. The Venetian master Titian is viewed to disadvantage alongside the Florentine Michelangelo (an opinion which reflects Michelangelo's attitude to Titian though not the reverse). Likewise, Flemish painting, though treated occasionally with polite enthusiasm, receives far less credit than many Italian artists in the fourteenth century would have allowed it. To correct this emphasis, it is almost enough to think of the so-called *Arnolfini Marriage* by Jan van Eyck (1390–1441) which represents possibly the wedding in Flanders of members of an Italian merchant clan, or else of his *Virgin*

Figure 5   Giovanni Antonio Amadeo, *Façade of the Certosa*, Pavia, 1473-first half of the 16th century. French travellers in the 16th century such as Philip de Comynes seem to have preferred this style to the more austerely geometric style of the Florentine Renaissance. With permission from Scala.

of the Chancellor Rolin (Plate I). Van Eyck's painting immediately displays an interest in light and landscape that Italian painters were to find especially compelling. Equally it adopts an attitude to the natural world which is itself at one with International Gothic sensibility yet proves no less significant to the development of High Renaissance art. The viewer encounters here not the presumption of human control over – or recreation of – the natural world such as Vasari admires in Michelangelo but an attention to the finest manifestations of texture, glint, sheen. Rules or even intuitive discipline are less important here than sheer pleasure in the abundance of the world.

Then, finally, the resilience of Renaissance culture depends (as Vasari is by no means disposed to allow) upon a sensitivity as much to the dark as to the light, to the irrational as well as to the rational. Compare Plates II and III, the first of which is a detail from Michelangelo's Sistine Chapel ceiling, representing the Delphic Sybil, the second a painting entitled *Dulle Griete* (that is, 'Crazy' Griete) by the Flemish contemporary of Vasari and Michelangelo, Pieter Breughel. The first is everything that Vasari believes the Renaissance should be. Michelangelo draws freely on architectural and sculptural allusions but also shows an informed understanding of the pull, lift and torsion of the human body. The result is a figure that is neither simply classical nor obviously natural. The figure reflects Michelangelo's pursuit of a formal air and grace which has nothing to do with mundane activity. But beauty here is no trick of the light or appeal to sentiment. It is founded upon a rigorously intuitive logic that builds the head and its headdress out of lozenges of green and grey around the firm blocks and ovals of the face. Indeed beauty itself is in some sense the subject of this painting: just as the Sybil 'a pagan oracle' could rise above history and participate in the unfolding of Christian revelation, so formal beauty itself, as created by Michelangelo, claims a prophetic rather than historical role.

Against this, Breughel's painting with its demented allusions to peasants, to the pots and pans of a lunatic marching resolutely out of Hell might by some be regarded only as a subversive Northern alternative to the taste decreed by Italianate humanism. It is not. This alarming work is no less the product of humanism than Michelangelo's, and its conception may well have been determined by the spirit of the humanist circle to which Breughel belonged in Antwerp. This circle – gathering at a time when Spanish oppression was especially fierce – took its cue from Erasmus; and its temper can be gauged from the words of Breughel's friend, the geographer Abraham Ortelius (1527–98) who, despairing of the extremes he saw displayed around him by Catholics and Protestants alike, declares that: 'Everyone wishes to be called but not to be good; everyone wishes to teach others but not to humble himself.' Breughel's own response (as also in *The Blind Men*, Fig. 32) summons up outrage at the madness that folly and avarice (witnessed in Griete's clanking holdall) has loosed upon the world and its inhabitants. Yet this world is depicted with skill and style which draws as much upon Southern as Northern technique. Breughel had travelled in Italy as far south as Naples (and a Madonna by Michelangelo was housed in Bruges). Here in *Dulle Griete*, line, volume and architectural construction are as exact as they could be. So too manifold forms of light – as cultivated by Van Eyck – appear here in the gleam of metals, the shimmer of stagnant rivers and spurts of volcanic flame. But eyes and vision here – as in the empty monocular surmounting the mouth of Hell – are agents of demonic possession; and luminous details now become knife-points and shards of glass. Painterly sophistication and humanist learning here combine to express the humanist's agonized perception of how far from humane the world can be. This terrible knowledge rises as far above history as Michelangelo's Sybil and produces a vision that might have terrified even Machiavelli.

RENAISSANCE PAST AND FUTURE

> Always dressed in the most beautiful red cloth . . . he was the neatest of men . . . at table
>
> he ate from the finest of antique dishes . . . his drinking cup was of crystal . . . to see him
>
> at table, looking like a figure from the ancient world, was a noble sight indeed.

These words written towards the end of the fifteenth century by Vespasiano da Bisticci – a dealer in manuscripts – invites us to see the perfect example of early Renaissance man in Niccolò Niccoli (1367–1437), who was a Florentine merchant of some standing, as well as being (at least in Vespasiano's opinion) the reviver of Greek and Latin letters.

The picture we are offered is one of consummate urbanity; and there can be no doubt of its appeal, especially if we think of self-fashioning as the primary characteristic of Renaissance Man. Yet the limitations of that view – which Vespasiano and Niccolò would presumably have shared – will by now also be apparent. It hardly seems likely for instance that Niccolò Niccoli would have been comfortable in the company of a Michelangelo who, in *The Last Judgement*, painted his own distorted features on the flayed skin of St Bartholomew. Still less would his *élite* vision have been able to encompass the hysteria and feminine power that Breughel contemplates in his portrayal of *Dulle Griete*.

Yet madness, melancholia, martyrdom, pain and penitence contribute as much to the art and thought of the Renaissance as do manners and decorum. As in the *Orlando Furioso*, so too in *The Ship of Fools* by Sebastian Brant of Strasbourg (1457–1521) or else Erasmus's *Praise of Folly*, lunacy is viewed with varying degrees of satire and irony. For some indeed, the creative act itself is the product of self-abandon. As will appear, blindness and drunkenness are represented by Neoplatonists such as Ficino as the way to superior insight; Melancholia, for Michelangelo and Dürer alike, is the very condition of genius; and Hamlet acts as chorus to this agitated scene.

There is then a subtext which cannot be ignored; and Renaissance scholars in recent years have been very fruitfully concerned to lay this subtext bare, emphasizing in particular three factors that characterize the Renaissance mind.

The first is located deep in a political and economic humus, where banking, commerce and propaganda may all be found to contribute to the flourishing of artistic achievement. Merchant–aesthetes such as Niccolò Niccoli were plainly unembarrassed by their own affiliations with the world of money. But – for good or ill – the most obvious respect in which the Renaissance prefigures the modern world is that it consolidates the foundations of a capitalist economy and demonstrates how easily one can overlook (or disguise) the hidden nexus of power, wealth and artistic or moral endeavour beneath the veil of conspicuous consumption. Even Machiavelli does not seem to have understood the extent to which economic forces may have been as important as military interests in shaping the social order; and the nineteenth-century historians – in celebrating the rationalism and individualism of Renaissance culture – revert sympathetically to the surface of this capitalist order at the expense of its dialectical depths.

Following from this one should not expect that Renaissance institutions would be moved by libertarian or democratic considerations. It is true that the language of republican liberty was cultivated in the merchant oligarchies of Florence and Venice as early as the thirteenth century. But Machiavelli in his own day revealed how platitudinous and indeed soporific conceptions of liberty could become in the mouths of a ruling *élite*; Utopias in the Renaissance, as will appear, could assume totalitarian characteristics; and even Carnival, where the popular voice might be expected to speak, could easily be employed – in the hands of, say, the Medici – as a device to channel and divert disruptive energies. Nor does religion – at least in the first instance – offer a release: Luther, along with Calvin, was vehement in his denunciation of popular disorder (as, for example, in his treatise *Against the Robbing and Murdering Hordes of Peasants*; and the Lutheran Dürer, while interested as many Northern artists were in the depiction of peasant life, could also devise a monument celebrating victory over the Revolutionaries, surmounted by a cowherd with a knife between his shoulder-blades.

Then finally there is the crucial question – bearing not only upon conception of political justice but also upon the very idea of what a human being might be – of the social position and representation of women in the Renaissance. In aristocratic circles, there can be no doubt that many women did receive and benefit from an education as good as or even superior to that of their brothers. Indeed, it will be suggested in Chapter Three that if we now seek an exemplar of the Renaissance Individual then Marguerite of Navarre – sister of the French King, Francis I – may well be regarded as such. But the prevailing mood of the period in this regard is set by the virago, or woman warrior, who, in a shifting perception which encompasses ambiguity, danger and uncomfortable comedy, dominates so many scenes from Ariosto and Tasso. Likewise, in political reality, Isabella of Spain is designated 'King' by the Pope of the day; Elizabeth I – daughter of the intellectually forceful Ann Boleyn – in her speech at Tilbury declares: 'I know I have the body of a weak and feeble woman, but I have the heart and stomach of a king.'

Up to a point it is of course anachronistic to expect that Renaissance thinkers could themselves have answered all the demands that critics in later ages have laid at their door. It would equally be foolish to suppose that demands of a political, economic or social nature could either explain or detract from the influence that the art of the period continues to exert over the imagination of its audience. On the other hand, a great tradition is characterized as much by the questions it bequeaths as by the conventions, sympathies and (sometimes) complacencies that it corroborates. In this sense it can only enhance our appreciation and engagement with the Renaissance vision that we should discover here, along with much that is familiar, much that is strange and as yet unresolved.

And much is strange about the Renaissance mentality – even for instance about the very conception of rationality – that might be supposed to provide a universal link between ourselves and our progenitors. Indeed, if there is any common feature to the many philosophies that the Renaissance produces, this may well reside, as Foucault suggests, in the belief that the world is ordered according to 'a chain of occult corre-spondences, sympathetic resonances and the visible marks of invisible analogies'. On this view, the Renaissance could not remotely be described as a scientific age; to enter such a world at all requires us to adopt the mentality as much of the magus as of the scientist – or else the skills of an anthropologist, alert to the patterns of tribal behaviour, rather than those of the estate agent seeking for desirable and comfortable properties.

More will be said to justify this contention in Chapter Four. Here, however, one may conclude – as one means to continue – with questions and with examples. What does it mean, for instance, that Francis I, the founder of humanist France and early architect of the modern French state (Fig. 6), should sanction a celebratory portrayal of himself in androgyne form as a bearded lady? Or why in the image depicted on the front cover of this volume should the English miniaturist Isaac Oliver choose, at the end of the Renaissance, to depict the image of a lover whose very clothing – though classical in its toga-like drapery – is woven out of tongues of flame? And why are the verses that surround this noble yet suffering head drawn here quoted from Petrarch, a poet who wrote in the vernacular 250 years before this image was painted?

The answer in the first case will require us to invoke the principles of analogy and correspondence, and to recognize – as many of the philosophies examined in Chapter Two will allow – that Francis here claims mystically to resolve all contradictions –

even those of gender – in his sacred being. In the second case, the answer is at one with arguments that I shall offer in every part of this volume: a man caught in a process of prismatic transformation from past to future, consumed yet unconsumed, tragic yet graceful, traversed by contradictions and questions, yet precisely in being so, brilliantly alive.

Isaac's elegant miniature represents in its own small way the characteristics of almost all the works of art that are studied in Part Two of this volume; and, having begun with Ariosto, who contemplates with such graceful irony the madness that affects the greatest of heroes, I shall end with Shakespeare whose plays reveal, sometimes comically but also tragically, the dynamic contradictions that often lie hidden beneath the surface of Renaissance civilization. Part One, however, considers how characteristics such as these also developed during this period in libraries and schools, at courtly entertainments and religious *autos-da-fé*; this account will begin where the Renaissance itself began, in the early formation of the commercial city.

Figure 6 Androgynous, *Portrait of Francis I*, (detail). Bibliothèque Nationale, Paris.

NOTES

It is still worth reading Jacob Burckhardt's *The Civilization of the Renaissance in Italy* (translated by S.G.C. Middlemore, London, 1995) not least because his views raise so many questions pursued by subsequent scholars. Excellent and sympathetically critical readings are to be found in Peter Burke's *The Renaissance* (Basingstoke, 1987), *The European Renaissance: Centres and Peripheries* (Oxford, 1998) and the *Italian Renaissance: Culture and Society in Italy* (Cambridge, 1999). Eugene Rice (with Antony Grafton), *The Foundations of Early Modern Europe 1460–1559* (New York, 1994) gives a comprehensive reading of the political and social history, as do G.R. Elton, *Reformation Europe 1517–1559* (London, 1963) and J.R. Hale in *Renaissance Europe 1480–1520* (1971) and *The Civilization of Europe in the Renaissance* (London, 1993). Hale's edited volume, *A Concise Encyclopedia of the Italian Renaissance* (London, 1981) is invaluable throughout for specific topics. On the Renaissance city, here and throughout, see Fernand Braudel's *Civilization and Capitalism* translated in three volumes by S. Reynolds (London, 1981–84). For definitions of the Renaissance, see especially Erwin Panofsky, ' "Renaissance"

– Self-Definition or Self-Deception?' in *Renaissance and Renascences* (London, 1965), pp. 1–35. For **Burgundy**, Christopher Cope, *Phoenix Frustrated: The lost kingdom of Burgundy* (London, 1986); Richard Vaughan, *Philip the Bold* (London, 1979), *John the Fearless* (London, 1979) and *Charles the Bold* (London, 1979). Derek Pearsall's *Gothic Europe 1200–1450* which precedes the present volume in the series *Arts, Culture and Society* contains a great deal of valuable material on the Northern Fourteenth Century, including Flemish and Burgundian culture. For **Northern art** see Jan Białostocki's *Il Quattrocento nell'Europa settentrionale* (Turin, 1989). A useful collection of translated texts (from which I quote Pico's *Oration* and Vives' *Fable*) is *The Renaissance Philosophy of Man*, ed. P.O. Kristeller *et al.* (Chicago and London, 1945). For **Ariosto** see C.P. Brand, *Ariosto* (Edinburgh, 1974) and A.R. Ascoli, *Ariosto's Bitter Harmony: Crisis and Evasion in the Italian Renaissance* (Princeton, 1987). For **Machiavelli**, see especially Quentin Skinner, *Machiavelli* (Oxford, 1981) and Felix Gilbert, *Machiavelli and Guicciardini* (London, 1984). For **Vasari** see Patricia Lee Rubin, *Giorgio Vasari: Art and History* (London and New Haven, 1995). Penguin translations are available for all of these authors. **Recent critical approaches** are exemplified by Lauro Martines, *Power and Imagination* (London, 1984), Stephen Greenblatt, *Renaissance Self-Fashioning* (Chicago, 1980), and *Marvellous Possessions* (Oxford, 1992), and Lisa Jardine's *Worldly Goods* (London, 1997). Recent works on the representation of women in the Renaissance are Pam Benson *The Invention of Renaissance Women* (Pennsylvania, 1992) and P. Tinagli, *Women in Italian Renaissance Art* (Manchester, 1997). For **M. Foucault**, see *The Order of Things: An Archaeology of the Human Sciences*, trans. Alan Sheridan (New York, 1970).

part one

THOUGHT
AND CONTEXT

chapter one

CITIES, SPACES AND
INSTITUTIONS

THE PIAZZA AND POLITICAL IMAGINING

In the 1450s, Leon Battista Alberti – architect, social theorist and the author of treatises on both painting and sculpture – devised a plan for a terrace of city houses that might, in a perfect city, have surrounded the piazza of a marketplace (Fig. 7). In this design, Alberti identifies a number of the aesthetic principles that had already begun to display themselves in the construction of both civic and private build-ings in Florence and that subsequently would be fundamental to the formation of Renais-sance taste. In Alberti's eyes, the function of architecture is 'to prescribe an appropriate place, exact numbers, a proper scale and a graceful order for whole buildings and for each of their constituent parts' so that in its siting, lineaments and angles the edifice should immediately communicate an effect of propor-tion (*Re Aed.*, I, i, p. 7). Similarly, the city at large should exhibit an orchestrated relation-ship between buildings which, while continu-ing to respond to the demands of 'convenience dignity and beauty', also encourages the many different activities at play in the social nexus. Squares, for instance, will be designed 'for the

Figure 7 Leonbattista Alberti, *Terrace to surround a Market place*, from *De Re Aedificatoria. VIII* c.1450 (illustrated from Italian translation, C. Bartoli, 1550). This figure is reproduced by kind permission of the Syndics of the Cambridge University Library.

exposing of merchandise in times of peace but also for the exercises proper to youth and equally for the laying-up of supplies in war-time' (*ibid*. IV, viii). In order to achieve such a harmony, the ambitions of citizens will of course have to be governed by a measured understanding of the whole. Such restraint, however, will not preclude an interest in ornamentation and stylish display. Columns are an especially important feature, allowing the architect to demonstrate an understanding of both mathematical proportion and classical forms of embellishment.

In architecture such as this, no less than in Ariosto's *Orlando Furioso*, order and variety, display and discretion appear as prevailing characteristics of the Renaissance mentality; indeed in Alberti's marketplace, mathematical expertise and classical erudition would have been present to the eyes of his fellow citizens, even while they were shopping. This particular marketplace was never built. But Alberti was responsible for public works in Mantua, Rimini and Rome as well Florence (Fig. 13); and his influence – combining with a renewed interest in the writings of the Roman architect, Vitruvius – spread progressively throughout Europe at large. Variations on Alberti's Florentine formula were subsequently performed by Bramante (in the rebuilding of Papal Rome), by the Bolognese architect Sebastian Serlio (who carried Renaissance motifs to France, England and Poland), and above all by Andrea Palladio whose influence was to extend as far as eighteenth-century America.

The significance of these developments cannot be limited to the area of architectural taste. For, properly understood, the Renaissance concern with the delineation and decoration of urban space is the visible expression of an ethical and eventually political concern that animates all aspects of life, whether intellectual or social, in this period. To be human in the Renaissance is essentially to participate in the public life of the piazza. Indeed, for Alberti (drawing upon notions he discovered in Cicero) the proportions of a city should themselves reflect and magnify the proportions of the human body. Correspondingly, it is through its performance on the public stage that, as a social self, the individual discovers its true destiny. 'Glory', as Alberti declares, 'is to be sought not in the realm of private leisure but in the public spaces of a city.' The meaning of glory differs from culture to culture, sometimes being sought in monastic contemplation of divine creation, sometimes in the salon, or science laboratory. For Alberti, glory means unambiguously the excellence that human beings may cultivate in their secular existences. For him the public spaces of the city – echoing with the achievements of heroes past and present, of orators, warriors, merchants and gymnasts – is the stage on which the whole gamut of human activities are nurtured, pursued and applauded.

The City, then, is the point of intersection between theory and practice, word and deed, mind and marble and mortar. To say this is in part to emphasize that the growth of cities throughout Europe was initially fuelled by vigorous economic advances. Nor was Alberti – the builder of marketplaces – unmindful of this. On the contrary, he speaks of money itself without the least embarrassment. Money is for him a 'bait' but also a 'source of nourishment'; so far from being the root of all evil, money is the lifeblood of everything that matters: 'whoever lacks money lacks almost everything'. Money is necessary for everything. It would nonetheless be simplistic to suppose that conspicuous consumption were the catch-all explanation of Renaissance culture. Better say that there occurred in this period a unique (if highly unstable) alchemy of money and intellect. Ideas themselves will here prove saleable; but money is often no more than a catalyst, facilitating but not entering into a chain reaction of artistic and intellectual excitements.

The potentialities of Alberti's thinking are realized as much in the imagination as in the pocket. Henceforth, visual artists were able to produce plans for ideal cities conceived with mathematical rigour on classical principles (Fig. 8); and painters such as Botticelli, Mantegna or Perugino (Fig. 9) were quick to include exuberant and sometimes fantastic representations of architecture in their paintings. Likewise, the period is rich in conceptions of Utopia or of Golden Worlds – often with reference to Plato's *Republic* or to the classical pastoral; and if Shakespeare's theatre is called the

Figure 8   Luciano Laurana (designer; probably painted by Piero della Francesca), *View of an Ideal City*, late 15th century, Panel, 60.5 × 200.5 cm. Galleria Nazionale delle Marche, Palazzo Ducale, Urbino. With permission from Scala.

Figure 9   Perugino, *Christ giving the Keys to St Peter*. Fresco Sistine Chapel, Rome. With permission from Scala.

Globe, then this is because it seeks to assemble an audience in microcosm and re-create in fictional space its own understanding of the actual world. As William H. Sherman has written, there are 'striking parallels between the "wooden O" of the Renaissance theatre and the "wooden world" of the Renaissance ship'; and explor-ation, trade and travel in this period would demand, alongside artistic imaginings, very considerable advances in cartography and navigational aids to encompass newly discovered territories.

In conjunction with these imaginative and scientific configurations, the Renais-sance witnesses a whole series of experiments in the formation of ethical, political and religious space. Rome is reconstructed on decidedly theatrical principles; Calvin conjures up a severe Utopia on the shores of Lake Geneva; and as geographical (and ultimately astronomical) space expands under the impulse of economic and dynastic or national ambition, so political theory also develops in response to the many pres-sures and possibilities that were revealed in this expansion.

Around 1500, the Florentine Guicciardini declared, in a mood of panic and alienation, that there was too much space in the world; and well he might, for the spaces beyond Florence were shortly to be filled with vertiginous displays of hungry dynasticism. Conversely, at the end of the period, the political prisoner Tommaso Campanella (1568–1639) – the author of the Utopic *City of the Sun*, who in his own time was also described as the new Machiavelli – is happy to justify a use of all the devices of mod-ern warfare in Imperial adventures to ensure the diffusion of knowledge and science, arguing the fundamental human right is the right to know. Since then, the Western mind has been characterized by a desire to encompass all conceivable space and fill it with the evidence of its own supposedly civilized achievement. The contradictions in this ambition are evident, as William Blake was to recognize when he raises his voice against the clangour of 'mind-forged manacles' that resonate in London on the banks of the 'charted' Thames. This was eighteenth-century London. Yet in retrospect it is by no means impossible to discern in Alberti's Florentine commitment to mathemat-ics and money remote anticipations of these sounds. And certainly the sounds will grow louder as one travels (in sections three, four and five of this chapter) from a court such as Urbino, to the palace of Francis I at Fontainebleau and on to the consistories and chancelleries of Geneva and Rome, observing in each place how the patterns of institutional control were intimately linked with the architectural designation of space. Alberti himself would not, however, have wished to hear this, even though his own Medici patrons were in this regard as in many others precursors of a larger European development. Alberti, throughout the early part of his life, had been an exile. He understood at first hand how hard it is for a human life to flourish in isola-tion from the universe of civic activities. To him, Florence was still in some measure a sacred place, where the Florentine tribe could cultivate the forms of thought and art that other generations would turn to other uses.

Figure 10   Medieval Towers of San Gimigniano, Tuscany. With permission from Scala.

THE FLORENTINE FORMULA

The Florence to which the exiled Alberti returned was changing rapidly. Its medieval cityscape – like those of most Italian cities, including Rome – had been dominated by a stark forest of towers, such as are now seen at San Gimigniano (Fig. 10). These towers were once the clan houses or strongholds of feudal families, and stood as the expression of mutual suspicion as well as of a desire to outbuild the neighbours. But insofar as the feudal nobility had begun to move into the city at all – attracted by the possibilities of merchant adventure – they also represent the beginnings of a new order.

To Dante, this moment was the cataclysmic origin of a decadent age where avarice, envy and pride would defile the sacred territory of the city, unleashing the forces that led to his exile. But the exiled Alberti a hundred years later saw things differently. From as early as the thirteenth century, Italian intellectuals – in particular Florentines such as Dante himself – had shown a profound interest in the revival of interest in Roman Law, and Ciceronian rhetoric was simultaneously a focus of intellectual attention. By the end of the fourteenth century, the city had developed a jubilant conception of its new-found possibilities. Leonardi Bruni (1370–1444), for instance – an Aretine by birth who had been drawn to Florence and eventually served as its Chancellor – writes his *Laudatio Florentinae urbis* of 1401 in praise of the Florentine constitution, its government and even its bureaucracy. Orsanmichele had been trans-

Figure 11   Filippo Brunelleschi, *Ospedale degli Innocent*, begun 1419 and completed mid-15th century. Piazza della SS. Annunziata, Florence. With permission from Scala.

formed from a commercial warehouse into a church. Masaccio and Donatello (see Figs 3 and 44–48) were now energetically at work. And most important, from Alberti's point of view, architects were now beginning to open up and ornament the spaces of the city in a highly distinctive style.

In particular, Filippo Brunelleschi (1377–1446) had shown a capacity to build in a manner that responded to classical models while subtly adapting these models to the interests and ambitions of contemporary Florence. In Santo Spirito he designed a Church with many of the qualities of a Roman basilica. In the Pazzi Chapel he delicately adapted Roman domestic architecture to a space that fitted the Gothic precincts of the great Franciscan Church of Santa Croce. Among the most graceful of Brunelleschi's creations is the Foundlings Hospital with its portico of Corinthian columns (Fig. 11).

The most significant of Brunelleschi's works, however, to speak politically as well as architecturally, is the high, red dome of the Duomo (Fig. 12). This was the largest dome to be erected since the Pantheon in Rome; and classical aspirations speak clearly in its lines. Yet its somewhat ovoid shape, along with a Gothic tension in its ascent, was also to insert itself into the vernacular memory as an inspiration to Michelangelo when he came to build the dome of St Peter's. To Alberti, the Florentine dome was a structure 'rising sheer above the skies, yet ample enough to cover with its shadow the people of all Tuscany, built without aid of cross beams . . . an artifice

Figure 12   Filippo Brunelleshi, *The Dome at the Cathedral at Florence*, 1420–1436. With permission from Scala.

to surpass modern or even perhaps ancient times'. Structure and engineering skill are here accorded due appreciation. So, too, are politics and ethics: the dome encompasses the whole region of Tuscany in its protective embrace; and – as a symbol of ascendancy – even rises *above* the Heavens. Unlike a Gothic tower, diminishing towards the sky, this edifice articulates space, both vertical and lateral, as though the horizontal space were its own political possession.

Whenever Alberti speaks of churches, the term he invariably employs is the Latin – therefore profane – term 'temple'. He also expresses a fervent desire that any modern temple should be illuminated not by 'the feeble and guttering light of tapers' but rather by fenestrations that could orchestrate 'majestically' the natural light of the sun. Yet the secularism implied in this view should not lead one to ignore a darker and more troubled obverse to Alberti's enthusiasms. This is evident whenever he speaks – as in his satire *Theogenius* – 'of how the ether is besieged by an unbelievable clamour of holy vows: Apollo's path is encumbered, Juno's court wholly covered by them'. Here, it seems, human stupidity defiles the purity of the pagan skies with its superstitious chantings and prayers. The suggestion must be that, secretly, Alberti entertained a desire to preserve the clarity of geometric construction from the untidy contamination of human folly.

This surreptitiously dictatorial tendency is confirmed when Alberti sets himself in *Della Famiglia* to celebrate the family principles that sustained the great Alberti clan in their mercantile endeavours – he himself being an illegitimate offspring. Despite a skilful employment of dialogue-form, which allows him to explore many different facets of the family ethos, Alberti speaks with unfailing admiration of the autocratic discipline exercised by the Alberti patriarchs. This is particularly evident in his discussion of the women of the family. Wives will be chosen for their virtue and for the honour they bring. They will be instructed in the secrets of the household, with the aim of enabling them, in their turn, to exert a rigorous supervision of the activities performed by lesser members of the family and its servants. This is *masserizia*, the care of resources and control of domestic space, which both male and female members of the household all display. Women nonetheless make no contribution to the patriarchal debate.

Activity is the key word in Albert's ethical vocabulary. For him, all things in creation are in a constant state of motion: fish are constantly swimming, bees forever in flight; and so in their own lives should human beings be. Seen in a positive light, such a demand is the source of an energy displayed to good effect in the life of the piazza. A concern with the profitable use of time will re-emerge in many guises – not least that of Calvinism – throughout the Renaissance: it is one aspect of Renaissance secularism that it should seek to bring to fruition every least seed of possibility that the temporal world affords. It is equally possible, however, to see here a driven and even anxious cast of mind – reflecting perhaps the insecurities of an exiled, illegitimate and sometimes misogynistic Alberti. If 'money makes everything possible', so too 'the man who knows how not to waste time knows everything'. 'Even a blind man can turn a rope-maker's wheel'.

All of this may suggest that Albertian culture is merely a façade. But if it is a façade then it is one that human beings can never do without. Thus the most characteristic of Alberti's own architectural works is the frontage of Santa Maria Novella, which reconciles geometric experiment with a lively respect for mercantile realities and an ability to harmonize rather than to set at odds the classical past and medieval past (Fig. 13). One of the greatest inspirations for this design was the geometric patternings, suggested not only by the classical arts of proportion but also by the façade of the twelfth-century Florentine Baptistery that still stands in the centre of Florence (Fig. 42). Alberti's conception shows great respect for the original gothic edifice. The great curving buttresses that surmount the rectangle show equal respect for mercantile interests: seen as sails, they allude to the emblem of the Rucellai merchants who commissioned this structure.

Comparable forces – in harmonious discord – are also present in the larger history of Florence; and it is no accident that Alberti found favour with the Medici family. Of the brilliant achievements that flowed from Medici patronage more will be said later

Figure 13 Leonbattista Alberti, *Façade of Santa Maria Novella*, c.1456–70, Florence. With permission from Scala.

in speaking of artists who worked for them, such as Donatello and Michelangelo. Yet the successes of Medicean Florence rose on the foundations of *masserizia* – or good housekeeping – and of family pride cannily sustained over a couple of centuries. The Medici had arrived as immigrants in Florence in the 1200s; and in the sixteenth century they were to move on to an international stage by the acquisition (in collaboration with invading forces) of Dukedoms, Papal thrones and eventually of marriage alliances with the French Royal House. In the fifteenth century, however, Cosimo de' Medici (1389–1464) was deliberately unostentatious, pursuing a policy which (although it did arouse enmity) was aimed at the careful management of an international banking network and (in Florence itself) at the cultivation of influence rather than naked power. The fifteenth-century Medici were never in a constitutional sense the rulers of Florence. Rather, they ensured their dominance by controlling the committees of the oligarchic, though ostensibly Republican, machinery of government. In the early years, Medici influence was spread through advantageous marriages in the local market; later, they secured a sure hold on the electoral register; and by the mid-fifteenth century – especially under the direction of Lorenzo Il Magnifico (1449–92) – the Medici palace itself was likely to be the venue for ambassadorial or diplomatic encounters rather than the civic buildings of the Republic. But just as Cosimo desired to be known simply as *Pater Patriae* – Father of the Fatherland – so too the Medici palace, seen from the outside, with its rusticated walls and heavy projecting roof, has something of the grim restraint of a fortified money-box. Inside, however, there was all the apparatus of an aristocratic court.

In this respect, the Medici led a double life, participating with enthusiasm and profit in the city that Alberti admired, yet opening the way to a new form of social organization – centred less on the city than on courts and courtly practices – which would contribute directly to political changes of ultimately international dimensions as the century turned from Quattro- to Cinquecento.

COURTLY VARIATIONS: THE EXAMPLE OF URBINO

By the middle of the fifteenth century the surges of economic development that initially fuelled the development of Venice, Florence and Milan had produced a reconfiguration of the Italian political map. Many small and hitherto autonomous city-states had been absorbed into the hegemony of the three great powers (Rome being largely dormant till the Papacy returned there in 1420). With the Franco-Spanish invasions of Italy further readjustments would occur. For a short period, however, the chances of war and political negotiation produced a number of small but independent courts administered by hereditary dynasties; and these were to exert an influence especially in matters of culture on an international scale quite disproportionate to their size – which in population may often have been between 15,000 and 30,000 inhabitants.

Pre-eminent among these courts were Mantua, Ferrara and Urbino, ruled respectively by the Gonzaga, Este and Montefeltro dynasties. These autocratic families were free to make claims to noble rank, as the Medici of Republican Florence certainly did not allow themselves to do; and one important way in which power and the arts came into fruitful association in these courts was in the celebration of marriage alliances between noble houses. Moving away in manner if not in substance from the notions of bourgeois *masserizia*, the courts tended to intermarry, bringing women into prominence and also producing the elaborate nuptial celebrations in which arts and artists of all kinds would be enlisted. Henceforth, aristocratic women were increasingly influential as patrons of the arts and followers of the humanistic pursuits that gravitated around these centres. In Mantua, for instance, Isabella d'Este (1474–1539) not only encouraged the works of Leonardo and Titian but also – as will be seen in Chapter Eight – played an important role in the development of Italian music. More generally, the courts provided an atmosphere in which artistic and intellectual experiment (improvising on the Florentine theme) helped to disseminate these cultural advances throughout all Europe. It was in Ferrara under the Este dynasty that the Renaissance epic first developed, as a medium in which poets such as Boiardo, Ariosto and later Tasso could celebrate the strengths – and also suggest the tragic weaknesses – of Renaissance culture. However, for a short period of thirty or forty years in the second half of the fifteenth century, the smallest of these courts was also the most influential. This was Urbino.

In the fortunes of Urbino, the dominant figure is Duke Federigo di Montefeltro (1422–82), who – though an illegitimate son – assumed power over this mountainous domain (nominally under the control of Rome) in 1444. Federigo's enormous fortune was almost entirely dependent upon his activities as a military expert. Geographically, Federigo's lands lay in close proximity to Venice; and his marriage to Battista Sforza allied him with Milan. But his private army operated most effectively in support of the Florentine Medici. So formidable was Federigo's fighting capacity that, during the peace that prevailed in the later Quattrocento between the three major Italian powers, his income was secured by protective agreements *not* to engage in battle. In this same period Urbino enjoyed especial esteem abroad. England in particular – under both Yorkist and Lancastrian rulers – sought to win influence in Rome by honouring the ruler of Urbino, who remained in high favour with the Papacy. Edward IV of England lacked representation in the Roman Curia and, in the year that Federigo was made a Duke by the Pope, correspondingly bestowed on Federigo the Order of the Garter. In 1506, Federigo's son, Guidobaldo, was accorded the same honour by Henry VII – who at the time was seeking Papal approval for a marriage between the widowed Catherine of Aragon and his second son Henry. In return, Henry Tudor received a painting by Raphael – whose father was the court poet of Urbino – depicting St George and the Dragon. (This gift formed the first contribution to what are now the Queen's Pictures.) English interest in Urbino continued when Henry employed the Urbinese Polydore Virgilio (with only qualified success) to write a history of England that would applaud the newly established Tudor dynasty. An equal or greater beneficiary of Urbinese talent was the Papacy and Rome. Raphael would execute his most ambitious work under papal patronage; and Bramante, also born in Urbino, was probably the finest architect of High Renaissance Rome (Fig. 22).

Urbino in this period attracted as well as provided genius. Alberti visited Urbino; he may have been consulted on the rebuilding of the Duke's palace and certainly left a copy of *De Re Edificatoria* in Federigo's library. Piero della Francesca worked here producing, among other pieces, the great celebratory depiction of Federigo and his wife, Battista (see Fig. 14). But the court also attracted Northern artists such as Justus of Ghent and the Spanish painters such as Pedro Berreguete. As for tapestries, by the end there were works by twenty Northern weavers in the Ducal inventory.

Of all the intellectuals who worked at Urbino none was more impressed by the myths and achievements of the Montefeltro clan than the Mantuan Baldassare Castiglione (1478–1529), author of *The Book of the Courtier* (Fig. 1). Nor, on an international scale, was any thinker of the period more influential than Castiglione in defining the nature of the Renaissance court, or in suggesting how courtliness might itself become a catalyst in the shift from civic culture to the dynastic and ultimately national politics of the sixteenth century.

Where fifty years before Alberti wrote a treatise on the mercantile family, Castiglione, offers an account – in delicately dramatized form – of conversations that may have taken place among the courtiers of Urbino, concerning the nature of courtliness, the place of wit in courtly life, the position of women at court and the ethical and political influence that a courtier might expect to exert in his dealings with his sovereign. Castiglione's *Book of the Courtier* was the first of many Renaissance conduct books, by authors such as Stefano Guazzo and Giovanni della Casa along with an English version of Castiglione's own work by Sir Thomas Hoby (1530–66). Indeed the genre proved so popular with the nouveaux riches in their search for the secret of gentility that aristocrats began to fear it would devalue their own cachet. Castiglione, however, so far from offering merely a manual of polite behaviour, insists upon the subtlety and indefinability of true courtliness and simultaneously ascribes to those who possess this quality a central role in political and cultural negotiations. Courtliness depends upon the cultivation of *sprezzatura*. 'Nonchalance' might be one translation, 'artless art' another. Yet Castiglione's own word is itself a neologism or term of art, hardly meant to be understood save by those who already understand it. Only those who practise *sprezzatura* will know what it is. Yet possession of it can be a matter of life and death at the Renaissance court. In circumstances where there were no constitutional checks on monarchical behaviour, a certain inwardness – as of those that 'speak the same language' – with the style and character of a ruler was the only way in which a courtier might introduce moderation or good advice into the councils of state. The telling word or graceful gesture in the corridors of power could easily be the most effective means of political representation. So, too, the courtier's own survival might depend upon his success or failure in attracting or sustaining the attention of his lord. At the very least *sprezzatura* – as a form of 'courtly performance' – contributes, as Ariosto demonstrates, to the political theatre of the court.

Castiglione, in his time, proved to be a far more successful politician than Machiavelli. It was he who received the Order of the Garter on behalf of Duke

Figure 14   Piero della Francesca, *Profile Portraits of Federigo da Montefeltro and his wife Battista Sforza*, c.1478, Panel, 47 × 33 cm. Uffizi Gallery, Florence. With permission from Scala.

Guidobaldo; and at his death he was himself due to be offered a cardinal's hat. Indeed, the skills of the courtier are immediately visible in his description of the court of Urbino, which simultaneously disguises the realities of brute politics and knowingly and willingly promotes a myth or idealized picture of the court and its inhabitants. By Castiglione's day, the great age of Federigo was over; and Urbino had, for a short time, felt the effects of political reality under the rule of the Machiavellian, Cesare Borgia. This may account for a certain elegant melancholia in Castiglione's tone. Yet with a witty lightness of touch – or *sprezzatura* – Castiglione confects an animating image of a city and a court which can still cast light in the midst of surrounding calamities. Conscious that 'Urbino' means 'little city' (a microcosmic Rome) Castiglione adjusts geography (but still with a modest tonality) to present the 'little' city of Urbino as 'almost' in the middle of Italy. Its location is in the mountains and therefore 'not as pleasing' as some might be. Nevertheless, the city benefits (as Alberti would have wished) from 'the healthiness of its air' and is surrounded by fertile and fruitful land (*Il Cortegiano*, Prologue). Above all, Urbino is represented by its Ducal Palace which 'many consider to be the most beautiful in all Italy'. Significantly, the palace seems to be 'less a palace than a city in the form of a palace': in both geographical and political terms the courtly culture is moving away from the urban arena; it remains nonetheless a term of praise to associate that culture with a civic ethos.

The Ducal Palace of Urbino is set on the summit of a crag, elevated still further by two towers of a northern, even romantic design. The Duke's balcony lies between these towers allowing him (as is suggested in Piero's portrait) a confident outlook over his own territories. There is power here – but none of the secrecy which characterized the regime of Cosimo de' Medici. At the same time, there is also discretion and balance – reflecting Albertian precepts yet advancing beyond them in a lightness of touch that shows itself immediately in the courtyard designed by the Dalmatian architect, Luciano Laurana (Fig. 15). This space is dominated by an elegant piece of classical epigraphy which, in proclaiming Federigo to be its maker, unambiguously asserts his absolute authority. Yet the courtyard seems to have been open to the public in Federigo's day. Beyond this there runs the sequence of rooms that leads eventually to the private quarters of the Duke. Again, the plan of many of these rooms – where Castiglione locates his courtly debate – are at one with an Albertian interest in the orchestration of large and small spaces and dark and light. They also demonstrate the extent to which architectural space was thought to contribute to the mood and mental well-being of those that moved within it. Yet in this light it is remarkable how restrained in dimension – though rich in ornament – the private rooms of the ruler prove to be. Though eventually giving out onto Federigo's triumphal balcony, the suite – comprising chapel, bathroom and study – is meditative and symbolic in character. Rising as if from a purifying immersion in the bathroom and jewel-encrusted chapel, a narrow staircase leads to the study that is wholly decorated by marquetry

Figure 15   Luciano Laurana, *Courtyard, Palazzo Ducale*, c.1465–after 1472, Urbino. With permission from Scala.

panels (Fig. 16) depicting in rare wood both realistic details (including a squirrel) and the emblems of scholarly activity such as compasses and lutes. *Sprezzatura* is here exemplified in the graceful accomplishment that allows the volumes and textures of the natural world to be depicted in a medium as rigid as wood might seem to be. The linearity of wooden panelling responds to perspectival rules expressing, at one and the same time, the controlling power of human vision and the delight one may take in illusion or *trompe l'oeil*. The Duke was a soldier. But the image of himself that he wished to cultivate was that of the scholar, humanist and sage; and illusionistic skill enabled him to promote that image.

Piero's portrayal of Federigo conceals (as do all other portraits of him) the disfigurements that affected his right profile. So too the court poet (and father of Raphael) Giovanni Sanzio constructs a mythic programme in which the illegitimate Federigo can be seen as the Child of Jove, who in his posthumous triumph is greeted by the most illustrious messengers of Mars along with the singing of all the Muses; 'and at his right, I saw Pallas, her dress delicate, rich and noble'. Propaganda of this sort will become common currency as the courts of the Renaissance transform themselves into seats of absolute power. Yet it would be wrong to obscure with cynical hindsight the extent to which, in the Renaissance itself, 'magnificence' – greatness in ambition and expense – was a virtue, uniting lords and subjects in the common

Figure 16   Intarsia Panels from the *Studiolo* of Federigo da Montefeltro, 1470s. Palazzo Ducale, Urbino. With permission from Scala.

pursuit of glory. One of Federigo's most impressive possessions was his collection of rare and costly manuscripts. Federigo seems not to have lost touch, in the course of his political and military career, with an early education in the schools of humanism, nor for that matter with a practical interest in Albertian housekeeping. Indeed, there are signs that he cultivated a certain domestic benevolence of demeanour in conscious rivalry with the notoriously tyrannical Sigismondo Malatesta – whose court at Rimini, lying some forty kilometres from Urbino, espoused a flagrant interest in displays of pagan power. Where Sigismondo inhabited a fortress-like palace on the edges of Rimini, Federigo located himself in the centre of his city. Similarly, the aristocratic women of the Ducal court seem to have enjoyed a role far freer than that of their bourgeoise counter-parts in Albertian Florence. Castiglione's debate is directed by the women of court; and Federigo's wife Battista not only enjoyed a humanist education but was also entrusted with the government of Urbino (along with the power to sign treaties) in periods when her husband was absent. Sigismondo's wife Gentile (in keeping with the temper of her own particular court) was reputed to be an Amazon in battle, a 'Penthesilea'.

It is striking that, alongside the emblems of an Imperial Eagle that Federigo adopted, he should also have favoured the motif of the Sweeping-Brush. This betokens a fanatical concern with everyday hygiene – which apparently extended to the checking of the fingernails of his servants and to a concern with drains – but also an attitude to his subjects which might well have combined good housekeeping with military discipline and paternalism.

More precise political diagnoses are hard to make. But that in itself is an indication of the political character of the court. For a short time, in the late 1400s, political discourse could be silenced by expedient political play and patronage; the courtly arts could perform to practical effect upon the internal issues of the state and promote the interests of the state persuasively in the international arena. Such arts would continue to be prized – and be necessary – throughout the sixteenth century. However, as states grew in size and ambition, new discourses were required to advance and define the political purposes that they embodied.

DYNASTIES, NATIONS AND STATES: THE FRENCH EXAMPLE

From the small world of Urbino, Castiglione – as a courtier and diplomat – moved with ease into an international arena that, by the beginning of the sixteenth century, had broadened to accommodate the political ambitions of France, of the Habsburg Empire and, to a lesser degree, of Tudor England. Among the protagonists in that arena who most impressed him, one was Francis I of France whom he met in 1515 at Bologna and again at Pavia in 1524, shortly before Francis was captured and imprisoned in Madrid by his Spanish opponents. An early version of *The Courtier* is dedicated to Francis and contains an encomiastic portrait of his princely virtues. The same work, however, praises Henry VIII of England; and in later years Castiglione would transfer his allegiances to Charles V, Habsburg Emperor and ruler of Spain. It was through Charles's influence that Castiglione expected to become a cardinal.

Such courtly tergiversations point alike to the changing character of political realities in the early sixteenth century and equally to the resilience and continuing importance of the courtly ethic to new political developments. It is in this period that France, Spain and Tudor England began to develop as nation states, and religion itself in the sixteenth century would soon be an occasion for bloodshed: partisan battle-standards would wave over the Catholic Empire of Spain and the Protestant powder-barrel of England, while simultaneously drawing France into the quagmire of civil strife. Correspondingly, issues of space and institution here move beyond both city and court to embrace dynastic ambitions to contemplate forms of organization that anticipate the expansionist and ultimately absolutist monarchies of the seventeenth century. Spain in particular developed a code of honour that embodied an extreme and punctilious understanding of courtliness – as well as devising a tightly efficient system of bureaucratic control. But it was France under Francis I that first displayed the cultural possibilities of the new ethos and, drawing still on the vocabulary of Italian political thought, laid the foundation of monarchical polity.

Francis's own grandmother was Valentina Visconti, born into the ruling house of Milan. Indeed Francis himself – being effectively ruler of Milan from his accession in 1507 until 1521 – could easily be regarded by Italian courtiers as an Italian prince; and many of the courtiers who appear in the *Cortegiano* sought refuge at Francis's court. In Europe at large the agitations of the period combined with the growing pressure of absolutist states and religious controversy brought about a considerable movement of displaced intellectuals, artists and men of conscience. France exported its own flock of intellectual refugees. (Du Bellay went to Rome and Clément Marot spent

Figure 17   Stair case in Francis I's wing of the château at Blois, 1515–1524. Roger-Viollet.

time in Ferrara before arriving in Geneva.) But it also offered sanctuary to many others, especially those who were skilled in the courtly arts. The preferment they received was often ecclesiastical in character – exemplifying the nepotism and abuse of Church offices that so scandalized Luther. However, the currency of exchange was essentially secular and in that regard contributed to the development of an international market in ideas and styles. In the course of Francis's reign, Italian artists as diverse as Raphael, Serlio, Primaticcio and Cellini all had some association with Francis's court; and Leonardo died at the manor of Cloux given to him by Francis I (after the artist had devised, among other things, a mechanical lion for court entertainment).

A major consequence of this exchange was architectural. At Blois (Fig. 17) – as later more extensively at Fontainebleau – an attempt was made to reconcile Italian motifs with the existing lineaments of Northern, and predominantly Gothic, frameworks. Venetian and Milanese examples – with their own inclination to arabesques and intricacy of design line – were much preferred to the austere volumetric geometries of Florence. Correspondingly, Francis, though a warrior by disposition, had been trained in humanist schools and displayed, in common with his provincial counterpart Federigo, a great interest in book collection. His Ambassador to Venice was commissioned to look for Greek manuscripts; and by the end of his reign his library contained some 3,000 manuscripts in Latin and Greek and 150 printed books. These volumes formed the basis of the French National Library; and it was Francis who first established the principle of Legal Deposit. This might be viewed as an early attempt at absolutist control of the press; and at one point in his reign Francis had reason to know how subversive public placards could be. At the same time, Francis's interest in scholarship was sufficient to allow some latitude even to Protestant thinking and to Northern forms of humanism. His sister Marguerite had probably received a better humanist education than he had himself and, like Anne Boleyn, was to promote the cause of Protestant experiment. But Francis (unsuccessfully) invited Erasmus to France, and was pupil and patron of Guilluame Budé (1468–1540) who became almost the equal of Erasmus in his cultivation of the Greek language.

Francis, then, may rightly be considered a humanist prince and as such was successfully able to transform both French culture itself and the Italian model that he had initially adopted. The French King after all inherited a realm and not merely a 'little city'. In contrast to the territories ruled by Charles V of Spain and Henry VIII of England, this realm was relatively stable, unembarrassed by over-extension or by problematical succession. Francis indeed was endowed with some of the ceremonial accoutrements of divine right. It was his prerogative to receive the Eucharist in the form of wine as well as bread; his powers could be seen as the thaumaturgical powers of a priestly magician (Fig. 6); and an anonymous court poet, celebrating the nomination of Francis as heir to Louis XII in 1506, describes the dedication of an altar to 'Saint' Francis within the 'Temple of France'.

At the same time, in the practical and philosophical organization of his kingdom there were issues that could not simply be contained within the idea of a city or even of a court. Faced with a very large realm and the remnants of a feudal aristocracy, Francis needed to develop a style of Court Progress in which, as he travelled through his kingdom, the realities of power could be articulated in visible and symbolic display. Châteaux such as Blois provide one illustration. So too did Francis's cavalcades – which might involve the movement of several thousand horsemen and knightly followers. Benefiting from taxation laws established in previous ages, Francis (though an expansive and therefore expensive monarch) never needed to summon the Estates. In any case, his authoritarian temperament disinclined him to do so. Yet the same temperament seems also to have conspired with his aura and interest in chivalric endeavour to ensure a cohesion in France which contrasted greatly with the subsequent descent of the country into the Wars of Religion.

A forthright statement of Francis's political position might be found in the words addressed by his Chancellor Poyet to the *parlement* of Rouen in 1540: 'The king is not asking for advice as to whether or not his laws are to be observed: once the prince has decreed them, one must proceed; no one has the right to interpret, adjust or diminish them.' Pronouncements such as these are self-evidently absolutist in tendency. They also betray, however, a certain understanding of how Law should command assent in and for itself; and to that degree Poyet's words anticipate a juridical vision of the State as being an entity distinct from its citizens and rulers alike. By the end of the century this view would be explicitly proposed by Bodin and subsequently by Hobbes; and developments in Spain, Geneva and Reformation Rome were all to contribute to the growth of that position, leading decisively away from the particularities of civic and courtly polity.

There were, however, those in France (including Rabelais) who were ready to address their courtly advice to the French sovereign and, specifically, to analyse the shifting relationships between hereditary monarchy, nation and state.

One such is by Claude de Seyssel (1450–1520), Bishop of Marseilles and one-time member of the Paris Parlement, who in 1515 presented the new King with a treatise on *La monarchie de France*. Seyssel insists that the King is ordained by God. But he also allows in a spirit of moderation that there must be checks upon absolute authority. Some of these checks derive from the general traditions within which any sovereign must be thought to act, as also from the rules of succession and from the duty to preserve the royal patrimony – all of which are conditions underlying any particular reign but also independent of it. Other limitations derive from the social pyramid that 'assigns to each stratum of society its proper status and its accompanying rights and obligations'. Seyssel, then, is concerned not only with the conservation and augmentation of the monarchy but also with *la police* in the form of the checks, balances, customs and good advice to which a ruler must always be attentive.

A different emphasis emerges from the writings of Guillaume Budé. Serving as Francis's court humanist, Budé's tendency was to speak in terms of honour and glory – familiar from the writings of other humanists such as Alberti and Erasmus – but also to emphasize the ultimate authority of the King. Such a position would harden in the thinking of Du Moulin who declares that the king's majesty is 'a living law', 'a corporeal God within his own kingdom'. Budé, however, characteristically voices this recommendation through an insistence upon prudence and upon a need to regard the local constitutions established in any one country. This in effect admits an alliance between absolute power and expediency. For 'prudence' can be taken to mean that a certain pragmatism may enter the actions of a ruler so as to temper any impractical or over-scrupulous devotion to justice. Nor need a modern sovereign be bound by the example of Rome. As one of a line of legal humanists, Budé strikingly calls into question the universal validity of the Justinian Code of Roman law – which was greatly admired by late medieval writers such as Dante. Any code needed to be interpreted in the historical context of its culture; the consequence was that the sovereign of any country might claim the right to develop his own autonomous (or better, autochthonic) forms of authority.

To speak – with Seyssel – of the checks and balances inherent in an institution or to recommend – with Budé – cautiously Machiavellian 'prudence' in defence of monarchical power is to anticipate a debate which would continue into the seventeenth century and far beyond as absolutisms, reasons of state and demands for democratic representation begin to dominate the political scene. However, the implications of such shifts – prior to the establishment of any legal, parliamentary or academic forum for discussion – were less likely to appear in the conclusions of formal philosophy than in those relationships between power and ceremony which Renaissance courtiers were especially trained to choreograph. Examples could be found in Spain, England and Rome. This development is not unique to France as Henry VIII's palaces can tesify. Indeed Francis was to enter into cultural as well as

Figure 18   Hans Holbein, *Solomon Receiving the Homage of the Queen of Sheba*, c.1535. Silver point, pen and brush on vellum, 24.9 × 19.7 cm. King Henry VIII considered himself to be a Solomon-figure, particularly in his dealings with the Church. This drawing dates from a year before Henry assumed spiritual guidance of the Church. The Queen of Sheba represents the new obedience that Church was to owe to Crown. The scene is redolent of the sexual politics that were to characterize the courts of both Henry and Francis I, while also displaying a mannerism of style that was to be cultivated in England and France during this period. The Royal Collection © 2002 Her Majesty Queen Elizabeth II.

political contest with the English. But the workings of ceremonial politics – which often involved a cultivation of sexual politics (Fig. 18) – would reach its apogee at the court of the French King Louis XIV in the seventeenth century; and it is in the France of King Francis, or more specifically at Fontainebleau that the seeds for such a development were sown.

Francis I had been captured at the Battle of Pavia in 1525 by his Spanish adversaries and imprisoned in Madrid. On being ransomed, he returned to France with a determination to centralize his power in the environs of Paris rather than to engage in foreign adventure. One expression of this was the palace he built (now destroyed) in the Bois de Boulogne, known with grim irony as the *Madrid*. But it was Fontainebleau that was to endure, in a state of constant development over the coming generations, as a focus both of authority and of courtly ceremonial.

If Fontainebleau symbolizes an appetite for centralization, then it also proved to be a point of confluence for humanist and artistic currents running from the North as

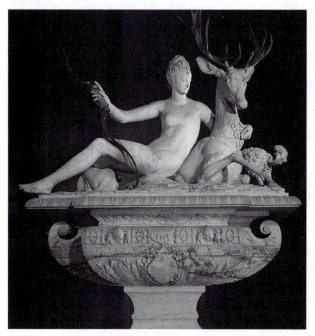

Figure 19   Studio of Jean Goujon, *Diana with Stag* (originally from the fountain of the Château of Anet), c.1549, Marble 211 × 258cm. The Louvre, Paris. The Bridgeman Art Library.

well as from the South. Fontainebleau is not a city nor even an urban court. It was and remains a forest lodge, inviting chivalric pursuits – and more responsive in its architectural design to earth and vegetation than any Italian court would ever be (Fig. 22). Already, André Thevet had begun to represent Valois France in terms of a destiny drawn from its rural roots, speaking of Angoulême, Francis's birthplace, as a promised land and an earthly paradise, fertile and abundant with fountains and swans. Fontainebleau translates this vision into architectural form. The most striking of Francis's own commissions ensures that the gallery should itself be composed not of stone nor be decorated with gilding in the Tudor style but constructed in panels of exotic timber, 'finely wrought' (as Francis told an English ambassador in 1540) 'with divers colours of natural wood, as ebony, brazil'.

Internally, Fontainebleau came, over the years, to be dominated by highly decorative stuccos and a programme of designs – focusing on Diana – which recalls both the theme of hunting as entertainment and the erotic charge which both pastime and politics openly generated in this period. In the art of the school of Fontainebleau, Diana is seen, often, fondling the stag she has subdued; nymphs castrate satyrs; twin ladies – naked yet cool, poised and witty in their sexual display – gaze almost full face at the onlooker, as though the onlooker might himself be the voyeur, Actaeon (Fig. 19). Even the famous silver salt-cellar by Cellini depicting Venus and Vulcan turns classical myth (and poses derived from Michelangelo's Medici chapel) into silvery suggestions of post-coital repose) (Fig. 20).

The political function of Fontainebleau is most apparent in its external features. In preferring Fontainebleau to the Louvre, it seems evident that Francis had recognized that the Louvre lacked sufficient space for formal entertainment. Nor is this to suggest frivolity but rather a recognition – universal throughout Europe – that entertainment was an occasion for Magnificence or propaganda. Here, as later at Versailles, the gardens and lakes at Fontainebleau were laid out with an eye to the theatrical events that might be performed in their perspectives.

It was here that artists such as Serlio and Cellini revealed their political importance. Serlio – who travelled throughout Europe with a facile portfolio of Italianate stylemes – dedicated his *Books of Architecture* to Francis; he was also a designer of ideal stage-sets (Fig. 74). Cellini too had an equally vivid sense of the imaginative strokes that an artist might effect in the interests of his patron or his own advancement. So an increasingly familiar feature of Renaissance gardens, the grotto, makes a notable appearance in Fontainebleau (Fig.

Figure 20   Benvenuto Cellini, *Salt-Cellar*, 1540–44, Gold and enamel, 26 × 33.5 cm. Kunsthistorisches Museum, Vienna. Roger-Viollet.

21). Art here conjures nature to provide a civilized frisson in the face of dark and dangerous forces. Of course, there really is no danger and civilization is there to assure us of that. But in the grotto our earthy, dank and shadowy origins can be experienced anew in a witty allusion to their profundities.

In cultural style, the school of Fontainebleau contributed greatly to developments in the international vogue that has subsequently been termed Mannerism – the 'stylish style'. In this (as will appear in Chapter Six) motifs originally conceived by Michelangelo and Leonardo were adopted and transformed – often with virtuoso exaggeration – into objects of knowing good taste. Such exaggerations, in their cultivation of sinuous and dramatic line, proved (as at Fontainebleau) consistent with a continuing interest in Gothic design; indeed the chivalric finesse of International Gothic here joins the flow of Italian invention to promote a fashion which, in its own international way, was to dominate European taste in the later decades of the Renaissance.

But, if Mannerism is a knowingly stylish style, then it is so because it knows (in part) that its place is assured by an inherently political programme. It is now that the *coup de théâtre* comes to be associated with the *coup d'état*. Machiavelli recognized that the exercise of power involved a command of untruth and illusion. But in France throughout the sixteenth century there were followers of Machiavelli who realized (often pretending, in Machiavellian fashion, not to be followers at all) that effects of spectacular propaganda were essential to the well-being and order of the state. These were not the only channels through which Machiavelli's thinking was diffused: by the end of the period, others, such as Botero, would produce a practical even commercial

Figure 21   *The Grottos of Fontainebleau,* early sixteenth century. © Photograph RMN –
Lagiewski.

Machiavellianism, envisaging how cities – not unlike London – might be ruled by a
resident prince in the midst of a merchant community. This development pointed
rather to a future that would be more fully expressed in the mercantile expansion of
Dutch and English interests in the seventeenth century. Francis and Fontainebleau
also point forward, albeit remotely to the theatrical even ritualistic absolutism of
Louis XIV. In its dynastic phase, however, the Renaissance is characterized by experiments – still courtly in character – that thrived on the possibility of cultural display
and recognized that absolute power needed to express itself obliquely through checks,
balances, conversation and the enjoyable impressions induced by the play of art.
Other institutions – notably Geneva and Reformation Rome – were to contribute
more directly to the advance of both absolute power and conceptions of statehood.

CITIES OF GOD: UTOPIA, GENEVA AND ROME

In the sixteenth century, the institutions of state, becoming ever more clear as to their
political purposes, made ever greater demands on the inner-life conscience of the
individual. For Alberti, it was unthinkable that any conflict should arise betwen personal and public glory: we live our lives to the full only in the piazza. Increasingly,

however, in an age of increasing absolutism – where notions of the Renaissance 'individual' were also growing stronger – this confident equation refused to yield an answer. As will be apparent in the case of the mystics and political activists (discussed in Chapter Four), there are certain claims that cannot be satisfied by stylish participation in the civic or courtly theatre. Even poets (discussed in Chapter Six) sought at points in this period to protect their imaginations by retreating into a world of pastoral fiction. Yet Fontainebleau had already staked a claim to that region for its own political purposes.

In political terms – or as a battle for space – there is no more vivid expression of the dilemma than the works (and life) of St Thomas More. More is a saint. He was also a courtier and a member of the early-modern civil service. Yet the only good place he can find is that which he devises for himself in the punning words of his title: *Utopia* – a 'good' place but also 'no' place at all. In his unfinished history of *Richard III* (1513–18?) More had contemplated the extent to which absolute power might encroach upon the sacred places of a national realm and the inner being of its inhabitants. In *Utopia* the place he makes for himself, illuminated by learning, ironic wit and covert urbanity is, significantly enough, a place where all things are open unambiguously to view. Here there are no corridors of power – of the sort in which More himself was to thrive and ultimately die; all things are communal and readily identifiable for what they are. Family joins with family in a familiarity that makes all distinctions of dress unnecessary and transmutes even gold into a material appropriate for the making of chamber-pots. But is such communal openness a blessing or a bane?

There are many ironies and hauntingly unresolved questions that follow from More's depiction of a perfect society. Some of these are as ancient as Sophocles's *Antigone*, and so perhaps should be numbered among the defining contradictions of the human condition: How are the needs of the self and the needs of the state ever to be reconciled? It is, however, in the sixteenth century that the modern form of the question first begins to be formulated. Erasmus (as will be seen, pp. 109–15) attempted in his *Enchiridion* to make inner virtue the source of all glory; Machiavelli (as has already been seen, pp. 16–17) saw no virtue at all in minds that had not the *virtù* to contribute to public glory. The question becomes yet more acute in an age of Indexes and Bibles: now the very words one uses in print or in prayer may be scrutinized simultaneously by censorious authorities and by those who seek inspiring stories of virtuous spirituality. And that question, of course, continues: as Machiavellians, we still see the need for politicians to dirty their hands in the public interest but we also seek stories that will speak (as More's still does) of courage or love and inspire a confidence in a realm of life beyond mere utility.

More's own book (as also his life) leaves as its greatest legacy an unresolved irony as to how we should locate ourselves in response to these contradictions. In the institutional world itself, however, there were two institutions that set out confidently to confront the issues that More, Erasmus and Machiavelli had traced out in their personal visions and consciences. These two institutions were John Calvin's Geneva and the Counter-Reformation Rome. Being entirely innocent of irony, these two Leviathans were just as likely to exacerbate as to resolve the dilemma. Both sought in practice to restore an ethical conception of human existence to a world enthralled by degenerate power and deluded by the sophistications of courtly practice. So (despite theological differences) there was in fact a remarkable similarity between the ethical purposes of Geneva and Rome in the sixteenth century. Yet once these purposes are themselves encoded in institutional power the tragic difficulty of maintaining any such purpose once more reveals itself – and even more when institutional practice proves to be as adroit and (in the Machiavellian sense) as 'virtuous' as it began to be in the course of this period. To view Puritanism or Tridentine Catholicism in their institutional guise is to recognize that an honest pursuit of realpolitik may itself be more ethical than spiritual absolutism. Or so it might seem from the success in England of Elizabeth I and her flexibly Machiavellian reign. Yet both Geneva and Rome, in its claim to universal jurisdiction, sought to build communities in which human beings could be truly free and flourishing. And for good or ill their influence persisted more vigorously into the European future than the example of any Italian city or French monarchical palace.

To the Calvinist Reformer John Knox (who established his own form of holy city in sixteenth-century Scotland) Geneva 'is the most perfect school of Christ that ever was in this earth since the days of the Apostles'. By the time of Calvin (1509–64) who arrived there in 1536, Geneva had already demonstrated an appetite for religious and political reform. Against the background of their own distinctive style of civic humanism, the cities of Switzerland had responded to the reforming zeal of Ulrich Zwingli (1484–1531); and, in 1527, the burgers of Geneva threw off their allegiance to the Dukes of Savoy, to join the Swiss Alliance. Henceforth, Switzerland was to be a place of refuge for free thinkers and exiles, among them the Frenchman Jean Cauvin (or Calvin). Indeed under Calvinism, Geneva grew in size, between 1550 and 1562 from 10,000 to 17,000 inhabitants.

Calvin, unlike Luther, was a humanist in intellectual formation. He had been educated at the Collège Montaigu where Rabelais, Erasmus and Loyola also studied: and, with something of a courtly eye to the main chance, he kept alive his prospects in France by dedicating writings to Francis I and maintaining links with the King's sister, Marguerite. Notably Calvin's major work was his *Institutes*. The title recalls works by Quintilian and Erasmus and designates an educational programme, or, as John Knox puts it, a school rather than a political philosophy. Calvin's own powers of argument and the clarity of his style (which was to contribute considerably to the development of French prose) allowed him in the *Institutes* to produce a far more concise and intellectually cogent account of the Protestant position than Luther ever achieved. All of which may explain the appeal of Calvin's thinking to intellectuals as diverse as Sir Philip Sidney, Edmund Spenser and Clément Marot (who, after exile in Ferrara, where he wrote erotic poems, also won acceptance in Geneva on the strength of his translation of the *Psalms*).

The ultimate purpose of the *Institutes* was to establish on earth the possibility of an Augustinian city of God, in which the wickedness of humankind would endlessly be remembered but where also the utter dependence of human beings on God would be translated into a glorious realization of saving grace. The doctrine of predestination may not have been as crucial to Calvin himself as has subsequently been suggested. However, this doctrine was an important bulwark in the citadel, intended to shore up the fragility that even the faithful were bound to acknowledge. Similarly, the institutional structures of government and congregational discipline that Calvin introduced were themselves meant as an acknowledgement that religious awe was the fundamental principle of all human society. This principle – which Calvin discerned even in pagan culture – ensures that virtue need never conspire with the corrupting power of the secular world. Thus in the *Institutes of the Christian Religion*, Chapter xxv (quoted here in a translation by Hugh T. Kerr), Calvin writes:

> If the Scripture did not teach that this office extends to both tables of the law, we might learn it from heathen writers; for not one has treated of the office of magistrates, of legislators and civil government, without beginning with religion and Divine worship. And thus they have all confessed that no government can be happily constituted unless its first object be the promotion of piety and that all laws are preposterous which neglect the claims of God and merely provide for the interests of men.

In conjunction with the lucidity of his religious thought, Calvin possessed a remarkable capacity for political organization. Between 1538 and 1541 – when he finally won acceptance from the burghers of Geneva – Calvin had spent time in Strasbourg (itself regarded sometimes as a 'New Jerusalem') under Martin Bucer (1491–1551); and from Strasbourg he brought back to Geneva a conception of the indissoluble relationship that must exist between religious and civic organizations, along with a talent for the day-to-day implementation of this vision. From now on, as part of the bargain which Calvin struck with the Genevan magistrates, government of the city was to lie in the hands of four categories of minister – doctors, pastors, deacons and elders – all meeting regularly for discussion in consistory and no doubt for purposes of mutual surveillance.

'Anyone who sings indecent, dissolute or outrageous songs or dances the fling . . . shall be imprisoned for three days and then brought before the Consistory.' These words are taken from the *Register of the Company of Pastors*, and capture the grim profile that has come to be recognized as Calvinistic. Yet the line which Calvinism sought to tread between charity and chastisement was finely drawn; and to Calvin himself the theocratic – or, to us, totalitarian – aspects of his government were seen as expressions of divine love. In the words of a modern apologist 'The Consistory really tried to assist everyone in its city-state to live the kind of life that God intended people to live ... and to ensure that there were real networks of caring'. In consequence, Puritans were among the first to frown on the whims of personal benevolence and to insist that charitable relief should be administered by the State.

Similar qualifications are necessary in discussing Calvin's attitude to religious imagery. There is no doubt that Calvinism did set itself against the luxuriance of imagery that flowed from the Catholic Church and from the increasingly manneristic fountains of Renaissance culture. In fact Tridentine Catholicism also sought to moderate the artistic or secular exuberance of artistic fantasy; and a certain chastity of dress – where clothing might be black though exquisite in texture – came into fashion among courtly mannerists of the later sixteenth century. Yet Calvin was *not* opposed to the beauty of material things per se, and in Book III, chapter 16 of the *Institutes* he inveighs against 'the inhuman philosophy' that despises the loveliness that God has given to gold, silver, ivory and marble, and 'deprives us of lawful enjoyment of Divine beneficence'.

For all that, the strains of a tragic Utopia are perceptible whenever Calvin addresses such central themes of humanist thinking as the theme of liberty. In faith and theological intention, Calvin's conception of liberty must be that human beings are only free in their relationship to Divine Glory; and on this view, restraint and restriction in the temporal world define the very condition of our emancipation. Nor is Calvin deaf to the demands of democratic suffrage. In practice, however, he vigorously defended his own authority against the anarchical freedoms displayed in the Anabaptist tendency. There is also the telling case of Michael Servetus, who – fleeing from Geneva after theological disagreements with Calvin – was extradited on Calvin's request from Catholic France. Executed in effigy by the French for his Protestantism, Servetus was actually burned at the stake for heresy in Geneva on 27 October 1553. Calvin may have attempted – humanely perhaps, but unsuccessfully – to commute the sentence from burning to beheading.

The Servetus case is only one of thousands – involving Catholics, Protestants and civil powers alike – that illustrate the tension between institution and individual conscience in the sixteenth century. But fault lines are similarly visible in the two great legacies that Calvinism bequeathed to the social thinking of subsequent generations: the notions of the family and the notion of honest work.

Within the city, Calvin saw the family as the fundamental unit of social order. (Alberti would largely have agreed with him.) Likewise, marriage – which in its

courtly and dynastic form had a profound influence on politics and culture throughout the Renaissance – becomes a matter of especial importance in Puritan thought.
So it was also in the ethics of Tridentine Rome, where the sacrament of marriage now
took on new significance. But Calvin follows the revolutionary example of Luther and
insists that priests themselves should be married: the family thus becomes the revolutionary cell of Puritanism, compact with energies that expressed – in place of both
Catholic sacramentalism, or even Albertian *masserizia* – an active compliance with
providential purpose. God himself is constantly represented by Calvin as a nurse, a
mother, a father who gives good things. Free adoption through divine grace into the
family of God is the most central tenet of Calvin's philosophy. Such an adoption is the
assurance on which the chosen ones base their confident understanding of predestination. However, so far from inducing the complacency or sloth this confidence
encourages fruitful activity (as Alberti also would) in which an appreciation of the
familial bond between God and the individual is joyously realized.

This ideal is enthusiastically expressed by the English Puritan, Joseph Hall:

> The homeliest service that we doe in an honest calling, though it be but to plow, or digge,
>
> if done in obedience, and in conscience of God's Commandements, is crowned with an
>
> ample reward; whereas the best workes of their kinde (preaching, praying, offering
>
> Evangelical sacrifices) if without respect of God's injunction and glory are loaded with
>
> curses. God loveth adverbs; and cares not how good but how well.

Thus Work as such replaces both the sacraments and also the works of piety and liturgical observance that the Catholic tradition embodied; and the reward – or glory – of
this virtuous labour is that, in one's family as also in relationship with God, each
human creature should become an 'adverb' to the absolute verb of divinity.

In essence, Calvin's thought gives vivid expression to a concern that the Renaissance always displays with energy, activity and community. Yet taken out of context
these same thoughts can later produce the work ethic, the commodification of time,
the capitalism and egoistic individualism which Calvin himself would doubtless have
deplored. Calvin vigorously attacks all forms of greed. Money in particular is one of
the 'dreams and phantasms' that the human mind dangles before its own eyes, to
obscure the demanding truths of the spirit. As for the individual conscience, this is
only such in relation to the community out of which all individuals are born: 'all our
conceptions, deliberations, resolutions and undertakings ought to be consistent with
the benefit and advantage of our neighbours' (*Institutes*, Book II, chapter 12). Alberti
would not have disagreed.

The social implications of Renaissance thinking are in large part communicated to
the future through Calvin's Geneva. A strong current of revolutionary thinking ran
out from Switzerland to the Dutch Republics, then on to John Knox's Scotland and

finally to Cromwell's Revolution – which subsequently provided an example to the French Revolutionaries. Moreover, it was Calvin whose thinking laid the foundations both for the North American ethos – as well as for colonial South Africa. Equally significant in subsequent centuries is that 'sanctification of the everyday-world' that Calvinism envisages. As will appear in Chapter Four, it is this conception that delivers the created universe to the attention of the scientific worker; the very word 'technology' begins to be used in a Calvinist context to designate the work we must do in the world that God has given us to redeem from corruption and render significant in the perspective of eternity.

In all these respects, it is Geneva rather than Florence, Urbino or Fontainebleau that most directly anticipates the modern world. Yet Geneva was not the only city that projected Renaissance thinking into our future. Its unlikely twin in this respect was Tridentine Rome. Indeed, it has been argued (by Quentin Skinner) that, while the most advanced thinkers of early modern Europe 'were in general professed Calvinists, the theories that were developed by Protestants and Puritans – especially in political philosophy – were couched almost entirely in the legal and moral language of their Catholic adversaries'. It is therefore to Rome – with its expansive conceptions of space, liturgical imagery and time-honoured authority – that one must now return.

In the minds of Roman Catholic thinkers – gathering at the Councils of Trent between 1545 and 1563 – one of the most profound counter-arguments against Protestantism was that it made the Church 'invisible'. This is no trivial objection. Along with Luther and Calvin, there were many reformers in the Catholic Church itself who wished to make a bonfire of the Renaissance vanities. One such was Savanarola, whose campaign against the Medici involved a desire to restore the ancient form of Republican rule to Florence. However, the issues raised by the Protestant schismatics went deeper than any objection to ascetic iconoclasm or even the promotion of a political ideal. In rejecting the visible character of the Church, Protestantism seemed to endanger the very conception of the Church as the intermediary between the human community and its divine maker. Priests over the centuries have proved fallible (and worse). Nonetheless, the priesthood remained in Catholic theology the custodian of traditions that began with Christ's own ministry, and also of the sacraments and liturgical exercises that the Protestants sought to abolish: so too, the visible images that the Church had long cultivated were the means established by Christ to articulate in historical time the continuing relationship between Creator and human creature. Thus, while a movement for ecclesiastical reform had begun at least as early as the twelfth century, the Franciscans who dominated that movement had positively encouraged the belief that the natural world in which human beings live could be taken as an expression both of a rational order and also of the love that existed between humanity and God. Indeed the Franciscan movement exerted a decided influence (as in the works of Giotto) on the growth of the very naturalism in representing the physical order that lay at the heart of the Renaissance in Italy.

A reinvigorated belief in the potential sanctity of the visible universe and likewise an intense concern over liturgical imagery as the defining characteristic of a Christian community were seminal features of the thinking that characterized the Councils of Trent. The Jesuit Cardinal Robert Bellarmine declares that the Church is itself as much 'a visible and palpable assembly of people as the people of Rome or the kingdom of France' (*Concerning Councils*, pp. 317–18), and the consequences of such a position emerge in the institutional and ultimately legal concerns that the Councils of Trent displayed over questions that may now be described as questions of natural law and human rights. More immediately, similar consequences appear in the artistic and aesthetic principles that had begun – even before the Councils of Trent – to contribute to the reconstruction of Renaissance Rome as a city.

It is an indication of how closely connected liturgical, institutional and architectural considerations were to be in Tridentine Rome that in 1591 a funeral oration for the great urban planner Pope Sixtus V should speak of how the Pope had wished to see everywhere

> the most holy testimonies of our redemption and the images of the founders of the Apostolic See. He wanted the sight of these to animate the sacred images that he carried within his heart. And he especially rejoiced if ever the same thing should happen to us as we travelled through the city.

These lines allude to a tradition of Christian witness and also to an intensity of spiritual attention which might, it seems, transform any journey through the city into an emblematic pilgrimage. Such purposes correspond to practices – both architectural and devotional – that characterized the Roman Church in the final years of the Cinquecento; and it was Sixtus who prepared the city for the Baroque phase of its existence, opening streets akin to boulevards while insisting that these vistas should encourage a deeply inward and meditative exercise of the Christian imagination.

Comparable processes of urban and spiritual renewal had begun as early as 1420, when Pope Martin V – a member of the ancient Roman clan of Colonna – brought the papacy back to Rome after a century or more of residence elsewhere. Simultaneously, there began a rediscovery of the dignity of ancient Rome and an attempt to translate the images that archaeology had brought to light (at best) to the service of the Christian community, or (at worst) to the glory of the Pope himself.

The Rome of Pope Martin housed no more than a 17,000 inhabitants. There was no industry to enrich the city nor mercantile enterprise save for the pilgrimage trade; and the architectural fabric had degenerated – as Martin graphically describes (in a papal bull dated 1425) – into a midden: even in the most beautiful parts of the city

Roman tradesman 'have been throwing entrails, viscera . . . rotten meat and fish, refuse, excrement and other fetid and rotting cadavers into the streets and piazzas'. For all that, the idea of Rome and its glory in classical times had endured in the minds of poets and artists; and attention had begun to be paid in the early Quattrocento by visitors such as Brunelleschi, Donatello and Ghiberti to the details of its sculpture and architecture. Now – for reasons perhaps of hygiene as well as self-aggrandizement – Martin claimed authority (as *magister viarum*) over the Roman streets, and was followed by a succession of Popes with similar ambitions.

The civic centre on the Capitol was eventually redesigned by Michelangelo between 1538 and 1564. But before that the Churches of the city had often assumed (as Alberti would have wished) the lineaments of a classical Temple or Basilica. The Church of San Pietro in Montorio (1482–1510) (to follow Loren Partridge) had 're-captured something of the full complexity of ancient Roman architecture: sculptural malleable walls, pilasters that express sculptural forces and a varied but unified sequence of interior and exterior volumes'. More remarkable still is the Tempietto in the precincts of San Pietro designed by the Bramante of Urbino in 1502 (Fig. 22).

Rome, then, was poised to reclaim its privileges as a sacred place, standing at the point of intersection between past and present and surveying a future in which it would reclaim universal jurisdiction. It was a city, and shortly – under the Popes of the High Renaissance – was to become an absolutism, with as strong a sense of Empire as of spiritual aspiration. However, for a period of fifty years or so – a time corresponding to the greatest moral decadence and the greatest artistic fervour – Rome was also a court. Or rather it was many courts, each court ruled by a cardinal and likely – since the cardinals of Rome were themselves almost invariably members of aristocratic families – to possess its own character and pursue its own ambitions. Years before Castiglione wrote his *Book of the Courtier*, there existed a conduct book for cardinals, *De Cardinalatu*, which attempted to combine advice concerning both spiritual and social conduct – counselling, for instance, that scarlet vestments should be worn to symbolize a determination to defend the faith even to the point of bloody martyrdom: *usque ad effusionem sanguis*. On the other hand there were ample targets for satirists to aim at, as Roman poets such as Pasquino (writing in Roman dialect) quickly discovered: 'Just as if it were winter still/ Pius burns Christians like sticks of wood/ to get himself ready for the heat of Hell.'

There can be no doubt that the often competitive patronage between the cardinals and even between one pope and another produced an atmosphere of extreme excitement and productivity in the realm of art. Yet the moral corruption of the period – along with the organizational chaos arising from the proliferation of princely cardinals – also produced a desire for radical reform. Not all popes and cardinals were scoundrels; and the Lutheran schism – along with the cataclysmic Sack of Rome in

Figure 22 Donato Bramante, *Tempietto*, authorized 1502, completed after 1511. San Pietro in Montorio, Rome. At least two strands of Renaissance culture are united in this building: its model was the Roman Temple of Hercules Victor which had been excavated between 1471 and 1484; its execution was nonetheless highly original and the patronage which supported it was that of the Catholic Sovereigns of Spain, Ferdinand and Isabella, who clearly recognized the need for a place at the centre of a newly refurbished international capital. With permission from Scala.

1527 – concentrated the mind of the Church, leading it through the Councils of Trent to a vigorous programme of both spiritual and managerial self-appraisal.

The immediate effects of the Tridentine reforms were ethical rather than theological in character, generating an austere rigour in pastoral government. In the late six-teenth century, it would have been difficult to decide which was the more puritanical regime, Calvinist Geneva or Milan under the rule of the sainted but disciplinarian Cardinal Carlo Borromeo (1538–54). In the longer term, however, the Councils may also be seen to have contributed considerably to the development of an ever-more urgent debate in jurisprudential terms about the nature and exercise of absolute power.

Since the Middle Ages the Church, organizationally, had been in the forefront of bureaucratic practice. Now, however, it faced a particularly complex challenge, involving a need to overcome both internal and external dislocation. At the Council of Constance, meeting from 1414, the Church had displayed its institutional inventiveness in envisaging the possibility of rule by conciliar debate rather than by papal fiat. The Council of Trent preferred to reassert the primacy of Papal authority. Simultaneously, the Church prepared to respond to a world of mercantile expansion and Empire, as well as to govern the implications of the printing press by the establishment of the Index and the Inquisition.

It was this phase of Catholic history that also produced the Society of Jesus and, at the Council of Trent itself, a remarkable debate of far-reaching significance in regard to the rule of law as also in regard to the demands of Natural Justice. Of the founder of the Jesuits, St Ignatius, more will be said in Chapter Three. Here, it is enough to recall that Ignatius studied at the same humanist school in Paris that produced Calvin, and that – along with a chivalric and military understanding of hierarchy as an organizational principle – he also nurtured conceptions of glory, virtue and personal activity which were closely comparable to those that have been found in Alberti, Calvin and Machiavelli. For the Jesuit, however, the field in which he was to pursue such conceptions was fundamentally the field of the religious imagination – expanding to fill the spaces of both the city and the greater world with its meditations and to bring new life to the essential images of the Christian tradition. Thus the Jesuit Church of the Gesù in Rome is capacious enough for preaching to large congregations. Yet it is also designed to accommodate such liturgical (some might say theatrical) practices as the Forty-Hour Devotion or the Exposition and Benediction of the Eucharistic Host, as well as to encourage acts of private piety. Words were important to the Jesuits. But so too, in this community, was the 'gaze that saves' in devout attention to sacred objects. The artistic and architectural consequences of such developments are to be found in the great volumes and resonantly emotive images of such Baroque artists as Bernini, as also in some Late Renaissance works by Tintoretto and El Greco.

Correspondingly, the Jesuits in a spirit of religious adventure committed themselves to a world-wide mission. By the time of Loyola's death in 1556, the Jesuit order included over 1,000 members; and by 1626 there were about 15,000 Jesuits throughout the world and some 440 colleges associated with them. It is pointless to deny that these missionary expeditions colluded often enough with colonial and mercantile interests. Yet they were also the product of a powerful if tragically dangerous belief that there was an inbuilt propensity to truth in all human beings, a core of conscience that could be brought into play (as against Calvinistic notions of predestination and the prevailingly Protestant sense that all human effort was as nothing in the perspective of the divine will). Moreover, it was the Jesuits who understood, however confusedly, the need to accommodate themselves to the cultural traditions that they encountered in China and India as well as in the New World. In theory if not in practice, the aspirations of the Jesuits are consistent with concerns that are, as we shall see, characteristic of humanist thought to discern the possibility of truth in every kind of myth from every kind of culture.

Rightly suspicious as we now may be of cultural imperialism (or even of Universalism), the Renaissance characteristically encouraged such notions; and while this led often enough to flagrant abuse, it is precisely here that some of the most fundamental principles of modern justice were established. Infamously, there were theologians who could attempt to justify the worst excesses of imperial expansion, slavery – witness the pronouncements of Ginés de Sepúlveda at Council of Vallodolid (1550), which justified Christian hegemony on principles drawn from Aristotle and the slave-owning civilizations of ancient Greece. On the other hand, the debate could also produce countervailing argument that contributed directly to the development in later jurisprudence of conceptions of Human Rights and Natural Law. Notably, it is Spanish theorists who in the course of the Tridentine Reformation spoke most persuasively against the excesses of Spanish Imperialism. Even Isabella of Spain had expressed distress over the emergence of colonial slavery. But the forces ranged against oppression were mustered mainly by Dominicans such as Francisco de Vitoria (1483/92–1546) and Domingo de Soto (1495–1560) and later the Jesuit Francisco Suárez (1548–1617).

Drawing upon notions of natural law originally developed in the thirteenth century by St Thomas Aquinas, these thinkers now produced a conception of natural rights that was to prove of central importance in subsequent centuries. In Aquinas, these thinkers discovered the idea of a hierarchy of law deriving ultimately from the eternal law of God. Natural law is implanted in all human beings by God and all human beings have the capacity to respond to that law. For Suárez, the law is written in our minds by the hand of God himself; it exists as a 'habit' in us, and no human law enunciated for judicial purposes can ever be just if it is not compatible with this greater law. Indeed, according to Vitoria in his treatise on *Civil Power*, the law of nations, in harmony with natural law, is a set of precepts 'created by the authority of the whole world' which serves to ensure 'that there are just and convenient rules for every one in it' while De Soto (with the agreement of Suárez) declares 'All men are born free by nature'.

A particular characteristic aspect of Catholic thinking is that in theory at least it allows a competence to human will and reason that Protestant thinkers (again in theory) could not and consequently was able to envisage an effective division between secular and ecclesiastical power. The Catholic aim is not a theocracy such as Calvin proposed for Geneva but rather the foundation of a state in which human beings have a God-given right (and obligation) to discover and sustain laws of their own, in terms of their traditional understanding of law. It is also true that human beings will realize their humanity – or freedom – through a free involvement in the social and legal community. This understanding is, of course, hard to sustain when the perception of human good becomes confused, as it did in the Renaissance, by competing claims of ethical, political, material and individualistic interest. For all that, questions formulated first at the Council of Trent will reverberate in the jurisprudential writings of Grotius and also find a remote resonance in the work of Rousseau.

THE DOMAIN OF TASTE

The issues that have so far arisen in this chapter concern the relationships that existed in the Renaissance between small local communities (where a city such as Florence might comprise no more than 90,000 inhabitants and other such as Ferrara as few as 30,000) and the growing power of governmental institutions, national and international. There is, however, another domain – impossible to gauge in extent or number. This is the domain of taste (taste being a notion that some would trace to the seventeenth-century Spanish Jesuit Baltasar Gracián (1601–58). For aesthetics and taste are also capable of forming communities, with some pretension at least to be independent of any political agenda. It is true, as we have suggested throughout, that the arts may quite consciously contribute in a period such as the Renaissance to the *coup de théâtres* by which a state defines itself. The very fact, however, that the arts at this time were subject to regulation already reveals a degree of autonomy that political authorities had reason to fear. And, whatever the ideological attitudes of Geneva and Rome might have been towards secular imagery, there remained undiminished the appetites that lead artists and antiquarians in the fourteenth century to respond to the monuments of the classical world – and since then these have been expressed in adventures such as The Grand Tour (itself intended precisely to cultivate Taste) or sharpened by novels such as George Eliot's *Daniel Deronda* or E.M. Forster's *Room with a View*. In the sixteenth century itself, 'Rome' – as a rhetorical trope – could be appropriated to designate the triumph of enemies of the historical Rome such as Geneva (which was described as a 'New Rome' as well as a New Jerusalem) and countless smaller competitors.

In the domain of taste, the most enduring legacy was that of Palladian architecture, which, developing principles that were first defined by Alberti, also provides a resource for later builders – whether in Thomas Jefferson's America or in countless airport hotels – who wished to assert their ideals or their authority in classical trappings. Palladio himself (1508–80) meditated deeply on the example of Rome. He trusted, as did Alberti, to the ways in which a rational and mathematical understanding of proportion might reveal the underlying laws of natural construction. At the same time, he is both passionate and highly imaginative in his contemplation of Roman examples, and also understands very clearly the connection between architecture and the celebration of political power. He writes of how on his first visit to Rome the ruins (still for the most part buried) were 'more worthy of observation than I had first imagined them to be'; he was 'greatly moved by these enormous remains' and also saw in them 'a luminous example and testimony to Roman *virtù* and grandeur'. It is this that underlies his attempts to reconstruct in drawings – which are both precise and, often, fantastic – the outline of Roman buildings as they might have been (Fig. 23).

Palladio's classicism was also highly responsive to the demands of the sixteenth-century ambience. Though born in Vicenza, Palladio recognized that nearby Venice

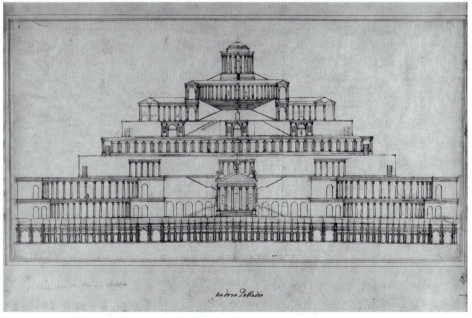

Figure 23   Andrea Palladio, *Idealised Elevation of the Forum and Sanctury of Fortuna Primigenia*, Palestrina. British Architectual Library, RIBA, London.

must be the stage on which he principally worked. For four hundred years, Venice had maintained itself in magnificent independence from the rest of Italy, developing – along with an Eastern Empire – artistic schools of its own and an enviable reputation (compared with contentious cities such as Florence) for civic order under a mercantile aristocracy. Its honorific title as 'Serenissima' reflects this; and Petrarch in the fourteenth century can speak of Venice as 'the home of justice, liberty and peace'. Following the Sack of Rome in 1527, deliberate efforts were made, especially by the Doge Andrea Gritti, to wrest from Rome the artistic kudos that the Popes had won for it. Gritti's success was considerable – attracting an influx of intellectuals who formed a circle around such figures as Titian and Tintoretto.

It was this new, artistically ambitious Venice that Palladio principally served – while still retaining an attachment to his origins in Vicenza, where he belonged to a circle of important humanists. His humanist inclinations are amply demonstrated in the frontage he supplied for the Palazzo (or as Palladio preferred to call it, the Basilica) della Ragione (1549–1614) in Vicenza. Here a high Medieval roof is combined with arcades in the lower storeys which are both monumental, in a classical spirit, and airy in a spirit of courtly gracefulness. However, his greatest influence – flowing to the rest of Europe out through the channels of Venetian prestige – came from the Churches he designed in Venice and the country houses he built for Venetian nobles on the mainland. With a fine understanding of architecture as a celebratory medium, he designed San Giorgio Maggiore (1566) to dominate the view across the channel from San Marco and the Doge's Palace. With an equal sense of both refinement and light-heartedness he built the extremely influential Villa Rotonda (originally Villa Capra, begun in 1550) with a raised portico on each of its four fronts – from which the surrounding countryside appeared in pleasing vista, and endless variations of light, shade, breezes and temperatures could be savoured (Fig. 26).

Palladio's Venice was as much a theatre for civilized living as Rome was for religious display; and it is no accident that one of his earliest followers outside Italy was the architect Inigo Jones, known also as a designer of Masques in Jacobean and Caroline England. This element of theatricality also points to one of the principal ways in which Renaissance Taste was disseminated (and ultimately domesticated). For from an early point, architectural motifs proved capable of imitation in the innumerable royal processions and entrées that accompanied the progress of itinerant rulers. So in the account that the French poet Maurice Scève gives of the entry of Henri IV into Lyons (which had a thriving Italian mercantile community) the scenery was constructed to display obelisks, victory columns and triumphal arches; and tableaux were enacted in front of painted perspectives. Likewise, the architect most responsible for the diffusion of Renaissance design, Sebastiano Serlio, was also a designer of ideal theatrical sets. Serlio visited Fontainebleau, but also travelled as far as Cracow and Poznan, leaving there traces of Renaissance style in the highly receptive minds of Polish intellectuals.

Figure 24   Bernardo Rossellino, *Cathedral*, 1459–62, Pienza.

Two final examples may here indicate how the architectural programme of the Renaissance – with all its political and intellectual implications – could prove its flexibility and adaptability. One is the city of Pienza, built by Pius II on his accession to the Papacy; the other is the Gate of Honour in the College re-founded in Cambridge by John Caius.

Pienza (originally known as Corsignano) was the birthplace of the Aeneas Silvius (originally Enea Silvio) Piccolimini (1405–64). Born of a relatively obscure family, Aeneas Silvius prospered both as a cleric and as an exceptionally worldly humanist; his artistic taste and a moving concern for his own roots led him to rebuild his native village as a miniature city, in a style that displays many of the best characteristics of the early Quattrocento. Though the architect of the city was Bernardo Rosselino, Alberti was employed in the Pope's secretarial staff; and, in the span of half a dozen buildings around the piazza of the miniscule Cathedral, the design sketches out the fundamental principles of order and symmetry that Alberti enunciates in *The Ten Books of Architecture* (Fig. 24). There is erudition here but no grandiosity. Indeed, to a remarkable degree the design of the city – and in particular of the cathedral – can be shown to respond to purely physical considerations, such as currents of air, changes of temperature, and above all the play of light (Fig. 25).

The Pope himself (in tune with Alberti's dislike of ecclesiastical gloom) declares that 'the first charm of a house is light' (and, after travelling to York, he writes of York Minster: 'a cathedral notable in the whole world for its size and architecture and for a very brilliant chapel whose glass walls are held together by very slender columns'). Here the South proves receptive to the North; and the result in the cathedral of Pienza is a remarkably lucid building that alludes to Neoplatonic light symbolism but also

Figure 25 Bernardo Rossellino, *Door to Pienza Cathedral*, 1459–62, Pienza. I am indebted to Peter Ungar for the illustrations of Pienza. Ungar associates the architecture of Pienza with Alberti's words: 'Here is mild air and quiet'.

remains deeply attentive (as the architecture of power would increasingly fail to be) to the preconceptual sensitivities of the ordinary human frame.

The last example – which also points forward to the theme of Chapter Two – shows education as a means of cultural transmission. In 1544 the English physician John Caius returned to England after some fifteen years of practice and study in Italy with a considerable (if conservative) reputation and a growing fortune. Twenty years later he went back to his old College in Cambridge, and set out to refound the College now known as Gonville and Caius (Fig. 27). Cambridge, unlike Oxford, is a essentially a Renaissance foundation, favoured not only by Henry VIII in his educational ambitions but also by Erasmus, and soon to be the centre of medical research with the discovery by William Harvey – another fellow of Caius College – of the circulation of the blood in the early 1600s. It is, however, the Gate of Honour – through which undergraduates passed for the conferral of their final degrees – that here best expresses the concerns of the second founder of the College. An educational community here becomes worthy, at least in the eyes of its founder, of all the dignities that once attached to Rome. The arch is a miniature triumphal arch, designed, probably, by John Caius himself. Yet miniaturization does not lead here – as it does in Pienza – to a purely classical design but rather to a lively eclecticism. This may suggest some acquaintance with Serlio's prescripts; and the pillars, pediments and obelisks on the upper storey (while being very precise in their reference to Roman motifs) also bear some resemblance to those to be found in the Entry of Henri into Lyons. By the mid-sixteenth century Renaissance principles had been so thoroughly assimilated that they were the language in which any European would speak in expressing his best aspirations.

NOTES

The indispensable account of political philosophy in the period is Q. Skinner, *The Foundations of Modern Political Thought* (Cambridge, 1978). See also Hans Baron, *The Crisis of the Early Italian Renaissance*

Figure 26   Andrea Palladio, *Villa Rotonda (Villa Capra)*, (begun 1550; finished by Vincenzo Scamozzi), Vicenza. With permission from Scala.

(Chicago, 1975), and J.H. Hexter, *The Vision of Politics on the Eve of the Renaissance: More, Machiavelli and Seyssel* (London, 1973). **Social conditions**: J. Le Goff, *Time, Work and Culture in the Middle Ages* (Chicago, 1980), also Richard Quinones, *The Renaissance Discovery of Time* (Cambridge MA 1972). **Travel** gets less attention in these pages than the topic deserves: see Robert Brenner, *Merchants and Revolution* (Cambridge, 1993). I quote William H. Sherman's excellent contribution to the forthcoming *Blackwell Companion to Renaissance Drama*, ed. Arthur F. Kinney. Here, as also in Chapter Two, Charles Taylor's *The Sources of Self: The Making of Modern Identity* (Cambridge, 1989) provides an excellent philosophical diagnosis of the period (I quote the words of James Hall from Taylor's discussion of Puritanism). For **Alberti**, see *On the Art of Building in Ten Books*, trans. Joseph Rykwer *et al.* (Cambridge, MA and London, 1981) and Antony Grafton, *Leon Battista Alberti* (London, 2001). For **Renaissance shopping**, R. Goldthwaite, *Wealth and Demand for Art in Italy 1300–1600* (Baltimore, 1993). For the **Medici**, see J.R. Hale, *Florence and the Medici: The Pattern of Control* (London, 1977). For **Urbino**, see Cecil H. Clough, *The Duchy of Urbino in the Renaissance* (London, 1981). For **Castiglione**, see Wayne C. Rebhorne, *Courtly Performances* (Chicago, 19X7), J.R. Woodhouse, *Castiglione* (Edinburgh, 1978) and Virginia Cox's Introduction to Hoby's translation (from which I quote) (London, 1992). On the importance of **Urbino's marquetry**, see A. Chastel, *Studios and Styles: 1450–1500* (London, 1965). Giovanni Santi's *La vita e gesta di Federigo di Montefeltro* appeared in the

Figure 27   *The Gate of Honour*, 1575. Gonville and Caius College, Cambridge.

Vatican in 1985, ed. Luigi Michelini Tocci. For **Francis I**, see R.J. Knecht, *Francis I* (Cambridge, 1982); also J. Poujol, ed., *The Monarchy of France* (Paris, 1961) and *Humanism and Letters in the Age of François Ier* (ed. Philip Ford and Gillian Jondorf, Cambridge, 1996). For **Fontainebleau** see Jean-Jacques Lévêque, *L'Ecole de Fontainebleau* (Neuchâtel, 1984). For **Thomas More**, see the outstanding essay by Colin Burrow, 'Literature and Politics under Henry VII and Henry VIII', in *The Cambridge History of Medieval Literature*, ed. David Wallace (Cambridge, 1999), pp. 793–820. For **Calvin** and Calvinism, I quote from *A Compend of the Institutes of Christian Religion by John Calvin*, ed. Hugh T. Kerr (London, Lutterworth Press, 1965), p. 207. See also John H. Bratt, ed., *The Heritage of John Calvin* (Grand Rapids, 1973), Charles H. George and Katherine George, *The Protestant Mind of the English Reformation* (Princeton 1961) and Andrew Pettegree *et al.*, *Calvinism in Europe 1540–1620* (Cambridge, CUP, 1994), esp. p. 34. On **Rome**, see P.A. Dempsey, ed., *Rome in the Renaissance: The City and the Myth* (Binghampton, NY, 1982), p. 360; Loren Partridge, *The Renaissance in Rome* (London, 1996), from whom I quote; B. Hallman, *Italian Cardinals: Reform and the Church as Property* (Berkeley, 1985); Denys Hay, *The Church in 15th century Italy (CUP)*. For **the Counter-Reformation and the Jesuits**, see H. Outram Evennett (ed. John Bossy), *The Spirit of the Counter-Reformation* (Cambridge, 1968). Accounts of the theories of human rights are to be found in J.H. Parry, *The Spanish Theory of Empire in the Sixteenth Century* (Cambridge, 1940), pp. 57–69, and John Finnis, *Natural Law and Natural Rights* (Oxford, 1980). For **Taste**, I follow Hans-Georg Gadamer, *Truth and Method* (trans. revised by Joel Weinsheimer and Donald G. Marshall, London, 1989); see also T. Eagleton's *The Ideology of the Aesthetic* (Oxford, 1990) for arguments on the revolutionary effect of the aesthetic, and Burke (forthcoming) on the 'Domestication' of the Renaissance. For **Palladio**, see James J. Ackerman, *Palladio* (2nd edn, 1979). For the **Entries**, see Maurice Scève, *The Entry of Henri IV into Lyon, September 1548*, a facsimile with Introduction by Richard Cooper and contributions by M. McGowan (Tempe, Arizona, 1997). On **Sebastiano Serlio**, see his *On Architecture*, trans. Vaughan Hart and Peter Hicks (New Haven & London, 1996). On **Pienza**, see Charles R. Marsh, *Pienza: the Creation of a Renaissance City* (Ithaca & London, 1987) and Peter D. Ungar, 'Pienza under the sign of the hour-glass: A study in observation and perception' (dissertation, Cambridge University, 1995).

chapter two

EDUCATION, IMITATION AND CREATION

BOOK-LEARNING IN THE RENAISSANCE

If cities, courts and empires were the sacred territories of the Renaissance tribe then the Book was its totem. To speak of the Renaissance at all (at least in its early phases) is to speak of the recovery of classical writings – Latin at first, then Greek and Hebrew – through zealous book-collecting, assiduous scholarship and painstaking attention to the historical and linguistic details of ancient but newly discovered texts. Such philological activities may now appear to be recondite, unworldly or else merely tangential to the spheres of power and politics.

There were those in the Renaissance itself who might have agreed, delighting in the scholarly cultivation of secret and exclusive influences. Shakespeare's Prospero can indulge his arcane studies, to the point of self-destruction. Yet even Prospero, before he finally drowned his book, came to realize the extent to which his books had given him authority in the very world of political confusion from which at one point he sought to abdicate. His historical counterparts discovered the same.

Books in the Renaissance proved to be not only a refuge but also a source of unexpected advancement – even of magic – in spheres that ranged from politics and religion to history and geography. It has indeed been suggested that the impulse leading to the exploration of the New World lay not merely in a greed for gold or spices but also in a desire for marvels – amply satisfied by Columbus's narratives – that had originally been stimulated by the countless stories of chivalric adventure flowing from Spanish presses. Thus the book became a tool as well as a totem, and – whether in manuscript or, later, in printed form – prised open an ever-widening field of activities (Fig. 28).

73

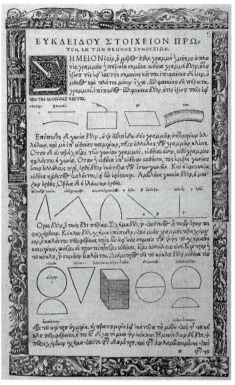

Figure 28 Euclid, *Elementarum*, 1537. Basel.
This figure is reproduced by kind permission
of the Syndics of the Cambridge University
Library.

An early indication of how central books
would become is to be found in the career
of Coluccio Salutati (1331–1400). Coluccio
was Chancellor of Florence at a period when
the Florentine Republic was threatened by
despotic Milan and when correspondingly its
sense of its own Republican culture was especially acute. The representations of David and
Goliath by Florentine artists such as Donatello
and Michelangelo are one expression of this
sentiment (see pp. 184) But Coluccio's own
activities in the interests of the city similarly
combined politics and scholarship in a politically impressive and wholly practical fashion.
Coluccio himself was not a Florentine by birth.
He trained as a lawyer, absorbing the most
advanced – and increasingly marketable – skills
of secular learning, particularly in rhetoric,
that were available in the fourteenth century
at universities such as Bologna. In Florence he
entered, with an enthusiasm that employed
to good effect the resources of the state for
intellectual purposes, on a programme of
book-collecting and philological scholarship.
The first public library independent of monastic institutions was open to scholars by 1444,
under the patronage of Cosimo de' Medici. But
the trade in manuscript books – along with resources for commercial copying – were
well advanced throughout Europe before this date. Coluccio by his death had acquired
some 800 manuscripts and had begun to cultivate the scholarly and editorial techniques which would subsequently be employed in the collation of material from multiple copies and the encouragement of disciplined habits of reading. Orthography was
one of Coluccio's specific concerns. It was he who ensured that an effective teacher of
Greek was available to Florence in the figure of Manuel Chrysoloras (1350–1415),
who spent three years in Florence between 1397 and 1400 teaching, among other
adult pupils, Coluccio's successor as Chancellor, Leonardo Bruni. The political and
even military significance of these advances was registered in the rhetoric and public
letters of Coluccio which were admired as far afield as Richard II's England. Even the
enemies of Florence, the Milanese Visconti, could recognize that a letter from
Coluccio was so inspiring as to be worth a thousand cavalrymen.

By the mid-fourteenth century, the Renaissance cult of the written word was both intensified and modified in its implications by the invention of printing. The compelling mystique of the manuscript book was challenged – sometimes to the chagrin of aristocratic bibliophiles such as Federigo da Montefeltro who refused to have printed books in their collections. Indeed the early versions of books often imitated manuscripts (possibly for convenience in design) to the point of being scarcely distinguishable. But – in a characteristically renaissance conjunction of craft, economic pragmatism and intellectual urgency – print developed its own technology (and its own alliances with political power). Chemistry had its part to play in developing alloys that were durable enough for repeated use in type. (Compounds of lead, tin and antinomy came to be favoured in the sixteenth century.) Special skills developed to deal with Greek type, with cartography and with musical scores, which required the superimposition of multiple lines of type. Techniques in woodcut, etching and engraving were refined. By the late 1470s, merchants such as the Strozzi had begun to realize the commercial potential of book-trading. By the early sixteenth century Aldus Manutius (?1450–1515) had turned Venice into the busiest printing centre in Europe, publishing something like 130 editions between 1495 and 1515. These included a five-volume Aristotle in Greek (1495–98). Aldus also began to introduce octavo volumes roughly the size of the modern book, intended for portable reading. These were usually editions of the Latin classics. But Aldus also published (in varying sizes) the works of vernacular writers such as Dante and Petrarch. By the time of the Reformation, printing was recognized by Luther as a gift from God, ensuring the extraordinary rapidity with which his own ideas were disseminated. By 1546 3,400 editions of the Bible had appeared in High German and about 430 editions in Low German – producing, on a print run of 2,000 copies, a total of something like a million available texts. Book prices were in fact rising at this time, which suggests a vigorous demand. And Aldus's *Aristotle* would have cost between a tenth and an eighth of a schoolmaster's annual salary. But octavo volumes of vernacular works could easily be equivalent in price to the daily wage of a middle-rank artisan and so affordable to the determined. The possibility of private opinion, formed in private attention to texts of one's own choosing, was, however remotely, becoming apparent.

None of this should suggest that printing produced any sudden democratization of knowledge. Much would depend upon what a printer saw fit to print or considered important. News, for instance, of the discovery of the Americas was relatively slow to spread; outside of Spain – with its appetite for the chivalric and marvellous – there were perhaps few printers before about 1550 who understood what the fuss was all about. It is true that by the middle of the sixteenth century printing had become sufficiently subversive in its implications for authorities throughout Europe – Protestant and Catholic alike – to seek to control the publication of books – so successfully in some cases that manuscripts themselves became a channel of agitation.

Yet print alone, without a mentality that understood and was receptive to its implications, would not itself have created any revolution at all. This mentality, closely associated with developments in educational practice, had their remote origins in the fourteenth century.

In this regard, a particularly significant episode occurs in the life of Poggio Bracciolini (1380–1459), a young member of Coluccio Salutati's circle. In the course of a career that took him as an exile to England, Poggio served the Papal Court as Secretary. In this capacity, he travelled to the great Council of Constance, which had been called to reconcile the differences between schismatic Popes and anti-Popes. This Council itself proved to be a fertile meeting for intellectuals from the whole of Europe and, while attending, Poggio pursued his own intellectual interest in the recovery of ancient manuscripts; and on a trip to the monastery of St Gallen in 1416 he chanced upon a particularly interesting cache:

> There in the midst of a great mass of codexes, I discovered Quintilian safe and sound, though entirely covered with mold and dust. These books were not in a library as their dignity demanded but practically in a dungeon, miserable and dark.

This passage rings with a fastidious distaste for the monastic life that also appears in Poggio's *De Avaritia* and *Contra Hypocritas*. Against this prejudice, it has to be said that the monastic orders had played a crucial role in the preservation of classical literature; and certainly by the time of the twelfth-century Renaissance connoisseurs such as Abbot Suger of Saint-Denis, had shown their own appreciation of that inheritance. Yet one of the greatest shifts in mentality that appears in the early Renaissance is a shift away from the dominance of monastic culture, in the sphere not only of religious practice, but also of educational programme. It is true, as will appear later in this chapter, that the contemplative life makes a reappearance in humanist form in the Neoplatonic philosophy of Ficino. On the other hand, the enthusiasm that impels Poggio may be scholarly but is also far from contemplative in its appetite for antiquarian rummagings. Poggio went on to copy out the manuscript he had discovered for the benefit of intellectual friends such as Bruni and Niccolò Niccoli, employing as he did so the elegant italic script (rather than a Gothic hand) which some have considered, because of its easy adaptability to printed type, to be among the most crucial achievements of early Italian humanism. These very activities, however, precise even pedantic as they may appear, also stand as expressions of a spirit which would effectively ally the realms of scholarship and classical learning with the practical demands of ethical and political existence. Henceforth it would be a civic and human duty to follow knowledge and to communicate it efficiently to one's fellows.

It is no less important that the book on which Poggio's eyes had lighted was Quintilian's *Institutio oratoria* ('The Education of an Orator'); and, though an incomplete version of this work had been available in Florence since before 1396, Poggio's discovery punctuated an important shift in conceptions of education. Poggio himself proved to be a somewhat conservative scholar (who failed for instance to see any point in learning Greek). However, examination of Quintilian's text confirmed that the study of eloquence – cultivated now by a precise understanding of words checked closely on the page – had once been and could again become a central feature in a civil and secular education. Quintilian (AD 35–95), out of deep respect for Cicero (106–43 BC), had wished to restore Latin rhetoric to its former glory and had devised his programme of education accordingly. His Renaissance followers could now follow suit, with the intention of producing the public man 'who can really perform his function as a citizen and who is fitted to the demands both of private and public business' (*Institutio oratoria*, 1, pr. 10).

From this point on, the study of the book goes hand in hand with the development of a new style of educational practice. This was at first guided by the initiative and enthusiasms of individuals such as Poggio, especially those who had been impressed by the extraordinary example of Petrarch (see below pp. 82–8). Almost at once, however, the usefulness of such learning in city and court – and its power to attract intellectual prestige to both community and scholar – was widely recognized. There were after all many princes whose private tutors had given them the *élite* instruction that only a humanist could command. Only in the sixteenth century did humanist education reach a wider audience and then mainly in the North, often under the patronage of powerful Protestants. It was for instance Erasmus's purpose to produce a species of Christian Gentlemen (though St Ignatius had similarly humanistic aims in founding the Society of Jesus). So too in England, Henry VIII, pursuing his own strategy of political and religious reform, founded Trinity College at Cambridge on principles that derived directly from the new learning, while Edward VI confirmed the trend with the establishment of his Grammar Schools. Elizabeth I was tutored by the humanist, Roger Ascham, who perceived in his particular style of learning a way, through the Monarch, of rectifying the manners of the nation at large.

It needs to be emphasized that humanism as an educational programme was pursued in private tuition and in schools rather than in universities. The universities themselves – though eventually modifying their syllabuses – continued for many decades to provide the sort of teaching that had characterized the revolution of the thirteenth century, when thinkers such as Albert the Great and St Thomas Aquinas had first invoked Aristotle in defining the principles of Christian rationalism. Much that now counts as Renaissance philosophy was in fact a product of the continuing rigour in logic and speculation that Scholastic philosophy had brought to the universities. But the education offered by the humanists, with their emphasis particularly upon

Quintilian's rhetoric and an attention to the detail of written texts, was analogous to the course that a Conservatoire of Music might now offer in competition with academic courses in mathematics, physics or theology. The discipline in the latter case aims at abstraction, hypothesis and communal inquiry; in the former, its purpose is performance – the articulation, through skills well learned, of the voice of original sensibility.

In practice, children were accepted for tuition at the age of about 14, though some could begin as late as 22. The course could then last as long as seven years, progressing from a detailed study of the Latin (or later Greek) language in point of vocabulary and grammar to an ever-closer engagement with the rhetoric, literature, history and philosophy of the ancient world. Time was also found in many curricula for recreation and for polite activities such as dancing and game playing, which would equip the student for entry into the courtly circles that Castiglione describes. In some curricula – such as that devised by Vittorino da Feltre (1378–1446) who in 1423 set up a school of some 70 pupils at the Mantuan court by invitation of Gianfrancesco Gonzaga – Greek mathematics was taught as an alternative to the Aristotelian logic which dominated the Scholastic syllabus.

A detailed picture of such studies is available in an account of the courses offered by Guarino da Verona (1374–1460), compiled by Guarino's son, Battista. After a brief spell in Florence (1410–14) – where his excellent knowledge of Greek seems to have excited the envy of Florentine intellectuals – Guarino in 1429 became tutor to Leonello d'Este at the court of Ferrara. Though Guarino himself insisted upon the importance of Greek (translating Plutarch's *On the Education of Children* and revising Chrysoloras's Greek grammar) Latin was still the staple of his teaching. The programme would begin with the reading aloud of Latin texts; Guarino always insisted that pronunciation and delivery were matters of importance. This reading led on to the analysis of parts of speech and recognition of inflections. From the outset, emphasis was laid upon detail, repetition and memorization, in which – over years of drilling – the book was constantly open before the eyes of the student: 'the teacher must not be satisfied with going over them once but must train the boy's memories by going over the material again and again'. Once the linguistic fundamentals were established, the course moved forward to a study of the substance of the texts, where material might be found in the history, literature and moral philosophy of the ancients not only for intellectual pleasure but also for moral or rhetorical profit in assembling examples, anecdotes and points of reference for future use. Here again the focus of attention was the word on the page, which, when it was submitted to microscopic attention by an enthusiastic teacher could yield a wealth of cultural information. A comment on lines 43–4 of Virgil's *Georgics* I (in the notes of John Free, one of Guarino's English students) finds it necessary to speak of what an 'annus' – or year – is before even touching on the topic of 'spring':

vere novo gelidus canis cum montibus umor

liquitur et Zephyro putris se glaeba resolvit,

(In fresh spring-time, snow melts from the white mountains and the hard earth grows soft and rich in the west wind.)

vere novo: the word *annus* comes from *annanein* ('renew', 'recover') because when the sun returns to the same degree, then the year has passed. Romulus began the year from March; hence he called the first month of the year by his name, since he is called the son of Mars. The second he named after Aeneas from whom the Roman nation is descended. . . . And because the Roman people were divided into two parts, that is into the elders or *seniores*, and the younger, he named May from the elders (*maioribus*) and June from the younger (*junioribus*).

Possessed of elocution, word-power, rhetorical know-how and a store of useful information (as well as the ability to dance) the Renaissance scholar could confidently go out into the court or piazza and make his mark. Many did; and Guarino writes (in his *Epistolario* I, p. 263) with pedagogic complacency to a former pupil who had become military governor of Bologna:

I understand that when civil disorder recently aroused the people of Bologna to armed conflict you showed the bravery and eloquence of a soldier as well as you had previously meted out the just sentence of a judge. . . . You owe therefore no small thanks to the Muses with whom you have been on intimate terms since your boyhood. . . . They taught you how to carry out your tasks in society. Hence you are living proof that the Muses rule not only musical instruments but also public affairs.

It was once supposed that the educational programme of the humanist was aimed at cultivating 'the whole man' and providing the individual with the freedom to be himself (or, in the case of courtly sisters, 'herself' as well). There is some truth in this. After all, the teachers must themselves have been – if they were to sustain and propagate syllabuses as tedious as Guarino's will now appear – charismatic individualists, capable of winning attention, as though in some literary master-class, and of recommending themselves (as did figures such as the Medici tutor, Poliziano) to the inward councils of an aristocratic circle. The very popularity of humanist teaching is also compelling evidence of its liberating power: scholars from Hungary were attracted by it, while in the fourteenth century English aristocrats such John Tiptoft, Earl of Worcester (1427–70) could escape from Balliol College in Oxford and cross paths, in his search for humanist learning, with the son of a Bristol merchant, John Free (1430?–65), also originally from Balliol. In a similar way, those supposedly universal factors of human nature that the Renaissance was credited, once, with discovering look plausible in the perspective of a humanist classroom. Not only were the pupils drawn from the widest geographical spectrum but their attention also was unanimously trained upon texts that spanned the temporal divide between ancient and modern societies. By the mid-fifteenth century, there were – as will be seen in section three below – philosophies in abundance that did encourage such a view.

For all that, there is reason to be suspicious, as recently critics have been, of a form of universal learning that could so easily ally itself with the local manifestations of power. Humanist rhetoric could often provide a dazzling gloss for very rough purposes and prove, in its application, very far from humane. The very relationship between master and pupil was often expressed in metaphors of sovereignty; and the liberal use of the whip seems to have been essential to success in these liberal programmes. At the very least, highly complicated cross-currents could arise in the relationship between a court humanist and his aristocratic pupil.

A case in point is that of the Scottish humanist George Buchanan (1506–82) in his relationship with his pupil, James VI (later James I of England). Buchanan himself was a humanist of the highest European standing. Author of Latin plays, translator of Greek, associate of the French *Pléiade* and admired by Sir Philip Sidney, Buchanan's influence stretched as far as Hungary and won the good opinion of the poet Balassi. As for his native Scotland, Buchanan would gladly have seen its language replaced by Latin. None of which prevented him, in a peculiarly authoritarian regime, from reminding his pupil, who was the son of the executed Mary, Queen of Scots, of 'the bloody nest from which he had come'. Nor would it be difficult (following P. Bushnell) to trace from such moments of brutality the curious psychological complexion that James brought to the government of England. Under James, in savage reaction against his tutor, Buchanan's books were banned. Yet the King, who in his *Basilikon Doron* (1599–1603) bequeathed a notion of Divine Right to his son, also wished to be a tutor to his own nation, instituting what Alexander Pope would call a 'pedant reign' and encouraging, in this case, not the Latin that Buchanan would have wished upon Scotland but the English vernacular:

> It is a king's duty and privilege to develop his country's language; for it best becometh a king to purify and make famous his own tongue; wherein he may go before all his subjects as it setteth him well to do in all honest and lawful things. (*Basilikon Doron*, trans. C.H. McIlwain *op. cit.* p. 48)

One product of this tangled humanist tale was the Authorized Version of the Bible, another perhaps was the execution of Charles I.

Discipline, power, precise imitation and memorization, these are the characteristics of humanist education. Their rigidity – at least to a post-Romantic or twenty-first century point of view – will at once be apparent. Indeed, even by the end of the sixteenth century the imitation of printed books produces the utter dissolution of books themselves in the picaresque fantasy of Cervantes's *Don Quixote*, while Shakespeare in his early comedy *Love's Labour's Lost* shows how rapidly all pretensions to humanist learning will evaporate in the heat of sexual stimulus. Yet Cervantes and Shakespeare are both the products of the humanism that they both deride. Moreover, Rabelais – who will feature alongside Cervantes and Shakespeare in the final chapter – at one and the same time displayed an unbridled relish for his native tongue which will resonate through all his French successors in the sixteenth century and a passionate enthusiasm for the freedom revealed by the new learning.

For Renaissance thinkers, there seems to have been no incongruity between imitation and creation. This may now seem a paradox. But it is a position characteristic of many arts, above all perhaps, as Chapter Five will suggest, of the visual arts. But here, on the borders of education and literature, an especially pertinent illustration is offered by the genre of Comedy. Comedy began in the classroom, where Latin plays were organized to combine all the components of the humanist syllabus: performance, attention to the details of language, courtly pastime. Humanists themselves wrote plays for performance in Latin; and, even when vernacular comedy began to appear – as in Ariosto's *I Suppositi* (1509) or Bibbiena's *La Calandria* (1513), imitation was the key and in many ways the very source of comic effect. A modern author may take a plot from an ancient or even contemporary source; and if the original plot hinged upon long-lost twins, then the next version would introduce a pair of twins and the next a pair of twins of different genders – or even pairs of transvestite twins (as in Bibbiena's play). Twinning – as only Shakespeare perhaps was subtle enough to realize in plays such as *A Comedy of Errors* and *Twelfth Night* – is itself a device in which imitation and identity are at issue. Yet to any playgoing audience the virtuosity that an author displayed in his treatment of received material would itself have been a source of pleasure, where creation was the more apparent in being a variation on a well-known theme. In comedy, too, academic artifice was reconciled with increasingly sharp observation of the everyday world. Sanctioned by classical example, the writer of comedy could set himself to imitate, realistically, the *mores* and foibles of his own contemporary ambience.

A dramatist such as Ben Jonson is a vigorous classicist, who in *Timber* produces his own educational theory. Yet he is also – in *Bartholomew Fair* or *The Alchemist* – a spirited and searching observer of the urban scene in sixteenth-century London. In his case, as throughout the Renaissance, 'imitation' is probably an inappropriate term for a procedure that involved not merely copying but rather a shaping or toning of the mind through the exercise of humanist erudition. A better word might be 'innurition', by which is implied a process of learning, digestion and vigorous or well-fed response to the needs of the moment. Quintilian himself supplies authority for such a view in his description of legal rhetoric:

> Although it is essential to bring into court a supply of eloquence which has been prepared
> in advance in the study – and on which we can definitely rely – there is no greater folly
> than the rejection of the gifts of the moment. (*Institutiones*, xvi, 6)

This can be matched by statements from any number of Renaissance humanists, at least those of the more creative tendency; and Erasmus carries the metaphor of 'feeding' to characteristically witty, even nervy, conclusions when he writes in his *Ciceronianus*:

> The speech which moves the listener must arise from the most intimate fabric of the body
> . . . you must digest what you have consumed in varied and prolonged reading and trans-
> fer it by reflection into the veins of your mind rather than into your memory or your note-
> book. Thus your natural talent, gorged on all kinds of food will itself beget a discourse.

To Erasmus even translation was more than a matter of accuracy. We learn a language with the utmost precision in order to be even more precise in the articulation of our thoughts. So the Latin prose and poetry that humanists wrote tended to take on a much more personal colour than mere imitation would have warranted; and Machiavelli fed his audience on the raw meat of classical example so that in the political present their actions might manifest an appropriately vigorous *virtù*.

There are new opportunities in all of this, cultivated anew by humanist thought often in conscious opposition to the achievements of scholastic philosophy. The book – to be read, revered and re-created – was certainly in many ways a source of liberation. But it brought with it its own viruses, delusions and possible misdirections of energy. And to see what these might have been, one may turn to the earliest, subtlest and (save Erasmus) most influential of the humanists, Francesco Petrarca. Section three then moves to a period when Neoplatonic thought, in the writings of Ficino and Nicholas of Cusa, seemed to develop an answer to the problems inherent in the humanist programme. Section four returns to two examples – one early and one late – Lorenzo Valla and Ramus who exemplify the characteristic features of the movement.

'I DO NOT ADORE ARISTOTLE'

The potentialities and pressures implicit in scholarly humanism are already visible in the writings of Francesco Petrarca (1304–74). Petrarch more than any other single individual may be regarded as the founder of an international interest in humanist culture, and was recognized as such as early as the 1560s when his name is quoted alongside Erasmus's in the lecture notes of a Protestant student at Christ Church, Oxford.

Son of a Florentine who, like Dante, was exiled by the Black Guelfs, Petrarch – though eager to be known as a Florentine – rarely wished to return to Florence. He could have returned. Florence particularly towards the end of Petrarch's life had emerged with some confidence from the heroic but tumultuous years of the late thirteenth century; and one sign of this was a devoted circle of admirers – including Coluccio Salutati, Poggio Bracciolini and Giovanni Boccaccio – who sharpened their humanist appetites and promoted the prestige of Florentine culture in correspond-ence with Petrarch. Petrarch, however, thrived as an intellectual celebrity on the international stage and preferred to allow his prestige to work from afar. From the age of seven he lived at Avignon (where, when he was twenty-three, he first encountered Laura), making his home at a villa in Provence until 1353. However, his frequent trav-els took him throughout France and Italy, notably to Milan, which at this time was in fierce political contention with the Florentine Republic.

Petrarch is now best known as a lyric poet, lover of Laura and progenitor of innu-merable Petrarchan poets throughout Europe in the fifteenth and sixteenth centuries. His importance in this regard will become apparent in Chapter Six. But Petrarch him-self viewed his own lyric poems with a mixture of shame and fascination. In his own eyes, as in those of his contemporaries, his achievement lay in his Latin works, the never-to-be completed *Africa*, a series of treatises on intellectual and ethical issues, a work of history, *De Viris Illustribus*, and a copious correspondence addressing the central concerns of scholarly and ethical humanism.

The tenor of these works may, in a number of ways, be taken to reflect a response on Petrarch's part to the conflicting influences in his years at Avignon, where the Papacy had taken up residence under the French sphere of influence. It was here that Petrarch found Laura – possibly an ancestress of the Marquis de Sade. But the city was also a place of international exchange in the intellectual market, where books and manuscripts were already attracting lively attention. To Italian eyes, the Avignon cap-tivity was an insult to the sovereign claims of Rome, as both a spiritual and secular capital. Certainly, Petrarch witnessed a profound disorder in the 'Babylonian' courts of predominantly Gallic popes; and his attacks on the Papal corruption would win him a ready hearing among Northern Protestants. (Petrarch himself was in holy orders – and was also the father of two illegitimate but apparently devoted children.)

The troubled history of the period that immediately precedes the fifteenth-century Renaissance was vividly exemplified in the circumstances of Petrarch's early life, the more so because these same years span the appalling irruption of the Black Death (in which Laura herself was carried off). Yet Petrarch – unlike his predecessor Dante and Boccaccio, his contemporary – developed neither the political imagination nor the polemical diction to address these issues directly. On the contrary (and in common with many subsequent humanists), he turned to scholarly solitude and to books to construct a history beyond the brute facts of the medieval city with its economic exuberance, its clamorous partisan conflicts and inescapable manifestations of human frailty.

A similar fastidiousness and desire for intellectual seclusion is also evident in the main thrust of Petrarch's philosophical attacks, aimed at the rationalistic synthesis that scholastic philosophers had achieved during the thirteenth century. This synthesis had been founded on the use of Aristotelian logic and science in the exploration of a Christian universe; and the essential technique of the schools had been one that depended less upon private study in a library than on communal and often oral debate between teachers and students. Petrarch, displaying the incipient individualism of the humanist, objects time and again to the noisy and entangling disputations that in his view characterized these schools. 'In too much altercation, truth is lost,' he declares, in a letter to Tommaso Caloria, citing the authority of Varro. More important still is Petrarch's insistence (in his treatise *On His Own Ignorance*) that he 'does not adore Aristotle'. It is with this slogan that he marks his assault not so much on Aristotle himself – who as a classical Greek deserved the respect of any humanist – but rather upon the over-systematic use that scholastic philosophy had made of Aristotelian texts.

Among the principal targets of Petrarch's disdain are the English and Scots who in Medieval Oxford pursued a regime of metaphysical speculations that, to the humanist eye, seemed increasingly barbarous. There is also a certain bravado in all this; Petrarch consciously pits himself against the overwhelming example of his Florentine antecedent, Dante, who had claimed that Aristotle was the 'master of those who know'. Petrarch, without always anticipating the consequences of his own thought, now begins to construct an alternative to the adoration of Aristotle that was to resonate throughout the Renaissance.

A quintessentially humanist feature of this development is Petrarch's objection to the far-from classical character of Scholastic Latin, loaded as Petrarch saw it with jargon and lacking all fluency of phrase. Aristotle himself still deserved to be studied but in authentic versions such as those that began to be printed in Greek around 1500. In reading Aristotle, as with any other classical author, the purpose of study must be to improve the quality of one's own prose and rhetorical powers. Linked to this insistence, however, there was a more radical programme. For Petrarch was concerned with a conception of knowledge itself that was neither speculative, logical nor metaphysical but rather ethical in its character. Correspondingly, he set himself to develop a form of intellectual presentation which – free from the technical vocabulary of scholasticism – could speak directly of the truths that most closely reflected human nature itself. 'What is the use,' he inquires, 'of knowing the nature of quadrupeds, fowls, fishes and serpents and not knowing or even neglecting man's nature, the purposes for which we are born and whence and whereto we travel.' Significantly, these words are quoted from Petrarch's treatise *On his own Ignorance (and that of many others)* – and one notes here, for discussion in Chapter Four, how far from scientific Petrarch's humanism is. Petrarch's concern is to define and defend a particular mode of understanding that vigorously rejects mere curiosity or the desire for information in favour of moral truth; and this concern is bound to resemble ignorance in the eyes of a rationalist – whether scholastic or scientific. For Petrarch, the goal of intellectual activity will not be achieved by the pursuit of logical conclusions but rather in the urgent communication of a profound insight into the needs and values of the human heart:

> The true moral philosophers and useful teachers of virtue are those whose first and last intention is to make the hearer good. . . . It is safer to strive for a good and pious will than for a capable and clear intellect. It is better to will the good than to know the truth. The first is never without merit; the latter can often be polluted with crime and then admits no excuse. (*ibid.*, trans. H. Nachod in Cassirel *et al.*, *The Renaissance Philosophy of Man*, *op. cit.* p. 101)

At this point it becomes clear why eloquence and rhetoric must, to humanists of the Petrarchan school, be more than a matter of ornamental flourish. It is only through words – well-chosen and inspiring – that others may be persuaded to see, contemplate and enjoy the truth that the moral philosopher lays before them. Love of words leads to love of goodness: for it is eloquence rather than argument that 'stings and sets afire and urges towards love of virtue and hatred of vice' (*ibid.*, 103); and 'what is the use of knowing what virtue is if it is not loved when known?'

There is much here – concerning both virtue and rhetoric – that will find an echo in the humanist thinking of Erasmus and beyond: and defences of 'ignorance' – in a period which also witnessed undoubted advances in technological rationalism – will continue to be mounted in the name of Socratic modesty, or sophisticated esotericism or mystic fervour. Nonetheless, there is much here that is highly problematical, as Petrarch himself certainly realized; and the problem may – conveniently if all too briefly – be summarized by a consideration of two authors, Cicero and Augustine, who were as important to most subsequent humanists as they were to Petrarch himself. The former – a classical orator – reveals to Petrarch the extent to which a self is constituted by its outward relationship to other selves, past and present, in a community of ethical purpose; the latter – a leader of the early Church and one of its most enduringly influential theologians – looked inward to a self which could not truly achieve the goodness of its own selfhood if it knew and was known in goodness by God. The two positions are complementary but could also be perceived in certain lights as profoundly incongruous.

So, on the one hand, Petrarch talks to the past in his reading of Cicero and discovers there – in common with all other Renaissance humanists – that the living self may be nurtured by ancient words, realizing in consequence its own responsibility to utter words of a similar resonance to its own community, present and future. (It has been said that if Petrarch is the father of the Renaissance, Cicero is its grandfather.) Fame and glory – denoted by the laurel crown that Petrarch indefatigably seeks – are the temporal channels of moral influence and may, even, seem to bestow a sort of immortality on human beings. How is one, then, to distinguish between the moral influence of a classical writer such as Cicero – or Plato – and a Christian interlocutor? This, for Petrarch, is the abiding question: 'I am certainly not a Ciceronian or a Platonist but a Christian. I even feel sure that Cicero himself would have been a Christian' (ibid., 114–15). Yet Cicero was not a Christian. Nor was Plato. So what are their Renaissance admirers to make of them?

This is not a question that Petrarch easily resolves; and it runs in parallel with another that almost forbids logical resolution, concerning not our secular relationships but rather the ground of our being in God. The self may be a brilliant receptor of intertextual influence. But what is a self in itself? And what is the source of, or reason for, its brilliant receptivity?

It is St Augustine who articulates this question for Petrarch, as also for the Protestant Reformers who succeeded Petrarch. St Augustine (354–430) recommended himself to Petrarch's mind not least because he had been a professor of Rhetoric, and had himself struggled to understand the allure of the classics at a point in history – the early centuries of the Christian era – when the claims of the classics were living claims, expressed in Imperial power over territories such as Numidia (now Algeria) where Augustine was born. Similar sympathies would have been evoked by Augustine's early entanglement in the conflicts of love and lust; and the Confessions in which Augustine records these troubles would finally have spoken to the inner self that Petrarch seeks to liberate from delusion and pride. But the simple answer which Augustine, like Petrarch, found it all but impossible to recognize, is that the self, even (or especially) the self of a talented individual, remained eternally a gift from God, to be sustained not by argument or even the brilliance of human words but inwardly in prayer and willing self-abnegation. St Augustine prays: 'Unchanging God let me know myself, let me know you' (Soliloquia II). These words acknowledge the essential truth, which is that a created intellect exists only to discover and delight in its Creator. Prior to any use that the created mind may put itself to, there is the fact that it is created; and therefore has no other raison d'être than its Creator.

On the fullest understanding of this position, the only possible life for a human being would be life of monastic prayer and contemplation. Petrarch recognizes this whenever he considers, with a troubled conscience, the example of his brother Gerard who had indeed entered the monastic life. But Augustine had lived in an age of hermits, whereas Petrarch had to seek his own solitude in a culture which had not only produced the beginnings of urban clamour but also was shortly to abandon the monastery under the influence of the Augustinian monk, Martin Luther. In any case, the divided mind of Petrarch was itself largely responsible for a new understanding of the value of human beauty, human creativity and indeed human individuality. Those are the values that Cicero and Plato had revealed to him. How then to reconcile this conflict?

One answer lies in the implicitly mystic philosophies of Neoplatonism, developed – as section three will suggest – by thinkers such as the Florentine Ficino and the German Nicholas of Cusa (Cusanus). Another recourse – to which Petrarch inclined – lay in a certain form of Stoicism which had classical cachet and from Petrarch's time onwards was adopted increasingly by Renaissance thinkers as an ethical fall-back or political default position in the face of extreme perplexity, contributing directly to the growth of a commonplace morality in schools, courts and parliaments. For Stoicism invited us to reconcile our own being to the being of Universal nature, exerting a rational control over ourselves so that our wills may be reconciled to the greater will of Creation. In Petrarch's words:

> Were you to find someone so vigorously possessed of his reason as to order his whole life by it, subjecting every desire, every impulse of his soul to its rule, in the full conscious-ness that reason alone is that which distinguishes him from brute beasts and that he alone deserves to be called human who lives by its light; and who at the same time is con-scious of his mortality as to keep it daily in his mind's eye, regulating his entire life with death in its view, so that despising all perishable things of this world, he aspires only to a life in which grown to new heights of rationality he will cease to be mortal, then at last you could say that you had truly and profitably understood the definition of man. (*Secretum* I, trans. Foster, *op. cit.* p. 166)

In time, such ideas came to be associated with the legend of the Labours of Hercules. (An early instance occurs in the thinking of Coluccio Salutati.) For Hercules was not a god but became a God by his own strivings in the temporal world.

Petrarch is honest enough never wholly to embrace the heroic intoxications of the Hercules myth. For him the fullest reflection of the inner conflicts into which his thinking led him is found, as we shall see, in his vernacular poetry – which oscillates constantly between the cultivation of eloquence and the language of private prayer. In a similar way, the form of Petrarch's prose writings proves highly significant for the humanist future. The Petrarchan treatise aspires continually to the condition of dia-logue. Abandoning scholastic debate, Petrarch seeks civilized conversation. The most important of his philosophical statements are cast in the form of letters that aim at intimate persuasion, or else in the Dialogue that he conducts in the *Secretum* (or *Secret Life*) between one aspect of himself (called Augustinus) and another by name

Franciscus. Unsurprisingly the dialogue is never resolved. Yet henceforth, with the discovery of Plato's *Dialogues*, that form – along with correspondence and orations – is to become the medium in which truth – of a moral kind – is communicated throughout the Renaissance by men such as Pico, More and Tasso. These developments – along with an increasingly confident Platonism and a Socratic sense of irony – will be perceptible in the two thinkers, Ficino and Cusanus, who may be said most convincingly to have developed a coherent philosophy out of the manifold promptings of humanist scholarship.

PLATONIC POSSIBILITIES: FICINO AND CUSANUS

Petrarch imagines a life of contemplation, pursued in an ideal landscape removed from the noise of cities and the contentiousness of the scholastic debating hall. Such seclusion was in practice secured for the intellectuals of Medici Florence when Cosimo de' Medici began to encourage them to meet, as members of a 'Florentine Academy', in a villa some three or four miles from the centre of Florence. The meetings that took place there foreshadowed many that would punctuate the intellectual life of the Renaissance, resulting finally in such institutions as the French Academy founded by Cardinal Richelieu in the seventeenth century. However, in the fifteenth and sixteenth centuries these academies were rarely formal institutions. They were akin, rather, to the circles and cenacles that Shakespeare derides in *Love's Labour's Lost*, and often gave themselves silly or knowingly pretentious names such as 'The Thunderstruck' (at Siena) or 'The Enflamed' (under Sperone Speroni at Padua).

The temper of the Florentine group was set by Marsilio Ficino (1433–99), tutor to Lorenzo il Magnifico who was offered full use of the Careggi villa at Careggi by Cosimo de' Medici and under Cosimo's patronage made it a centre for the translation and discussion of Platonic texts. Unlike Petrarch, Ficino was born in Florence and never set foot outside the city. He eventually became a priest and canon of the cathedral of Florence. But – as the son of a physician – he came in the course of his career to combine a practising interest in medicine with a passion for mathematics, magic and music. He was also a vegetarian.

It is some indication of how most of these great concerns came together in Ficino's career that, once, when a group of writers had met dolefully to discuss the apparently invincible advance of the Turks against Western Christendom, Ficino should have 'picked up his lyre and by his music immediately [given] back to the company its confidence and strength'. This performance was not merely a matter of social nicety: through his music Ficino was able, in a way that was simultaneously medical and magical, to restore a sense of proportion in his audience and reconcile them with the life of the universe at large. Underlying such moments, however, there is the great synthesis between Platonic – or Neoplatonic – thinking and Christian belief that Ficino achieved in his own philosophical writings. Where Petrarch – suspicious of intellectual system – opens himself at his most sincere, to an unending play of moral contradictions, Ficino celebrates Thought itself as the vital principle of true existence and offers a view of the universe in which microcosmic human beings and macro-cosmic truth can exist in an orderly interrelationship, if they are able to respond to the secret wisdom which he embodies in his philosophy. Indeed, in this universe, contradiction itself becomes a dynamic principle.

At the heart of Ficino's philosophy (as of his medicine, mathematics, music and magic) is a development of Platonism which occurred in the hands of the Neoplatonic philosophers in the early Christian era. Neoplatonism had a place in Augustine's thinking; and combined with the traditions of Christian mysticism to exert a strong influence on the Twelfth-century Renaissance, as for instance in St Bernard's sermons on *the Song of Songs* – in which human love becomes an allegory for mystic love of the Divine – and later on the cosmological imagination of Dante Alighieri, where Neoplatonic thinking is fused with an Aristotelian rigour in analysis. But humanist scholarship added its own dimension to these developments when, with a character-istic appetite for original texts, Ficino produced his translation of the greatest of the Neoplatonists, Plotinus, an Egyptian who lived in Rome between AD 204 and 270.

Drawing less upon theorems and logical questions than poetic enthusiasm and mystic eloquence, Plotinus imagines a universe that is constituted of and sustained by pure thought and pure love. Plato in the *Symposium* had pictured intellectual love as the fundamental motivation of the soul in its search for knowledge. Plotinus extends this motivation to the cosmos at large. Thus, from eternity the Divine Mind is in love with the utterly simple Unity that lies even beyond its own being; and its contemplation of that unity is also the beginning of a plurality which emanates down in hierarchical order – simultaneously unified and diverse – through all the ranks of thinkable or lovable existence. The human soul occupies a central place in this hier-archy. It is an 'amphibian' (*The Enneads*, I, 8, iv, 31), living between the spiritual and material expressions of existence. The soul, however, 'can awaken to itself' – as Plotinus longs to do – 'and escape from the body'. This awakening is love; it is love that responds to the manifestations of order and beauty that appear even in the shadowy world where the human being at first exists; and love is tested – as in some initiation ritual – for its power to discern the hidden evidence of ultimate harmony. Through the contemplation of such signs, the mind then rises to an ever-more sim-ple but ever-more intense contemplation of primal Oneness. Thus where Aristotle offers us a cosmos of causes and effects, always open to the lines of logical investiga-tion, Plotinus portrays a cosmos of circles or interconnected spirals where contradic-tions are resolved in the vision of a unity beyond all being and becoming. Truth is measured by the extent of our participation in that unity. Plotinus declares:

It is not that the Supreme reaches out to seek our communion; we reach towards the Supreme. . . . We lift a choral song to God. In this choiring, the soul looks upon the well-spring of Life, well-spring also of Intellect, beginning of Being, fount of Good, root of all Soul. (*ibid.*, VI, 8–9)

So, in his turn, Ficino writes

Every mind lauds the round figure when it first encounters it and knows not wherefore it lauds. So too in architecture we laud the symmetry of the walls, the disposition of the stones, the form of the windows and doors; and in the human body the proportion of its members; or in a melody the harmony of tones. If every mind approves of these and if it must do so even without knowing the reason for its approbation, it can only be because of a natural and necessary instinct. The reasons for these judgements are therefore innate in the mind itself. In appreciation of beauty and knowledge of beauty the human mind places itself between God and the world and thus encompasses itself for the first time in a true unity. (*Theologica platonica* XI trans. in Cassirer, *op. cit.*, pp. 63–4)

This is Socratic – to the extent that Socrates is confident that geometrical principles can be understood even by a slave in the marketplace. Yet in Ficino's response to Neoplatonic thought, there is another – some might say elitist – strand which, in seeking the refinements of secret knowledge, embraces contradiction itself as a way to truth. The dynamism of the Neoplatonic universe depends upon the constant interplay between unity and plurality; and this dynamism reveals itself to the human mind at its mid-point in the hierarchy whenever, under the sign of beauty – or musical discord – the point of correspondence between one sphere and another is perceived and re-enacted by the passionate intellect. Such a response, however, is possible only among those who are prepared to abandon commonplace understanding in the interests of a higher, even occult, reason. The intellectual dynamism of the Neoplatonic universe will be seen by those spirits who are capable in rapture of rising above mere geometry to a condition of ecstatic contemplation or love: 'Love unites the intelligible intellect to the first and secret beauty by a certain life which is better than intelligence'. So in his paraphrase of *Enneads* VI, vii, 35, Ficino writes:

The mind has two powers. . . . The one is the vision of the sober mind, the other is the mind in a state of love; for when it loses its reason by becoming drunk with nectar, then it enters into a state of love diffusing itself wholly into delight; and it is better for it thus to rage than to remain aloof from that drunkenness.

The task of the chosen spirit is to speak as if it were an oracle, an enraptured seer or a prophet about the harmonies it has perceived in the cosmos. So logical contradiction ceases to be an impediment to truth; and 'learned ignorance' becomes the mark of the chosen spirit. Michelangelo took this teaching to heart. But the justification for music, mathematics and magic – and the synthesis of all these practices – are all also to be discovered in this doctrine:

> Orpheus in his book of hymns asserts that Apollo by his vital rays bestows health and life on all and drives away disease. Furthermore, by the sounding strings, that is their vibrations and power he regulates everything: by the hypate, the lowest string, winter; by the neate, the highest string, summer; and by the Dorian, that is the middle string, he brings in spring and autumn. So since the patron of music and discoverer of medicine are one and the same god, it is hardly surprising that both arts are often practised by the same man. In addition, the soul and the body are in harmony with each other by a natural proportion, as are the parts of the soul and the parts of the body. Indeed the harmonious cycles of fevers and humours and the movements of the pulse itself also seem to imitate this harmony. (*The Letters of Marsiliso Ficino*, ed. in trans. P.O. Kristeller, p. 142)

On this account, proportion is the common concern of mathematics and music – as indeed it had been since Pythagoras's time and was throughout the Middle Ages. For Ficino, however, this becomes a way to reconciliation with the cosmos. Mathematical number corresponds to the underlying nature of the intellectual universe. Music brings that unity to act in harmonizing the microcosm and the macrocosm. But this is the effect of magic too. It may be noted in the passage above as elsewhere Ficino anticipates the notion of a heliocentric universe, where Apollo – the Sun-God – beams his rays on the passively receptive earth. There are those who see such sentiments as contributing to a cultural mood that would at the least prove favourable to Copernican cosmology; and certainly Ficino, as a physician, displays none of that suspicion of doctors or scientific curiosity that Petrarch displays in his treatise 'against physicians'. Yet Ficino's position remains resolutely wedded to the possibility of magical practice and to a mythical language in which the trance of true intellect can be induced. Apollo – one recalls – enraptures his true devotee to the extent that in myth of Marsyas, the satyr Marsyas is flayed alive so that his outer form can be filled anew with the influence of the deity. So too in magic (or in 'white' magic) the magician opens himself to the currents of life which run through the Universe and – so far from controlling them as the black magician would attempt to do – brings them harmoniously to fruition. In *De vita coelitus comparanda*, Ficino writes:

Nature is itself a magician. The farmer prepares his field and seeds for gifts from heaven and uses various grafts to prolong life in his plants and change it to a new and better species. The physician, the scientist and the surgeon bring about similar effects in our bodies. . . . The philosopher who is learned in natural science and astronomy and whom we are wont to call a magician likewise implants heavenly things in earthly objects by means of certain alluring charms used at the right moment. (Trans. Brian P. Copenharer in 'Astrology and Magic', ed. Schmidtl and Skinner, *op. cit.*, p. 274)

On this view, the whole cosmos – animated at all levels of its hierarchy by dae-mons, astrological correspondences and angelic intelligences – exists in a constant state of coherent activity. Human beings are at the centre of this cosmos; and even the most technical and craftsmanlike of human activities may properly be understood as a contribution to that synthesis.

A similar understanding, however, may also illuminate the relationship between one human being and another. For here too – given always that Ficino attributes true intelligence only to those chosen spirits who desire to enter the circles of intellec-tual love – a harmony is possible which extends between past and present, between culture and culture, and even between Plato and Aristotle. Plato and Aristotle are said both to agree that music is a way of harmonizing the activities of the soul and cosmos. But in this way too wisdom might be seen not as a matter of altercation or controversy, which even after the end of the disputatious Middle Ages could easily occur (as it still can) in scholarly discussion between peevish Platonists and acrimoni-ous Aristotelians. Truth lies in harmony, in participation and reconciliation; and even scholars in a mood of true syncretism can look enthusiastically for the corres-pondences between Classical thought and Biblical thought. Ficino can also translate with fervour the Greek writings of the mythical Hermes Trismegistus, who was identified with the Egyptian god Thoth. This identification was of course wholly mis-taken. Yet the mistake stimulated an interest in the ancient origins of all wisdom which itself became a characteristic of the fifteenth century – whose ruling deity, it has been said, was Hermes himself, God of merchants but also of physicians and 'hermeticists', leader of souls to their heavenly origins. Florentines such as Pico della Mirandola now began to explore the secrets of pseudo-Egyptian writings and the Cabbala.

Among his fellow humanists, Ficino found a ready reception. Erasmus admired his command of Greek and the breadth and syncretic implications of his work; as in England did John Colet, the founder of St Paul's School, who corresponded with Ficino and wrote: 'we can enjoy the divine mind through various ideas and seek it through various traces'. So, too, his work was read enthusiastically by Leone Ebreo (referred to by Cervantes in the opening pages of *Don Quixote*) who speaks of how the

Figure 29   Sandro Botticelli, *Primavera*, c.1482, Panel 203.2 × 315 cm. Uffizi Gallery, Florence. Ficino writes: 'Venus, that is to say *Humanitas* . . . is a nymph of excellent comeliness, born of Heaven and more than others beloved by God all highest. Her soul and mind are Love and Charity, her eyes Dignity and Magnanimity, the hands Liberality and Magnificence, the feet Comeliness and Honesty. The whole, then, is Temperance and Honesty, Charm and Splendor'. With permission from Scala.

passions and fury of love may lead one to union with the divine. Just as significant is Leone Ebreo's own life-story: a Portuguese Jew (*c.*1465–*c.*1535), he was driven out of Iberia by persecution, yet found his intellectual home in the Neoplatonic syntheses that Ficino offered.

It was, however, among artists and also courtiers that Ficino finds his most fruitful reception. Beyond his concern with music, Ficino was not himself especially interested in the arts. This cautiousness had a sanction in Plato's infamous banishment of the arts from his *Republic* and may, in turn, have contributed to the welcome response which Calvin gave to a philosophy that appealed to the inward rather to the outward eye. Nonetheless Ficino can speak of poetic *furor* as a way to truth, and of the beneficent power of magical statues and gem-stones. He also revives the metaphor in which Plotinus compares the changes in the cosmos to the changes in a dancer's body. None of which could fail to provide a wealth of suggestion to the poetic imagination.

Ronsard especially in his Odes evokes the magical powers of verse and dance. Sir John Davies in his poem *Orchestra* (1594) can compare the universe to a dance. And Shakespeare remotely feeds on Ficino's vision in *Much Ado About Nothing* and *The Winter's Tale* (see pp. 355–6).

In the more immediate arena of Italy, Ficino's philosophy was rapidly taken up in courtly circles. So Cardinal Bembo in the last book of the *Cortegiano* offers a rhapsodic account of Neoplatonic love as his contribution to after-dinner debate; and a rage developed for emblem-literature in which enigmatic mottoes attached often to pseudo-hieroglyphic illustrations invited the intellect to plumb the depths of such contradictions as *Festina lente* (where 'making haste slowly' would be illustrated by a dolphin twining around an anchor, or by the leaden weight of a cannon-ball being impelled by wings in its flight). Erasmus himself in Adages II, I, 1 speaks of *Festina lente* as 'a pretty riddle, particularly as it consists of contradictory terms', going on to speak of the dignity of symbols and (*ibid.*, 176) to discuss the dolphin and anchor emblem approvingly. A picture such as Botticelli's *Primavera* (see Fig. 29), executed in the Medici circles to which Ficino belonged, has in the past been taken (by Edgar Wind) to invite precisely the sort of hermetic reading that Neoplatonism encouraged and indeed to offer an allegorical summary of the main features of Neoplatonic thought. Recent readings emphasize the possibility of a more political reading. But there is no mistaking the figure of Hermes – the tutelary deity of Hermetic Neoplatonism – in the left-hand corner of Botticelli's painting.

In its own day, despite the excitement that Ficino's philosophy aroused among thinkers as different as Erasmus, Botticelli, Michelangelo and Bruno, Ficino's world-view is relatively conservative, enclosed in itself, sustained by the dynamics of intellectual appetite and love. Measured by the standards of scientific inquiry that in the seventeenth century began to dominate our understanding of the cosmos, Ficino's outlook is to say the least superstitious. But that may not be an accurate judgement. Like Petrarch, Ficino profoundly believed that the world we live in is not a world merely of brute facts. It is also a world of values and of ideas created or developed by the human intellect; and to participate in that world it will never be enough simply to recognize (as the curious scientist does) our genetic affiliations with it. The responsibility of human beings will be to create and nurture considerations of value – as they do in pursuing beauty – even if they are bound, in doing so, to abdicate the delusions wrought by the sober eye.

There is, however, one form of Neoplatonism that points to a somewhat more engaged understanding of our place in the world – exemplified above all by a thinker from the generation preceding Ficino's who is described by Kristeller in his authoritative book on Ficino as the most vigorous thinker of the age. This is the German Nicholas Cusanus (1401–64) whose thinking is sometimes associated (as Ficino's is, less convincingly) with that of Copernicus and whose work has recently been studied as an important key to the reading of Shakespeare's work.

Unlike Ficino, who never left Medici Florence, Cusanus was a figure of international standing. Born in Cues (Cusa) on the Moselle he became a cardinal in 1448 and was deeply and sometimes painfully involved in the conciliar debates that were aimed in the early fifteenth century at reconciling the warring factions within the Western Church, and also at bringing the West back into communion with the Greek Orthodox. These debates are reflected in the themes of Cusanus's philosophical work. It seems likely, however, that his earlier years were influenced by the *devotio moderna* which – developing in Flanders – insisted upon a disciplined observance of the example of Christ. This school had already produced mystics such as Meister Eckhart and the St Thomas à Kempis of *The Imitation of Christ* and – as will be seen in the next chapter – exerted an influence over Erasmus, Luther and St Ignatius Loyola. At no point in his subsequent career did Cusanus abandon the concerns that the *devotio moderna* had taught him; and he qualifies to be considered not only as a theologian but also in his own right as a mystic. At the same time, Cusanus was unmistakably a humanist. He studied at Padua, a leading centre of scientific investigation, and was closely linked with Leonardo da Vinci, and in the same wave of bibliophiliac fervour that led Poggio Bracciolini to unearth Quintilian, Cusanus discovered the Latin comedies of Plautus – bawdier works than the Terentian comedies that for some had been part of the education even of nuns in their convents. On the whole, however, where Florentine humanists tended to interest themselves in the rhetoric, history and literature of the classical world, Cusanus was drawn particularly to the science and philosophy of Socrates and Plato.

Like Ficino (who seems not to have read his predecessor's work) Cusanus depicts a dynamic universe that is constantly responsive to the creativity of the human mind. In this he was unquestionably influenced, as was Ficino, by the mystic tradition of Christian Neoplatonism, descending from the Dionysius the Areopagite (though the scholarly Cusanus probably recognized that this Dionysius was 'pseudo'). It is sometimes said that Cusanus was influenced by the works of the Catalan philosopher, Ramon Llull (Majorca, 1232/3–1316) who, himself drawing on Islamic writers, saw God's unity as constantly unfolding itself in the contrarieties of the temporal world. Llull also envisaged a Mediterranean unity of faith which would draw together Muslim, Jew and Christian in unity of religious purpose. Such notions certainly find a resonance in Cusanus's form of syncretism (as do the ideas of Nicholas of Oresme, working in Paris between 1345 and 1382, who had begun to stress the conjectural nature of all human knowledge). Yet these tendencies – simultaneously sceptical, generous and daring in their epistemological implications – were probably sharpened in Cusanus to a greater degree than in Ficino by a direct encounter with the thought of Plato and Socrates. In his philosophical writings, Cusanus is concerned with the ways in which the human mind approaches infinity; and the spaces of his cosmos are filled not with the angelic and demonic hierarchies which interest Ficino (though Cusanus does not deny their existence) but rather with the constructs that are born in the realm of pure thought from the interaction of certainty and uncertainty.

On his own account, the essential point of Cusanus's thinking came to him in a vision on his way from Constantinople. His itinerary needs to be noted. Constantinople was a place of peculiar contention between the Eastern and Western branches of Christianity and had been the cradle of the mystic tradition in Neoplatonic Christianity. It was also the city that would be overwhelmed in 1453 by the forces of the Ottoman Empire in a devastating blow to Western and Christian self-confidence. In the intensity of this highly charged atmosphere, and travelling over the Aegean Sea Cusanus achieved a vision: all incomprehensible things (*incomprehensibilia*) might be embraced in 'learned ignorance' (*De docta ignorantia*, iii, 12).

The phrase 'learned ignorance' has already appeared in Petrarch – whose work Cusanus may have known – and has its place in Ficino's conception of the blind love that embraces logical contradiction. In Cusanus's thought from the moment of his vision onwards the fundamental task of the human mind is to establish a knowledge of the only thing which fundamentally it can know, which is to say a knowledge of its own ignorance.

This may seem at first a sceptical or even obscurantist position; and certainly Aristotelian scholars of the period such as Wenck vigorously maintained that it was. Yet – in a spirit of truly Socratic humility – Cusanus is here undoubtedly looking for certainties, and correspondingly concerned to disclose the conditions under which the human mind can truly and freely engage in its proper activities. Cusanus is Socratic, too, in the wit and even comedy that runs through his philosophical writings. His titles are all inclined to be as paradoxical as that of his earliest work, and include the almost Joycean neologism of *De Possest*, where by combining the two Latin verbs *posse* (to be able) and *essere* (to be) Cusanus seeks to indicate the unthinkable nature of an infinity which can simultaneously be all and be capable of all (as finite beings never can). His prose too constantly aspires to recreate in thought the vertiginous action of unknowing, as when Cusanus declares that: 'Man is God. He is not God absolutely because he is Man: he is therefore a human God.' But Cusanus is also capable of a pithy appeal to common experience (a later volume is entitled *The Idiot* or 'Common Man'), abandoning the world of courtly enigmas and emblems for the Socratic marketplace, where he can point to a spinning top as the illustration of how utmost speed may be reconciled with the semblance of utmost stillness. Other works meditate on the translucency of beryl or the curvature of spoons.

Yet in all of these *jeux d'esprit*, there is a desire, sustained by mathematical considerations, to illuminate the nature of human knowledge. And where Aristotle has provided a logic of the finite (with its important but restrictive law of the excluded middle) Cusanus seeks to allow into his logic infinity itself – and all those teasings-out of thought that infinity elicits. Thus

> The intellect, which is not truth, never comprehends truth so precisely that truth cannot be comprehended infinitely more precisely. For the intellect is to truth as [an inscribed] polygon is to the inscribing circle. The more angles the inscribed polygon has the more similar it is to the circle. However, even if the number of its angles is to increase *ad infinitum*, the polygon never becomes equal [to the circle] unless it is resolved into an identity with the circle. (*De docta ignorantia*, iii, 12)

All knowledge, then, is seen as a matter of measure and comparison – applied to a transcendent object which is itself beyond measure. (One recalls that John Donne, evoking the Last Judgement, speaks of 'the round earth's imagined corners'. See also Dürer's *Melencolia*, Fig. 58.) Up to a point this implies the mystic abandonment of the rational mind in the face of divine infinity. Yet the mystic life – as will be seen from the case of St Teresa – may indeed seek the utmost intensity of relationship with the divine, yet rarely involves the abandonment of the world itself. It certainly does not in Cusanus's case. To be sure, we do need to abandon the crutches of Aristotelian logic. The alternative, however, is not mere feeling. On the contrary, Cusanus insists that mystic love itself would not be possible without knowledge, albeit the knowledge of our own ignorance. As for the temporal world, Cusanus now proceeds with an exhilarating confidence to fill it with mathematical constructs or hypotheses and a liberated understanding of competing but coherent discourse.

In mathematics, one needs to wait for the seventeenth-century advent of calculus for the mathematical mind to habituate itself to the notion of infinity. Till then, Cusanus constantly constructs thought-experiments around the notions of unity, of the absolute Maximum and the absolute Minimum, of Identity and Otherness: 'The First Beginning is triune-prior-to-all-number. And if you cannot conceive of the fact that it is prior to number, the reason is that your intellect conceives of nothing whatever without number.'

While plainly couched in terms of Christian theology (as much of Newton's thinking was to be) Number here – in the perspective of learned ignorance – emerges as the one true element in which the human mind can operate. Equally there are the beginnings of a notion of mathematical hypothesis which – when conjoined to experiment – will provide a foundation for seventeenth-century science.

At the same time, such thinking has direct consequences in regard to some of the themes that are traditionally regarded as most central to Renaissance thinking. Cusanus's vision offers a radically new conception of the human individual and also of the culture that human beings build for themselves; and in each case it is Cusanus's understanding of the relativity of created being which proves to be the source of liberation. To quote the account offered by Cassirer as a paraphrase of Cusanus's own words in *De docta ignorantia*, II, 2, fol. 38:

> In the cosmology of Cusanus the universe dissolved into an infinite multiplicity of
>
> infinitely different movements, each circling around its own centre and held together by
>
> their relationship to a common cause and by their participation in one and the same uni-
>
> versal order. The same is true of spiritual being. Every spiritual being has its centre
>
> within itself. And its participation in the divine consists precisely in this centring, in this
>
> indissoluble individuality. Individuality is not simply a *limitation*; rather, it represents a
>
> particular *value* that may not be extinguished or eliminated.

So, in appropriate paradox, we possess our individuality precisely because we are not possessed of the absolute Maximum but rather possessed, each in each, by a Maximum that exceeds our power to measure. It is our acknowledgement of this paradox that ensures our participation in the unfolding of universal possibilities.

Another way to put this is to invoke the celebrated analogy that Cusanus draws between the gaze of God and the forward gaze of a portrait (remembering always that this is an analogy constructed by a human mind and not in any way a final definition). Meditating on a self-portrait by Rogier van der Weyden (now to be seen only in a tapestry copy), Cusanus considers how all who meet the eyes of the portrait believe these eyes to be looking directly at them. Learned ignorance will teach us here that we shall know nothing of how we are observed unless we know that others too are observed in the same way. Or else we might say with Cusanus:

> When a man attributeth a face unto Thee, he does not seek beyond the human species.
>
> In like manner if a lion were to attribute a face unto Thee, he would think of it a lion's,
>
> an ox as an ox's and an eagle as an eagle's. (*De visione Dei*, VI)

All of which might confirm us in the folly of our individualism or specie-ism unless we are prepared also to recognize that we are only what we are because others are too.

Such an understanding has practical as well as metaphysical implications, especially for our dealings with cultures other than our own. So – in his own version of cultural syncretism – Cusanus asserts that all cultures must be seen as being envisaged by the source of truth. This position is all the more remarkable in that by 1453 the culture of Islam had terrifyingly opposed itself to the culture of Christianity in the Ottoman assault upon the city of Constantinople. But where Ficino had dallied with the mythical Hermes Trismegistus, Cusanus on his travels to Constantinople had vigorously sought out copies of Qur'ān; indeed, it has been suggested that his notion of 'one faith and many observances' derived from an Islamic source. So within two months of the fall of Constantinople it is both unsurprising and yet astounding that Cusanus should have written *De Pace Fidei*, a dialogue set in the presence of the Word of God, where a cast of Arabs, Persians, Tartars and even French, English and Italians all come in search of the peace of faith.

> You who are infinite power are none of those things which you have created; nor can any
> creature grasp the concept of your infinity, for there is no proportion between the finite
> and the infinite. . . . Therefore hide yourself no longer O Lord. If you deign to heed our
> plea, the sword, and the bilious spirit of hatred and all sufferings will cease; and all will
> know that in the variety of rites there is only one religion. (*De Pace Fidei*, I, v).

This may not be as liberal as at first it seems; Cusanus, for instance, has been shown to be less sensitive to the alterities of foreign tongues than such lines might have led one to suppose. Yet a recognition that diversity of discourse may indeed be the source of human creativity throws into tragic relief the historical consequences of that same diversity.

In one aspect, Cusanus's view has much in common with the view that Plato expresses in the *Laws* (803–4) when he declares that 'God alone is worthy of supreme seriousness, but man is made God's plaything and that is the best part of him'. Such a view is consistent with an understanding of 'serious play' that runs through the Renaissance from Ariosto to Erasmus, from Cervantes to Shakespeare. But Cusanus's position involves no world-weary smile at the self-delusions of humanity. In Cusanus's cosmos God alone made things; human beings make ideas and it is the very act of human nature to fill the universe with these ideas, diverse as they may be. So in his *De Ludo Globi* (*The Game of Spheres*) (1488) Cusanus invents a game in which players aim at a target with a bowling-ball that in one hemisphere has been hollowed to a concave. We aim at truth, knowing something of the peculiar mechanics that will, of necessity, govern the trajectory of this bowl. Yet each throws with a different weight and heft, adapting a knowledge of mechanics to their own position, physique and touch; and no general rule will ever say how the bowl should be projected.

Such considerations must finally return to their theological origins. The Trinity – beyond number – is the source of all numerical possibilities. But the Trinity is also the Incarnate God whom Cusanus would have come to contemplate in the *devotio moderna*. And the ultimate mystery – known by all mystic imitators of Christ – is that the game we play is one that must be played in the temporal and historical world. It is there that the ever-shifting map of our pilgrimage is laid out, through the comic discovery of a Plautus manuscript and the tragic experience of Constantinople. Cusanus depicts a cosmic comedy of relativities and asks us to learn through alienation and tragedy the ignorance that will allow us to assume our ever-differing role in the cosmic game.

TEXTS AND TEXTBOOKS: VALLA AND RAMUS

Between them, Ficino and Cusanus turn the contradictions that Petrarch first unleashed on the humanist mind into exhilarating occasions for intellectual advance. Ficino and Cusanus offer – as far as humanism ever did – a coherent alternative to the scholastic systems of the thirteenth century. In common with all humanist writings their works remain dependent upon the cultivation of the word, poised for a moment in the productive flow of discursive activity; and Sir Francis Bacon recognizes this when he expresses his characteristic mistrust of eloquence, and seeks to go beyond the wiles of word-play by instituting a fully scientific form of knowledge (see pp. 144–6). However, until the seventeenth century, the Renaissance mind, displayed through its poets, narrative writers and dramatists, continues to swim with vigour and confidence in – and sometimes against – the currents of language. Later chapters will pursue this theme in regard to writers such as Rabelais and Ronsard, Montaigne, Cervantes and Shakespeare. Here, however, in concluding this account of humanism as an educational programme, two authors deserve all-too-brief attention for their practical and very influential achievements in the library and the classroom. These are Lorenzo Valla (1407–57) and Pierre de la Ramée, known as Petrus Ramus (1515–72).

Valla's career is an indication of how transferable (to use the modern university phrase) the skills of the humanist had become within fifty years of Petrarch's death. It is also true that the advent of printing ensured a wide diffusion of Valla's often-controversial ideas and procedures. Born in Rome, Valla taught for a time at Pavia under Milanese overlordship, became Secretary in Naples to Alfonso of Aragon in 1437 and returned to Rome as a papal secretary and university professor in 1448. His philosophical and academic works were comparably wide-ranging. He dealt with the problem of Free Will, from an angle which was both anti-scholastic and antirationalistic, evoking pagan myth for a Christian purpose – as for instance, in his insistence that, while the oracles of Apollo may tell us what is going to happen, that does not logically mean that they themselves determine what will happen. Similarly, Valla mounts a vigorous attack against a growing tendency in humanist thought to conflate the Christian and Stoic moralities, and argues (in *De Voluptate*) that Christianity in its true nature and Epicureanism are entirely compatible: in common with Epicureanism, Christianity must ultimately concern itself with Beatitude, which is to say, with happiness and, supremely, with joy.

However, Valla's most important and influential works were those that gave confidence and intellectual purpose to the philological and scholarly pursuits of his fellow humanists. In this field, his most spectacular success was the *De falso credita et ementita Constantini donatione* of 1440, in which Valla demonstrated on stylistic grounds that Constantine's gift of Temporal Power to the Church had been an eighth-century forgery. Henceforth, the Reformers – Protestant and Catholic – were armed with scholarly evidence in their assaults upon the corruption of the Church. In a similar manner, Valla set himself to clarify the abuse of scholastic terminology – or jargon – which had so offended Petrarch. In particular, he mounted a full-scale attack upon the linguistic tendency to create nouns out of adjective by the addition of an '-itas'. Such terminology not only breaches the canons of good Latin style but might well convince us that certain categories actually existed in substantial fashion when in fact they are merely products of human ingenuity.

Though Valla himself remained within the Church, a number of his works were eventually put on the Index. He was also attacked as a 'fanatic' by Poggio Bracciolini for his devotion to the educational rhetoric of Quintilian at the expense of Cicero. None of this, however, could impair the development of the philological and educational methods to which Valla so conspicuously contributed. Erasmus in particular was deeply influenced by Valla's (editorial) *Annotations to the New Testament* as well as by his *Elegantiarum libri* ('The Elegancies of the Latin Tongue'); and, of late, Valla has even been compared with Wittgenstein in the concern he displays to avoid conceptual abstraction and to examine the function of words as we actually use them. In his own day, it is true, that Valla – always preferring Latin to Greek – could speak of the 'great sacrament' of the Latin language. Yet part of his preference for Latin came from its solidity of reference and the resistance it put up against the speculative tendencies of Greek. For Valla as for Petrarch, the purpose of scholarship in its concentration upon the word was to develop highly refined sensitivity to the nuances of common sense. The grammar of ordinary language – when fully analysed – must always be allowed to rule over the merely artificial constructions of logic. Dialectic on this view had now to take instruction from the rhetorician.

Similar considerations proved to be consistent with certain developments in the educational field – culminating in the work of Ramus – that were encouraged in the early sixteenth century by humanists such as the Dutch Rudolphus Agricola (1443/4–85) and the Spaniard Juan Luis Vives (1492–1540). Agricola in particular was influential in ensuring that academic courses with a humanist bent became a recognized part of the university curriculum; and his text book *De Inventione Dialectica*, first published in 1515, came to enjoy extreme popularity in the 1530s. On Agricola's recommendations, the central concern in both logical and rhetorical studies was henceforth to be a study of Topics – of those considerations, that is to say, that thinkers or speakers needed to take into account in any discourse on any topic. (The topic of 'definition' survives whenever an author begins with a reference to the Oxford English Dictionary.) But in giving prominence to these analytical exercises in the planning and structuring of material, Agricola displaces pure logic of an Aristotelian kind in favour of a procedure which is likely to make an argument clear and persuasive in such practical circumstances as a court of law. Equally, he replaces the reliance upon logical certainty with a realistic understanding of the claims that might proceed from and contribute to common sense. To an Aristotelian this might look like a compromise with the demands of mere opinion. But Cusanus has shown that opinion – or 'conjecture' – represents the true character of human argumentation. Mysticism is one expression of that understanding. But Agricola shows how far the same understanding may also be adapted to the practical purposes of schoolroom, lecture-hall and judicial court.

It was, however, in Ramus's work that attempts such as Agricola's to revise the syllabus and endow oratorical practice with new significance were pursued most systematically and with the greatest animus. To Ramus himself – an ardent self-publicist – it might well have seemed that he had in fact succeeded in replacing the whole discredited system of medieval philosophy with a system of his own. His abiding purpose, he declares, is to put the logical arts to 'use': 'After my regular three and a half years of scholastic philosophy . . . I went back to my study of rhetoric. My aim was to put the logical books of [Aristotle's] *Organon* to the service of erudition' (*Sch. dial.*, Lib IV in *Sch. in lib. art.* (1569), cols 155–6).

Born near Soissons, Ramus (1515–72) was educated under an Agricolan regime where rhetoric was emphasized. In 1551 he was elected Regius Professor of Rhetoric and Philosophy at the Collège Royale of Paris. In 1561, he became a Calvinist and he was murdered in the St Bartholomew's Day Massacre of 1572.

Ramus's whole career seems to have been almost wilfully controversial, beginning with attacks on Aristotle and continuing in a series of very energetic and very popular lectures, punctuated by animadversions on his contemporary colleagues. Knowing, as Erasmus did, how to make a name for himself, Ramus put these lectures into printed form – effectively as textbooks; and the popularity of these volumes ensured that throughout Europe their author's influence was quickly assimilated into educational practice, and was carried to the New World by Puritan devotees. A case can be made for the influence of Ramism on English metaphysical poetry; and Milton wrote his own version of Ramus's work, *A fuller institution of the art of logic*.

In one aspect, Ramus's thinking can be seen as a response to the great proliferation of knowedge that the Renaissance had by now produced and also as a recognition of the resources available in the printing of texts. A method was needed to organize the exuberant volumes of scholarly material and to reduce subjects to manageable form. On this view, Ramus's genius lay in the production of study-guides, methods of reading, mnemonic devices and key-notes for authorial organization – all to be available in printed form. Thus the core of Ramus's practice involves the breaking down of any subject – in response to the considerations embodied in topical analysis – from its most general aspect to its most particular implications. This dichotomous keying of a subject could easily be reproduced in the form of a graphic table, so that the reader might find a path through the subject by linking one topical question to another. In composition a similar series of bracketed subdivisions would open (probably in a more disciplined way than a spider-diagram does) the paths that an argument on that particular subject should properly pursue (Fig. 30). As for oratory, Ramus's own success in giving extempore lectures of inordinate length must have exemplified the value of this method for the delivery of sermons, harangues and philosophical orations.

However, as well as being an *aide-memoire* or a source of 'finding subjects', the dichotomous method could also be seen – as Ramus was not slow to claim – as a way of providing a new dialectical understanding of how we should orientate ourselves in the world. In common with Agricola and Valla, the starting point in Ramus's logic is not some hypothetical system but an inspection of subjects under a scheme that – unconstrained by Aristotelian principles – might well reveal facets and aspects that would not otherwise have been

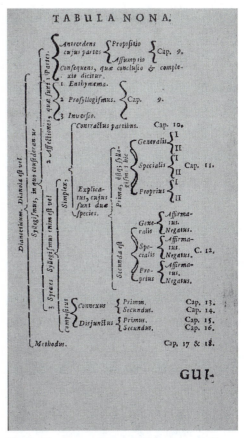

Figure 30 Petrus Ramus, *Dichotymous Table from Dialectae*, 1574. This figure is reproduced by kind permission of the Syndics of the Cambridge University Library.

brought into consideration. Logic in such a method is encouraged to be natural rather than formal logic; and rhetorical urgency might lead in directions that a syllogism would never have allowed. One has only to think of the Euphuistic style in Elizabethan England or even of Shakespeare's own restlessly 'dichotomous' inclination to divide concepts and multiply terms to see what, remotely, Ramism might produce. Yet Ramus himself maintained an implicit suspicion of – or at least a desire to control – the unruly word. It is a characteristic of Ramus that he seems to have included the philological and artistic Italians among his enemies, maintaining that he himself was a Platonist and endowing a Chair of Mathematics at his own university. His concern was as much with the spatial or diagrammatic display of words as with their physical utterance. So far from being responsive to the aspects of sound which characterize oral delivery – in significant silences, inflections and cadences – Ramus's ambition (and the source of his success) seems to have been the construction of flow charts in which the channels of thought might be tabulated with little reference to the pronunciation of words that Guarino, for instance, at the beginning of the period had insisted upon. That concern with the space of the printed page would have its descendants in all those scholars of the seventeenth century who sought, under many different schemes, to codify the knowledge that they had inherited from the ancient world. As for the Renaissance itself, we have yet to consider the extent to which, in competition with the humanist penchant for library and page, the word in this period was accompanied by music, by the oral and aural enrichments that Rabelais and Montaigne can bring to their writing, or, above all, by the rhythmic and visual semiotics of Shakespearian theatre.

NOTES

In general *The Cambridge History of Renaissance Philosophy*, eds Charles B. Schmitt and Quentin Skinner (Cambridge, 1988) gives an excellent introduction to the topics discussed in this chapter. For **Books and Education**, P.O. Kristeller (among many important papers), *Renaissance Thought II: Papers on Humanism and the Arts* (New York, 1965), Lucien Febvre and Henri-Jean Martin, *The Coming of the Book: The Impact of Printing*, trans. David Gerard (London, 1976), Paul S. Grendler, *Schooling in Renaissance Italy: literacy and learning 1300–1600* (Baltimore, 1989) and Anthony Grafton and Lisa Jardine, *From Humanism to the Humanities: Education and the Liberal Arts in Fifteenth- and Sixteenth-Century Europe* (London, 1986). (I quote from Grafton and Jardine on Guarino's teaching methods.) Also W.J. Bouwsma, *The Culture of Renaissance Humanism* (Cambridge, MA, 1957). For **Coluccio Salutati** see Ronald G. Witt **Hercules at the Crossroads** (Durham, NC, 1983). For **Buchanan** and **King James VI. I** see I.D. McFarlane *Buchanan* (London, 1981); C.H. McIlewain, *King James: Political Writings* (Cambridge, MA, 1918) and R. Bushnell, *A Culture of Teaching* (Ithaca and London, 1996). For **Petrarch and Augustine**: quotations are from Cassirer (ed.) *op. cit.* See Kenelm Foster, *Petrarch, Poet and Humanist* (Edinburgh, 1974), Nicolas Mann, *Petrarch* (Oxford, 1983), Charles B. Trinkaus, *In our Image and Likeness: Humanity and Divinity in Italian Humanist Thought*, 2 vols (London, 1970). For **Augustine** see Peter Brown, *St Augustine of Hippo* (London, 1967), Charles Taylor, *The Sources of the Self: The Making of Modern Identity* (Cambridge, 1989). On the importance of **the dialogue** in the Renaissance see Virginia Cox, *The Renaissance Dialogue* (Cambridge, 1992). For **Ficino**, see esp. P.O. Kristeller, *The Philosophy of Marsilio Ficino*, trans. Virginia Conant (New York, 1943), p. 12, *The Letters of Marsilio Ficino*, Prof. Kristeller (London, 1975), and Edgar Wind's classic study, *Pagan Mysteries in the Renaissance* (London, 1967), from which I quote. Wind's view of Botticelli's *Primavera* is no longer uncontested but it offers a plausibly enigmatic reading. For **Plotinus** see *Enneads*, trans. S. Mackenna with introduction by E.R. Dodds (London, 1966). For **Cusanus** see Ernst Cassirer, *The Individual and the Cosmos* (originally Berlin, 1927) from which I quote from the Harper Torchbook ed. (New York, 1965). For translation of Cusanus's *De Docta Ignorantia*, see Jasper Hopkins (Minneapolis, 1981), also

Hopkins's *A Concise Introduction to the Philosophy of Nicholas of Cusa* (Minneapolis, 1978). For *De Pace Fidei*, I quote from the edition by James E. Biechler and H. Lawrence Bod Lewisto (Queenston/ Lampeter, 1990) published as *Nicholas of Cusa: On Interreligious Harmony*. See *Nicholas of Cusa and the Renaissance*, ed. Thomas M. Izbicki and Gerald Christianson (Aldershot, 2000). For a valuable application of Cusanus to literary texts, see Ronald Levao, *Renaissance Minds and Their Fictions: Cusanus, Sidney and Shakespeare* (Berkeley, 1985). For **Valla**, see *Cambridge History*, *op. cit.*, esp. pp. 648ff. For **Ramus** see the exceptional volume by Walter J. Ong, *Ramus: Method and the Decay of Dialogue* (Cambridge, MA and London, 1958). For the influence of Ramus, Perry Miller, *The New England Mind: From Colony to Province* (New York, 1953) and Rosamund Tuve, 'Ramus and Metaphysical Poetics' in *Renaissance Essays*, ed. Paul O. Kristeller and Philip P. Wiener (New York, 1968), 267–302. For the tendency of Shakespeare's language to split dichotomously see Frank Kermode's analysis in *Shakespeare's Language* (London, 2000).

chapter three

REFORMATION AND THE RENAISSANCE INDIVIDUAL

THE LIMITS OF HUMANISM

The most fundamental achievement of Renaissance culture was the intellectual pro-gramme pursued in the cities, libraries and courts of Italy by thinkers such as Petrarch and Valla. This programme was further enhanced by the interest that was shown in school education by Northern humanists such as Colet and by the writings of Erasmus. Employing for the most part the lingua franca of Neo-Latin and aided by the development of print technology, the humanists established among themselves a Europe-wide consensus. This proved to be the seed-bed for such highly original thinkers as Bruno and Montaigne (see p. 150 *et seq.*) as well as presenting a challenge to vernacular poets from Ariosto to Shakespeare. Figurative artists likewise were fre-quently inspired by (and sought to vie with) the oratory to which humanist education had given a central position, and responded enthusiastically to the myths and fictions that the classical world had now been made to yield. Music, too, enjoyed the kudos that thinkers such as Ficino had bestowed on it and developed a particular interest in the relationships that existed between the rhetoric of the word and the rhetoric of musical form itself.

For all that, the humanist enterprise was in certain respects highly conservative in its intellectual and social character and could even be something of an impediment to advances in areas beyond its own philological sphere. One such area, as will be seen in the next chapter, is that of scientific thinking. It is not after all immediately obvi-ous how a culture as concerned as humanist culture was with poetry, myth and magic could abet the cause of science. A similar question arises in the area of religious thought – the more so because the texts to which the humanist paid homage were, for the most part, classical and therefore pagan in origin. Of course, Cusanus and Ficino were themselves Christian thinkers, indeed they were both priestly members of the Church. Moreover, there was one central feature of humanist practice that was to prove central in the hands of Erasmus, probably the greatest of all humanists, to the developments in religious practice that dominated the sixteenth century. The great motto of humanists such as Valla had been *ad fontes* – 'back to the originals' – encouraging its adherents to rediscover through textual and scholarly criticism the primary character of classical sources. This same scholarly spirit was now to inspire a review of the Christian scriptures and lead to a profound interest in the supposedly authentic history and original character of Christian teaching. Yet there were revolutionary implications in this development; and these would hardly have appeared at all if there had not simultaneously been at work in the period certain revolutionary energies that would not rest content with the urbane deliverances of the humanist scholar.

Popular legend acknowledges this when it pictures Martin Luther on 31 October 1517 striding to the doors of the University church in Wittenberg and nailing up ninety-five arguments against the authority of the Pope, attacking in particular the Papal practice of selling Indulgences (whereby living members of the Church could secure merely by money donations the expeditious release from Purgatory of their dead relatives and friends). 'Why', Luther asks, 'does the Pope not empty Purgatory for Love rather than Money?' In fact, it seems unlikely that the event was anything like as dramatic as legend suggests. Luther may simply have posted up on the regular academic notice board a list of questions that he intended to discuss in his university lectures, continuing a theme that he had been developing as early as 1514. Nonetheless, Luther's contemporaries – allies and enemies alike – were quick to represent his actions as revolutionary, using the resources of print and woodcut to promote their cause; and, whatever Luther's original intentions might have been, he quickly became the focus for reforming tendencies which were pursued with far more deliberate purpose than the principles of humanism had ever been.

The consequences of the Protestant Reformation were manifold. Some of these (as outlined in the Introductory chapter) were political, offering a new instrument for kings such as Henry VIII to employ in pursuit of national ends. Others were social, particularly as Calvin – always more radical in his thinking than Luther – began to build a new form of ecclesiastical institution which was well-adapted to the interests of a modern bourgeoisie. It must also be emphasized, as will be seen in the following chapter, that the obstacles to scientific advance that humanism had in some measure created were overcome by the revolutionary thrust of religious thinking in both its Protestant and Catholic manifestations. Equally important, however, was a re-examination and re-definition of an issue that in subsequent centuries came to be associated particularly with the achievements of the Renaissance period: namely, its triumphant cultivation of personal individuality. Throughout the fourteenth century, the ideal of the courtly individual had dominated the European imagination (sometimes at the expense of a Machiavellian or Castiglionian deviousness). At the same time, the notion of a private self – cultivated no longer in monasteries but rather at the reading desk or in the bookshop – had also begun to exert a claims for attention. With the Reformation, a decisive change would take place in the relationship between the public and private facets of the human personality. For the Reformers were acutely aware of the pretensions to which humanist culture might lead in its public aspect. Popes were more likely to be patrons of the arts than to be saints; even the ethical self-sufficiency that was cultivated on heroic or stoical models by humanist pedagogues would need to be questioned if it was not to ignite the fires of complacency or arrogance. Now conscience – in the sense of an Augustinian submission to the inner voice of God – was called to declare itself and be tested upon the public stage.

Throughout the early years of the Reforma-tion Luther's troubled but vibrant personality was never far from view so that, alongside his theological arguments, vivid accounts of his personal behaviour were likely to have at least some influence on the course of public events. From this point, European culture develops progressively a supposition that the public eye must be brought to discover the private self – delivered in seventeenth-century character literature, eighteenth-century novels, and twentieth-century gossip. Our concern is less with the processes of reciprocation than with the supposed nucleus of an inner truth. In the sixteenth century, however, the deliverances of inner being were likely to encounter a more violent form of inspection. As will be seen in the third section of the present chapter, those individuals who in the early Renaissance shaped themselves above all else to play a part in the civic arena or on the stage of courtly performances were just as likely in the sixteenth century to become martyrs – whether Catholic or Protestant – pursuing an inner call and fulfilling their destinies in the fiery theatre of an executioner's pyre. The voices of suffering,

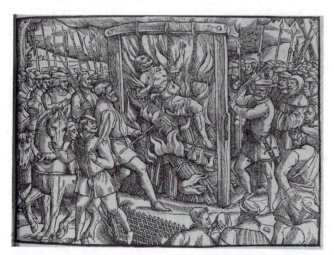

Figure 31   From John Foxe's *Acts and Mouments of the Christian Martyrs*, London, 1563.

exile and alienation express humanity just as potently in the sixteenth century as the confident tones of courtiers, heroes and conquerors. Indeed it will be seen that some of the subtlest representatives of this period are women such as Marguerite of Navarre and St Teresa of Avila, who – while accommodating themselves to the public institutions of the day – also speak with a peculiar understanding of the margins, or even prisons, that define the boundaries of the human condition.

First, however, one must turn to the group of men – Erasmus, Luther and St Ignatius – who in the course of the sixteenth century contributed most notably to an expansion and redirection of humanist culture.

ERASMUS, LUTHER AND ST IGNATIUS

If the great humanist Erasmus had had his way there would never have been a Reformation at all; nor did Erasmus ever seem to understand the need for the extremes to which Protestantism drove its division with Rome. He was not alone in his incomprehension. Luther himself seems not at first to have understood the full implications of the reformation he had unleashed. Correspondingly, the Church – in the heat of a highly charged political and economic moment – may too readily have condemned Luther for heresy, and thus failed to realize that Luther's thinking was, at worst, merely a schismatic variant on traditional positions or, at best, the expression of a desire to return to certain fundamental doctrines that could easily have been accommodated within the theological perspective of Catholic orthodoxy.

These are points that Erasmus himself was quick to make. In a letter of 1524 to Duke George of Saxony (whom Luther derided as a 'poltroon') Erasmus agrees that in its outward forms and in the style of its thinking the Church has grown corrupt: 'The world was besotted with ritual. Scandalous monks were ensnaring and strangling consciences. Theology had become sophistry. Dogmatism had grown to madness.' He also agrees that, at the outset, Luther (with whom at the time he was still in correspondence) had been rightly applauded for his attack on the abuse of indulgences. By now, however, Luther had begun to display his 'vehement genius', 'taking everything to extremes' – to the extent of launching a series of personal attacks on Erasmus's probity. Popes, emperors and kings had been drawn into the fray. Luther himself had been 'spoiled' by his success. None of which was necessary at all. Writing to Luther's closest associate, Philip Melancthon (again in 1524), Erasmus insists that 'practices grown corrupt by long usage might be gradually corrected without throwing everything into confusion'. Had Erasmus himself been at the Diet of Worms he would have ensured 'agreement and compromise'.

In all of this there speaks a desire for the middle way – or a passion for peace – which inspires most of Erasmus's thinking and may be regarded as a direct product of his humanism. In the *Adages*, for instance, under the heading '*Dulce bellum inexpertis*', Erasmus declares:

> If there is anything in mortal affairs that is is to be approached with hesitancy that thing
> is war. There is nothing more wicked, more disastrous, more widely destructive . . . in a
> word more unworthy of man, not to say of a Christian. Yet, strange to say, everywhere at
> the present time war is being entered into lightly, for any kind of reason and waged with
> cruelty and barbarousness not only by the heathen but by Christians, not only by lay
> people but by bishops and priests.

Erasmus then goes on to observe that in the natural world mankind alone seems designed to enjoy a peaceful existence:

> [Nature] fixed murderous fangs to the boar . . . she armoured the crocodile on all sides
> with scales, the dolphins with fins for weapons, the porcupines she defended with quills,
> the ray with a sting. Only man was produced naked, weak, tender, unarmed, with very
> soft flesh and a smooth skin. Among his members nothing would seem to have been
> intended for fighting and violence. . . . On man alone she bestowed laughter.

For Erasmus, the middle way represents no feeble course, but rather a deep vision of human reasonableness and the rational possibility of collaboration between all human beings. Yet in the religious and political circumstances of the early fifteenth century such reasonableness had become hard to sustain and might itself become an occasion for persecution. In Norwich in 1531, Thomas Bilbnet, Fellow of Trinity Hall, Cambridge, was burned at the stake, having first confessed to the influence that Erasmus's Christian humanism had exerted upon him:

> At last I heard speak of Jesus, even then when the New Testament was set forth by
> Erasmus, which when I understood to be eloquently done by him, being allured rather by
> the Latin than by the word of God (for at that time I knew not what it meant), I bought
> it even by God's Providence.

To Erasmus, 'stakes and prisons are vulgar remedies'; and he laments the fact that 'two poor creatures have been burned at Brussels and the whole city turned Lutheran' (*ibid.*, p. 151). He himself never came to such extremes. Nor was his thinking or religious development ever impelled by those moments of violent revelation that drove the young Luther (as will shortly be seen) to long for ultimate certainties and seek a cure for his guilt-ridden temperament by entering an Augustinian monastery.

For all that – and however unwillingly – Erasmus was precipitated into violent controversy with Luther, while also finding eventually that his books were prohibited by the Catholic Index. The very moderation he sought to cultivate was to draw him into a direct confrontation with new manifestations of political and religious fervour.

Erasmus – the son of a priest and his concubine – spent his early years at a school administered by the Brethren of the Common Life who had encouraged the growth of the so-called *devotio moderna* in the Low Countries. This movement (for which there were parallels in the South going back to the time of St Francis of Assisi) had developed a network of lay communities that remained under the aegis of the Catholic Church, but also encouraged a meditation on the example of Christ's earthly existence and insisted that this example should assume particular authority in the lives of its adherents. Thomas à Kempis in his *Imitation of Christ* seems to have shared in the spirit of the movement, while St Teresa of Avila – along with other Spanish spirituals of the sixteenth century – drew directly on this Northern example. As for Erasmus himself, he may have been suspicious of the extreme passion to which the *devotio moderna* might lead; and certainly in his role as an educational theorist, he came to detest the rigorous educational discipline that was followed in the schools of the movement. But the concern that the *devotio moderna* showed to cultivate a certain intense simplicity of Christian practice stayed with him throughout his life.

Transferring from his tyrannical school to the monastery at Steyn, Erasmus found that the austerities of the monastic life also abraded his sensitivities. This lifelong delicacy is no small point. To be sure, there were intellectual reasons for Erasmus's rejection of monastic culture. In common with the majority of humanists, he objected to the cult of scholastic theology and the barbarity of the Latin employed by thirteenth-century schoolmen. Thus, when he eventually arrived in Paris he was to seek out humanist scholars rather than scholastic philosophers, as he was also to do in his visits to Italy. Likewise, Erasmus displayed a considerable understanding of the courtly attractions that humanism could exert, becoming associated, for instance, with Giovanni de' Medici, later Pope Leo X. (It was Leo who on his election declared that he now intended to enjoy his God-given office – only to find himself confronted by Luther and the outbreak of the Reformation.) A certain care of the self was always a characteristic of Erasmus's humanism. Indeed he admired the work of Lorenzo Valla not only for Valla's elegant Latin style and his *Annotations to the New Testament*, but also for his intellectual Epicureanism. Correspondingly, his own narrative style in the *Colloquies* shows a marked attention towards, and pleasure in, the varieties of gesture, gait and voice that could characterize the behaviour of the human person. It was this delicacy and fastidiousness that led him to obtain the right to leave his monastery and abandon clerical dress in pursuit of what may well be regarded as a more generous and humane conception of the intellectual life.

Yet no sooner had Erasmus freed himself from the monastery than the pressures that had attended humanism since the time of Petrarch began to reveal themselves. Some of these pressures were themselves in the exhilarations of the success that he achieved with the publication of his *Adages* and the *Enchiridion*. Erasmus always knew (as Luther eventually would) how the new possibilities of printing allowed the humanist to cultivate an international self-image; and he thrived on this knowledge. At the same time, just as Petrarch was often self-reprovingly concerned about his own pursuit of the laurel, so too in Erasmus's case the printing press – considering his own facility in writing for it and in propagating the fame it brought him – proved an ambiguous instrument of self-advancement. As with Petrarch, there was in Erasmus a profound concern with sincerity, directness and simplicity of address. Yet the very publicity that he gained – along with the associated demands of unwanted contro-versy – was to complicate his scholarly and meditative existence.

Some of this is evident in the work that initially secured Erasmus's international reputation, the *Enchiridion*. This work (the title of which means both 'handbook' and 'stiletto') was intended to define an energetically practical pursuit of Christian virtue and to demonstrate (at a time when notions of political and military glory were growing ever the stronger) the ways in which truly Christian Glory might be achieved. St Ignatius, in founding the Society of Jesus, would demonstrate in a very literal sense, the possibilities of Christian heroism. For Erasmus, too, if less adventurously, the essential weapons in the pursuit of Glory are prayer and knowledge; and know-ledge, as the *Enchiridion* emphasizes, must be allowed to encompass the very works of pagan philosophy that might seem to present a distraction to the Christian mind:

> And whatever good advice even a pagan author gives ought not to be scorned, seeing that
> Moses did not spurn the counsel of his father-in-law, Jethro. Literature shapes and invig-
> orates the youthful character and prepares one marvellously well for understanding Holy
> Scripture, to pounce upon which with unwashed hands and feet is something akin to
> sacrilege.

Here (as well as a characteristic concern with hygiene) Erasmus envisages a pro-gramme for intelligent reading that he pursued in his own work throughout his life, allowing both Scripture and classical literature to feed his passion for words and nuances. Yet in a number of ways 'nuance', in a period as volatile as the early six-teenth century, became a knife-edge – dextrously traversed in the study but more dan-gerous in the outside world; and Erasmus immediately encountered difficulties even among his fellows in the Catholic Church when he began to publish his philological and interpretive annotations on the Scriptures.

Originally inspired by Lorenzo Valla's *Annotations* – which Erasmus saw through the press in 1505 – Erasmus came to realize that, if a simple and authentic Christianity were to be regenerated, then the Christian would need to get as close as possible to the Greek of the original text – closer even than St Jerome had in his

Vulgate version. This understanding was strengthened by Erasmus's experiences in England, where he observed how Greek was cultivated by John Colet in the reading of biblical texts. Thus having laboriously acquired a knowledge of the Greek language, Erasmus set himself the task of translating (into Latin) a new version of the Scriptures, accompanied by his own paraphrases and commentaries.

Yet even before his version of the New Testament was published, opposition had arisen to his methods and findings, which ran from Spain (in the objections raised by Cardinal Ximenes) to England (in the attacks launched by Edward Lee, later Archbishop of York). In some cases, these attacks arose precisely because the Vulgate itself had come to be seen as an unassailably authentic version of the divine word; and certainly scholastic exegesis had invested heavily in the exposition of this Latin text. In other cases, other scholars of a humanist bent had begun to analyse this according to their own contentious understanding of its emphases. Nor did Erasmus improve matters by representing himself, in an astute cultivation of his public image, as the new St Jerome or by claiming that even the Gospels themselves could not always be taken as an accurate record of Christ's own utterances.

At the heart of Erasmus's apparently disinterested scholarship, there were theological implications – of which he himself may not have been fully aware. Biblical texts were now to be read without the interpretive incrustations of scholastic thought. An example is his comment on Romans 1: 17. This verse was to be of revelatory importance to Luther in its insistence that the justice of God is revealed *ex fide in fidem*, 'from faith and into faith'; and Erasmus notes that we must subordinate our human understanding and trust to the divine words themselves; 'this phrase is directed against the philosophers' – which is to say, against those who supposed that systematic argument could replace that intimate reading which faith made possible and which in turn strengthened faith. To Luther this may have seemed an insipidly over-cautious adjustment. But from Erasmus's own perspective, the call to faith reflects an approach that admitted the continual vitality of the scriptural text. He never claimed that his own interpretations were final or authoritative. Repeatedly Erasmus declares that the version he offers is, in the end, no more than a version; and underlying his project there is the two-fold belief that human knowledge itself must never presume to absolute certainty. A continual unfolding or efflorescence of human discourse needs to be encouraged if the truth is progressively to flourish.

A significant illustration of this position is to be found in Erasmus's treatment of the first verse of the Gospel of St John. The Vulgate version reads (*with authorial italics*): 'In principio erat *Verbum*, et *Verbum* erat apud Deum et Deus erat *Verbum*.' Erasmus now suggests: 'In principio erat *Sermo*, & *Sermo* erat apud Deum, et Deus erat *ille Sermo*.' In his notes on this text, Erasmus insists that an equally appropriate translation of *logos* (in Greek) would have been *verbum* or *ratio*. Erasmus's own preference, however, emphasizes his concern with the discourse (*sermo*) and with a process of conversation rather than with the finality of a single word of power. Or else one may see here a preference for the spoken as against the written word (*verbum*). Creation is brought into being through its colloquy with the divine, just as divinity is itself eternally a generative act of speech. Thus in his paraphrase on St John's original, Erasmus writes:

> Since the nature of God immeasurably surpasses the feebleness of human intelligence, however talented and acute that intelligence may otherwise be, its reality cannot be perceived by our senses, or conceived by our mind or presented by our imagination, or set out in words. . . . To search out knowledge of the nature of God by human reasoning is recklessness. . . . But if it is granted to behold any part of these things, simple faith grasps it more truly than do the resources of human wisdom. . . . And there is no other object that more fully and clearly expresses the invisible form of the mind than speech that does not lie. Speech is truly the mirror of the heart which cannot be seen with the body's eye. But if we want the will of our heart to be known to someone, our wish is accomplished by nothing more surely or swiftly than speech. . . . And for this reason chiefly he first delivered his word, so that through it he might become known in speaking.

On this understanding, the relationship between God and the human mind can be expressed in terms of some of the most characteristic features of humanist thought, above all by attentive discourse and by a recognition – which Socrates and Cusanus would have confirmed – that true learning resides in a confession of human ignorance. Luther was later to intensify these notions – to the point at which they ceased to qualify as humanist notions at all. But Erasmus stops short of that, remaining in a realm where the very playfulness of human discourse may itself be regarded as its most productive feature. In that perspective, one of the most characteristic and influential of Erasmus's writings is the *Praise of Folly*, which was written rapidly (though later supplemented) for Sir Thomas More – and indeed opens with a good-humoured pun on More's own name and the Greek word for 'fool'.

In his *Praise of Folly*, Erasmus identifies – in a vigorously satirical style that owes much to Lucian (as does Rabelaisian style) – the absurdities of ceremonial practice that have come to mark the Catholic tradition and equally the distortions that characterize the work of overconfident intellectuals, be they scholastic philosophers or humanists, as represented in pettifogging arguments and ridiculous etymologies. In any case there are many matters which are so holy that they call for reverence rather than explanation with a profane tongue or the pagan subtleties of the heathen.

Satirical aggression, however, is not the predominant note of the work. On the contrary, Folly can be seen as a source of freedom, of humanity and indeed of Christian

Figure 32   Pieter Breughel, the Elder, *The Blind Men*, 1568, Canvas, 86.1 × 154.3 cm. Museo di Capodimonte, Naples. With permission from Scala.

redemption. Thus it may be folly to love the human self, considering its deficiencies and frailties. Yet without the folly of self-love there would be no graceful *sprezzatura* in any of our actions. Nor would married life be possible were it not for folly:

> Goodness me, what divorces or worse than divorces there would be everywhere if the
> domestic relations of man and wife were not propped up and sustained by flattery, jok-
> ing, complaisance, illusions and deceptions. (trans. B. Radice, p. 35)

Despite the evident sarcasm of this, the passage concludes in a witty extemporization that manifests its own form of compassionate foolishness in noting how 'a deceived husband kisses away the tears of his unfaithful wife' and 'how much happier it is for him to be thus deceived than to wear himself out with jealousy'. Indeed, all earthly existence depends upon a sense of humour and a capacity for the absurd: 'The propagator of the human race is that anatomical member which is so foolish and absurd that it cannot be named without raising a laugh'; and no woman, were it not for folly, would willingly accept the pains of childbirth.

At the same time, our spiritual as well as earthly existence depends on Folly. For as the book concludes, Erasmus combines emphases that occur throughout the Folly literature of the Renaissance with notions draw from the *devotio moderna*, to produce a profound exposition of our human dependence upon the folly of faith:

'Thou knowest my foolishness'; and fools have always given great pleasure to the Gods. God himself makes this clear enough when he proclaims through the mouth of the prophet 'I will destroy the wisdom of the wise and reject the intelligence of the intelligent'.

Thus finally it is to 'Folly alone' that forgiveness of sins is granted – folly to forgive, folly to have the faith that participates in forgiveness.

When Breughel depicts the blind leading the blind into a ditch (Fig. 32) he captures – in an Erasmian spirit of both comedy and compassion – the frailty and yet solidarity of the human condition. Rabelais – a devoted reader of Erasmus – and Montaigne went on to offer their own versions and emulate Erasmus in the cultivation of a linguistic folly of mercurial invention – as did Shakespeare, more remotely, in a number of his tragedies and comedies.

Turning to Luther, it is immediately apparent that he too is buoyed up – as is the movement that he inaugurated – on the sixteenth-century passion for words and also by the mania that printing could induce. He wrote more – and to judge from his *Table Talk*, perhaps, talked more – than any German before or since; and where Erasmus, up to a point, calculated his own success, Luther in the early stages of the Reformation seems to have been swept along by an appetite among his followers for printed propaganda. News of the Lutheran controversy spread with remarkable speed and was impelled or even exaggerated by a general appetite for controversy. Luther himself was more than able to ride with and outpace that tide. Rhetoric, irony, parody, a fine sense of audience, a powerfully scatological streak and a taste for paradox are all part of Luther's linguistic make-up – to the extent that he might just as fittingly be compared to Rabelais as to Erasmus. Worthless documents uttered by his opponents are said to have been 'sealed with a sausage'; priests who suppose that they, uniquely, have the right to administer the sacrament are 'cake-eaters' whom Luther counsels to 'eat cake and crud'. Yet Luther also writes with great simplicity for his own children, and in *News from the Rhine*, can combine satire with a delicately poetic inventiveness, as when he speaks of a trade in relics which offers for sale: 'two feathers and an egg from the Dove of the Holy Ghost', 'three flames from the burning bush that Moses witnessed' and 'five brilliant chords sounded by David's harp'. (These phrases find analogues in Boccaccio's *Decameron*, Day VI, 10.)

While energies such as these had something in common with the animating forces of humanism, Luther's formation was not itself humanistic in character, nor was the implication of his thinking. To be sure, he drew on the resources of philological expertise and – as well as admitting an early admiration for Erasmus – he retained, as his closest associate, Philip Melancthon, a scholar whose erudite surname is itself an elegant Greek version of his native *Schwarzerd*: 'Black Earth'. However, where the Swiss branch of Protestantism – under Zwingli, Bucer and Calvin – drew directly on the humanist tradition, there is at the heart of Luther's own thinking a profound rejection of that 'care of the self' that expresses itself in civic humanism and also forms so conspicuous a part of Erasmus's intellectual temperament. For Luther it is axiomatic that, if we are to love ourselves, we should first hate ourselves. For only by doing so can we realize the absolutely liberating truth, which is that human beings are wholly dependent in faith upon the grace of God, who even before we know it has redeemed us from our state of utter sinfulness.

It is this contention that leads Luther into his most vigorous disagreements with Erasmus. For Luther is prepared unswervingly to deny that human beings have any moral contribution to make to their own salvation. In *De Servo arbitrio* (On the Slavery of the Will) Luther enunciates the apparently brutal truth that the human will is itself a source of enslavement and can only be free when it knows that this is so. Against this argument, Erasmus complains that God has created human beings not only with a propensity for peace but also with a capacity for working by their own intelligence and love towards a reconciliation with divine discourse. This will become a characteristically Catholic position, defended above all in the heroic spirituality of St Ignatius Loyola. However, neither Luther nor those who follow him will countenance any such confidence in human worth. Human pretensions to ethical dignity are as nothing compared to the recognition, in religious awe, of our complete dependence on the Atonement wrought by Christ.

For Luther himself, his advance towards this revelation was gradual, as was his realization of its consequences for his relationship with the Catholic Church. And in no small part that progress towards understanding was due to a far more willing involvement with the life of the Monastery and the thinking of Medieval theologians than Erasmus would ever have tolerated. Struck (in a terrifying thunderstorm) by an early desire for salvation, Luther sought redemption initially in the community of Observant Augustinians at Erfurt which he entered in 1505. Indeed, so far from resenting the monastic regime as Erasmus did, he seems to have been almost over-conscientious in pestering his fellow monks for advice about how best to cleanse himself from guilt, not yet acknowledging that his own efforts could never – on the understanding of his later thinking – be effectual. In the monastery, Luther's reading would at the outset have been scholastic in character; and he also seems to have relished the sort of debate and controversial cut-and-thrust that so offended the humanist sensibilities of Petrarch. Subsequently, the vigour of Luther's style may in some measure be due to his addiction to the intoxications of oral delivery, as for example in his *Table Talk* and in the vivid marginal glosses with which he punctuated the texts he presented for formal discussion. At the same time, the finesse of his thought, his ability to live with the utter daring of paradox, derives from a mind which – without being itself the mind of a mystic – drew upon the great mystic traditions of St Bernard and the Pseudo-Dionysius, who both knew that the way to God was the negative way, requiring an utter emptying of the self in the face of Divine Love.

Such an understanding led Luther back (as it had also led Petrarch, though less so Erasmus) to the writings of St Augustine. But going still further *ad fontes* – and availing himself of Erasmus's biblical scholarship – Luther by 1515 had begun to prepare a set of lectures for delivery at the University of Wittenberg on St Paul's *Epistle to the Romans*. This implies that a shift had already occurred in the Wittenberg syllabus away from scholastic argumentation towards a certain style of 'biblical' theology: the Scriptures would no longer be cited merely in support of authoritative philosophical positions but rather be read in their own terms as a source of continual revelation, in which one part of the text might be expected to throw reliable light on another. Thus – rather than debate set questions of an Aristotelian, Thomist or Scotist variety – Luther would prepare printed handouts of the text with spaces for annotations and dictated comments, lecturing in this way (at 6 am on Mondays and Fridays) between Easter 1516 and Summer 1517.

The purpose of these lectures, in Luther's own words, was 'to learn to breathe and confide in the righteousness of Christ . . . and therefore to learn Christ Crucified'; and at the core of this teaching – yielding the illumination that he had sought since he first entered the monastery – was the verse of St Paul in Romans 1: 17: 'he shall gain life who is justified by faith'.

Of this same verse Erasmus, almost simultaneously, was writing in his own paraphrase:

> Although the power [*of God conferring salvation*] was offered first to the Jews, soon it was spread among all the nations of the world so that all might acknowledge their own unrighteousness and seek the righteousness of God, whether they be Scythians or Britons. . . . This righteousness does not depend upon the superstitious cult of idols or on the legal ceremonies of the Jews. Rather it comes from faith.

Erasmus here displays a characteristic interest in the continuance of rational discourse; while resisting the dangers of idolatry as vigorously as Protestants thinkers would, he evidently shares with many of the Italian humanists a confidence that faith may be discerned in cultures other than those of the Christian world. In Luther's interpretation, however, there is no such generous syncretism. Nor any such trust in human discourse. His passionate conviction is that faith is a participation in the righteousness that God – and God alone – secures for us through the Atonement:

> Human teachings reveal the righteousness of men, that is, they teach who is righteous and how a man can be and become righteous before himself and his fellow men. But only the gospel reveals the righteousness of God (that is who is righteous and how a man can become righteous before God) by that *faith alone* by which one believes the word of God.

From this point on, Luther never ceases to emphasize that human beings are at their best when they are passive in the hand of the divinity and properly obedient to the divine utterances of the Scriptures. The notion that our works of any kind – whether moral, intellectual or liturgical – can create an impression on God or weigh in an eternal balance has now to be wholly abandoned. Hitherto, the Church had increasingly encouraged the notion that God had established a covenant with human beings in which a schedule of activities – under the guidance of the priests of the Church – might, in justice, contribute to our justification in the eyes of God. Luther now inverts such thinking. On his understanding (to quote Carter Lindberg): 'We do not do good works in order to be acceptable to God. Rather we do good works because God has made us just.' Nor is our faith in Christ a matter of belief in any set of formal propositions or itself an intellectual or moral achievement that we can be proud of. Rather, it is an acceptance of the mystery – so often obscured by the 'fleshly' or 'this-worldly' pride of human beings – that is enacted in the Atonement by Christ in his acceptance of the Cross.

Two questions immediately present themselves. The first is how such a doctrine could ever be seen as a 'liberation'; the second is how so self-effacing a position should have produced the revolutionary consequences that followed in the politico-religious climate of the sixteenth century.

As to the first question, there can be no doubt that for Luther himself (as also subsequently for Calvin), the doctrine of faith immediately lifted away the burdensome notion that there was any formal standard – supposedly set by God but actually administered by priests – against which one could govern and regulate one's own existence. Now the duty of the Christian is to realize that every human being, participating through faith in Christ's redemptive action, is already saved, and that our task in religion is to discover, in and through the reading of Christ's words, something of the extent of that salvation. Thus, we recover the spiritual depths of the *Psalms* (which, until he turned to St Paul, had largely guided the development of Luther's thinking) where joy is the recognition of dependency:

> Let my cry of joy reach thee, O Lord,
>
> Give me understanding of thy word.
>
> Let my supplication reach thee
>
> Be true to thy promise and save me.

Henceforth there is no need either for the contortions of scholastic philosophy or the traditional idols and ikons of devotion. Reading and song – in which the congregation at large will play an active part – were to constitute the new and flourishing profession of the faith (thus founding a new tradition, which would eventually find its centre in the devotional practices of works such as Bach's *St Matthew Passion*).

Similarly, as Luther soon came to realize, these considerations also called into question those religious works that lay under the control of the priesthood, along with all the intermediate apparatus of saints and liturgy. Good works for the Catholic involved not merely moral acts but also participation in the sacramental mysteries; and all these works were part of the covenant or contract that God made possible between himself and his creatures. Any such apparatus now came to seem – to the Protestant mind – both impious and redundant; and the number of sacraments – as Erasmus had anticipated – was consequently reduced from seven to three: Baptism, the Eucharist and Confession.

As to the second question, it needs to be recognized that an appetite for Reform had been growing for two or three centuries within the body of the Catholic Church, and that the impetus of the Protestant movements in the sixteenth century depended as much as upon political and social factors as upon religious or intellectual ambition. The term 'Protestant' in fact derives from the protest uttered at the Diet of Speyer in 1529 against the political machinations of the Emperor and his Catholic allies. Luther himself does not seem to have acknowledged the extent to which his thinking belonged to a reforming inheritance that went back at least to St Francis and included such figures as Savanorola, Wyclif and Hus. Nor did he admit the extent to which the nominalist tradition – which in its various forms derived from the work of William of Ockam – underlay his own thinking. In a similar way, Luther viewed with great suspicion both the social disturbances movements (fomented by men such as Thomas Müntzer) that came to surround his preaching. He was also extremely suspicious of the theological radicalism that developed – largely independent of his own theology – particularly in Switzerland. He was especially appalled when the humanist zealot Zwingli attempted to reduce the Eucharist to a mere commemoration of the Last Supper. Luther may have objected to scholastic explanations of transubstantiation. But that was largely because they were, precisely, explanations, and thus further evidence of a fleshly presumption that the truths of the spirit could be embodied in argumentative form. Luther himself characteristically declared that 'if I cannot fathom how the bread is the body of Christ, yet I will take my reason captive to the obedience of Christ, and – clinging simply to his words – firmly believe that the body of Christ is in the bread'.

For all that, when Luther – as a good pastor, concerned for his congregation – violently reacted against the Sale of Indulgences, he identified a point of intersection between theological and social considerations. The sale of indulgences may, from a Papal point of view, have been a useful remedy for near-bankruptcy, wrought by the demands of running an increasingly international state; and the notion that one could buy one's way out of Purgatory represented an obvious contamination of spiritual concerns by the new language of the Renaissance marketplace. It also brought into scandalous relief a form of religious practice that was governed by secondary and often superstitious agencies. Luther's own protector, Frederick the Wise of Saxony, hoarded no less than 17,443 relics in his castle church at Wittenberg; and his support for Luther may in some measure have derived from his resentment at the flow of local revenue away to papal coffers in pursuit of pardons. On the other hand, there was no mistaking the subtle corruptions perpetrated by the Dominican pardoner Tetzel, who would carefully assess the prices that a local economy would stand before beginning his campaign for the sale of indulgences.

Add printing to this mixture and the situation became extremely volatile. And, even if Luther did not rebelliously 'nail' his Ninety-five Theses against Indulgences to the door of the Wittenberg Church, the myth of a flagrant act of rebellion was quick to ignite the imagination of the times, leading to student unrest and the burning of Papal Bulls. As to Luther's German translation of the Bible, which appeared in September 1522, 3,000 copies were sold in a month and reprints had begun to appear by December; in all, between 1517 and 1520, some 300,000 copies of Luther's works were sold. There were at this time something like 400,000 readers in a population of 16 million Germans, most of these readers being concentrated in the towns. But such readers were also the leaders of opinion; and, given that there was a well-established network of travelling preachers, the movement readily, though more slowly, trans-ferred itself to the countryside.

Luther's own contribution was to stir controversy and to shift his own controver-sial position in response to the panic that the Papacy (unnecessarily perhaps) experi-enced in response to his initial declarations. Luther himself when he heard that the Pope had become interested in the case expressed a certain panic of his own at the thought of how far matters had gone. But the debate soon moved to new ground, under the influence of Prierias's *Dialogue against the Arrogant Theses of Martin Luther Concerning the Power of the Pope*. The Papacy, having only recently reasserted its central authority against the possibility of Rule by Council, was over-eager to make dis-obedience to the Pope a matter of heresy rather than schism; and Luther was thus provoked into adopting (as Erasmus recognized) extreme anti-papal positions which were subsequently taken up – in pursuit of political and economic advantage – by those rulers and factions who wished to be free of Papal dominion. As for Luther him-self, his final position – as he expresses in characteristically strenuous terms – was not to seek partisan advantage or intellectual kudos but an utter certainty configured around the abnegation of the self:

I ask that men make no reference to my name; let them all call themselves Christians not Lutherans. What is Luther? After all the teaching is not mine. Neither was I crucified for anyone. . . . St Paul in I, *Corinthians* 3 would not allow Christians to call themselves Pauline or Petrine but Christian. How then should I – poor stinking maggot-fodder that

I am – come to have men call the children of Christ by my name. Let us abolish all party names and call ourselves Christians, after him whose teaching we hold. (From *A Sincere Admonition by Martin Luther to all Christians to Guard against Insurrection and Rebellion*)

The forces that produced the Protestant reformation had been gathering for many centuries before Luther precipitated their release. In that perspective, the Catholic response to the reform movement was not simply a defensive counter-thrust to the impact of new thinking but rather an articulation of long-standing concerns that had first arisen in the Catholic mind itself. The response led those who remained within the ancient Church to attempt a clarification and re-affirmation of tenets that were central to the Catholic inheritance – involving a strengthened justification of the sacramental authority of the priesthood, a clear analysis of what it means to form one's thought within an interpretative tradition and a renewed emphasis upon the intercessory power of the Virgin Mary. Implicitly, perhaps, the Catholic Reformation at the Councils of Trent sought to adapt the Church in organizational – or managerial – terms to a new world order which now included nation-states, Empires and capitalist adventure among its political structures. In many respects, the Catholic Reformation, while seeking a new clarity in its dogma, laid greater emphasis on moral reform than on doctrinal innovation. Indeed (as was suggested in Chapter Two) there were strong similarities in terms of moral rigour between the Catholic and the Calvinist versions of reform. In regard, particularly, to an emphasis on sexual probity, both Catholics and Calvinists identified certain very simple (and in practice over-simplified) moral principles that could easily be adapted to the moral government of large social units – and thus prepared the way for a modern obsession with sexuality as the central issue in commonplace conceptions of moral conduct.

When St Ignatius was invited to Calvinist Geneva to discuss theology with Beza, he was greatly impressed by the moral discipline displayed in the city, even though with hindsight he managed to convince himself that such strict displays were illusions of virtue wrought by the devil. (He was also greatly shocked when his hosts offered to find him a Calvinist wife.) Nor were the doctrinal emphases of Catholic and Calvinist thinking wholly incompatible. Both contributed to a concern with the workings of Providence and even predestination that was to colour very profoundly the general culture of the late sixteenth century. St Ignatius admits that 'no one can save himself without being predestined and without having faith and grace'. At the same time, he enters a note of caution, recognizing that an over-confidence in one's predestined redemption may well 'induce laziness and negligence'. Against the Protestant disparagement of human works, the Catholic Reform – as in Erasmus's objections to the Lutheran view of human impotence – sought to maintain a high conception of the dignity of human action as the agent of providential design. In particular, the Society of Jesus founded by St Ignatius Loyola, attempted to reconcile the demands for reform with an elevated conception of human learning and indeed of human heroism that clearly drew upon some of the most essential strands of Renaissance humanism and literary taste. The Jesuits were instituted as an order not of monks and friars but of working priests, thus endowed with the responsibilities of administering the sacraments and with a particular duty towards Papal authority. At the same time, the order was commissioned to pursue an educational as well as a spiritual mission, founding schools and universities throughout the Empires that had been opened up by the ambitions of sixteenth-century adventurers. Equally, the Jesuits were inspired by an heroic ethos that deliberately sought out difficult and even dangerous circumstances, testing their spiritual prowess often to the point of martyrdom.

St Ignatius himself (1491–1556) drew deep upon the traditions of humanist education and also upon the chivalric ideals that thrived particularly in sixteenth-century Spain and (before Cervantes made them the butt of his comedy) extended their influence even to the mind of the young St Teresa of Avila. Born into the Basque nobility, St Ignatius began life as a soldier and – until wounded at the siege of Pamplona in 1521 – seems to have practised the military and courtly arts to the point of dissoluteness. However, while recovering from his wounds he became convinced that he had been called to defend the Church in the world as a soldier of Christ. Loyola may never have read any of Luther's works. Yet in common with many of the Spanish spirituals of the period he had certainly absorbed the spirit of the Flemish *devotio moderna*. His intentions then of forming a religious order were in part inspired by a desire to renew the vigour of the Church Militant. In the medieval world, to speak of a soldier of Christ was to speak of a member of the monastic orders. Loyola preserved this notion, but also recognized that military hierarchies and military ambitions could well provide effective models for the organization of an active force for spiritual renewal. The Pope was to be seen as the pinnacle of this hierarchy, so that – along with the traditional vows that were taken by medieval monastics, Jesuits were required to acknowledge especial obedience to the Papal Throne to the point at which a Jesuit could declare: 'What seems to me white I will believe to be black if the hierarchical Church so defines' (Thirteenth Rule of the *Spiritual Exercises*). So too a special devotion was reserved for the Virgin Mary, as the courtly Lady of chivalric adventure; it was on the feast of the Annunciation that Loyola exchanged clothes with those of a beggar and dedicated his sword to the service of the Virgin. On the other hand, the active life of the Jesuits required that the monastic understanding should be absorbed into the very hearts of the new soldiers of Christ, and be available beyond the confines of a physical cloister in whatever arena their adventures might lead them to enter. Here the inwardness of Erasmus's Christian humanism – especially as expressed in the *Enchiridion* – exerted an undoubted influence on St Ignatius's thinking.

St Ignatius was no more concerned than Erasmus to offer a systematically doctrinal account of his own thinking. Indeed it is central to his vision that the corruptions of the Church and the possibilities of renewal depended not upon dogmatic re-definition but rather upon a revitalization of the spiritual responsibilities of the individual. Thus the *Spiritual Exercises* are intended, when performed under the guidance of an experienced master, to bring the essential narratives of Christian belief into the very core of the psyche, by a training aimed at the emotions and the imagination as much as at the rational mind:

> The instructor should limit his discourse to a brief summary statement of its principal
> points. For then the one who is making the contemplation may find something that will
> make it a little more meaningful for him or touch him more deeply. . . . It is not an abun-
> dance of knowledge that fills and satisfies the soul but rather an interior understanding
> and savouring of things. (*Spiritual Exercises*, para. 2)

Thus St Ignatius himself recommends that on the first day and in the course of the first Contemplation

> I will see all the different people on the face of the earth, so varied in dress and in
> behaviour. Some are white and others are black; some at peace and others at war, some
> weeping, some laughing and others sick, some being born and others dying.

Against this generous vision of human variety and human need, the pupil will then envisage the power of the Trinity and the generosity of the Virgin Mary, so that, 'according to the need I feel within myself, I may more closely follow and imitate Our Lord who has just become incarnate'. And with this inner incarnation one may simultaneously go out along the paths of the world and deeper into the understanding of the providential story:

> The second prelude is to form a mental image in my imagination of the road from
> Nazareth to Bethlehem. I will consider its length and breadth and whether it is level or
> winding through valleys and over hills. I will behold the place of the cave of the Nativity,
> whether it is large or small, whether high or low and what it contains.

To a scholastic thinker, such as St Thomas Aquinas a contemplative practice so committed to the workings of the imagination would have been utterly incomprehensible. Yet even apart from its religious implications – which are in keeping with the renewed attention to liturgical practices such as the display of the Host in Benediction – St Ignatius's thinking is an intense expression of a mentality that was to characterize many artists and poets, Protestant as well as Catholic, in the later decades of the sixteenth century. The sensitivity with which Renaissance culture particularly in Italy

Figure 33   El Greco, *St Domenic Kneeling Before the Crucifix*, c.1595–1600, Oil on Canvas, 120 × 85.9 cm. Sacristy of the Cathedral, Toledo, Spain. The Bridgeman Art Library.

displays the visual sphere of experience, is itself progressively turned inward to the contemplation of those highly charged images that the mind itself can generate in the paintings, for example, of an El Greco (see Fig. 33) or the poetry of a Góngora.

FROM PURGATORY TO PYRE: CONSCIENCE IN THE MIDDLE AGES AND RENAISSANCE

When at the end of the Middle Ages Dante pictured Purgatory, he imagined it as an island in the southern hemisphere. For him, this spiritual realm existed in space and time and was inhabited by souls who willingly accepted penitential suffering as the way in which they might become once more – as human beings were originally intended to be – 'free, upright and whole'. The sign that a penitent individual had arrived at renewed perfection was the pleasure that she or he took in his or her own nature: Dante imagines the Garden of Eden to have been located on the summit of Mount Purgatory; and as he enters that garden, he is told by his mentor, the classical poet Virgil, that he should now 'take pleasure as his guide' (*Purgatorio*, XXVII).

In common with many of the Protestant reformers – some of whom were quick to cite his work – Dante detested the thirteenth-century manifestations of papal corruption; and he clearly anticipated the ways in which the very conception of Purgatory would eventually become an abomination, a means of extortion – associated with indulgences and the sale of pardons – by which the Church could extend its priestly power and increase its revenues. For all that, Dante's own highly original response to this outrage was very different from that which developed in the Renaissance and Reformation, in regard especially to its conception of the potentialities of the human individual. For Dante, the penitential life is one in which the human individual seeks self-knowledge and renewed self-love in the confident understanding that it is capable of both. But love, knowledge and a true conception of the human self are, in Dante's case, revealed by an increasing understanding of our relationship to other beings in the human community, in the natural world and ultimately to the Creator. This is why Purgatory is set at one remove from God's presence in a world of time and place, where the single soul is able to orient itself by reading all the signs that are offered to its eyes – by other penitent souls, by the stars, by the moods and meanings of the passing hours, by ritual observance – so as to assume its appropriate place in the created order. There is little room for guilt in the psychology of Dante's penitents; there is a great deal of opportunity for ritual, in which all penitents participate in the public and communal enactment of providential purposes.

When compared with such a model, the Renaissance self – from the moment that Petrarch (see esp. pp. 223 *et seq.*) consciously dissociates himself from the Dantean world – thrives on and propagates an understanding of its own divisions, sometimes in self-approbation at the subtlety of intrinsic energies, but often in a guilty awareness of how far these energies can lead the individual away from other human beings, from God and from a coherent understanding of its own potentialities. So, on the one hand, the early Renaissance – again largely through Petrarch's example and the resuscitation of Augustinian considerations – invents the notion of the inner self. Our relationship to God is to be discovered in the heart rather in the communal world where ritual and scientific observation – along with the ministrations of priests and scientists – might lead it to truths located beyond itself. However, the inner heart, seeing itself as the meeting place of the divine and the human, may come to mistake what we now call its subjective or private constructions as the final end of all its inward explorations, especially when it can corroborate that understanding by private reading, private scholarship and the cultivation of artistic experience. And when it realizes this, then Petrarchan guilt – or even *angst* – becomes overwhelmingly a mode of self-apprehension. With Luther guilt itself becomes the very ground of our relationship with God. Where Dante in the *Purgatorio* demands that we should bring to fulfilment the inherent possibilities of our nature, Luther asks us to recognize joyously our utter worthlessness and simultaneously to admit that, just as God has created us, so he has redeemed us from ourselves. On that understanding, the self, supported by its inward faith in God (or on a Catholic view, by devotion to liturgical images) may, through an utter disparagement of self, again take up a triumphant position in a fallen world.

In the sixteenth century, hierarchical models – as a way of organizing thought as well as social and political practice – tend to disintegrate in favour of the claims of personal conscience. This, however, did not mean that institutional hierarchies themselves disappeared. On the contrary, many were surreptitiously strengthened, the more so because they were now sustained by forces of money, power and bureaucratic control which had yet to be fully analysed – as they have been in subsequent centuries by economists, political theorists and sociologists. Dante in exile had looked back at Florence and had recognized that his own political misfortunes were a result of the divisions wrought by avarice or, as one might now say, by a proto-capitalist economy. For him hierarchy, so far from being a form of tyranny, represented a way in which the diverse talents necessary for the health of any social order could be orchestrated and directed to harmonious purpose. In the Renaissance, where individuals lived increasingly in a world of international organizations – of Empires and of Churches with universal ambitions – and where censorship, Indexes and Inquisitions bore down upon the very words that fed the private conscience, dissension would itself become the way to truth. Lacking the possible retreat into an ideal city – and justifiably suspicious of monastic notions of obedience and poverty – the sixteenth century became, in consequence, an age of the martyrs, both Protestant and Catholic, who found that they could only record their inner convictions in acts of opposition to ecclesiastical or institutional power. Hutter for instance could declare in *Brotherly Faithfulness* to the Moravian authorities: 'God has not given the government power to demand obedience of us in matters of conscience'; and when brought to the test the Renaissance produced forms of witness and penitence very different from those that Dante had envisaged. Failing the rituals of communal confession or the fear of eternal judgement which Dante dramatizes in the *Inferno* and *Purgatorio*, new and horrible forms of confession (involving execution and torture rather than threats of eternal fire) began to characterize the culture of the sixteenth century. Words themselves became in a literal sense a burning matter; as books were incinerated, so too were those who wrote or read them. In the Low Countries the resistance offered to Spanish domination were fought around positions that were no longer merely territorial or dynastic but rather ideological, as in their own way were the French Wars of Religion. Individuals drew on the explosive chemistry of the book and conscience, and were met by increasingly subtle technologies of censorship and persecution.

Burckhardt speaks of the Renaissance as a time when 'swarms of individuality' were released from the anonymously tribal cultures of the Middle Ages. At the same time he recognizes that one of the principle expressions of Renaissance Individuality was the unconstrainedly despotic behaviour of many Renaissance princes. This touches on a dilemma that Machiavelli relished but which also displays itself in Calvin's Geneva and is perhaps felt ever more acutely in the modern world as part of its inheritance from the Renaissance: how are we to organize to the advantage of human individuals the power that human beings themselves generate in knowledge and technological control? We need to be as suspicious now of any triumphalist conception of the human self as the Renaissance sometimes was of hierarchical authority. Yet, repressing the celebratory tones of Burckhardt's interpretation, it is possible to see in the Renaissance itself an often-painful but also productive realization of the ironies and contradictions that underlay the lives of both individuals and communities.

St Thomas More, for instance (see pp. 54–5), may rightly be taken as an example of heroic probity in the face of institutional power. Yet in *A Dialogue Concerning Heresies* (1529) where he attacks Tyndale for his translation of the Scriptures, More in his own institutional role shows himself to have been a fervent advocate of inquisitorial and persecutional methods. Selfhood here is braced between and destroyed by the competing claims of conscience and governmental efficiency. On the other hand, the period witnesses, in England particularly, the establishment of a distinct and confident sense of nationhood. And this sense was nurtured in large measure by an adherence in pursuit of conscience to vernacular versions of the Bible producing, in the ever-changing climate of Tudor religious policy, the terrible but triumphant catalogue of public suffering that Foxe records in his *Book of Martyrs* (see Fig. 31).

Such tensions in their productive as well as their painful aspect could run to the farthest corners of Europe. For instance in Poland throughout the fifteenth century no one was executed by burning; and the Jagiellonian dynasty, extending its highly cultivated rule around the outer rim of Europe – often in encounters with hitherto pagan civilizations – deliberately adopted a policy of religious and ethnic toleration. In 1432 the great Rector of the Jagiellonian University, Paweł Włodkowic (cited by Anton Hilckman) could declare:

> The Church does not allow the expulsion of infidels from their lands or the use of pressure to bear against them. . . . They are in truth God's creatures and faithless. That is why a way must be found of agreeing with all men; for they are all God's lambs of whom it was said: 'Feed my sheep.'

It has to be said that by the sixteenth century, however, even Poland had succumbed to the appetite for persecution; and in retrospect it might seem that the policy of toleration was itself a reflection of the desire on the part of the Jagiellonian rulers to assert their own jurisdiction over the activities of the Polish warrior classes. Nonetheless, there is clearly some way in which this points forward to thinkers such as John Locke; and by the end of the seventeenth century the idea of a tolerant society in which the rights of the individual as a self-sufficient – or economic – entity were recognized began to be articulated more decisively than they ever could be in the ferment of sixteenth-century Europe. A particularly telling instance of this occurred (as recorded by Grell and Scribner) at Ringingen, South Germany, in 1505. A certain Anna Spülerin was accused of witchcraft, was tortured and disfigured in mind and body; and yet by legal appeal she was able to establish her innocence and even set a money price (of some forty times the current annual salary for German professors) on the compensation she claimed. Here the terrible pursuit of the private self through witchcraft trials mingles with a real sense that a system of justice, linked to a sense of the monetary recompense, is at last beginning to emerge.

Comparable instances – where confession itself becomes, often simultaneously, a means of pursuing a legitimate interest in an inner biography and of testing the self against the claims of public discourse – will emerge in a number of ways in the art and literature of the period, in the stories of imprisoned poets such as Surrey and Tasso – who in prison pleaded to be subject to Inquisition so as to establish his sanity – and not least in the confusions suffered by Shakespeare's Hamlet. Here, however, we may turn finally not to Burckhardt's heroes but rather to other voices, which – in being the voices of women – speak from their own peculiarly marginal position in the social order, with an especial sensitivity to the currents that shift around the borders of institutional culture. The first in St Teresa of Avila, the second is Marguerite, Queen of Navarre and sister of Francis I of France.

St Teresa is now known as a mystic – often by virtue of the sculptor Bernini's famous representation of her in a pose of orgasmic rapture – or else as the author of an apparently very spontaneous account of her own religious experiences. Yet both descriptions ascribe to St Teresa characteristics that she in all likelihood would not have ascribed to herself. 'Mysticism' is now viewed as a nineteenth-century conception – from the same vintage as Burckhardt's conception of the Renaissance Individual – in which the soul is supposed to achieve an exceptional even heroic understanding of its own relationship to God. In more recent interpretations, mysticism is more likely to be represented as an intense commitment to the fundamental teachings and practices of Christ; and this is consistent with St Teresa's own insistence upon humility and upon the pursuit of highly practical expression of Christian example in the human world. Nor is it likely that St Teresa would have recognized her own *Life* as the piece of biography or intimate self-revelation which subsequent generations have taken it to be. The Church itself – alarmed by the disruptive implications of St Teresa's radical spirituality – was quick to assimilate her to an exemplary position as a model of supposedly feminine spirituality. In a similar way, as notions of unitary personality have taken hold – influenced by the cult of the novel and the development of models for biographical narrative – readers have increasingly emphasized the 'freshness' or 'spontaneity' of St Teresa's colloquial voice and the telling detail of her prose – thus protecting themselves from the implications of a work in which 'person' is defined rather by the processes of prayer and confession than by the affirmation of identity.

St Teresa writes with St Augustine's *Confessions* always in mind, at the behest, and under the guidance of her own confessor. At all points she submits her work to the scrutiny of her religious superiors, admitting that these writings may be fit only to be burned: 'I should not like them to be burned, however, before they have been seen by three persons known to Your Reverence.' As to the core of her inner being, the self that St Teresa depicts is one that is always in motion – 'I saw the devils playing tennis with my soul' – and where indeed there is no self at all that is not responsive to the demands made upon it either by God or by the community of the religious:

> But now – glory be to God! – though many speak ill of me out of their zeal for right-
> eousness and all kinds of things to my face, I care very little because I believe the Lord
> has chosen this means of benefiting some souls. (*Life*, trans. J.M. Cohen)

Throughout her writings, Teresa adapts a *persona* of humility. This may in part be seen as a necessary piece of rhetoric, designed to allow her sometimes-dangerous discourse to circumvent or infiltrate institutional opposition: characteristically, she will frame her utterances with a phrase such as 'being a woman and writing only what I have been commanded . . .'. It may also be that a similar rhetoric resulted from her awareness – at a time of anti-Semitic persecution – of her own Jewish ancestry. For all that, her writing becomes a means of continual exploration, aspiring to the condition of prayer, as in St Augustine, but also of submission to the public eye in which the self, so far from being any simply definable essence, is understood dialectically as the point of intersection between inward and outward being.

In her public role, St Teresa was no less aware of the social eye than those who in the Renaissance paced the very different boards of the courtly stage. Indeed her visions (like those of El Greco) are just as likely to be visions of the glory of the Church as of her own intimate connection with God, as when she sees, among many similar visions, the Society of Jesus marching triumphantly in Heaven under white banners. In this regard, St Teresa's reforms within the Carmelite Order were markedly different from those represented by the Spanish *alumbrados* who had begun to cultivate a separatist spirituality in Spain, drawing heavily on the example of the *devotio moderna*. St Teresa certainly fell under suspicion from the Inquisition as did her follower, St John of the Cross – who was imprisoned for nine months in 1577 (and who later described his captors as his great benefactors whose actions had led him to 'a plenitude of light and consolation' (see Fig. 34)). The concern of both St Teresa and St John had nonetheless been to tighten rather than to challenge the discipline of her own order as an agent of the faith and to negotiate a selfhood within the structure of the Church itself.

At the same time, the Inquisition may rightly have recognized in Teresa a representative of the *béguine* mentality that had led to the formation of communities of women, unified in the belief that the example of Christ could be realized anew in the life of earthly individuals. Throughout Europe at this time, women mystics – and their counterparts in the supposed realms of witchcraft – had become especially prominent in encouraging such forms of religious practice. In St Teresa's mind this tendency combined with the example set by her much-respected mentor St Ignatius to produce

OH, BLISSFUL NIGHT! OH, SECRET NIGHT! WHEN I REMAINED UNSEEING AND UNSEEN, WHEN THE FLAME BURNING IN MY HEART WAS THE ONLY LIGHT AND GUIDE

Figure 34 These verses from the twenty-fifth chapter of St John of the Cross' *The Dark Night of the Soul* allude to the drawing by St John which is now only to be seen in the Convent of the Encaracion at Avila, Spain. Christ, in this intense, dark and almost brutal vision is seen obliquely from above as if the contemplative participation in suffering could raise the soul to transcendent vision.

an understanding of Christianity in which the affections, the imagination and a concentration of bodily senses were themselves as significant as the pursuit of book-learning or argumentation: 'I am sorry for those who begin with books alone. For it is strange what a difference there is between understanding a thing and subsequently knowing it by experience', writes Teresa (*ibid.*, p. 93). The body itself – with all its ailments and frailties becomes the location of a battle that defines the human person. In the Late Middle Ages, the body had only rarely been thought of as opposed to the soul: indeed, for Dante it would have been logically absurd to argue any such thing: for him, as for all Aristotelians, the soul was simply the animating principle of embodied individuality. But Renaissance platonism had greatly encouraged a more dualistic conception of the human person. Now St Teresa (along with other thinkers such as Montaigne) began to find in their concentration on the bodily passions a way to make the body itself an eloquent witness of spiritual aspiration. The body in its suffering – as in Teresa's many accounts of her illnesses – may resonate with an awareness of the evil that afflicts us. But the body too may be brought into sympathetic relation with the suffering body of Christ himself. The inward self and the physical self are at one in realizing anew a kinship with the crucified God:

When I made that inward picture in which I threw myself at Christ's feet, and sometimes also when I was reading, there would come to me unexpectedly such a feeling of the presence of God as made it impossible for me to doubt that he was within me, or that I was totally engulfed in Him. This was no kind of vision; I believe it is called mystical theology. The soul is then so suspended that it seems entirely outside itself. The will loves; the memory is, I think, almost lost, and the mind, I believe, though it is not lost, does not reason – I mean that it does not work but stands as if amazed at the many things it under-stands. For God wills it to realize that it understands nothing at all of what his Majesty places before it. (*ibid.*, p. 71)

The self, then, can only realize itself through an awareness of its own nothingness. Such paradoxes might perhaps be expected of a Christian mystic. They also articulate an understanding, which has its antecedents in the logical games played by Nicholas Cusanus and eventually in the joyous asceticism of Luther's far from mystical theo-logy. There is, however, no more fluent or sustained expression of this theme than that which concludes the great poem *Les Prisons*, written by Marguerite of Navarre (1492–1549):

> Qu'en ce Tout là toy, Rien, experimente,
>
> Qui sans finer tousjours croist et augmente,
>
> Las! tu ne veulx ou nous peulx respondre!
>
> Si grant plaisir as de te sentir fondre
>
> Et de te perdre en ce Tout amoureux,
>
> Sans le quel Rien est tousjours langoureux.
>
> (*Les Prisons*, Canto Three, 4895–4908)

(You know, as Naught in All, which it foments, that endlessly increases and augments! To us you won't or cannot answer send? So great's your pleasure as you come to blend/And lose yourself inside this loving All,/Without which Nothing always comes to pall,/In whom you've pleasure of such amplitude.)

Marguerite stood at the very centre of power in early Renaissance France, acting on occasion as Regent of the realm and regularly being involved in matters of the highest diplomatic importance. Her own literary work was voluminous and many-faceted, including (in all likelihood) her own variations on the Boccaccian prose *novella*, the *Heptaméron* and the early *Miroir de l'âme pécheresse* – which was condemned by the theologians of the Sorbonne for heretical tendencies. Marguerite was also the admired patron of writers as diverse as Rabelais, Marot, Scève and Calvin and – in common with other women of an intellectual cast such as Ann Boleyn – she conceived a profound interest (evident throughout *Les Prisons*) in Protestant thought which resulted in the development in France of a style of 'courtly Evangelism'.

For all that, penitence is the central principle of identity in Marguerite's thinking, as also is the desire that she shares with St Teresa to transform the prisons of body and institutional power into a training-ground for the flight towards the All-ness and Nothingness of God. Notably, the second Canto of *Les Prisons* concludes with an exceptionally subtle reading of Dante's *Commedia* that reflects Dante's own understanding of how liberty is to be sought through the penitential ascent of the Mountain of Purgatory 'whose shoulder's draped in verdure fresh and clean/Already by the sun's rays he had seen' (*ibid.*, Canto Two, 1669). Here – in a style that draws constantly on the allegorical modes of the *Romance of the Rose* – Marguerite, in common with other French poets of the early Renaissance such as Marot, refuses to make any sharp break with the language and idiom of the Medieval tradition (see pp. 236–9). Nonetheless, she does insist (*ibid.*, 1676) that the Scriptures – in this case the Gospel according to St John – provide a more 'authentic' view of penitential liberty than Dante can; and there can be no doubt that Marguerite's conception both of penance and of the selfhood that penitence defines is markedly different from Dante's. This is a self that must abandon all sense of its own power to cooperate with the workings of the divine mind – as expressed in the vocabulary of nature or liturgy – and rediscover its own interiority through an understanding of its own self-imprisonment: Marguerite will weep so as to 'rust up' the hinges of her own prison (*ibid.*, Canto One, 144) since this is the way to a knowledge of God: 'as your grip approaches maximum in heavy irons, the sweeter you become' (*ibid.*, 152–3). It is a self that lives above all on the word and the book – and books and words simultaneously feed the self and also produce their own particular form of intellectual prison. To Dante – who in this respect is at his most characteristically scholastic – the Universe itself, and all the created things that it contains – is finally seen in Paradise as a book divinely sanctioned for the human eye to read and understand in its advance towards spiritual understanding. Marguerite, as a humanist, glories in the realization that the element in which the human mind will thrive is that of words rather than things. She shares this understanding with Erasmus. But she also knows that the institution of language, being the only medium in which nature allows the mind to work, is itself a form of confinement – at least until one realizes penitentially that it is so. Thus at one point Marguerite can construct a great tower or shaft of books in her mind from which to survey, with an all-but Faustian (and phallocentric) enthusiasm, the possibilities of human learning – '*Ung piller fiz de livres beaulx et grans*' Canto Two, 1911):

Je m'voloys par la philozophie

Par tous les cyeulx, puys la cosmographie

Qui me monstroit la terre et sa grandeur

Faisant mon cueur courir de grand ardeur.

(ibid., 2077)

(I flew through philosophy,/through all the heavens, then through cosmography that showed me the earth and all her grandeur, making my heart race with ardour.)

Yet she also derides those who purport, by their interpretations of Scripture, to teach the Holy Ghost its own business (*ibid.*, 1968); and on the top of the bibliographical tower – demanding her constant attention – is a book bound in the skin of a lamb and freshly spotted with drops of bright vermilion blood – *Gouttes de sang très vermilion et nouveau* (*ibid.*, 2010–12). This is the word of the crucified Christ. And it is through a reading of that book – or else through being read by it – that the prison of words may yield to reveal the all-creating nothingness. Here merely numerical identity dissolves into paradox: 'HE WHO IS, imagined truly, is seen within this Androgyne' (*ibid.*, 2636). (One recalls that her brother Francis allowed himself to be represented in androgynous form as a sign of his mystic majesty.) Now 'drunk on ignorance', Marguerite sees not, as Dante would, a book that binds together all the universe – but one 'unbound, and open wide', and this unbinding is also the condition of freedom (*ibid.*, 3258) as the word of God seizes and shapes the mind: thus she writes, recording Christ's words of humility: 'A thrilling radiance fair to behold/Its blaze and strength such power did unfold/As feeble eyes could not sustain' (*ibid.*, 2205–6). It is here in the all and nothing, as expressed in Christ's Incarnation that the true nature of being is revealed and what it means to say 'I am'. For Marguerite, God is repeatedly declared to be (as Moses and St Thomas Aquinas also asserted): He who is: *Celluy qui Est* (*ibid.*, 2674) – He Who Is. Now, Marguerite sees this 'I am' in all things and in all books: 'I can look upon no discourse in which I do not find him on all sides'. And it is this vision that allows her – accepting negation – to become herself the true Child of 'I am' (*ibid.*, 3228) and truly free from prison: 'For Nothing fears no prison or closed door' (*ibid.*, 3463).

NOTES

Owen Chadwick, *The Reformation* (London, 1964); Carter Lindberg, *The European Reformation* (Oxford & Cambridge MA, 1996); John Bossy, *Christianity in the West 1400–1700* (Oxford, 1985); J. Raitt, *Christian Spirituality* (London, 1982); A. McGrath *Reformation Thought* (Oxford, 1993); Heiko A. Obermann, *Forerunners of the Renaissance* (New York, 1966); R.W. Scribner, *The German Reformation* (London, 1986); R.R. Post, *The Modern Devotion: Confrontation with Reformation and Humanism* (Leiden, 1968); Brian Cummings in *The Cambridge History of Medieval English Literature*, ed. David Wallace (Cambridge, 1999). For **Erasmus**: Raymond Himelick, *The Enchiridion of Erasmus* (Bloomington,

1963); *The Collected Works of Erasmus: New Testament Scholarship*, ed. Robert D. Sider (Toronto/Buffalo/London, 1984); Margaret Mann Phillips (trans. and ed.), *The Adages of Erasmus* (Cambridge, 1964). *Paraphrase on John*, trans. and annotated Jane E. Phillips (Toronto/Buffalo/London, 1991). *Praise of Folly* (trans. Betty Radice) (London, 1971). Quotations are from the aforementioned texts. Works on Erasmus include: Richard L. DeMolen, *Erasmus* (London, 1973); J. Huizinga, *Erasmus of Rotterdam* (London, 1952); Lisa Jardine, *Erasmus, Man of Letters* (Princeton, NJ, 1993); Albert Rabil Jr, *Erasmus and the New Testament: The Mind of a Christian Humanist* (San Antonio, 1972), pp. 16–17. The quotation from Bilbnet appears in in T. Dorey's *Erasmus* (London, 1970). For **Luther**, *Lectures on the Romans*, The Library of Christian Classics, Vol. XV, trans. and ed. Wilhelm Pauck (London, 1961) from which I quote. James Atkinson, *Martin Luther and the Birth of Protestantism* (London, 1968); H.G. Haile, *Luther: An Experiment in Biography* (Princeton, 1980); A. McGrath, *Luther's Theology of the Cross* (Oxford, 1985); John M. Todd, *Luther: a Life* (London, 1982). For **St Ignatius**: A. Lynn Martin, *The Jesuit Mind* (Ithaca, NY & London, 1988). For **Pawel Włodkowicz**, see Anton Hilckman, 'A Forerunner of the Modern Doctrine of State' in *Poland and Christian Civilization*, ed. Jerzy Braun (London, 1985), from which I quote. For **St Teresa**, J.M. Cohen, trans., *The Life of Saint Teresa of Avila by Herself* (London, 1957), from which I quote. Gillian T.W. Ahlgren, *Teresa of Avila and the Politics of Sanctity* (London, 1996). For **Marguerite of Navarre**, see Claire Lynch Wade, *Marguerite of Navarre: Les Prisons* (New York, 1989) from whom I take all extended quotations.

chapter four

SCIENCE, ART AND LANGUAGE: A CONCLUSION TO PART ONE

RENAISSANCE RATIONALITY

On the understanding of Renaissance culture that first established itself during the nineteenth century (and continues to attract support) the period from 1400 to 1600 saw the development of an unprecedented confidence in the ability of the human mind to realize its own potentialities and to exert its control over the universe in which it was located. For those who favour this point of view the supreme exemplar of Renaissance rationality is Leonardo da Vinci, who was concerned not only to observe the details of the human form and to represent its beauty but also to experiment with passionate curiosity in the fields of science, engineering and technology.

As will appear in the third section of the present chapter, this argument is by no means inconsistent with conceptions of reason, science – and genius, too – that Leonardo himself was inclined to propagate; and Galileo declared that he had learned more from Leonardo than he ever did from Aristotle. There are, however, grounds for caution here. Leonardo can hardly be regarded as a typical case; and it is by no means obvious that Renaissance conceptions of human rationality are wholly consistent with conceptions that have developed in the course of subsequent centuries. Increasingly since the eighteenth and nineteenth centuries, our view of reason has been dominated by a tendency to take scientific activity as the measure of rational activity and to suppose that the true mark of the human mind is its capacity for unprejudiced experiment, disinterested analysis and logical argument. Yet, on the evidence of foregoing chapters, the dominant concerns of Renaissance culture were rhetoric, persuasion, poetry and prayer. The public spaces of Renaissance cities and courts echoed with oratory, inspired by a study of the classics; the private world likewise was animated by a conscientious attention to the ancient words of Latin, Greek and biblical texts.

Rationality in this perspective seems better to be understood as a mode of discourse than a mode of investigation or analysis. In discourse, we seek to participate in a continuing pursuit of common interests. We enter into conversation with ourselves and with others, with past, present and future – or sometimes with God. And the purpose of these conversations is not to establish some supposedly neutral point of observation where the facts about ourselves or the world we live in may be accurately assessed but rather to reveal the sympathies, values and visions of beauty that sustain our characteristically human form of life. Petrarch knew this in his cultivation of eloquence; Ficino and Cusanus knew it in their devotion to a world of myth, of magical correspondences and of learned ignorance. Nor can one ignore the profoundly original energies that were unleashed by the religious reformers of the sixteenth century. In all these cases an irrational act would be one that denied any entry into fruitful discourse.

It would scarcely be appropriate, then, to describe the Renaissance as a period of Scientific Revolution or an Age of Reason. If there was a scientific revolution, then this – drawing no doubt upon certain developments in Renaissance thought – can more convincingly be dated to the seventeenth century – inaugurated by Galileo (1564–1642) and Sir Francis Bacon (1561–1626) and promoted by Newton and Descartes, Boyle, Hooke, Pascal and Leibniz. It was in this later century that the disciplines of experimental method began to be properly understood. In this same period, mathematics came to be recognized as the appropriate medium in which to form scientific hypotheses. Through a combination of mathematical and experimental rigour, the scientific mind was now able to distinguish itself from a mentality in which literary and linguistic study were the dominant factors. It was from this foundation, corroborated progressively by the eighteenth-century Age of Reason and the Enlightenment, that the Nineteenth Century was able – in an apparently neutral spirit of historical assessment – to project upon the fifteenth and sixteenth centuries its own conception of what reason was supposed be.

There were, then, at least three main strands in the intellectual texture of the Renaissance mind. One of these may undoubtedly be characterized – at least in retrospect – as scientific or technological; and this did indeed, through Leonardo, link the Renaissance to a Galilean future. But the second – most characteristic of the early part of the period – was woven by humanists in their educational programmes; and a third – which dominated the sixteenth century – was the revolutionary fervour of religious reformation. Nor is the relationship between these strands as simple as hindsight might suggest it was. Only on a very loose understanding of the term can 'humanism' be regarded, unambiguously, as the ally of scientific thinking. How could it be when 'learned ignorance' was one of its central principles? Nor was there any unqualified or ideological opposition in the period between science and religion. Local oppositions undoubtedly did occur. Yet Calvinism, as was seen in Chapter Two, displayed a strong interest in technology; conversely, as late as the mid-seventeenth century, Newton regarded the spiritual omnipresence of God as the foundation and guarantee of his physics.

In the second section of the present chapter, it will be argued that if there was a scientific revolution in the seventeenth century then in large measure this was a consequence of the religious revolution that dominated the sixteenth century. But the complications in the temper of the Renaissance itself are illustrated by the crucial case of the Polish scientist, Mikołaj Kopernik (1473–1543). As early as 1523, Copernicus had begun to develop a heliocentric view of the universe. His theories, however, only attracted serious attention towards the end of the century; and the delay was a result neither of literary humanism nor of ecclesiastical censure. Humanists such as Ficino who were devoted to the myth of Apollo the Sun-God would not have taken exception to Copernicus's notions. As for the Church, Copernicus was encouraged to publish *De Revolutionibus Orbium Coelestium* by the Catholic Cardinal Schonberg of Capua and (more persuasively) by the Lutheran Georgius Rheticus. Copernicus himself addressed the work to Pope Paul III, who accepted it without any disapproval of its heliocentrism. But scientists proved less receptive. Even a figure as significant in the history of astronomy as the Dane Tycho Brahe (1546–1601), whose techniques for the measurement of relative cosmic distance in practice did as much to undermine the Aristotelian world picture as Copernicus ever did, considered the Copernican system to be a 'physical absurdity'. In this case, it is clear that, while scientists are never wholly immune to their own forms of professional obtuseness, the means to arrive at a proper assessment of scientific findings – through disciplined experiment and mathematical argument – had yet to be fully developed.

It is for reasons such as this that in the final section of this chapter neither of the two figures offered as representatives of Renaissance thinking will prove to be Leonardo, even though both of these figures, in their own day and since, have sometimes been thought of as scientists. The first of these is Giordano Bruno (1548–1600), the Dominican friar, philosopher, playwright and (probably) spy who, having been excommunicated by the Catholic, Lutheran and Genevan congregations, was burned for heresy in Rome in 1600. Bruno professed a profound admiration for the works of Copernicus – to the extent that Copernicus's work seems only to have been put on the Index of Prohibited Books in the early seventeenth century as a consequence of Bruno's vigorous support for it. Yet Bruno's own thinking is influenced equally by the science of the Latin poet, Lucretius, and is expressed just as fully in his comedy

Il Candelaio and by the *Cena dei Ceneri* as by his brilliant but fanciful cosmological philosophies.

Bruno may be taken here as a representative of a group of figures who in the later sixteenth century worked with highly original if not always verifiable results on the borders of science, magic and philosophy: these include the Swiss Paracelsus, and the Englishman John Dee. And, if Bruno proved his case, he did so not through mathematical method but rather through his martyrdom. (Galileo was to take a different course.)

More significant still is the figure of Michel de Montaigne. Montaigne undoubtedly is concerned with recording experience as it flows beneath his observant and experimental eye. Yet the language of Montaigne's *Essais* – of his 'essays' and attempts – is itself constantly generative, denying the reader anything of the stability that a scientific trial might be supposed to offer in its appeal to experimental demonstration or to mathematics. If, as has been suggested, Renaissance reason invites us to participate in a discourse rather than to analyse a state of affairs, then it is Montaigne whose work illustrates most fully what this might mean.

Before turning to the great figures of Leonardo (who will here be set alongside the Flemish master Jan van Eyck and the great anatomist, Andreas Vesalius), Bruno and Montaigne, one must first look more closely at the cross-currents of science, art and language that flowed around them in the sea of Renaissance rationality, paying particular attention to the contribution that Sir Francis Bacon made to an understanding of the thought of the period.

SCIENTIFIC HUMANISM AND RELIGIOUS SCIENCE

In the field of science as in every other field of Renaissance thought, the period witnessed no sudden or decisive departure from earlier practice. A comprehensive review of the history of science would necessarily take into account an earlier and truly scientific renaissance that occurred during the ninth century in the Arab world, where optics and mathematics became particular points of interest. Medieval thinkers had already begun to study and transmit the Muslim inheritance to their Renaissance heirs. Attention likewise would need to be given in any full account to Franciscan thinkers – particularly at Merton College, Oxford where optics, mathematics and experimental science had begun to flourish as early as the thirteenth century under the guidance of figures such as Roger Bacon. Most important of all, it would be necessary to acknowledge the influence of William of Ockham and the various forms of nominalism proceeding from his philosophy which anticipated both the religious and scientific thought of the Reformation. It was Ockham who sought to remove all intermediate causes between God and the laws of nature and to insist upon a primary attention to the particularities of existences. And it was this position that (in the sphere of theology) encouraged the possibility of a direct relationship in faith between the human mind and the divine while simultaneously (in the sphere of science) promoting a detailed investigation of the phenomena and design that constituted the observable universe. Nor, finally, can the continuing importance of Aristotle be overlooked. To be sure, the Aristotelianism of the medieval schools eventually generated too tidy an explanation of the world, as if we had inherited from Aristotle all the logical apparatus that we needed to determine the 'causes' that sustained the created cosmos: and this confidence would certainly need to be questioned if science were to thrive. Yet Aristotle himself had been above all else a biologist (in contrast to the speculative and mathematical Plato), concerned with an unprejudiced attention to the phenomena of the world; and there were schools particularly at Padua where liberating forms of Aristotelian thought were cultivated with considerable enthusiasm.

That said, humanism from Lorenzo Valla to Sir Francis Bacon continued to expand the range of scientific and technological possibilities, not least in response to the many developments that were taking place in the spheres of commercial, political and military or nautical activity. Valla in particular nurtured a critical habit of investigation and began to envisage alternatives in the scientific as in the religious sphere to the cult of authority that by the end of the Middle Ages had begun to stifle independent inquiry. A similar cult was by no means unfamiliar among those humanists who sought to establish a classical precedent for every action they might perform. In common with other humanists – including even Petrarch – Valla, as a bibliophile and antiquarian, delighted in having copies of the works of classical mathematicians and scientists on his shelves (Fig. 28) – even if he could not read them or fully realize their implications. Book collecting contributed directly both to the prestige and range of scientific study in the Renaissance, as thinkers came to recognize how the classical world had included scientific and technological topics in its diverse field of intellectual interests.

At the same time, humanism at its most penetrating favoured a certain precision of observation and inquiry. Such precision may initially have been be displayed by scholars and artists in their reflections on literary texts, as also on the details of classical drapery or epigraphy. However, this same habit – as illustrated above all by Leonardo – contributed very directly to the gradual development of a scientific mentality. This is particularly evident in medicine. Leonardo's interest in the working of human anatomy is well known. But other artists shared this interest. Antonio Pollauiolo (1457–98) was dissecting corpses while the medical syllabus was still dominated by the supposedly authoritative writings of the classical Galen-whose works had been championed by humanists even though practising scientists came to question it. And practice slowly allied itself with professional forms of medical inquiry. This was after all a period in which medicine encountered a completely new spectrum of experimental challenges – as well as an abundance of corpses. The Black Death ensured this in the early years, as did the onset of syphilis, which returned from the New World with Columbus's crew in the sixteenth century; and through-out, modern weapons such as the pike, arquebus and artillery produced unpreced-ented types of wound. In this case, there were appalling occasions for testing the competence of remedies that had often been derived from the classical textbooks; and eventually debate and controversy were to lead away from the ancient nostrums towards an ever greater reliance upon first-hand experience.

However, precision was also a feature of the most abstract and theoretical form of science, mathematics. Mathematicians in their search for ever-more simple formulae would eventually carry forward into the scientific sphere an appetite for elegance and beauty, which was by no means unconnected with the humanist sense of the com-mand that the human mind could exercise over its own constructions. It is indeed the mathematician Girolamo Cardano (1501–76) who declares – displaying a mathemat-ician's appetite for finesse – that he seeks 'that fundamental precision by means of which one may explain many things through a few cases, or render vague facts clear, or state in certain form facts formerly doubtful'. In common with many of his period Cardano could combine magical practices with his pure science – and included among his experimental procedures vigorous pinchings of his own body to ascertain what the limits of his tolerance were. Nonetheless in a vast output of medical and magical studies Cardano also found time to write a detailed account of cubic equations, the *Ars Magna* of 1545. His was one of many contributions to the development of algebra in the period, and proved as controversial with fellow scientists as science has often been. In subsequent centuries, however, it has been suggested that Cardano – some-times known as the gambling scholar – was capable of anticipating the later work of Pascal and Fermat.

Medicine and mathematics were the two dominant forms of science in the Renaissance, and between them they anticipate, respectively, the experimental and theoretical disciplines that in later centuries would become central to the practice of science. Both had already a recognized position in academic and professional institu-tions: Mathematics shared a place with Music in the University curriculum – both being concerned with number and proportion. (One notes that Medicine throughout the period was considered a professional art, while painting in its association with mathematics came to be thought of as a science.) By the end of the period, however, science – especially in its technological aspect – had certainly made great advances; and scholarly curiosity had broadened to accommodate the many 'miracles' and won-ders that were flowing now less from a religious source or even from the world of classical antiquity but rather from the New World and new astronomical observation.

In practical terms the huge development of cartographical science was one such development. But the educational syllabus itself grew correspondingly wider; Agricola wrote treatises on mineralogy and in 1562 the Elizabethan colonist Sir Humphrey Gilbert proposed an academy – for the younger sons of nobleman – that was intended especially to accommodate technological learning: 'Whereas in the Universities men study only school learnings, in this Academy they shall study matters of action meet for present practice of both peace and war.'

For all that, humanism in itself was just as likely to impede as to advance the causes of religion and science. Notably one of Ficino's associates in the Florentine academy, Pico della Mirandola, was to oppose the notion of astrological influence and collaborate in the mid-1480s with the educator Poliziano in pursuit of a question posed by the humanist Poliziano himself which looked with some scepticism at ancient authority: 'I began to wonder, most learned Poliziano, if these ancient observations were derived from natural causes or from the credulity of the vulgar.' This is of course to ask again what part myth and literary enthusiasm could contribute to the development of science. It is also, however, to suggest the extent to which movements for religious reform (whether Catholic or Protestant) may have been necessary if the scientific revolution of the seventeenth century were to be possible.

This may seem an unlikely proposition to those who have become accustomed (as many have since the nineteenth century) to suppose that science and religion are, at best, entirely separate aspects of human thinking or, at worst, inimical one to the other. Nor is it immediately obvious how an emphasis – particularly in Protestant thinking – upon the characteristic fallibility and even ignorance of human beings could contribute to the development of scientific confidence. Yet it is Albert Einstein, writing at the mid-point of the twentieth century (in words quoted here from the epigraph to Hailes's study of Martin Luther) who declares:

> The religious attitude towards truth is not without its influence on the total personality of scientific man. . . . The researcher recognizes as a matter of principle no authority whose decisions or utterances can lay claim to 'truth'. . . . A man who dedicates his best powers to things outside himself becomes, from the social point of view, an extreme individualist who, in principle at least, relies on nothing but his own judgement. . . . Intellectual individualism and scientific aspiration appeared at the same moment in history and have remained inseparable since.

The 'moment' to which Einstein is here referring is the sixteenth century; and in his emphasis upon the 'individualism' encouraged by the religious thinking of that period he offers his own testament to a traditional conception of the Renaissance ethos. Yet it is not enough to suppose that individualism alone was the stimulus to scientific advance. Up to a point, certainly, the concern with personal conscience that developed in the Renaissance – carried to the point of martyrdom in some cases – must have contributed to the development of scientific confidence and courage. On the other hand, the Renaissance self, or more specifically the Reformation self (as depicted in the previous chapter), was more acutely aware of relativities than Einstein here seems to allow. And, arguably, it was this awareness – involving a recognition both of human ignorance and of the corruption of the world – that contributed as much as did 'extreme individualism' to the development of science.

Above all, it was necessary, if this development were to take place, that the human mind – at least in the scientific field – should rid itself of a propensity to the making of myths and even of a desire to attribute ethical value to the neutral world of facts. A thinker such as Ficino presented a profoundly orderly and also dynamic view of the Universe; and undoubtedly this vision encouraged the mind – as in its own way had the medieval world picture to which Ficino's is akin – to look for laws, correspondences and architectonic principles in this cosmic system. Yet the enthusiasm which Ficino – in whom love was an intellectual principle – brought to this task is an indication that his purpose was to discover a world of values rather than facts, and to enhance the sense of human orientations in a sympathetic environment. There was little sense in this world of the possibility of the surprise that the mind of the scientist might feel on encountering the discomfiting excitement of a hard reality. Ficino's world is too orderly, too enchanted by the vision of order itself, too closed in its own intellectual and magical construction, to challenge the mind to scientific exploration. The same might be said even of Cusanus, who otherwise comes close to the scientists of his own day (and even on a certain understanding to Einstein) in his thought-experiments with infinity and relativity. Yet even the world that Cusanus depicts might ultimately seem to be closed in the rhetorical play of its own Socratic ironies.

Against this – though drawing on both the precision and the capacity for intellectual daring displayed in the fifteenth-century Renaissance – the Reformation envisages a profound and liberating simplification. Returning to a biblical understanding of the created world – and rejecting the hierarchical universe that both medieval and humanist thinking had encouraged – the Reformation insists that the cosmos, so far from being sustained by a multitude of forces and intermediaries, was in fact the creation *ex nihilo* of a single Deity. To that degree, the universe may be assumed to possess an intrinsic order that justifies the mind in its desire to establish natural laws. Yet the God of the Scriptures is utterly transcendent to that creation. Indeed, on one extreme account, creation since the Fall is itself a region of sin, utterly worthless (as Calvin would suggest) until transformed by the honest labour of the faithful. Or else it is a world in which each created object *per se* is worth attention as the handiwork of God, offered now for admiring investigation – nowhere more so than in the investigation of the human body in sickness and in health. In either case, the responsibility of the human mind is to treat the world as a world in itself, discovering its uses, its laws and its possibilities without any supposition that the purposes of that world had been pre-established according to some comprehensibly human design and equally without any superstitious fear that the world might suddenly reveal itself as coterminous with the divine. Any such revelation will come on a wholly different level, in relationships of faith and conscience. Not knowing the ultimate is itself the spur to knowing what we can know.

The strongest voice raised by humanism itself against the humanist programme is that of Sir Francis Bacon (1561–1626). Pursuing an interest above all in experimental science and in useful technology, Bacon in *The Advancement of Learning* launches an attack on both monasticism (which cuts the mind off from direct contact with the natural world) and 'the rubbish and bother' of scholastic Aristotelianism, where proof was related to the logical investigation of traditional and authoritative pronouncements. Such thinking can produce nothing but mental fictions – the 'Idols of the Theatre' (IV, 32); and Bacon's first concern is to eradicate all systematic preconceptions so that the empirical and 'rational' faculties (IV, 19) can pursue a steady and experimental inspection of the facts of nature (IV, 32). At the same time, Bacon also attacks the humanist cult of eloquence. It is this that has produced the 'Idols of the Marketplace' – which is to say those distortions of empirical perception that occur under the influence of persuasive rhetoric. In science at least (IV, 254–5) 'all that concerns ornaments of speech, similitudes, treasury of eloquence and such like emptiness' are to be utterly dismissed. Only thus would science be able to exert its domination of the world and serve the interests of human advancement.

When the Royal Society was founded in 1662, under the influence of Bacon's writing, it took as its motto *Nullius in verba*, which suggested its determination to withstand any merely authoritative pronouncement on scientific matters and equally to resist the delusive charms of rhetoric. In these respects, the Society follows quite deliberately in Bacon's footsteps, as it does also in its predominantly puritan concern to see learning (in Bacon's words) 'as an effectual inducement to the glory of God', and 'a singular help against unbelief and error'. To that extent, a new age has begun, the more so because, following an early seventeenth-century surge in the study of mathematics, it was increasingly understood that mathematics – alongside empirical experiment – could provide a discipline of thought, free from the contamination of rhetoric, in which to form and prove hypotheses. It was this combination that provided the basis of a true scientific revolution and made possible Galileo's great claim that the universe is 'a book written in a mathematical language' (*Il Saggiatore*, 1623) – wanting all to be informed, in the vernacular, about these new discoveries.

Bacon himself, in common with most of his Renaissance antecedents, falls short of Galileo's vision. Indeed, in his emphasis on observation and experiment, it seems that he is apprehensive that mathematics itself might prove a new form of scholastic or theoretical entanglement – hence the marked suspicion that he displays towards the work of Cardano who is 'a weaver of cobwebs, for ever in contradiction with all things and with himself'. On the other hand, despite such limitations, there is also to be observed in Bacon a generous sense of a spirit of collaboration in the interests of scientific rationality that not only points towards the ethos of the Royal Society but is also ready to sympathise with scientific enterprise wherever it may be found – nowhere more strikingly perhaps than in the praise that Bacon reserves for the Jesuits of Coimbra University. Between between 1592 and 1598 a band of Jesuit scholars – whose influence was to be felt deep into the seventeenth century – had come together at the most ancient of the Portuguese universities to recover the natural philosophy of St Thomas Aquinas – deriving from these writings their own understanding of nature as an orderly entity responsive only to those who explored its intrinsic patterns. It was presumably to these scholars that Bacon was referring when he writes:

And we see before our eyes that in the age of ourselves and our fathers, when it pleased God to call the Church of Rome to account for their degenerate manners and ceremonies and sundry doctrines obnoxious and framed to uphold the same abuses; at one and the same time it was ordained by Divine Providence that there should attend withal a renovation and a new spring of all other knowedges. And on the other side we see the Jesuits (who partly in themselves, and partly by emulation and provocation of their example, have much quickened and strengthened the state of learning) we see, I say, what notable service and reparation they have done to the Roman see. (*The Advancement* of *Learning*, Book I.)

Here the re-interpretation of 'idols' to which both Protestants and Catholics had contributed releases a scientific spirit that in Bacon's mind becomes that spirit of enlightened liberality which (not infrequently) characterizes the rational endeavours of ages more scientific than the Renaissance itself was able to be.

LEONARDO, VAN EYCK AND VESALIUS

What, then, of Leonardo da Vinci? Unlike his great rival Michelangelo, Leonardo drew remarkably little from the world of humanist learning. He learned Latin only in his later years and chose the vernacular (almost without predecessor, save Dante in the *Commedia*) as the medium in which to elaborate his most complex philosophical and artistic conceptions. Indeed there is a profound antipathy in Leonardo's writings to book-learning as a form of knowledge. Conversely, he displays an unabated enthusiasm for experience and observation as the most authoritative of teachers and also the beginnings at least of a realization that mathematics (in the form at least of geometric mensuration) might be the best instrument to employ in the pursuit of accurate record: 'experience is the mistress of all those who wrote well'. Indeed, at one period in his life (around 1502) he was said to be working so hard at Geometry that his mathematical experiments made him impatient with painting itself: 'he would lose his temper at the sight of a brush'. Equally Leonardo can declare that there is no certainty in sciences when mathematics cannot be applied; he contrasts the constructions of mathematics favourably with those of the theological mind.

One result of this interest was a devotion on Leonardo's part to perspectival drawing and similarly to the exact analysis of anatomical detail. In this he was at one (as will be seen in Chapter Five) with theorists of the visual arts such as Alberti and practitioners such as Piero della Francesca. But Leonardo went further than most in the range of phenomena he thought fit for observation and in the complexity of the constructions he wished to investigate. For not only was he prepared to think of stains on walls as containing an intrinsic pictorial interest but also, in drawing or writing about the natural world, he showed a marked attention to the phenomenon of dynamic gradation – for which the mathematics of his day had no convenient formulae. Effects of light – progressively moving towards the distances of a landscape – were as interesting to Leonardo as effects of architectural line, and so too were the subtle registrations of *chiaroscuro* necessary to produce the smile of a Mona Lisa; the

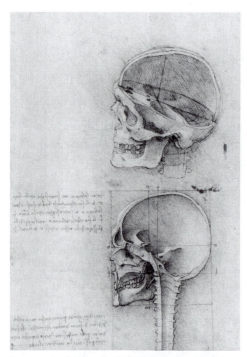

processes of decay attracted his attention, so that in depicting a skull he is concerned not only to establish its volumetric measure but also to represent a texture which leads one to perceive, as he puts it, 'the very death of the bone' – as if its organic structure were as interesting to him as its geometric form. (Fig. 35). Above all perhaps, Leonardo is interested in recording and analysing the ever-changing rhythms of fluids and water (Fig. 36). Here his eye challenges itself to see the laws implicit in pure flux; and flux itself is recognized to be one of the principles on which the natural world is constructed. Indeed the human being itself, while being observably a skeletal frame (which famously can be inscribed in a Vitruvian circle), can also be seen in Leonardo's terms as a hydrodynamic system with internal 'lakes' of blood and sap rising in it as springs rise on mountainsides. As for the behaviour of water itself, this taxes Leonardo's powers of observation and calculation to the limit. In one passage he summons up no less than sixty-four terms to describe the effects of

Figure 35   Leonardo da Vinci, *Section of a Skull*, 1489. Pen and Ink, 18.3 × 13 cm, Black Chalk 6 1/4". The Royal Collection, © 2002 Her Majesty Queen Elizabeth II.

'rebound', 'circulation', 'elevation', 'percussion' and destruction' that are to be found in a great deluge or waterfall. But he can also trace the movements to be found in the rising of bubbles:

Figure 36 Leonardo da Vinci, *The Deluge Formalized*, after 1513. Black Chalk 16.3 × 21 cm. The Royal Collection, © 2002 Her Majesty Queen Elizabeth II.

> The air which is submerged together with water ... returns to the air penetrating the water in sinuous motions. When the air enclosed within the water has arrived at the surface, it at once forms the figure of a hemisphere and this is enclosed within an extremely thin film of water. This occurs because the water always has cohesion in itself.

Such examples point to a markedly analytical attention towards our experience of the natural world, with consequences that can be illustrated if one compares Leonardo's *St Ann, the Virgin and Christ* (Plate VIII) with Van Eyck's *Chancellor Rodin* (Plate I). Van Eyck himself deserves to be regarded as one of the most influential artists of the Renaissance – for his close attention to detail, to effects of luminescence and reflection, and to the carefully graduated landscapes that he introduces in the background of his paintings. Indeed, Leonardo himself probably derived a great deal from the Flemish painter, particularly in regard to the treatment of aerial perspective. Yet Van Eyck (to follow Erwin Panofsky's great account of Van Eyck's achievement) offers rather a reconstruction of the world than a mere representation of its visual features; and the principles guiding this reconstruction are recognizably those of a theological contemplation. Details – of objects, folds, sheens, scarlet headgear, lilies in a translucent vase, angel's wings – are enriched by colour so as never to be merely incidental contributors to some larger action but worthy of regard in themselves, as if they were part of the primary stuff of divine creation. We see with an eye disposed, by Van Eyck's colour and composition, to celebrate a plenitude of particular instances of being. In comparison, Leonardo's paintings are characterized by a crystalline chilliness animated rather by analysis than by contemplation. In the *St Anne*, as elsewhere, Leonardo effortlessly commands all the techniques that are necessary to create an emotionally vivid narrative – pose, mass, disposition in space. Yet (in the picture at large) the eye moves commandingly from a background – in which mountains are seen more for their function as exemplifications of haze and optical recession than as objects that might inspire or threaten – to a foreground of heroic figures. Here, similarly, attention falls upon the anatomical engineering which allows a virgin of gigantic proportions to sit upon and bend from the knee of an equally massive (yet elegant) St Anne. Coming to the detail, one finds in the curl of Christ's hair and the skull that it surrounds an interest in precisely those volumes and patterns that elsewhere Leonardo has depicted in his anatomical studies and in his drawings of water, just as the smile shows a characteristic interest in the slight depressions of flesh and the play of light and shade. Similarly organic whorls and annulations are traced in the fleece of the Lamb. The presence of this Lamb carries, of course, a conventionally symbolic reference to Christ as the Lamb of God. Yet nothing in Leonardo's treatment encourages the viewer to attend to that significance rather than to the demands of observation. Our pleasure is less in the object represented than in the precision of the artist's own constructions; and beauty here resides not in the compelling intensities that Van Eyck commands but rather in a control or even elegance in the composition of massive forces.

Van Eyck's painting breathes a religious intensity of attention that is wholly absent from Leonardo's work. Yet it would be misleading to suppose that this marked a difference between 'Medieval' and 'Renaissance' spirits or that Van Eyck – with his extraordinary attention to detail and indeed to the technology of oil painting – were less scientific than Leonardo. Conversely, if Leonardo himself is finally not a scientist of the seventeenth-century vintage, then the reason is that his mind is precisely not responsive to those movements in religious thought that would eventually challenge the cosmos of poetic mythology. To be sure, Leonardo possessed, along with a coolly observant eye, a vivid technological im-agination, capable of conceiving – if not always of delivering – helicopters, submarines and siege engines for subsequent generations to admire. But if he stopped short of scientific hypothesis, the reason must be in part that his thinking continued to be governed by certain mythic expectations of his own. For wherever he looks, Leonardo is seeking reflections of the human form. Even his water-drawings – where his attempt to capture invisible rhythms is at its most acute – can be transformed into the heroic image of a sea-god in human form riding his chariot through the waves (Fig. 37).

Figure 37   Leonardo da Vinci, *Neptune with Sea Horses*, 1503–4. Black Chalk 25.1 × 39.2 cm. The Royal Collection, © 2002 Her Majesty Queen Elizabeth II.

The myth that impels Leonardo is the myth – which no scientist could ever countenance – that man is the measure of all things. There is, however, another scientist of the period who dispenses with that myth while simultaneously demonstrating the benefits that might come to the human person – in the sphere of medical care – from a coolly scientific understanding of its constitution. This is the great anatomist Andreas Vesalius (1514–64), author of *De Humani Corporis Fabrica* (1543). Born in Brussels to a family of physicians who served the Dukes of Burgundy and, later, the Habsburg Emperors, Vesalius studied at Paris between 1533 and 1536, and later moved to Padua in the Veneto where at the age of twenty-three he was nominated Professor of Surgery by the Venetian Senate. It has sometimes been claimed that Vesalius – who was certainly capable of entering into controversy with his colleagues – is the revolutionary founder of modern observational science. This is something of an exaggeration. It is true, however, that, up to a point, he did withstand the contemporary interest in the writings of Galen. This interest provides an instance of the extent to which humanism could act as an impediment to the development of science. For Galen's sixteenth-century authority derived from the recent re-publication of his ancient texts; and those anatomists who accepted Galen's newly discovered authority considered it unnecessary ever to approach an actual corpse. The book of words was enough; and Vesalius can acerbically declare that he would be happy to suffer in his own person the number of surgical cuts that his Parisian master, Johann Guinther, had inflicted on any cadaver. It seems clear that Vesalius's own intention in deciding to subject the human body to the knife, was mainly to test and corroborate the theoretical speculations offered in the classical text. But in pursuing this practice, Vesalius drew with great skill upon countervailing resources in the Renaissance tradition, including a profound confidence in his own personal virtuosity, an understanding of the potency of the visual arts and of printing, and the support offered by the new religious temper of the Protestant Reformation.

In the first place, the anatomical lecture theatre was for Vesalius truly a theatre, in which (as illustrations of the period suggest) the anatomist would draw great and enthusiastic crowds by the display of his dexterity in dissection. Vesalius also realized the extent to which, by virtue of the printing press, the theatrical display of the anatomist could be made public knowledge and be brought to contribute (against the respect for ancient authority) to an understanding of how science might progress through the sharing of published information. Here the visual arts had a part to play. It seems likely that the anatomical figures who, with joyous lack of embarrassment, display their inner secrets to the open air, were engraved if not by Titian himself (as was once supposed) then at least by a member of Titian's workshop; and along with his collaboration with the great art of his time, Vesalius chose his printer with an unerring eye for the possibilities of the printed page. This printer was Johannes Oporinus of Basel who not only produced Vesalius's own studies with peculiar clarity of line but was also himself accustomed to the daring acts of controversial gesture. He

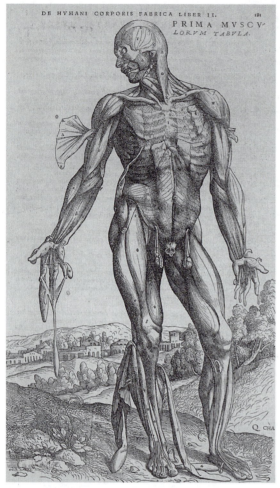

DE HVMANI CORPORIS FABRICA LIBER II. 181
PRIMA MVSCV-
LORVM TABVLA.

Q. CHA

Figure 38 Andreas Vesalius, *De Humani Corporis Fabrica*, Tenth Plate of Muscles, Basle 1543. This figure is reproduced by kind permission of the Syndics of the Cambridge University Library.

had already been imprisoned for printing the Qur'ān – being released only on the intervention of Martin Luther.

Then, finally, there is the support that Vesalius himself received from Protestant quarters. Though himself a practising Catholic (who, in 1564, performed a pilgrimage to Jerusalem), Vesalius has inscribed on the frontispiece of his own volume the words: 'We shall explore the ingenuity of the Artificer of the Universe as shown in the remaining parts of the human brain.' To ambitions such as these Luther's closest associate, Philip Melancthon, gives his ardent support, declaring in his *Oration in Praise of Anatomy* (1554) that in studying the human body 'You should imagine that you are led into a temple or some sacred place' (105). Likewise, writing a commentary on Aristotle's *De Anima* (alpha zeta rho), it is Melancthon who declares:

> Since God alone applied so much skill in fashioning the human body He wished His wondrous work to be seen so that we may understand that these mechanisms created and arranged so skilfully came into being by no means by chance but that there is an eternal and architectonic mind.

THE CRUX OF LANGUAGE: BRUNO AND MONTAIGNE

When we talk now of 'Renaissance men', we tend to think of Leonardo as the archetype. But Bruno in his own day proudly cast himself in that role. He was, he believed, a 'Mercury sent down by the Gods to illuminate humanity'; and he locates himself between Copernicus and Columbus as a man who could map both the terrestrial and cosmic world and offer – in works such as *De immenso* and *De infinito* – a peculiar insight into the physical and epistemological character of our dealings with the universe of things. Nor did his protestations fall entirely upon unheeding ears. In 1583, he presented himself to the University of Oxford 'as one whose work is applauded by all noble minds'. He eventually quarrelled with the university – as he did with almost every other great institution of the day – and left under suspicion of plagiarism. However, the time he spent in England in the circle of Sir Philip Sidney seem to have been particularly productive and is celebrated in his great dialogue, *La Cena dei Ceneri*.

Inspired by Cusanus as well as Copernicus, Bruno in his natural philosophy develops a conception of the universe that stands in marked contrast to the closed worlds of the medieval Aristotelians. The Aristotelian cosmos, on Bruno's understanding of it, was an aggregate of all that was structured and sustained in motion by the Primum Mobile. But for Bruno himself the universe has no centre and no circumference (his English opponents mocked his Italianate pronunciation of 'ci-'). There is an infinite number of possible worlds and so far from there being any unalterable character to the things that constitute these worlds, there is a constant generation and interpenetration of apparent entities, subject not to a hierarchical principle but rather to an organic law of constant decay, regeneration and reformulation. Moreover, we understand our world not by a calculation of universal abstractions but rather by an attention towards and active relationship with the particulars that momentarily emerge in this flux. On this understanding, to speak of 'Universal ladders' and orderly 'Chains of Being' is merely metaphorical fantasy. Rather, we must inspect the atomic world of mutation and contradiction if we are to orient ourselves and productively realize the intelligence that works in this flux. We too are particulars and our own intelligence will best be realized in abandoning all forms of arrogant resistance to the motions that speak in us as much in our own particular being as in the external and observable world. There can be no dualistic separation of spiritual reality from the physical shadow; our lives philosophical and otherwise are best understood as a participation in the cosmic rhythms that gives significance to all particular.

It would be easy to describe this view of the world in terms compatible with modern conceptions of sub-atomic structures, multiple dimensions and principles of uncertainty. Yet Bruno's own understanding is turned at all points to the fulfilment of magical, political and ethical ends. An indication of this is concern with the Art of Memory. In common with many Renaissance intellectuals (in a tradition going back, in modern times, to Ramon Llull) Bruno won high regard at the court, for example, of the French Henri III by claims he made for the capacity for memorization. Nor was this a matter simply of mental athletics. On the contrary, mnemonic art – in a way analogous to magic – allowed access to the unfolding totality of the world where one object must always (as in memory) be related to another: a thing recalls a thought, a place recalls a train of argument. In mnemonic practice the mind moves inward to create an understanding of – and participate in – the interplay of whole and part. Indeed in this respect there is something in common between the Jesuit practices of meditative internalization and the Brunian arts of memory; and Bruno himself vigorously attacks any Lutheran notion that the images we see must be repressed in favour of some purely spiritual apprehension. In our memory-systems the particular and the whole are summoned into active and productive life.

It is significant, therefore, that Bruno should have been particularly sensitive to two of the arts that, early and late, represented the most characteristic forms of Renaissance culture, painting and the theatre. Indeed in his great (if unperformed) comedy, *Il Candelaio* the *persona* in which he chooses to represent himself is that of the painter Giovanni Bernardo. For painting is acknowledged never to be an exact reproduction of the world beyond; yet precisely in its dynamic difference from the objects it represents, a painting stirs the intelligence into a movement which (as in the thought-experiments of Cusanus) is itself generative of further intelligence. This is a process that refuses to take the simple story as adequate but seeks to find plenitude in all the apparently superfluous detail that the picture contains. Philosophers, in Bruno's view, do likewise. Theatre carries similar implications. The mental image of the theatre was frequently used in Renaissance and classical arts of mnemonics, so that ideas and phrases – mentally placed at certain places in the architecture of the auditorium – could be recuperated at need. But theatre too as a play of particular images – all illusory yet all demanding attention – could be an emblem of Bruno's own philosophical principles. So in *Il Candelaio* Bruno includes many figures who by his own time had become standard types of human foolishness – the Renaissance pedant, the miser, the alchemist, the misguided lover – and their foolishness, even their squalor, is represented in the intense and varied texture of Bruno's dramatic language. Yet even idiocy has a particularity that can make it worth attending to. Thus it is the miserly idiot, Bartolomeo, who declares:

> Metals like gold and silver are the source of everything: these are the causes of words, plants and stones, flax, wood, silk, fruit, corn, wine, oil, everything desirable on earth depends on them. I give them this importance because without them you can have none of the others.
>
> This is why gold is called the substance of the sun and silver of the moon. Take these two planets from the sky and what happens to your generative powers, where is the light of the universe . . . I'll only value the one thing that gives value to all else. Money subsumes the very elements: he who lacks money not only lacks stones, plants and words but air, earth, water, fire and life itself. (*Candelaio*, III, i)

This may be a ridiculous and inauthentic account of the cosmic flux that Bruno is concerned to reveal. But we shall not know what true vitality is unless we can enter theatrically into an engagement with these particulars.

Such an understanding may finally explain why Bruno in his last days returned to Italy and exposed himself to the full rigour of the Inquisition. His actions have subsequently been represented as an heroic assertion of intellectual freedom. And Bruno certainly had his own conception of what intellectual freedom was. But the theatricality of his self-immolation may have weighed as heavily in his own mind as the defence of conscience. In any case, his philosophy, taken seriously, ensured that his being would itself be realized most fully in its re-entry into the flowing plenitude of an infinite universe. Nor would such apparently eccentric (but none the less real) heroism be out of keeping with one of the richest notions that Bruno conceived in regard to political liberty. In characteristic Renaissance fashion, Bruno sees an ultimate connection between justice and verbal acts of communication. For just as *Il Candelaio* (and also dialogues such as *La Cena*) show a remarkable sensitivity to various and varied forms of discourse, so for Bruno the liberation of discourse in ever-widening acts of communication is the proper function of justice.

It would be hard to pretend that Bruno had any influence beyond his time (though Schelling was to invoke his name in his own search for the mysterious truths of nature). Montaigne, on the other hand – who in his own, more self-questioning way was as concerned with the flux of things as Bruno – left a very vigorous, if also very ambiguous, legacy to subsequent centuries. Ben Jonson in *Volpone* notes how fashionable his writings were becoming during the first decades of the sixteenth century (by which time the Italian Florio had already translated Montaigne's work into an energetic English version). To some – from Bacon to the eighteenth-century Deists – Montaigne's concern with experience, along with an apparent appreciation of the design of divine creation, qualified him as a forerunner of early science; it is after all Montaigne who declares that 'there is nothing more shocking than to see assertion and approval darting ahead of cognition and perception'. At the same time, his encyclopedic attention to odd and even eccentric observations nourished a seventeenth-century taste for curiosities that in turn led on to the museum mentalities of the nineteenth century. (Montaigne's second-hand accounts of the behaviour of elephants were to be widely influential in the field of elephant literature.)

In another sense, Montaigne has until recently been particularly influential in contributing to a certain view of human 'character' as being determined as much by its quirks and contradictions as by its moral ambitions or political intentions. On this understanding, Montaigne brings to a conclusion that Renaissance 'care of the self' which has shown itself sometimes in the cultivation of courtly manners and sometimes in heroic acts of self-affirmation while also preparing (along with Cervantes and Shakespeare) for that fascination with the detail of human behaviour that finds its most obvious expression in the traditional novel, the frank autobiography (or the canny *curriculum vitae*). As will be seen at many points in the coming pages (especially in dealing with Cervantes and Shakespeare), the notion of 'character', though undoubtedly an important category in cultural and critical analysis, is one that needs to be treated with some circumspection if one is considering the Renaissance conception of the self.

Up to a point Montaigne's *Essais* do exert the appeal of sincere self-revelation. Montaigne will speak of his most intimate inclinations and characteristics: of his liking for one kind of food rather than another, of his propensity to travel sickness as well as to the awful affliction of gallstones. On the other hand, when Montaigne speaks of playing with his cat and wondering whether or not his cat is playing with him, he comes close to the Wittgensteinian realization that if a lion could speak we should not understand it, and the related understanding that our selves are determined not by some inner but communicable essence (be it feline or human) but rather by the forms of life that we construct for ourselves in our forms of language. Thus Montaigne has lately been represented above all as a writer whose very being is coterminous with the words he inscribes (in their many variant forms) on the pages of his *Essais*. The *Essais* would thus become not merely attempts to describe experience but experiments in pursuit of the possibilities that arise when the self is seen in terms of the constant unfolding of linguistic ambiguities and logical parentheses. Bacon would have disapproved. Yet in this regard Montaigne is at one with a culture that from Petrarch to Rabelais to Shakespeareare understood, as few other cultures ever have, the stresses and exhilarations of the language game.

Montaigne's life (1533–92) was lived at a point of confluence between the political, cultural and religious forces that dominated the sixteenth century. His father had fought with Francis I in his Italian campaigns; and, in common with many among the invaders, he had been deeply impressed by the cultural advances that he encountered there. The elder Montaigne had also read Erasmus's work on education and determined that his son should be brought up according to its humanist precepts. Indeed, Montaigne was taught to speak Latin before he spoke French, though from an early age he was also put to the charge of local country-people. Montaigne himself lived to see the violent consequences of humanism – wrought in part by the intellectual ferment of the Reformation – that appeared in the French Wars of Religion; and, though he remained a Catholic throughout his life, his sensibility was indelibly marked by an irenic (and Erasmian) detestation of the cruelty that could be caused by intellectual extremism and the single-minded pursuit of principle.

In some measure, the humanist ambitions of Montaigne's father were directly realized in Montaigne's early career. If a humanist education was meant to form the public man, then Montaigne proved particularly active in the political affairs of Bordeaux and Paris. Yet his *Essais* were written in retreat from the public stage; the sanctum of

his library and a mind stocked with the fruits of lifelong reading became the labora-
tories in which he explored and generated his own version of the Renaissance conscience. He now wrote in French; he now sought a self that could not simply be
satisfied with the formalities of the humanist programme. Indeed in his essays on
education, Montaigne insisted that his own children would have been better off educated in taverns – or in schoolrooms carpeted by leaves and blossoms rather than the
debris of the pedant's birch-rod (*Essais*, I, 25 and 26). Along with the dramatists of
his day – who increasingly represented the schoolmaster as a comic type – Montaigne
sees formal learning as an impediment to the natural and spontaneous unrolling of
the human self: 'men may be made stupid by too much learning' (*ibid.* I, 26, p. 184).
So, too, in the forms and language of his own writing, Montaigne, while aware that
experience will always elude the definitions that language might project upon it,
nonetheless seeks a style which is as fluid or mercurial as experience itself. Imitation,
as we have seen throughout, is at best for the Renaissance a matter of recreation, of
digestion and 'innurition': 'that which we rightly know,' says Montaigne, 'can be
deployed without looking back at the model' (*ibid.*, p. 171). In Petrarch and Erasmus
this produces a constant pursuit of elegance and refinement in their own phrasing.
Montaigne himself recognizes that 'all we do is look after the learning of others', but
that each writer must make a previous writer his own intimate associate. The result
(in contrast to the poise that Petrarch and Erasmus seek) is a constantly changing
stream of quotation, half-quotation, anecdote and parenthesis, where it is never easy
to establish the point at which an original text ends and Montaigne's own begins.
Memory for Montaigne as for Bruno is an active and generative power, leading us into
the flux of experience. On Montaigne's view, we should be 'steeped in knowledge' –
the emphasis being on the all-but physical 'steeping'. Nor should the words of a
philosopher ever be 'bloodless or fleshless' (*On Educating Children*, I, 26, p. 165).
Montaigne's own words never are. Read in French (and, sometimes, in the exuberant
English of Florio's translation) the arabesques of thought that Montaigne executes are
accompanied by a remarkably acute sense of language itself as a physical phenomenon
– sonorous, vibrant, and responsive to constant changes of tempo and rhythm.

   The self-knowledge, then, that Montaigne sought in his retirement from the public world was fed constantly by the shifting currents of language, new and old. In this
regard, Montaigne's inquiry was markedly different from that of the many others who
– almost as a matter of fashion in the sixteenth century – set out to 'know themselves'. For example, Sir Thomas Elyot, the English courtier and political theorist,
urges that anyone destined for important office should seek for self-knowledge, so
that, pragmatically, they might be aware of their own strengths and weaknesses as
they take their place on the public stage. There is, however, no such sense of judicious
self-description nor of normative self-control in the *Essais*. To be sure, for Montaigne
any time that is not spent writing of the self is a waste of time (III, 8, p. 1067). Yet

to write of the self is also to write of everything that is *not* the self and to discover the self precisely in doing so. Cusanus in contemplating the Infinite realized that our pursuit of it, while never complete, is endlessly – and playfully – productive of new thought. So too in Montaigne's pursuit of the self. For the moment of identity is penetrated by dependencies and alterities that deny us any stable self-satisfaction, but fruitfully reveal a further field of complexity: 'When the mind is satisfied, that is a sign of diminished faculties.' Indeed the human mind carries with it the intimate otherness of its own bodily nature which produces its own constantly surprising sequence of pains, quirks, curiosities and psychosomatic urges: the body – its hands and eyebrows – have their own language: 'And what of our eyebrows or our shoulders? None of their movements fails to talk a meaningful language, which does not have to be learned, a language common to us all' (II, 12, p. 507). Montaigne is no dualist; and, in regard to language, the very physicality of his writing – shot through with references to nerves, sinews, acts of eating and throbbing veins – prevents his philosophy from ever pretending that the mind could exert a deadening dominion over the totality of the human being. Thus when Montaigne writes an essay on some lines of Virgil (III, 5, p. 947), the mention of Venus leads not only to a commentary on the literary significance of the classical line but also to a frank (and sometimes misogynistic) investigation of his own sexual promptings.

On a simple overview, there is much in Montaigne's thinking that could easily be considered conservative in character. Indeed, he confesses – paradoxically enough – to a detestation of any change in his fixed routine of daily habits. Yet this same position is one in which scepticism and humility constantly intersect to produce a liberating understanding of human relativity. Nor can one safely attribute to Montaigne any dogmatic pursuit of sceptical principle. It was once common to identify distinct phases in Montaigne's career, in which by turns he could be seen as Sceptical or Pyrrhonic, Stoic and Epicurean. However, Montaigne himself declares: 'I gyrate'; and just as it would prove reductive to describe Shakespeare's similarly sceptical mind in terms of some definite philosophical allegiance, so in the case of Montaigne any such description would misrepresent the character of his own philosophical procedure and equally diminish the force of his example as a representative of intellectual life in Renaissance Europe. As we have seen throughout, this period saw a flight from systematic philosophy. Montaigne makes clear that the alternative to system is a subtle, sceptical but also humane and generous attention to the manifold possibilities and ever-varying codes by which human beings seek to govern their existences.

Nowhere is this clearer than in Montaigne's interest in habit and custom, where what is customary can also appear, to the sympathetic but foreign eye, curious and eccentric or even wonderful, simultaneously unseating and exciting the philosophical mind. So in the early essay on ancient customs Montaigne notes (citing well-remembered texts in support of anthropological detail) that 'the Ancients used to bath every day before dinner. It was as usual as our washing our hands' (I, 49, p. 332); 'they took a gulp of breath when they drank; they wiped their arses with a sponge fixed to the end of a stick' – and one such stick was once employed by a man condemned to the arena as an instrument of suicide on which he choked himself to death. Is it the Romans – so often our supposed exemplars – who were odd or are we? Or else, famously in speaking of Cannibals or Coaches, Montaigne's imagination – or capacity for wonder – seeks the logic that rendered apparently barbaric practices evidence of a civilization that equals or excels our own. From the New World Columbus brought back not only gold but marvellous tales and unheard-of objects (and persons). Indeed, to judge from his journals such curiosities were valued as highly as gold itself; and the fabulous could easily turn into a lucrative freak-show. It is this turn that Montaigne's thinking wholly forbids. Extending the range of sympathies which led earlier humanists to seek wisdom in, say, the lore of exotic Egypt, Montaigne looks at the customs even of the cannibals with an eye that discerns the inward (if surprising) rationality of their behaviour. Rationality, for Montaigne, is 'a dye that spreads itself through the whole of humanity' (*ibid.*, p. 126); and it is scepticism, humility and wonder that reveal the hue of such rationality even in the speech of a cannibal who – though destined for death – taunts his captors with his awareness of how his own forebears were nourished by the flesh of those who are about to feed on him:

> These sinews, this flesh and these veins – poor fools that you are – are your very own;
>
> you do not realize that they contain the very substance of the limbs of your ancestors:
>
> savour them well for you will find that they taste of your very own flesh. (*ibid.*, I. 31, p. 239)

In any case, is it any more cruel, asks Montaigne – with his habitual hatred of all forms of cruelty – to eat our victims rather than to torture them as the civilized European regularly does? There are many different expressions of rationality; and unity between us will only arise from a vivid and lively understanding of that difference.

The essay on cannibals is as close as Montaigne comes to enunciating doctrine or definitive position. Even his most extended and compendious essays – *The Apology for Raymond Sebond* and *On Experience* – reflect the form of Montaigne's thinking most closely in offering the reader the whorl and fingerprint of a constantly shifting mind rather than a credo or manifesto.

At the core of the *Apology* is the realization that, whether in reason or in faith, we must acknowledge that 'the natural and original distemper of human beings is presumption'. There is much in the central sections of the work that anticipates the anguish and irony of Hamlet's 'What a piece of work is man' or of Lear's determination to look the 'bare, forked animal' in the eye. But the same realization carries (as in Shakespearian tragedy) the exhilarating freedom of a truth truly seen and of perspectives consequently opening. Thus, suddenly, Montaigne can be amazed at the thought that a dog is just as capable of reasoning as a human being: deciding which path it should take at a crossroads in pursuit of its master, the dog employs 'disjunctive and copulative propositions', sniffing at two paths but not at the third – which must by exclusion be the right road to take (*ibid.*, p. 517). A similar insight produces a passage in which Montaigne describes the behaviour of nesting swallows with as much attention as Leonardo might bring to the description of a deluge. Yet he animates this description with a sensuousness of apprehension that is quite unlike Leonardo's attempted neutrality of tone and a wondering admission that human language can hardly capture such subtle formulations:

> Take swallows, when spring returns; we can see them ferreting through all the corners of our houses; from thousands of places they select one, finding it the most suitable place to make their nests; is that done without judgement or discernment? And when they are making their nests (so beautifully and wondrously woven together) can birds use a square rather than a circle, an obtuse angle rather than a right angle, without knowing their properties or their effects? Do they bring water and then clay without realizing that hardness can be softened by dampening? They cover the floors of their palaces with moss or down: do they do so without foreseeing that the tender limbs of their little ones will lie more softly there and be more comfortable? . . . Why does the spider make her web denser in one part and slacker in another, using this knot here and that knot there, if she cannot reflect, think or reach a conclusion?
>
> We are perfectly able to realize how superior they are to us in most of our works and how weak our artistic skills are when it comes to imitating them. (*ibid.*, pp. 508–9)

Whether in its view of swallows, spiders or cannibals, Montaigne's prose attempts to enter into conversation with the world around him rather than to assert any presumptuous control; and this, finally, is the character of the relationship that Montaigne invites his reader to form in reading his own text. This is no work of biography; nor is it in any sense a confessional piece. We are not told the truth *about* any situation or person, as if we were somehow observers attempting a neutral assessment or anatomy. Rather we are asked to participate in a truth, collaborating, as one might in a conversation, in the gradual and often surprising development of its implications.

It is this understanding of the interpretative interplay of conversation that, in the end, distinguishes Montaigne's position – and more generally, the thinking of the Renaissance – from the positions that over the last century have come to characterize the procedures adopted by philosophical and literary critics. To be sure, the Renaissance (and Montaigne above all) recognizes, in common with most twentieth-century philosophy, that human beings live and move in the element of language. Similarly (as the second part of this volume will often emphasize) recent studies of the Renaissance have effectively – and sometimes sceptically – called into question certain notions of rationality, presence and mimesis which have developed since the Renaissance and yet are in some measure alien to the period itself. For all that, the scepticism which is exemplified by Montaigne, and which could be discerned in many other Renaissance thinkers from Cusanus to Erasmus to Shakespeare, is a scepticism that leads us away from the voids and vacancies that, conventionally, have come to excite the modern mind. In the Renaissance, words were understood to imply relationship; a speaker speaks to an audience, even if the dialogue is an interior discourse between the self and God or the self and its own earlier manifestations. The condition of truth, in an age that had not yet committed itself completely to a conception of experimental or mathematical method, was a condition of trial and trust, an exploration (whether on the page or on the ocean) that would have been inconceivable or futile were there not others in the past, present or future who could listen to and nourish the exploratory impulse. In Montaigne's understanding we are 'enstoried' beings, present only in our own continuing narratives.

This is particularly evident in Montaigne's moving account of his friendship for Etienne La Boëtie. This essay contemplates many silences, fissures and dislocations. Death itself is supreme among these, so that now, in Montaigne's words:

> I merely drag on. The very pleasures which are proffered me do not console me; they redouble my sorrow at his loss. In everything we were halves. I feel I am stealing his share from him. (*ibid.*, p. 217)

Yet that is not all. The essay opens – in a passage that helps to characterize Montaigne's view of his own essay – obliquely with an account of how a painter in Montaigne's household will paint a dominant in the centre of a wall and fill the empty spaces around it with grotesques. Montaigne's own essays are analogous to these grotesques, always marginal, always interestingly odd. But the central emptiness is reserved for a masterpiece, which is La Boëtie, or more precisely it is the writing of La Boëtie on the Lutheran subject of the will, *On Willing Slavery* – known to others as *Against The One*. This work is absent, and the reason in part is that it has been suppressed by political censorship for its defiance of tyranny. But not only by censorship. For Montaigne himself, while offering to reproduce the work along with twenty-nine sonnets by La Boëtie, revises this intention, striking out the text he had once included or leaving gaps in his own essay to indicate where the words of his friend could have or should have appeared: 'I may perhaps still find a place for it elsewhere' (*ibid.*, p. 206).

Words, then, are subject to suppression. Yet they are only comprehensible because of the punctuation or spaces that distinguish one word from another. So the story of a human existence is a story punctuated by suppressions, silences and death. Friendship, like reading, represents an acceptance of this condition, and this acceptance itself turns the void into a story of human significance. Montaigne himself had been drawn to La Boëtie by words that speak of freedom and also of the paradoxes that show the will itself to be free in its willing engagement with the interests of others. But friendship itself is the form of such freedom. Indeed – quoting Aristotle – Montaigne declares that 'good law-givers have shown more concern for friendship than for justice' (*ibid.*, p. 207). Moreover, it is friendship that shows what it means to live 'against the one'. The strict claims of identity – of that which is identifiable and determinate – are all willingly denied in the mysteries of friendship as they are also in the willing act of reading where the interpretation of minds is only possible because of the physical marks of black on white or the articulation of vowels and consonants:

> The perfect friendship I am talking about is indivisible: each gives himself so entirely to his friend that he has nothing left to share with another; on the contrary he grieves that he is not twofold, threefold or four-fold and that he does not have several souls, several wills, so that he could give them all to the one he loves. That secret which I have sworn to reveal to no other, I can reveal without perjury to him who is not another; he *is* me.
>
> (*ibid.*, p. 204)

As Montaigne reads La Boëtie, so too – with scarcely less intensity – he reads the texts of all the authors whom he has 'digested' in the course of his self-education; and so too Montaigne invites us to read himself and his own *Essais*. We are involved constantly in an interpretative reconstruction where books do not merely offer us information or provide us with laws and norms of behaviour but rather induce the freedom of friendship, in which – both sceptically and with humility – one abandons the claims to single identity and, allowing oneself to be read by others, promotes the process – against silence, suppression and death – of becoming yet more human. There was much in subsequent centuries which was to resist and seek to arrest this process. Yet we recover it and release it whenever – as in the second half of this volume – one turns to the works that the Renaissance itself produced in art, music and literature and attempts to allow those other voices to echo again in the chambers of one's response: 'We live among the living and let the stream flow under the bridge' (III, 8, *On the Art of Conversation*).

NOTES

For **Science in the Renaissance**, see W.P.D. Wightman, *Science and The Renaissance* (Edinburgh and London, 1962); Antony Grafton, 'Humanism, Magic and Science', *The Impact of Humanism on Western Europe*, ed. Anthony Goodman and Angus Mackay (Harlow, 1990), pp. 99–117; Brian Vickers, *English Science, Bacon to Newton* (Cambridge, 1987); M. Boas, *The Scientific Renaissance 1450–1630* (New York, 1962); A.G. Debus, *Man and Nature in the Renaissance* (Cambridge, 1978); E.J. Dijksterhuis, *The Mechanization of the World Picture*, trans. C. Dikshoorn (Oxford, 1961); A Grafton, *Cardano's Cosmos* (London, 1999) and Oystein Ore, *Cardano The Gambling Scholar* (with a trans. of Cardano's Latin *Book of Games of Chance*) (Princeton, 1953). For **Science and Religion**, A. Koyré, *Galileo Studies*, trans. John Mepham (Hassocks, 1978); Harold P. Nebelsick, *The Renaissance, The Reformation and the Rise of Science* (Edinburgh, 1992); S.J. Tambiah, *Magic, Science, Religion and the Scope of Rationality* (Cambridge, 1990). For **Bacon**, Paolo Rossi, *Francis Bacon. From Magic to Science*, trans. S. Rabinovitch (London, 1968). For **Leonardo**, Martin Kemp, *Leonardo da Vinci: The Marvellous Works of Nature and Man* (Cambridge, MA, 1981), also trans. of Leonardo's writings (London, 1989); Kenneth Clark, *Leonardo da Vinci* (London, 1967). For **Vesalius**, see *The Illustrations from the works of Andreas Vesalius* with annotations and translations, ed. J.B. de C.M. Saunders and Charles D. O'Malley (London, 1950); C.D. O'Malley, *Vesalius of Brussels* (Berkeley, 1964); S. Kusukowa, *The Transformations of Natural Philosophy* (Cambridge, 1995). For **Bruno**, see Frances Yates, *Giordano Bruno and the Hermetic Tradition* (Chicago, 1964); D.P. Walker, *Spiritual and Demonic Magic from Ficino to Campanella* (London, 1958). For **Montaigne**, I quote from M. Screech (trans.), *Michel de Montaigne: The Complete Essays* (London, 1987); Dorothy Gabe Coleman, *Montaigne's Essays* (London, 1987); G. Defaux, *Marot, Rabelais and Montaigne* (Paris, 1987); J. Starobinski, *Montaigne in Motion*, trans. A. Goldhammer (Chicago, 1985); Philip Ford and Gillian Jondorf (eds), *Montaigne in Cambridge* (Cambridge, 1989); M. McKinley, *Words in a Corner. Studies in Montaigne's Latin Quotations* (Lexington, 1981).

part two

THE ARTS

Figure 39   Coppo di Marcovaldo, *Christ in Judgement* (detail), second half of 13th century. Mosaic, The Baptistery, Florence. With permission from Scala.

chapter five

THE FIGURATIVE ARTS

COMPETITIVE EYES

In Florence throughout the Middle Ages the most imposing object of visual beauty had been (and, for some, still remains) the Baptistery of St John. This great octagonal building was probably constructed on the ruins of a fourth- or fifth-century original. However, Florentine legend insisted that it had replaced a Roman Temple dedicated to Mars. The edifice served as a place of Christian worship but also as a forum for political activity. Charlemagne was received there in AD 786. And from an early date the Baptistery benefited from civil and mercantile patronage: the geometric design of the marble façade was sponsored, probably, by the Guild of Wool-Refiners around 1150. The interior is dominated by a mosaic standing some twenty-five feet high on the west face of its pyramidal vault that depicts Christ in Judgement (Fig. 39). This was completed around 1265.

In the eyes of the Florentines, the Baptistery bore witness to a proud heritage unbroken since the Roman foundation of their city. Its history also indicates the extent to which the early development of Florentine art was encouraged by civic and mercantile patronage. And in 1400 – continuing this long tradition – the city authorities decided to embellish the building further with a set of ceremonial bronze doors. They announced an open competition that attracted entries from artists such as Brunelleschi, Donatello and Ghiberti who have been celebrated in later times as the founding fathers of the Florentine Renaissance.

Two of the competition entries are still available to view (Figs 40 and 41); and comparing these with the *Christ in Judgement* it is evident that great changes had taken

Figure 40   Filippo Brunelleschi, *Sacrifice of Isaac: Competition Panel*, 1402–3. Gilded Bronze 53.3 × 44.5 cm. Bargello, Florence.

Figure 41   Lorenzo Ghiberti, *Sacrifice of Isaac: Competition Panel*, 1402–3, Gilded Bronze, cm. 53.3 × 44.5 cm. Bargello, Florence. With permission from Scala.

place between 1265 and 1400 in regard to pictorial style, choice of materials and even theological emphasis. Vasari leads one to expect this; and the mosaic displays many features that, on one view, the Renaissance is sometimes thought to have surpassed. Despite an occasional concession to naturalistic detail, this image, lofted in an austere but exhilarating atmosphere, is concerned less with the observation of the natural world than with the contemplation of a divine mystery. The hieratic image of Christ – in a pose that is simultaneously an embrace and a reminiscence of the Crucifixion – is here seen both as Judge and Saviour. The vitreous tiles of the mosaic are inwardly illuminated by a light from beyond their own confines.

In the door panels, however, light – which is itself a symbol of faith – gives way to bronze, and to the efforts of the craftsman who – skilled in the handling of fire and understanding the chemistry of molten metals – has brought to life in each case a highly distinctive narrative. The set theme for the competition was the story of the Sacrifice of Isaac at the hand of Abraham. This is a religious story, but one that demands to be told in terms of high emotion and heart-stopping drama. Divine Providence speaks here not through contemplation but rather through a cruel crisis and the immediacy of our human response.

Though Brunelleschi's rendering is now often said to be the more vigorous, it was Ghiberti who obtained the commission. And his victory reflects in a number of ways the prevailing taste of early Florentine connoisseurs. Ghiberti was a goldsmith and in terms of metallurgical technique his panel proved more perfect than Brunelleschi's. In style too the human situation is rendered with a greater elegance and grace than Brunelleschi chose to evoke. In Brunelleschi's version, Isaac's face is contorted with fear and the angel wrestles with his father's wrist. Ghiberti, however, shows Isaac raising his eyes in faith; and Abraham's knife has yet to enter the space illuminated by the angel. An intense but measured assurance in the handling of both material and story is the characteristic of Ghiberti's art. The citizens of Florence were apparently still impressed by good craftsmanship while also showing already a taste for a courtly *sprezzatura* of style.

Ghiberti in his subsequent career continued to cultivate such qualities, along with a developing response to the demands of pictorial narrative. He worked all his life on the Baptistery – being commissioned to execute a second set of doors when the first were completed. In the first set – as in the competition piece – he works lucidly within the frame of the Gothic quatrefoil and his figures are cast in lithe and courtly postures that recall the sculpture and metalwork of Burgundy and the International Gothic manner. In the second set, Ghiberti maintains the Gothic figure type. By now, however, he had visited Rome. His figures tend to be dressed according to the canons of classical drapery; and the frame he later adopts is a plain rectangle. This new device displays some attention to classical proportion. It also provides a coherent narrative setting in which – rather than contemplating the still point of eternity – the eye could

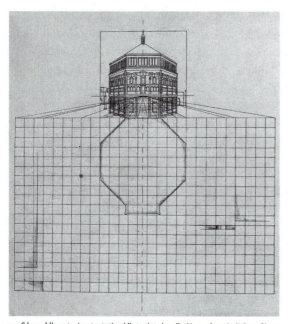

2 - Schema della costruzione prospettica della tavoletta brunelleschiana col tempio di Santo Giovann

Figure 42   Filippo Brunelleschi, *Perspectival drawing of the Florentine Baptistery*, early 15th century. Gabinetto dei Disegni e Stampe, Uffizi Florence. With permission from Scala.

trace the lines, flow and consequences of human interactions.

For all that, it was the architect Brunelleschi who – being responsible for the opening up of urban space in Florence (see pp. 36–9) – likewise contributed more to developments in the field of pictorial space. One day in 1420 – or so the story goes – while working on the construction of the Duomo, Brunelleschi looked across at the Baptistery and realized that it was possible, mathematically, to replicate the geometric lineaments of that building on a plane surface in perspectival form. Supposing that light travels in straight lines, then a straight line will connect the eye with the object of perception and thus form a pyramid of rays – with the eye as its base and an assumed point of infinity as it apex. The size and shape of objects as received in the visual image will be defined by their position within this virtual pyramid. Brunelleschi then insists that all the points that constitute an object in this visual field can be accurately transcribed onto a plane (as if the eye were not in fact rounded but rather as flat as a canvas). Figures could now be placed with confidence in relation to architectural designs and the components of an unfolding drama read as one might in looking out from a window over a piazza (Fig. 42).

Brunelleschi's observations were immediately welcomed by Alberti – whose own interest in the Baptistery had contributed to his design for Santa Maria Novella (Fig. 13), and subsequently developed by others – including Leonardo and Dürer – some of whom refined the mathematics of perspectival construction to the point of obsession. (Uccello is said to have kept his wife awake at night with his ponderings of perspective.) Calculations were subsequently extended to allow foreshortening in the depiction of human as well as architectural forms; and mechanical instruments devised to allow an exact reproduction of the visual pyramid on a 'window' of canvas.

The stylistic and technical developments that were signalled in the work of Ghiberti and Brunelleschi were echoed across Europe in sculpture and painting alike – not always, as will be seen, with the aim of producing a photographic likeness.

Before turning to examples, however, it is important to note another respect in which the Baptistery competition marked a turning-point. For the fact that there was a competition at all suggests that attitudes to art and the atmosphere in which the arts were practised was itself now changing. A secular arena had opened up in which the taste and judgement of fellow citizens of the artist were crucial factors in deciding who should receive a prize and what prices might properly be paid. The spirit of competition itself (in a sense that does not exclude collaboration) was in some measure to determine henceforth how the artistic action unrolled. Present would contend with past, city would vie with city, North with South. (At one point, certain Florentines even favoured a return to the outdated medium of mosaic – so as to compete with Venice where mosaic was a native art.)

At the same time, as the figurative arts came to be associated ever more with perspective, so too artists could claim a new prestige by virtue of their mathematical and theoretical science. This period, as described by Vasari (see pp. 17–20), was to see the transformation

Figure 43   Paolo Uccello, *Perspective Study of a Chalice*, 1430–40. Pen and Ink, 34.6 × 24.2 cm. Gabinetto dei Disegni e Stampe, Uffizi, Florence. With permission from Scala.

of craftsman-artists into intellectuals and later into the godlike artists of the High Renaissance. And the transition was driven by the vigorously confident ambition of particular artists. Quattrocento Florence might be compared to Paris in the avant-garde 1920s. Donatello, certainly, returning after a period in Padua, speaks with relish of the controversial and critical atmosphere that prevailed in the city – and could declare with his well-known irascibility that the finest thing Ghiberti ever achieved was to sell off a ramshackle farmhouse out in the sticks. A tumultuous expression of such cut-and-thrust would later occur when Leonardo and Michelangelo – who never concealed their mutual detestation – decided to debate the relative merits of their own favoured arts, Painting and Sculpture. To Leonardo 'Painting is the superior art because it is the more intellectually demanding, playing with both skill and intelligence on our sense of illusion and reality, making impalpable things palpable, flat things seem in relief, near things seem far'. In any case, sculptors get as filthy in their workshop as bakers in their kitchens. Against this, Michelangelo represents the sculptor as a hero engaged in a metaphysical duel, seeking endlessly to release pure spirit from the dead confines of material stone.

Such competitive words are common enough in all fields of Renaissance debate. Yet beneath their ritualistic aggression they articulate serious artistic aims and ambitions; and nowhere is this clearer than in the relatively sober motives that led the German Albrecht Dürer to visit Italy on two occasions and to seek, eventually, to outdo Italians such as Leonardo and Michelangelo themselves. Dürer shows particular interest in the Italian theory of perspective. Yet if representational technique had been his only concern, his journeys would hardly have been necessary. Early stirrings of Italian experimentation (as for example in Giotto and Duccio) had already attracted the attention of innovative Northern manuscript illuminators. Dirk Bouts (c.1415–75), moreover, could set his scenes – without resort to mathematical formulae – on chequer-board floors as an aid to the reading of the visual pyramid. Dürer, however, was clearly stimulated by the attraction of scientific and theoretical discourse for its own sake. Returning to Nuremberg he composed his own study of proportion – particularly in the representation of the human figure – and consciously sought to contribute to the advance of humanism in the German world.

Artists, then, progressively claimed a place at the heart of Renaissance culture. Indeed in doing so they precipitated – not always knowingly – a final competition on a high philosophical plane between Art and Nature. This issue was one that would be pursued in many other aspects of Renaissance culture (as for instance when Sir Philip Sidney declares that while History delivers a merely Leaden world, Poetry delivers a Golden world). But the question is in fact still wider than that. For it calls for a discussion of the very nature of representation or *mimesis* – of the relationship that exists between the natural object and the artistic image that reflects it. This question was first raised by the Greeks, and lives on especially in later centuries in a way that cannot fail to affect our understanding of the Renaissance arts. Thus Plato contends that the arts were to be exiled from an ideal Republic – on the grounds that the natural world is merely the shadow of an ideal world and the images of art merely the shadows of shadows. Some Renaissance thinkers would have been familiar with this argument; and some iconoclasts, such as Calvin, would have been largely sympathetic to Plato's argument. They could not, however, have anticipated fully the modern equivalent of Plato's position. For science has now put us in a position to inquire as to what, after all, should properly be regarded as the world of natural objects. We may observe and replicate the geometry of the Baptistery. Yet this says nothing of the atoms, neutrinos and quarks of which, as we now know, the building must be composed. Conversely, faced with a medical X-ray plate, we may reasonably ask whether this is any more accurate as a representation of the human person than a fuzzy family snap.

Questions of this sort are inclined to provoke anxiety, at least in those students of the Renaissance who suppose that here art confidently offers a true and transparent window on the world; and these students would no doubt also resist the suggestion that the Renaissance artist was reflexively aware of the philosophical problem or the formal strategies that the artist is bound to adopt in constructing, say, a perspectival viewpoint. Yet the Renaissance did have its own understanding of the issue and so far from experiencing anxiety drew upon this in producing some of its most ambitious works. Even the Aristotelian Leonardo, so deeply attracted to an observation of the natural world, nonetheless delights in the fact that the painter can represent objects on a flat surface as if they appeared in relief. To the Neoplatonist Michelangelo, as will be seen, such visual puzzles become the enigmas through which the artist can wholly recreate the present world in pursuit of a golden ideal. In any case, even the most mathematically perfect of perspectival constructions were known at the time to be purely conventional in establishing a single viewpoint. Renaissance artists did not know (as now we do) that light bends, but they certainly knew (as did their audiences) that we see stereoscopically with two eyes and not the one that squints into the visual pyramid.

None of this need to detract from the pride that Renaissance artists took in the invention of a (supposedly) commonsensical as well as a visionary world. Nor is it to deny that the common-sense or 'natural' viewpoint is unimportant or insubstantial. It is, however, to emphasize that in art at least we choose our modes of vision and place a value on what we see through the lens of art which is not determined by any supposition of technological accuracy. Masaccio in his depiction of the Holy Trinity in the Florentine Church of Santa Maria Novella uses the most advanced techniques of perspective to produce an image that asks us to meditate as much on the ultimate mystery of the Divine Being as did the Baptistery mosaic. In the Counter-Reformation Tintoretto employs similar techniques – combined with dramatic effects of Venetian *chiaroscuro* – to imagine a world where transformations of a miraculous or even sacramental kind are always possible: everyday objects in a supper scene can be transmuted on the instant into divine *visibilia*. Perspective here fulfils a function almost exactly opposite to that which it performed in the works of Ghiberti and Brunelleschi. Nor are we asked simply to check which vision more accurately corresponds to the world but rather to choose which world and which vision we are likely to value. In such a competition, we may even prefer to return to the values embodied in the Baptistery mosaic of the Duecento.

The diversity of possibilities that was opened up by the Baptistery competition may be confirmed by considering here two works which also reveal the principal terms in a debate which for most of the period would rage between the art of Florence (founded on drawing and proportion) and the art of Venice (founded on colour and light). The first is Piero's *Flagellation of Christ* (Plate IV), the second is Giorgione's *The Three Philosophers* (Plate V). Each work in its own way is profoundly enigmatic – and each in its strangeness has exerted a particular influence over modern taste.

In the *Flagellation*, Piero's use of perspective is so accurate that his measurements may be used in computer reconstructions to produce a coherently three-dimensional model of its architecture, of the circle on which Christ stands and of the coffered ceiling of the portico. Other features, too, acknowledge a Florentine influence. The modelling is sculptural but alert; figures are drawn in a way that allows attention to fall on distinct anatomical features, such as half-raised hands and wrists posed on hips or else the fall of garments under the weight of differing materials. The architecture of the columns is studied and well-informed.

Piero's conception, then, is wholly unified. Indeed its unity extends beyond considerations of perspective and proportion to an evident interest in the treatment of light. The sky is a Mediterranean blue, but delicately so; and the fall of sunlight, as shown by the shadows at the feet of the three foreground figures, is represented logically at something like 45 degrees from the picture-left. Yet the calculations of perspective, foreshortening and light contribute to no legible or coherent view across a piazza. On the contrary, the mathematics only emphasize a division between the interior and exterior scenes; and the logic of the emotions is just as hard to read. The flagellation itself is a moment of suspended animation, with a gilded classical statue in an heroic attitude contributing as much to the scene as any wince of pain or Christian passion. As for the three exterior figures, their eyes do not connect with each other, still less with the scene enacted over their shoulders.

It is at this point that, seeking to read as the Renaissance eye may have read, one might justifiably invoke symbolic, scriptural or even political considerations. One notes that the light above Christ is different in its intensity from the daylight outside – a sign like the circle on which Christ stands indicates that the moment of Passion is, paradoxically, a moment of reconciliation, of eternal truth and harmony. At the same time – considering the oriental garb of Pilate – the scene might refer to the Fall of Constantinople, or the breakdown of negotiations between the Western and the Eastern Churches, or else in scriptural terms, the three figures may be members of the Sanhedrin who had judged Christ to be worthy of death. Yet decisive interpretations on any of these lines might themselves be out of keeping with a Renaissance mode of seeing. At the very least the proliferation of interpretative possibilities reveals how far from transparent the pictorial window of the Renaissance could be. These possibilities may remind one that paradox itself – as we have seen in Chapter Two – was profoundly a part of both religious and courtly thinking in the Renaissance. A contemplative cast of mind would allow one to see the suffering of Christ as both the axial connection between time and eternity and also as a recurrent event in the history of fallible human beings. In this moment of seeing, time and space, light and line, dissolve into a suspended moment mirrored in the uplifted eyes of the three figures in the foreground. The answer here may be to seek no answer at all but to enter into the moment with the acuteness that Piero's pictorial style insists upon.

Giorgione's *Three Philosophers* is no less of a mystery, yet for wholly different reasons. Giorgione's style, in common with that of his Venetian successor Titian, depends less upon line than upon colour. His picture is unified, but not by linear means, and his figures are modelled into a landscape rather than being displayed against an architectural background. This is partly a matter of Giorgione's responsiveness to aerial perspective – to gradations of light in the sky, on garments and on faces – which creates a coherent atmosphere, slowly developing as the viewer recognizes its components. It is also a matter of technique. Giorgione did not draw his figures in outline as even a Florentine such as Leonardo does (despite his interest in *chiaroscuro*). Rather he works directly in oil, mixing, modifying and harmonizing colour with colour: gold, red, and green along with black and white form the basic palate of *The Three Philosophers* (as compared with the plum, pink, turquoise, gold, silk-green, ochres and blue of Piero's composition). Glazes contributed further to a unity of effect, though, like Titian, Giorgione seems also to have relished the feel of canvas itself as it channelled or high-lit his paint.

Such techniques have been revealed by an X-ray study of Giorgione's work. And it is sometimes supposed that research of this sort will also contribute to the deciphering of this work and its equally mysterious companion, the *Tempestà*. Yet if anything, such information only complicates the interpretation. Strikingly the figure in the foreground of the *Tempestà* itself is found to have been originally a naked woman transformed finally into a vaguely military vagabond. And *The Three Philosophers* seems to have been subject to similar if less radical alterations of drafting. All of which is consistent with a further difference between Florentine and Venetian art in respect particularly of the stories they have to tell. For, while Venetian art continued to be dominated by religious themes throughout the fifteenth century, it interested itself somewhat earlier than Florence in the possibilities of secular subjects and of subjects where landscape was as important as the actions designated by figures. In *The Three Philosophers* as in *The Flagellation*, the painter depicts a moment of stasis. But the ruminative calm of Giorgione's scene is quite different from Piero's – where there is still the notable possibility of descending whips and where intellectual inquiry seems to be drawn urgently into the solving of the mystery. It is, of course, possible to see Giorgione's work as an enigmatic and meditative representation of the Magi – though in that case the painter is claiming considerable intellectual freedom in dispensing with any depiction of gifts or even of a traditionally African Balthasar. Equally as the figures stare into the cave from the vantage-point of a superior light, there seems to be a plausible reference to the Cave of Plato's prisoners. Certainly one could no more mistake this scene for a realistic account of a day in the country any more than one could Giorgione's version of the *fête champêtre* or the *Tempestà* itself. However, we are invited into the scene less by the rigorously intellectual challenge that Piero poses than by an appreciation of finesse in technique, by the richness of a unique colour-world, by evocation and by the suggestions generated in the darkness of organic growth and the lucidity of human presences. It is sensibility rather than intellect that generates this mystery.

SEEING IN THE RENAISSANCE

One reason for the strangeness of both Piero's painting and Giorgione's is that they may, conceivably, have been meant to speak to the arcane tastes of an aristocratic audience. Devices – such as linear or aerial perspective – which now might be thought to allow us common-sense access to a common-sense world could easily have been intended, at least in some Renaissance paintings, to demonstrate the virtuosity of the painter or defend the painting from the unwelcome attentions of the common man. Such elitism – which directly affects the ways we see, or at least the ways in which we want to see – is available in a variety of versions. Leonardo, for instance, could maintain that the merest sketch of a painting should be enough to communicate the whole idea of a finished work to those who had the intelligence to read it aright; Michelangelo, as we shall shortly find, made an heroic virtue of courtly *sprezzatura* whereby immense technical difficulties are overcome with apparently effortless grace – to the applause of those in the know. But such expectations will, of course, determine what we look for in a painting and the values we place upon it. Seeing can never be innocent of social or moral considerations. Currently we are conditioned – or choose – to assess the world through our driving mirrors, or the leering frame of a Levi's advertisement. What then were the conditions under which the Renaissance eye, as exercised in the figurative arts, was obliged to – or chose to – envisage the natural world? Perspective is one such condition; and perspective – which so far has dominated the present discussion as it does so many other accounts of Renaissance art – can all too easily be regarded as an instrument of *élite* control, encouraging us by an illusion to think that our eyes may command the world around us. There were, however, other principles at play in the period. Some of these have become almost foreign to the modern eye (and some were far from elitist in their implications).

Consider, for instance, what it must have been like to buy and sell either goods or pictures in a Renaissance marketplace. Infamously, there were patrons of the time who chose to buy their paintings by the yard, and to stipulate in contracts how much gold leaf or what quality of lapis lazuli they wished to see in the finished product. But mercantile perception must also have been capable of its own particular and now-lost dexterities. Lacking modern units of measure and computational apparatus, the Renaissance eye had to be particularly skilful in 'gauging' the capacity, say, of a cask or of deciding on a weight from the evidence of size or material consistency. Seeing any shape there would have been much more readiness to translate it into its volu-

Plate I   Jan Van Eyck, *The Virgin of the Chancellor Rolin*, 1436. Panel, 66 × 62 cm. The Louvre, Paris. With permission from Scala.

Plate II Michelangelo, *Delphic Sybil*, 1510. Fresco, The Sistine Chapel, Vatican, Rome. With permission from Scala.

Plate III Pieter Breughel, the Elder, *Dulle Griete* (*Mad Meg*), 1562. Oil on wood, 115 × 161 cm. Mayer van den Bergh Museum, Antwerp, Belgium. The Bridgeman Art Library.

Plate IV   Piero della Francesca, *Flagellation of Christ*, probably 1460s. Panel, 59 × 81.3 cm.
Galleria Nazionale delle Marche, Palazzo Ducale, Urbino. With permission from Scala.

Plate V   Giorgione, *Three Philosophers*, c.1500–10. Oil on canvas, 123.5 × 144.5 cm.
Kunsthistorisches Museum, Vienna. The Bridgeman Art Library.

Plate VI   Rogier van der Weyden, *The Deposition*, c.1440. Panel, 219.7 × 266 cm. Prado, Madrid. With permission from Scala.

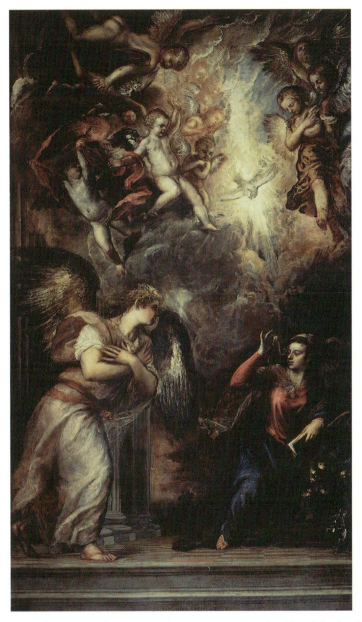

Plate VII   Titian, *The Annunciation*, 1565. 411.5 × 268 cm. Church of San Salvador, Venice. With permission from Scala.

Plate VIII   Leonardo da Vinci, *Madonna and St Anne* (detail), 1508–10. Oil on panel, 168.7 × 130.2 cm. The Louvre, Paris. With permission from Scala.

metric equivalent; and artists, through perspective and foreshortening, could play ingeniously upon this, inviting the viewer to interpret (repeating Leonardo's words) flat shapes as round, realities as illusion, illusions as celebrations of reality. Number too was a commercial skill; and Piero della Francesca is happy to recognize this in *De Abaco*, where his interest in mathematics led him to ask: 'Seven *bracci* of cloth are worth nine *lire*; how much will five *bracci* be worth?' and answers by applying the Rule of Three (also known as the Golden Rule or Merchant's Key).

In a similar way, the eye and hand in the Renaissance, responding to the material of both the natural world and of their own art, are likely to have been especially immediate, tactile and instinctual. In the modern world phenomena tend to come in bubblewrap; and there is little inclination to recognize the extent to which human responses are linked to a power of 'estimation' – to the preconceptual ability that a cat might display in jumping from roof to roof, in estimating spatial relationships, or in assessing the effects of darkness and light as beneficial or dangerous. But an exact and agile line drawn rapidly in fresco by Michelangelo or by Dürer with his burin draws on that unselfconscious skill, that instinctual power to assess and delimit the surfaces of wall or page that Vasari praises as *disegno*. The suffused tonalities of Giorgione's painting settle both eye and figure into a rich and nourishing habitat. Titian, on the other hand, in depicting the rape of Lucretia, will ring instinctual terror down the nervous system by an appalling clash between plush red breeches and the dangling orange socks that accentuate the rapist's lower body.

Other modes of seeing develop as the status and ambitions of the artist develop. Increasingly a work of art would be bought not for its intrinsic value – in yardage or costliness of material – but for the value added by the artist's own signature. Alberti indeed in his *Treatise on Painting* insists that 'Gold worked by the art of painting outweighs an equal amount of unworked gold'. Likewise the skill of the painter in mixing his yellows and white will itself be more valuable than yards of gold embossing. This is in part, of course, to favour a naturalistic rather than symbolic style of representation. It is not only that. On Alberti's view, we look at works of art and prize them for what the artist can do with the ever-shifting material of natural observation – seeing, in Shakespeare's phrase, 'the Fancy outwork Nature'. Nor need this exclude new forms of symbolic representation, arising in response to the intellectual ambitions of the artist. Piero may be a mercantile mathematician. But *The Flagellation* has already revealed the extent to which number-symbolism can govern his painting. As for colour, the choices that Van Eyck makes in, say, the *Arnolfini Marriage* could well be taken as allusions to the alchemical practices – or 'marriages' – working beneath the wedding of two merchant souls. The connoisseur might also appreciate the ways in which technical and symbolic art could produce their own significant combinations: white lead when mixed with ultramarine and azurite ensures an intense and permanent blue; but when this is used on the cloak of the Virgin Mary such a mixed colour could be seen as 'a symbolic act of worship', a recognition of how in the Incarnation divine candour animates human form.

Throughout the fourteenth and fifteenth centuries, the art of seeing called into play a range of simultaneously instinctual and esoteric impulses. And this is reflected in the work of the two theorists – Alberti and Vasari – who apparently did most to encourage a later emphasis on mimetic realism.

Important as perspective is to Alberti, far more important is *istoria*. *Istoria* can only very cautiously be translated as 'story' and certainly does not mean the sort of picture-narrative that modern art has called into question. The Renaissance would, of course, witness a growing interest in the depiction of 'stories' drawn from secular 'history'. *Istoria*, however, reflects a particular affiliation that the visual arts sought to claim in its own time with the arts of literature and rhetoric. Rhetoric seeks to persuade, literature to organize and shape our emotions, often to moral ends. Likewise in visual *istoria* the representation of admirable deeds will attract the eye and concentrate the attention in a pursuit of praiseworthy values. But in this sense *istoria* can be just as much a principle of pictorial composition as coherent perspective. Like a great dramatist, the painter of an *istoria* will create a rhythm of actions and emotions that runs coherently alike through the figures in a scene and invites the audience to participate in the meaning of the scene; or else like a stage director, the artist will ensure that the responses of a group or ensemble are varied yet consistent one with another, according to an inner logic of emotion and character. An example would be Masaccio's depiction of *The Raising of the Son of Theophilus* (Fig. 3).

Alberti, then, is concerned not simply that we should observe an action but rather that we should participate in its moral drama. Sometimes this participation will be encouraged by choric figures adopting gestures from public oratory. But it is also encouraged by a specifically visual technique that, for Alberti, is as central to the development of Renaissance technique as perspective is. This is 'circumscription'. In a unified group how do we mark off the shape and gestures of one figure from those of another? If groups are to be placed in rhythmic relation to one another, the rigid use of a primitive black outlining will hardly be sufficient. A subtler designation of difference and contiguity is needed; attention must be given to an exact registration of the direction of light and gradations of shade. Alberti himself suggests that the painter might proceed as if there were a gauze between himself and the figure he was painting that diffused its hard outline. It is this suggestion that is registered – along with stupendous perspectival effect – in, for example, Masaccio's *St Peter Healing with Shadow*. This painting could not even have been attempted without an understanding of *chiaroscuro* – and indeed a moral sense of *istoria*, in contemplating the miraculous power that the very shadow of St Peter could cast.

Turning to Vasari, one quickly discovers that he is no more wedded to perspectival construction than Alberti. His principal concern is with the *grazia* that is supremely exemplified by Michelangelo's command of *disegno*, by which he means a brilliant ability (or *sprezzatura*) that embraces the most difficult subjects – particularly in representing the human figure – and overcomes them by the vigorous inventiveness of his drawing. On these grounds, Vasari criticizes Uccello for wasting his considerable talent on drawing merely inanimate objects (Fig. 43); the truly taxing subject for a genius is foreshortening (as in the *Delphic Sybil*, Plate II). Conversely, when Vasari lights upon any instance of such *grazia*, he is often willing to extend the normally restricted range of his temporal and territorial sympathies. Giotto, for instance – in a mosaic now lost – displays *grazia* when, choosing to depict a storm on the Sea of Galilee in the inherently rigid medium of vitreous tiling, he succeeds in capturing the tumult of waters and flickers of emotions that are observed in a scene of shipwreck.

In Giotto's case – as constantly in Michelangelo's – Vasari looks, as Alberti would, to the enactment of a moral drama but also responds to the drama of the artist's own triumph over resistant material. Fresco-painting in particular represents an heroic contest with fresh and fluid substances and thus must be considered the most difficult and therefore most 'graceful' of the arts. Frescos are painted directly onto wet plaster and demand a rapid and ever-ready understanding of where a line should fall and of how a colour may look when dry on the following day (*On Technique*, p. 221). This predilection, however, does not prevent Vasari from seeing the inherent fascination of oil painting. Thus in a wonderful evocation of process, slow time and chemical expertise he writes (describing a painting intended for Federigo da Montefeltro's [*sic*] bathroom):

> This manner of painting kindles the pigments and nothing else is needed save diligence
> and devotion, because the oil in itself softens and sweetens the colours and renders them
> more delicate and more easily blended than do other mediums. While the work is wet the
> colours readily mix and unite with one another; in short, by this method the artists impart
> a wonderful grace and vivacity and vigour to their figures so much so that these often seem
> to us in relief.

Even here Vasari cannot finally resist judging painting in terms of sculptural form. Yet the sheer pleasure in material itself as it shifts beneath the artist's hand is witnessed on innumerable pages of his work, as for instance when he describes the character of travertine stone – not the most costly of materials – and delights in the shapes that mannerist artists (such as he himself was) can derive from it:

> The stone is all a kind of coagulation of earth and water, which by its hardness and cold-
> ness congeals and petrifies not only earth but stumps and branches and leaves of trees.
> On account of the water that remains within the stones – which can never be dry so long

as they lie under the water – they are full of pores which give them a spongy and perforated appearance both within and without. . . . Although [travertine] is coarse, it can be worked as freely as marble. . . . The Frenchman Maestro Gian . . . carved astrological globes, salamanders in the fire, royal emblems, devices of open books showing the leaves and carefully finished trophies and masks. (*ibid.*, pp. 51–2)

Turning now to the artists of the Renaissance themselves, our concern will be with representation and design but also with the competitive and experimental spirit that underlies at all points the great art of the Renaissance, beginning with a Southern sculptor, Donatello, and a Northern painter Rogier van der Weyden, who each in his own way showed a remarkably innovative understanding of stylistic and material possibilities.

EXPERIMENTATION IN MATTER AND FORM

Donatello (1386–1466), along with his younger and tragically short-lived contemporary Masaccio (1401–29), dominated the early Florentine Renaissance and translated the artistic possibilities revealed by the Baptistery competition into a sixty-year series of experiments in marble, bronze, wood and even moulded glass.

Consider, for instance, the *St George* commissioned by the Florentine Guild of Armourers and Sword-Makers, to be placed in an external tabernacle on the Church of Orsanmichele (Fig. 44). The figure of St George inhabits the vertical shadow of a high Gothic arch. He does not dominate this space (being only 6 foot 5 inches in height against a 12-foot background) but rather looks out from it, as if the darkness represented a source of faith and the fall of light – against which his brow is furrowed – designated a place from which danger might at any point emerge. A sword – now missing – would once have threatened this dangerous void. The shield bears a prominent Crusader cross. But the taut, even angular pose of the Christian hero is informed by a full if understated command of classical *contrapposto*. The 'story' here is simultaneously ethical and political; and as late as 1571 a Florentine commentator could speak of how the *St George* inspired 'elevated thoughts and greatness of soul in the young noblemen of Florence'.

Masaccio in the Carmine frescos (see Fig. 3) had responded enthusiastically to the call of civic pride and the demands of intelligent patrons. Donatello, likewise, in the *St George*, as at every point in his long career, is able to combine the demands of both the secular and religious imagination. Impelled by a confident sense of his own virtuosity and an appreciative reception (on the whole) from mercantile sponsors and the increasingly courtly Medici, Donatello is unmistakably Florentine in his

Figure 44 Donatello, *St George*, c.1415–17. Marble, height 426.6 cm. Bargello, Florence. With permission from Scala.

Figure 45 Donatello, *St George and the Dragon*, 1415–17. Marble relief on the *St George* Tabernacle, 39 × 120 cm. Orsanmichele, Florence. With permission from Scala.

formation, not least in his enthusiastic response to the material stuff of his own art. One of his statues – which has now disintegrated – represented 'Wealth', or *Dovizia*, and once stood in the Florentine marketplace. Another is the heraldic lion of Florence, the *Marzocco*. Another, of very different dimensions, is the brutal equestrian statue (the first since antiquity) of the Medici hit-man, Gattamelata. Likewise in his two representations of the Boy David, political considerations combine with religious insight to produce, as in the *St George*, a celebration of Florentine opposition to the Goliath of Milanese despotism which also articulates the joyous agility of the biblical victor. In this respect his Davids anticipate Michelangelo's well-known icon. Notably, however, there is none of the giganticism and taste for stupendous effect that in a later period of the Renaissance was to characterize Michelangelo's ambitions. Michelangelo may have wished to carve a colossal statue visible out at sea from the quarry face at Carrara. Donatello, with all his civic confidence, aims at responsive subtlety of technical design that accompanies and deepens his attention to psychological and ethical detail.

In technical terms the pediment of the St George (Fig. 45) is no less innovative than the statue above it. Here – in an agitated narrative of chivalric lances, scaly dragon wings and the fluttering robes of a damsel in distress – Donatello retains the fluidity and elegance of Gothic design but also, in sculptural competition with the art of drawing, produces a technique entirely his own – *rilievo schiacciato* – which allows marble to register effects both of movement and of atmosphere as if it were canvas beneath a draftsman's pencil or brush. The marble (which in this case was particularly costly) is not treated as a block from which to carve an unambiguously three-dimensional figure but rather as a fluid medium, sensitive to the fall of light and shade (as 'circumscription' demands). Perspective both – linear and aerial – is acknowledged in architectural orthogonals and shrouded crags. There is, however, no crudely naturalistic insistence on a single viewpoint. Rather, shifting in and out of an epic-romantic dream that recalls Ariosto's *Orlando Furioso* (see pp. 5–9), the panel claims the freedom to escape from the confines of commonplace perception and entertain a fascination with the very texture of its marble substance.

To some connoisseurs of the time (wedded perhaps to the craftsmanlike perfections produced by the goldsmith, Ghiberti) the originality of Donatello's technique could at times be mistaken for carelessness. Usually, however, an apparent roughness of texture proves to have been calculated to avoid inappropriate effects of sheen or to allow the luminosity of the material to reveal itself. Similarly, apparently disproportionate elongations in a figure were intended, it seems, to correct the positioning of the finished statue on a high vertical plane (as in the case of the stark and startling statues of the prophets Habbakuk (the *Zuccone*) and Jeremiah which were located in niches high on Giotto's *campanile*).

Technical experimentation of this order continued throughout Donatello's life, until (when almost blind) he produced the bronze-cast pulpits for the Medici Church of San Lorenzo, with the angles of drapery and anatomy incised as they might be in a twentieth-century modernist idiom. Donatello, however, was no less original in his choice and treatment of iconographical programme.

Two cases in point are the (apparently) Christian Annunciation in Santa Croce (see Fig. 73) (1433) and the (apparently) Dionysiac Singing Gallery intended for the Florentine Duomo (1433–39) (Fig. 46). The *Annunciation* offers a magnificent treatment of a symbolic door in the background of the scene, picked out in metals that texture the shallow, shaded space – so that (as in Ezekiel's prophecy) the *porta clausa* suggests both the unimaginable division between the Old Dispensation and the New and the equally unimaginable entry of God into the world through the delicate vessel of the Virgin Mary. The same door carries in its unadorned beams a plain and unambiguous Cross. But against this (reading outward from the gravitational centre) three other elements are in polyphonic play. The first is the classical dignity of both draperies and head. Then there is the gracefulness of the gesture – caught on the electric diagonal of the glance between Archangel and Virgin – in which, without resort to doves or rays of light, the emotions of awe, reverence, haughtiness, fear, tenderness and intimacy (as well as lightness of human movement contrasted with winged movement) are all legible. Then finally there is the exuberant fantasy of the surrounding frame. Here the columns themselves are scaled or feathered (in a manner which was described as *alla grottesca* by Vasari and would influence Michelangelo in designing the Medici Chapel), and finally burst into an architectural rhapsody combining ovoids, swirls, swags and (for colour-contrast) terracotta *putti*.

Putti in fine abandon are themselves the hedonistic protagonists of the Singing Gallery (Fig. 46). Here Donatello was in direct competition with Luca della Robbia. Indeed, his contract stipulated that he would receive forty florins for every panel that proved as good as the panels by della Robbia. But the contest is one of wholly contrasting styles not of representational skill. Luca's cool, smooth singers dressed like Roman boys with sentimentally recognizable faces, sing from behind a proscenium of classical columns; and their purpose in praising the Lord is unambiguously declared in words from Psalm 150 carved in elegant classical epigraphy. Donatello, however (working in from frame to narrative), introduces classical motifs in abundance, acanthus leaves, urns, egg-and-dart mouldings. But there is no structural balance or decorum; the whole edifice is supported on undulating surges of stone struts and topped by lath-like horizontals. The thin columns – in syncopated relation to the struts beneath – force the white marble substance to glitter through the dominant inlay of gold-coloured stones. The *putti* themselves advance in no single direction nor in relation to any fixed point of view; some have wings and some do not, but all engage in an anarchic dance that could express equally well either pagan glee or the jubilation that the Psalmist speaks of.

Donatello's inexhaustible interest in new forms of *istoria* as well as for new techniques could be illustrated by his work for the Church of St Anthony in Padua, which includes the *Tale of the Believing Donkey* in bronze, where tunnel-like perspectives open up a scene in which narrative vigour and psychological insight are both abundantly exemplified. Donatello even defended his relatively bland *St Louis* on the grounds of narrative propriety as an accurate representation of a boring saint. But Donatello's greatest gift – which he shares with the Masaccio of the Carmine *Expulsion* – is to concentrate narrative *istoria* into the psychological *istoria* of a single person. This implies no crude attention to the tics and eccentricities of his characters, but rather a coherent appreciation of the ways in which bodily movement, from toe to head, may flow to a single expressive rhythm. And nowhere is this more apparent than in the bronze *David* of 1440 and the wood *Magdalene* of 1454–55 (Figs 47 and 48).

Seen together, the two statues manifest a power of imagination on Donatello's part which reveals itself in the very material of which the figures are constructed. The *Magdalene* is in wood, a medium popular in the North but associated in Florence with unsophisticated artistry. Though originally gilded, the poverty of wood has an immediate relevance to the penitential poverty of the repentant whore. But the lines of Donatello's carving hint at fissures, cracks and gnarlings in the substance of the desiccated log; and, had the gilding and polychromatic colourings remained, the tension between surface brilliance and profound laceration would have been only more evident. That is not all. The statue keeps to a thin, tight vertical line, still reminiscent of the trunk from which it was cut: there are allusions here to growth as well as to utter degradation. By contrast, the *David* has been cast and then polished in a bronze which

Figure 46 Donatello, Singing Gallery, *Cantoria*, 1433–39. Marble and Mosaic, length 569 cm. Museo dell'Opera del Duomo, Florence. With permission from Scala.

is almost black in tone and yet, in all its supple planes, responds to glint and sheen. This is the first free-standing nude since classical times. Yet the effect is by no means simply classical. The casting itself is alive with the delicate suggestions of an eye accustomed to Northern detail and equally to a craftsmanlike interest in the challenge of differing textures or the subtle registrations in the casting: a garlanded hat, flowing hair, boots and the brutally bleeding head of Goliath would have tested the technique of any foundryman. Nor does Donatello restrict these effects for safety's sake to a single point of view. Where the *Magdalene* demands that we stay within sight of her hypnotically painful eyes, the very narcissism of David's pose – which parallels the confidence of the artist in his own creation – invites one to move around the figure, to observe the effects of burnish and changing reflections. Where the *Magdalene* is clenched around its vertical axis, the swagger of elbows and hips in the *David* open up

Figure 47   Donatello, *David*, c.1440. Bronze, height 158.1 cm. Bargello, Florence. With permission from Scala.

Figure 48   Donatello, *Mary Magdalene*, 1454–55. Wood with polychromy and gold, height 188 cm. Museo dell'Opera del Duomo, Florence. With permission from Scala.

an interest even in the spatial volumes that they designate, a moving cone beneath the left elbow, a streamer of space on the right, bordered by a lithe flank, an almost puny arm and a great flat broadsword descending to the booted foot.

The figures are no less subtle (and subtly different) in their iconographical and narrative implications. The *David* may still carry – as Donatello's earlier version did and Michelangelo's will later – patriotic implications for the Florentine citizen. Yet the technical finish of the work suggests that it was destined for the Medici circle, where connoisseurs would have been able to read it closely. In that circle it may be interpreted with an eye to the Neoplatonism that had begun to stir in mid-Quattrocento Florence. David's hat certainly could represent an allusion to the hat of Hermes, who, as we have seen, was the dominant deity of Neoplatonic esotericism, and whose victory over brute body may be echoed here in David's victory over Goliath. At the same time, just as the *Singing Gallery* captures the jubilation of the *Psalms*, so the *David* may be seen here not only as the forerunner of the Psalmist but also – with his unconcealed eroticism – of the ruthless lover of Bathsheba, who sent his mistress's husband to death in the forefront of battle – and then repented. The eyes and the cast of the head have a depth that cannot be captured simply by speaking of adolescent impudence. The *élan* of David's pose is countered by a gravity or even sardonic reserve in the lowered eyes and slightly wry lips.

This complex *istoria* runs parallel in a very different key from the figure of the Magdalene. Here eyes are empty, staring and anguished. Yet they are also the eyes of prophecy, as eager for meaning as the male prophets whom Donatello sculpted for the Florentine campanile. The figure is in a hesitant movement of advance between a temporal past and a Christian vision. The past is there in a still-perceptible beauty of bone structure, in slender fingers and wisps of hair. Yet this is all translated into vertical movement. The eyes and the gait may be lowered but not in utter degradation. The fingers – delicately parted rather than wringing themselves in despair – are indications of an ultimate sanctity. It is no more possible to overlook these signs than it is to ignore the harrowing gauntness of Magadalene's condition. But sanctimony or disgust alone would here be equally sentimental. The 'story' that Donatello traces is one that, through both pity and terror, enacts the whole drama of sin and redemption.

Turning from sculpture to painting and from Italy to Flanders, a figure appears who is contemporary with Donatello and who at times sets up as complex an interaction between painting and sculpture as Donatello does in his experimental *rilievo schiacciato*. This is Rogier van der Weyden (1399–1464). Rogier may have begun life as an apprentice to a painter of polychromatic statues. Yet in a review of his work assembled for the London exhibition in 1999, it was suggested that he should be considered the most influential painter in the fifteenth and sixteenth centuries.

This is a paradoxical as well as a startling claim, especially in view of a certain resistance that Rogier shows to the technical developments of Italian art in the

Quattrocento. Like Dürer, Rogier travelled to Italy and was indeed greatly praised by the Genovese humanist, Bartolommeo Fazio, for the emotive power of his painting. Yet the reasons for his journey seem to have been more religious than intellectual. (He presented himself in Rome during the year of Jubilee Year of 1450.) Nor did he ever again leave Burgundian territory. Working as intensely within this ambience as Donatello or Masaccio did in Florence, Rogier became the official City Painter of Brussels in 1435, responsible for works such as the tapestry executed in a style verging on the allegorical (extant only in graphic reproduction) that welcomed Charles the Bold to the city with a celebration of Justice. His success – social and pecuniary as well as artistic – subsequently won him the title of the first 'bourgeois' genius.

In a similar way, Rogier seems to have resisted some of the most striking innovations of his Flemish antecedents, most notably those of Jan van Eyck (1390–1441) and his (probable) master Campin (1380–1444). By Rogier's time, Flemish art – drawing initially on the concerns and techniques that are exemplified in illuminated manuscripts – had developed a deep association with the spirituality that eventually produced the *devotio moderna*, and also a searching interest in the phenomena of the natural world. As appeared in Chapter Four, Van Eyck contributed greatly to interests in light, landscape and portraiture in the Northern as well as the Italian world; and, after Rogier's intervention, painters such as Dirk Bouts (1441–75) returned to the legacy of Van Eyck, as did Hugo van der Goes (1440–82) – whose *Portinari* altarpiece of 1475–76 was brought to Florence by an agent of the Medici bank and is now exhibited in the Uffizi alongside Botticelli's roughly contemporary *Birth of Venus*.

Critics sometimes describe Rogier as a Gothic counter-revolutionary. And, while he did not violently oppose the Van Eyckian vision, a comparison of Van Eyck's *Chancellor Rolin* (Plate I) with Rogier's *St John Altarpiece* (Fig. 49) reveals an understanding wholly different from either his Flemish or his Italian contemporaries. The river in Van Eyck's painting leads back – as it will in his Italian followers – towards a landscape where distance is designated by aerial perspective and where the painter displays his ability to orchestrate an effortless recession of graduated light. In Rogier the river itself has little presence save as a symbolic adjunct to St John's baptismal act: Christ is baptized in the waters of life. Attention instead is concentrated on this act, as though on a thrust-stage in front of a proscenium decorated by symbolic *trompe l'oeil* figures of stone. In this space, undistracted by naturalistic effect, the true point of Van der Weyden's painting appears. This is the initiation of a sacrament: St John's legs are braced over the wholly unnatural divide between river-bank and arch. His hand rises gracefully from this rhythmically energetic foundation to trickle water on the head of Christ and, simultaneously, to catch the divine acknowledgement that spirals, more fluently than water, over the otherwise insignificant landscape.

This religious meditation is the product of extreme technical experimentation. The statuettes in the proscenium arch have this much in common with Donatello's *rilievo*

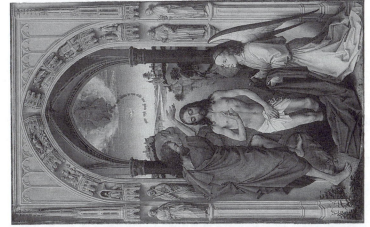

Figure 49 Rogier van der Weyden, *The St John Altarpiece*, c.1450. Each panel 76.9 × 48.2 cm. Kaiser Friedrich Museum, Berlin. Bildarchiv Preussischer Kulturbesitz.

schiacciato, that they play between the conditions of sculpture and painting. Yet Van der Weyden does not aspire to sculptural incisions as Donatello might to brush strokes; on the contrary the arch, having focused our attention, reveals that all figures save those involved in the divine action are hardly material at all, caught between paint and stone, between light and shade, volume and Gothic calligraphy. Conversely, in the execution of St John it is immediately clear that the human figure is as central – and as much the lightning-rod for emotion and significance as it will be in Michelangelo. Here with great narrative originality Van der Weyden compresses the moment of execution with the presentation of the Baptist's head to Salome. But the brutality of this synthesis is registered directly in the choreography of Salome's pose and the emotional posture of Salome herself. The rhythm here expresses both repugnance and a mincing complacency that reverberates from the thunderous object – itself weighted between life and death as it tilts on Salome's outstretched salver.

The faces that Rogier depicts in his many portraits are poised – though not wholly still – at a similar point of concentration; and formal austerity here, too, is at one with emotional complication. Van Eyck had presented character and sensibility in a descriptive fashion, as in the portrait of Chancellor Rolin (Plate I) where a firm but potentially brutal jaw is accompanied by eyes which are not wholly settled in con-templation of Christ. His *Man with A Red Turban* displays a sharp bone structure and a canny expression in contrast to a headdress which (unlike a similar version by Campin) is a fantastic confection of whorls, knots and folds all of which might at any point unravel. But Rogier's heads look at first as expressionless, as many of Piero della Franscesca's; between portrait and portrait, there are family resemblances here as if most of Rogier's sitters belonged to a clan of slightly reserved aristocrats. The heads are posed against plain, tinted surfaces. There is no attempt at narrative setting.

But, if this seems reductive, it also leads to an intensity of concentration on both paint and physiognomy. The still eye of the onlooker engages with the still gaze of artist and the tense or troubled gaze of the subject, framed first by the eye of the painter himself; and slowly the processes by which the heads have been modelled in shadowy oil paints and in-cisive lines reveal themselves. In *The Portrait of a Gentlemen* (Fig. 50), the head lifts in a sharp, taut diagonal (which is designated rather by angle than by movement of muscle); the eyes are held in a moment of attention – ready, receptive yet untouched with any identifiable emotion. By contrast, *The Portrait of a Young Lady* (Fig. 51) is settled or enclosed in her frame, her downward glance in run-ning parallel to the fine white of her wimple. The headdress performs no Van Eyckian tricks but is nonetheless a shape of great power, demanding and generating concen-tration. And so does the face which is composed or subdued, yet also smouldering, if not with crude passion then with possibilities that could prove either sensual or spiritual. Her lips are full, her hands (accentuated by a belt of the only red that the

Figure 51 Rogier van der Weyden, *Portrait of a Lady*, c.1450. Panel, 37 × 27.4 cm. Andrew W. Mellon Collection photograph © 2002, Board of Trustees, National Gallery of Art, Washington.

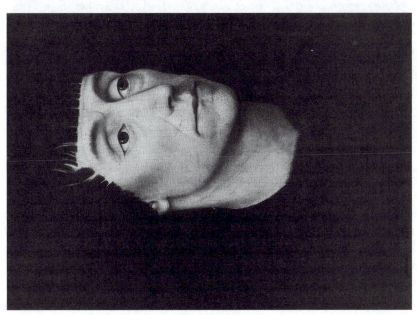

Figure 50 Rogier van der Weyden, *Portrait of a Gentleman*, c.1450. Panel 31.7 × 26 cm. Lugano, Switzerland. Coleccion Thyssen-Bornemisza, Prado. © Museo Thyssen-Bornemisza, Madrid.

portrait contains) are capable of nervous agitation, as promised by the elegant v-shape of her thumbs. Nothing has happened yet, any more than it has in the *Portrait of a Gentleman*; one can infer no history of past experience or biographical consequence. These are figures at a moment of test: pure being is gathered up in pure thought; and thought is the pure possibility of action.

Van Eyck, it has been said, is an explorer, Van der Weyden an inventor, Van Eyck a Christian humanist, Van der Weyden aware at all times of guilt and stress. Yet the attention that Rogier demands is not to phenomena but rather to the psychic motivations of human being. And this attention can itself prove to be a redemptive power. Consider *The Descent from the Cross*. (Plate VI). Here again Van der Weyden chooses not to place the action against a narrative landscape but rather against a highly formalized screen which, so far from creating a perspectival window, emphasizes the picture-plane. The body of Christ is anatomically exact and yet is presented flat to view without foreshortening. Faces, though sharply modelled, are remote from everyday emotion or sympathetic interaction: the very luminosity of their robes sets them apart from each other. Yet then once more the action is unleashed. The group is shaped by two curving figures distinct each from the other, the red-clothed St John gracefully impelled by solicitude and the Magdalene in red brocade sleeves and rich shimmering glaucous greens and blues, performing (like Salome) an incomprehensibly exotic dance of agony. And between these two figures there runs – flat across the picture-plane – a compositional pattern of knife-edged 'v's dividing figure from figure yet drawing them all – and the viewer – into an agitated unity of perception. There are great clefts between sump-tuous cloth and the stark lines of the ladder. There are fissures of the same shape even in the fall of fabric, while eye-sockets, brows, clenched fingers and collar-bones are chiselled to the same design.

But is this guilt? Compared with Donatello's Bacchic *Singing Gallery* it seems to be. Yet one thing that this panel does share with Donatello's work is a rhythmic dynamism of the utmost order. This is no sinking into or wallowing in self-recrimination any more than the *Oresteia* is. Indeed, compared with Van der Weyden's Magdalene there is even something conventionally pious about Donatello's Magdalene: her rags and bones are redeemed by praying hands and downcast eyes. But Van der Weyden's Magdalene is still dressed as a courtesan and dances like one, as Salome might. With this difference, that the dance in all its contorted energy appears in agonizing contrast to the corpse of the crucified Christ. It is as if the Magdalene were writhing in vital agony at the thought of being alive at all. The Greeks, too, might say 'It is better not to have been born'. But Christianity of Van der Weyden's kind demands that we live in conscious and expiatory attention to ever-new and unexpected rhythms. Rebirth is a process. Like the Renaissance itself, Van der Weyden makes new by re-inventing the old.

THE DIVINE ARTIST

The artists who had once been the craftsmen and, later, the bourgeois geniuses or intellectual *virtuosi* of the fifteenth century became in the early sixteenth century 'divine' beings. Pietro Aretino (1492–1556) – whose multi-faceted *oeuvres* combine a taste for satire and pornography with an elevated enthusiasm for the visual arts – applies the adjective to Michelangelo and to his friend Titian. (For Titian's portrait of Aretino see Fig. 59) Dürer was described in similar terms by his closest friend, the humanist Guillibaldo Pirckheimer (Fig. 56). The grandeur of the artistic calling now conspires and sometimes collides with the ever-more grandiose tastes of Popes and Emperors. Michelangelo's contentious record in tussles with the Pontiff over the terms of his various commissions is very well known. Dürer offered a Triumphal Arch of printed sheets to the Emperor Maximilian and Titian became extremely adroit (and extremely rich) in managing the demand for his work that flowed as much from Emperors in Spain as from Italian Popes and Dukes.

However, the notion of the divine genius was not simply an expression of hyperbolic self-congratulation between patron and artist. It was also a legitimate reflection of certain philosophical, cultural and proto-scientific conceptions of artistic activity specific to the High Renaissance. Some of these conceptions – as was seen in the case of Leonardo (pp. 145 *et seq.*) – were related to the prestigious liaison that arose at this time between art and science, in which artists might be expected to advance our not only observation of the world but also to contribute to the technological control promised by magus, engineer or Puritan work-master. Others were Neoplatonic in character, suggesting that the *furor* of inspired art was uniquely a channel for the creation and celebration of human values spun (in sometimes-spurious conjunction with religious values) out of the appetite for love and beauty. Others related to the claims (which may now seem wholly needless) that the visual arts could compete with rhetoric and epic poetry especially in the field of moral truth. In all of which, the 'divine' artist – or Renaissance man – was faced with a range of intoxicating ambitions but equally incompatibile realities.

The case of Leonardo has been examined in an earlier chapter. But the three representatives of artistic divinity in the sixteenth century to be considered now – Michelangelo, Dürer and Titian – all respond, though in different ways, to the play of concerns, intelligence and energy which the notion of genius vaguely designates. Dürer, for instance – though similar in many ways to Leonardo – brought back from his Italian visits not only an understanding of classical possibilities, derived in particular from the work of Andrea Mantegna, but also a profound sense of cultural mission and personal vocation. His own initials appear emphatically on all his works; and his intellectual aim was to attempt a wholesale reformation of Germany. He became in the fullest sense a humanist, praised as such by Erasmus. Yet, unlike Leonardo, his temper was religious; and his missionary zeal in the Lutheran cause ensured that his words were quoted in sermons by Melancthon. Titian, by contrast, was one of the least literary of the great figurative artists. He was a brilliant entrepreneur who knew how to organize not only a workshop but also a network of international art merchants and publicists, such as Aretino. Yet his success in this regard not only sharpened his eye to the social tastes and conventions of his time but also made possible the purely artistic freedoms that he claimed for himself. He would spend as long as ten years on a single painting – while his clients waited for genius to deliver. He became in consequence a visual story-teller of unexampled power, building layers of meaning into his long-meditated painting and was always inclined to tackle themes of a secular nature. By the end of the 1400s, Venetian painters such as Giorgione had begun (as we have seen) to address themes which sometimes had only the slightest anecdotal reference. Titian is at one with this tendency, and his *Venus of Urbino* was originally described as a 'lascivious painting' of 'a naked woman'.

In Michelangelo, however, the hallmark of his metaphorical divinity is a realization that the claim may from a Neoplatonic point of view indeed quite literally be true, and yet from a Christian point of view be wholly unmerited and constantly to be demonstrated and vindicated anew. Here is an artist who had been schooled in the Neoplatonic circle of Medici Florence, but who was also moved by a profound sense of Christian election and consequently by the prophetic words of Savanarola and the apocalyptic events of the Sack of Rome. Nor did a sense of the claims and significance of beauty (including his own physical lack of it) ever leave him.

In every one of Michelangelo's works, there is an enactment – sometimes in triumph, sometimes in pain – of the all-consuming realization that human beings can and need to pursue a new creation in spirit as well as in art. Hence the human figure is the unremitting focus of Michelangelo's work. In the *Doni Tondo* – depicting the Holy Family – realistic landscape is wholly displaced by a frieze displaying heroic gymnasts (all drawn with the intelligence of line that Vasari praises); in the *Crucifixion of St Peter* and *The Conversion of St Paul* hills and mountains are impressionistic washes around the fulcrum of torment or blinding inner vision. Even in his architectural works, a human face is discernible in the columns and windows of the Tomb of Leo X; and a dot added to an architectural moulding in a notebook can turn it into a grotesque profile.

It is, however, in his poetry and his sculpture that the implications of Michelangelo's position are pursued most powerfully. In the Medici Academy under the influence particularly of the humanist Poliziano, Michelangelo became an important poet in his own right, creating his own very knotty compound out of Petrarchan grace of phrase and Dantean energy, in Neoplatonic enigmas and scathing self-satire.

(Michelangelo, it is said, 'wrote things not words'; and famously, he parodies in his verses his own contorted ugliness as he paints the Sistine Ceiling suffering from goitre and lumbago.) Two poems in particular define his attitude to genius and art. In Sonnet 249, which celebrates the genius of Dante, Michelangelo portrays the very condition of genius as one of pain, rejection and melancholia: Dante comes down from Heaven (as Christ does); he then reascends (as the Neoplatonist might) to a vision of beatitude, yet on earth suffers exile and calumny at the hands of his fellow Florentines. *'Fuss'io pur lui!'* the poet concludes: 'Would that I were like him. Had I been born to such a destiny, I should exchange for his harsh exile, together with his virtue, the happiest state in all the world.' But the sculptor's own battle with the marble block may itself be seen as a battle between melancholic energy and the harsh unrealities of a physical world. In Sonnet 151 he writes: 'The greatest artist does not possess any conception which is not contained within the excess of a single piece of marble, though only a hand that obeys the intellect can reach to that idea.'

Matter or marble are good insofar as they contain within themselves infinite possibilities. But the good can only be revealed when the dead superfluities are carved away to release the spirit that the artist's intelligence has divined within it. This reflects a Neoplatonic but also a Christian understanding of both the intrinsic value of material creation and the liberating power of mind. Equally, these lines formulate the working method of Michelangelo himself, who would carve inwards from the face of a marble block constantly modifying line and plane till the 'idea' of a human form was drawn from its imprisonment in stone.

Difficulty and *terribilità* (which might roughly be translated as 'sublime terror') were qualities that Michelangelo's contemporaries regularly associated with his genius. This means in part that the subjects he tackled – as in *The Last Judgement* – were themselves implicitly awe-inspiring. It also means that for Michelangelo himself the same perception leads to an understanding of his own work as an action akin to both penance and prophecy, involving a constant engagement with the enigmas delivered by Christianity and Neoplatonism and promising always the possibility that difficulties will be overcome – in his own heroic version of courtly *sprezzatura* – by the grace of artistic intelligence.

The daring of the new colours revealed on the Sistine Ceiling is one indication of this. So too is the complex beauty of the St Peter's *Pietà* – a beauty that derives from a meditation on the paradoxes of life and death in which a youthful mother displays (with a gesture of both gravity and grace) the body of her Maker (older than she is) to the onlooker. In a later *Pietà*, Michelangelo carves his own features into that meditation, as likewise he paints them on the flayed hide of St Bartholomew in *The Last Judgement*. Correspondingly, *The Last Judgement* itself is surmounted by a portrayal of the prophet Jonah, in which an immensely 'difficult' foreshortening expresses the impact of vision on a man who (like Dante) had come back from the depths of utter

Figure 52 Michelangelo, *St Matthew*, c.1505. Marble, height 272 cm. Accademia, Florence. With permission from Scala.

nothingness. At large, the Sistine Chapel is the depiction of History itself as an initiation rite in which the perfect beauty of Adam is lost then recovered in a process that ends in the second coming of Christ in Judgement but also involves the pains and prophetic utterances that punctuate the whole of temporal history and now include the artistic activity of Michelangelo himself.

It is, however, in Michelangelo's sculpture that this spiritual and cultural drama is played out to most immediate effect. One example is the *Saint Matthew* (Fig. 52) Here the Evangelist is caught at the moment in scriptural history when he rises from his tax-desk to follow Christ. There is, of course, no tax-desk in sight. A book still embedded in stone may be a ledger but equally a gospel waiting to be written. The concern here is not with anything that resembles life as we know it but rather with the energies that are released in entering spheres of existence as yet undefined. The eye of St Matthew (in common with the eye of *Moses* in San Pietro in Vincoli) is already rounded and lucid; it directs both the rise of muscle and limb and also the plane that the statue would have followed had the artist brought it to completion.

In the present state of the *St Matthew*, it is easy to see how Michelangelo's technique involved a gradual lifting away of matter and progressive corrections, or conversions, of line – as in some rough pencil sketch – in pursuit of the original and also final conception. Whether or not this work, and others like it, were meant to remain unfinished is a continuing topic of debate – and also an enigma, ensuring that *difficoltà* and *terribilità* remain essential to our reading of Michelangelo's art. Yet even relatively finished works point to the same fundamental concerns with those unfinished processes in which hard stone and chisels are seeking out (in an all-but literal sense) unexpected moments of clarity. So, if finally one turns to the Medici Chapel (which is one of the most fully achieved and polished of all Michelangelo's conceptions) we find there too a meditation on themes of Mutability, Fame, Eternal Life and the mysteries of in-dwelling Divinity (Figs 53–55). These, since the time of Petrarch, had been central issues in the Renaissance tradition (see pp. 00); and Michelangelo – drawing on both Christian and Neoplatonic patterns of thought – translates them into a sculptural and architectural unity which simultaneously (and mystically) admits how insufficient human art must always be.

The Chapel, built between 1519 and 1534, was meant to house four corpses, including those of Lorenzo Il *Magnifico* (died 1492) and Giuliano Il *Magnifico* (assassinated in 1478). It eventually received only those of their decadent descendants, Giuliano, Duke of Nemours, and Lorenzo, Duke of Urbino.

The height of the original building has been extended by an additional storey; and architectural accents are executed in a grey limestone known as *pietra serena*. The upper storeys – which were meant originally to be painted with frescos – draw upon classical motifs and calculations but do so with great freedom of design, and fulfil no structural or engineering purpose. The windows, however, do allow for an optimum of muted light to illuminate the statuary. The tombs and their frames are carved in white marble. This architecture, too, is delicately fantastic, drawing on suggestions from Donatello but also anticipating the conscious elongation and elaboration of the Manneristic style. At the same time, it is here that the thematic concerns of the Chapel begin to register. Against the emphasis upon height, illumination and contemplative circles, the friezes and swags of the lower register allude to various textures in the physical world: foliage, the mane of miniature lions, an owl with downy plumage under the bent leg of *Night*, fish-scales on the pedestal of the tomb. Empty-eyed theatre masks complete the decorative programme; illusion is itself a factor here.

At the base of the tombs, it was once intended that there should also have been heavy statues representing the River-Gods. Had these been completed, they would have helped to express a preoccupation with material flux and the delusiveness of temporal things. Or else they could have been seen as the base of an ascending pyramid rising through the tombs of the mortal Dukes, on through the manifestation of temporal order to the immortal images that are provided in their sculptural *simulacra*, and higher still, on a Neoplatonic journey, back to their origins in the oneness of contemplation. Thus Michelangelo himself annotates his architectural plans with the words that in one case speak of his own desire for repentance at the approach of death (*Poems, op. cit.*, 51, pp. 39–40) – 'I have been betrayed by my fleeting days . . . but cannot repent . . . or prepare myself' – and in another with a eulogy to Giuliano:

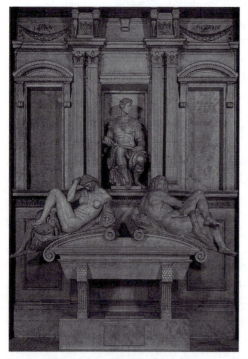

Figure 53–55 Michelangelo, *The Medici Chapel* 1519–34, with the tombs of Giuliano and Lorenzo de' Medici, Florence. With permission from Scala.

Day and Night speak, saying: We, with our swift course, have led to his death. Duke

Giuliano: It is therefore right that he take vengeance upon us. The revenge is this: that

we have slain him, and he in his death should take the light from us. (*ibid., no. 14, p. 11*)

In the first extract, the poet is as much entangled in a desire for Christian repentance as Shakespeare's King Claudius; in the second, he speaks – as Shakespeare will in his *Sonnets* – of Fame and Art as ultimate victors over Time.

If Time is defeated by Fame, this may explain why the four figures that represent Dawn and Dusk, Night and Day should all be so heavy with weariness and defeated by experience. If there is nothing other than Time, then Time is a tragedy. Night sags with sunken breasts and crease-marks as if, having borne too many children, darkness were the only place for her faded beauty. Day rounds on the world with defensive muscularity and angry yet unseeing eyes. Dusk is thoughtful but – sick of effort – he draws a blanket languidly around his thigh. Then, to start it all again, Dawn comes, with dark rings around her eyes and a heavy, seductive tug on her luxuriant bandana. For all that – and despite the awful range of experiences that Time engenders – time is a principle of regularity, of measure and order appreciable to intellect. Thus the four figures slipping around the arc of the tombs hint not only at motion and transience but also at the symbolic perfection of circularity.

The two figures representing Giuliano and Lorenzo stand in the pyramid at a point of confluence, between Descent and Ascent, Illusion and Vision, Repentance and Fame, gathering into their being all the experiences that are observable in the Hours of the Day – that drag us down into matter or sharpen us penitentially to truth. These figures dominate and are displayed by the surrounding architecture. Yet they are in no way meant to be naturalistic portraits. Nor were the less-than-illustrious characters of these two Medici Dukes (who in life were both bearded) likely to have resonated in the memory. The images are rather ideas drawn out of depraved actuality, representing (redemptively) the human psyche in two of its most fundamental modes, the mode of action and the mode of contemplation. One – Giuliano – is the active life, open and unhelmeted yet easily ready with his baton. This figure is elongated – as many figures subsequently will be in Cinquecento Mannerism – and displays something of the serpentine upward movement or 'figure of flame' that expresses for Michelangelo an aspiration to spiritual refinement. The other – Lorenzo – is the life of contemplation, shadowed by his helmet, heavy in his limbs. He is also a melancholic, guarding with his elbow a box which displays a bat as emblematic of the night. But (as Dürer will also show) *melancholia* is a creative power; and the lowered gaze of this figure collects energies from the region beneath, as human beings do, so as to offer them upwards.

Yet the Chapel has a horizontal as well as a vertical axis; the eyes of the Dukes also encompass in their downward diagonal the empty tombs which themselves stand opposite the altar. There is a hint of political allegory in this. The Chapel was constructed in the period when the Medici themselves – having risen from civic leaders to the heights of the Papacy – had now become involved in the violent history of post-invasion Italy. Michelangelo himself at times lay under the threat of assassination for the support he had at one time given to anti-Medician Republicans. The peace achieved in the Chapel is not an easy peace, but is rather expressed by the Mass for the Dead that at one time was said four times a day within its walls. Nor is its programme simply that of Neoplatonic aspiration. Here as throughout Michelangelo's work Neoplatonic considerations combine with a profound devotion to Christian understanding. So on the horizontal plane attention is directed – as in the early *Pietà* – towards the Madonna who surmounts the empty tomb; she too is driven by her own ascending spiral; yet the lunette on the wall above her would probably have carried a fresco of the Resurrection. As it is, she is a *Virgo lactans*, suckling an already muscular Christ-child. Neoplatonism speaks of an initiation into spiritual divinity; and Michelangelo responded to that. Christianity speaks of an Incarnation and a Resurrection which together locate divinity in the human body itself. Michelangelo's penitential creativity drew equally on that understanding. Time and all its experiences may weary us. But the rising up – as in *The Last Judgement* – is also a return to that field of energy, in the confidence that the artist's line might release its latent purposes.

In his unremitting attention to the human figure and lines of movement, Michelangelo sets himself aggressively at times against Titian who, he says, 'cannot draw' (though Titian himself learns much from Michelangelo, who himself according to El Greco was 'a worthy man, but he never learned to *paint*'). As for Dürer, here too Michelangelo proves scathing, even though Dürer's art depends, like Michelangelo's, on strength and finesse of line and figure. It was on his return from his second Italian expedition in 1507 (the first having been in 1505) that Dürer starts out upon his theoretical studies of geometry and human proportion. (Leonardo attempted a similar study; Michelangelo never did.) To Michelangelo, however, Dürer's book was useless and the figures it produced were 'as stiff as sticks'. By this time, Michelangelo had developed that fine contempt for rules and a confidence in the instinctual 'compasses of the eye' leading him to a concern with movement and gesture which, in his view, Dürer lacked but also – at worst – to exaggerated violence.

Dürer does not seem to have had any particular success in Italy, save with Giovanni Bellini. Yet as he carried back the results of his enthusiastic researches, he also began to make his considerable contribution to the development of German humanism, realizing the need, even, to devise a native German language for the discussion of artistic theory. (A spiral becomes a *Schnecklinie* – a 'snail-line'; a parabola is a *Brennlinie* or 'burning line'; two intersecting circles form a *Fischblase*, a 'fish-bladder'). He was equally responsive to the thinking of Luther; and his religious art is characterized both by personal intensity and a passion to speak through the lucrative but also missionary medium of woodcut and engraving, both of which permitted multiple reproduction.

Dürer was born to a family of Hungarian goldsmiths that had emigrated to Nuremberg in 1455. (His fascination with his own origins appears in his numerous portraits of family members and a recurrent emphasis on his own Magyar features.) Nuremberg was a centre of metalworking which, in addition, had developed a higher-tech industry in the making of geodesic instruments. The city had no tradition of engraving, but it was close to the new centres of printing such as the very flourishing town of Augsburg. Nuremberg was equally an important city in the political perspectives of the Emperor Maximilian I, with whom Dürer came to be personally associated.

The intention was that Dürer should follow in his father's craft; and up to a point he did, never wholly abandoning an interest in the decorative use of metals. At the same time, his prints themselves became a valuable source of income: 'The merchants of Italy, France and Spain are purchasing Dürer's engravings as models for the painters of their homelands', writes Johannes Cochlaeus in 1512. But developments in humanism and devotional style contributed to this diffusion. It was through his lifelong friendship with Guillibaldo Pirckheimer that Dürer had been encouraged to go to Italy and, while his response was both theoretical and intellectual, he also developed an appetite for visual and technical experimentation which, without yielding to the grand rhetoric of a Michelangelo, nurtures a peculiarly intense vision – part religious, part scientific – of his own place in the world.

The techniques in which Dürer experimented were manifold, and included water-colour and oil painting (for example, in *The Feast of Rose Garlands*, executed for German merchants in Venice). But line-work was his preferred medium. Here the play and resistance of material spoke directly to his hand and the resultant images could be read with the close intelligence of a text. In woodcut – as in typography – the blade pares away excess, leaving a raised edge to be inked and printed. The line is bold, even coarse; and Dürer tends to use this medium for religious subjects that stamp on the eye the intimate pathos of the *Small Passion* or the terror of the *Apocalypse*. (Titian was sufficiently impressed by Dürer's fineness of line to compete with him in, for instance, his *Moses Crossing the Red Sea*.) In Dürer's own hands the printed outline is refined by a sensitivity to the swell and shrinking that the knife itself produces in carving wood away; organic undulations appear in the mane of, say, a careering horse while a cross-hatching of finer cuts adds effects of *chiaroscuro* and texture to the bold description of a scene. Silver-point, on the other hand, required specially prepared paper and allowed no erasures (which makes it all the more remarkable that Dürer's earliest self-portrait should have been done in this medium). Engraving is a wholly different technique: lines are incised by a continual and flowing movement of the engraver's burin over a copper plate; and ink is poured into the grooves, but these can be so finely detailed by scratches and nicks as to produce an intrinsic scintillation into the finished plate. Etching works to similar effect: an acid-proof layer is applied to the plate and then cut away for a line or dot to be burned through in the acid bath.

These and other techniques – such as dry-point and silver-point – are 'difficult' in the now-familiar sense that they display the virtuosity – even 'divinity' – of the artist himself in his mastery of illusion. So Erasmus writes:

> Apelles was assisted by colours. Dürer, however . . . what does he not express in
>
> monochromes, that is, by black lines, shade, light, radiance, projections, depressions?

The accuracy of Erasmus's account can be illustrated by the engraved portrait of Pirckheimer (Fig. 56). One notes here the textured fur of the collar, and the light of an eye that not only expresses lucid intelligence but also bears a reflection of the window-frame out of which the sitter must be gazing. The same example – in which pathological obesity is turned by Dürer's hand into impressively concentrated mass – also illustrates a further point of difference between Dürer's aesthetic principles and those that prevailed in Italy. For where an Italian might have tended to take as his artistic subject an object already possessed of proportion and formal beauty, Dürer here – as in his drawings of walrus and rhinos – prefers to reveal, through the beauty of his own treatment, the visual interest inherent even in the lineaments of a grotesque. For Dürer, beauty is not a normative conception. Indeed, even his theoretical study of proportion is in some measure a study in comparative anthropology, concerning itself not merely with harmonious regularities but also with distinctive and sometimes eccentric body-shapes.

Yet if this suggests Dürer's confidence in the organizational and revelatory power of his own art, it also suggests an attentiveness, even a humility, in the face of the variety of the external world – modifying the impression of self-regard which Dürer not infrequently displays. Melancthon writes of him:

> In his youth [Dürer] liked bright and florid pictures. But after, he began to view Nature
>
> as an old man and endeavoured to look upon her native face (*naturae nativam faciem*); then
>
> he understood that her simplicity was the greatest glory of art. The which he could not
>
> attain and so said he was no longer an admirer of his own works.

One product of these contending impulses is the etching known as *The Great Cannon* (Fig. 2). Dürer himself appears in this dressed in Saracen costume (which the artist had borrowed from Bellini). Flamboyance, power and danger associate the artist with the destructive potential of the cannon itself, which is about to be trained on the village of Kircherenbach. Perspective – wonderfully realized in the sweep of the landscape – is an agent of control. Yet the details of the gnarled tree – as massive as the cannon itself – make claims on even the Saracen's attention, voicing a truth,

Figure 56   Albrecht Dürer, *Willibald Pirckheimer*, 1524. Engraving 18.1 × 11.5 cm. Metropolitan Museum of Art, Fletcher Fund, New York (19.73.119). In his Elergy on the Death of Dürer, Pirckheimer writes:

> Omnia Durero dederit fortuna secunda,
> Igenium, formam, cum probitate fidem . . .
> At nos praeservans aderit quum gratia Christi
> Hoc duce felices ingrediemur iter.

(Favouring Fortune bestowed on Dürer all good things, Genius, beauty, Faith unwavering. He with foresight will assist us through the grace of Christ; under his guidance we shall make our way.) Institute of Art, Chicago.

organic and older than machinery, which is replicated in bushes and wooden roofs throughout the scene. Dürer's perception remains firmly rooted in observation, clarity of line and organization, as, for instance, in the joyously simple diagonals in his drawing of Antwerp (Fig. 57).

Such attention to landscape or natural detail is wholly unlike Michelangelo. Yet direct comparisons between the German and the Italian are possible if one turns finally to the profound study of the nature of genius that Dürer pursued in the engraving *Melencolia I* (1514) (Fig. 58). The source for this image, as for Michelangelo's *Duke Lorenzo*, lies in Ficino's Neoplatonism. But where, underlying Michelangelo's art, there is the burning desire for unity of conception, Dürer in this engraving risks the depiction of a sullen storm, featuring a bat and a languid dog – traditional emblems of melancholia. The latter lie dejectedly alongside a clutter of the very devices of art and geometry such as spheres, polyhedrons, compasses, saws and nails which once might have been the instruments of constructive control. These devices are all skilfully textured but sometimes to the point of rendering an impression of imperfection

Figure 57 Albrecht Dürer, *Harbour at Antwerp*, 1520. Pen and Ink on Paper, 21.3 × 28.3 cm. Albertina, Vienna.

Figure 58   Albrecht Dürer, *Melencolia I*, 1514. Engraving, 23.9 × 18.9 cm. John H. Wrenn
Collection Fund, Insititute of Art, Chicago.

or roughness as in the face of the polyhedron or the famished rib-cage of the dog. Even the rainbow and the comet – portending hope in the one case and disastrous change in the other – emit a light that is eerie rather than refreshing. The lower world – if it is ever to have any value – needs to enlist the resources of the spiritual eye – as also in Michelangelo's *St Matthew*. But here the human eye flares in torpid anger. There is too much meaning in Dürer's *Melencolia*, too many instruments of measurement, too many allegorical devices. So the question which the image poses is not a specific question, admitting of any specific answer; it is rather as existential as Hamlet's famous 'To be or not to be . . .' – and as Petrarch's agonizing *accidia* had already been (see p. 82 *et seq.*). How are human beings to summon up from their own depths the forces of being which allow them to apply productively the whole apparatus of Renaissance technology? What lies beyond geometry to make geometry worth performing? There are answers to this question: some are Neoplatonic or even Socratic in character, admitting that we know nothing, or that we know best in a state of learned ignorance. Dürer's own answer in part lies in the companion-pieces *St Jerome* and *Knight, Death and the Devil* where the active energies of study and of crusade are fired in their different ways by the pursuit of Christian truth. But whether Socratic or Christian, these answers point in Dürer's case as in Michelangelo's to a humility that limits but also provides new focus for the talents of the Renaissance divinity.

Despite Aretino's justified encomiums, Titian does not share the intellectual passion that animates both Michelangelo and Dürer. One might indeed feel that his *Allegory of Time Governed by Prudence* (National Gallery, London) is a crystallization of Titian's businesslike philosophy. Nor do his self-portraits betray the penitence – or reasons for penitence – that Michelangelo's and Dürer's do and Rembrandt's will. Titian's inclination is to pride himself on the title of Imperial Count which he received from his most exalted patron, Charles V of Spain; and he is thought to have exaggerated his own longevity as a sign of peculiar status. His self-portraits in old age reflect a similar claim. For all that, Titian is perhaps the most powerful narrative painter of the Renaissance and also its most uncompromising in the portrayal of other persons. His very longevity and his extreme success at business and social advancement, brought him in touch with a range of persons and social concerns which expressed itself as much in analysis or even satire as in social climbing – nowhere more so, perhaps, than in his depiction in 1547 of Pope Paul III and his two nephews, where the senile cunning of a Pope, the reserved but dangerous authority of a cardinal and the oily courtliness of the second nephew are all put on show. The parody of underhand power-play is all the more cutting in that Titian's courtier genuflects in the pose of a classical discus-thrower. It is hardly surprising that the Papal family thought it better to keep this canvas out of sight. Such opportunities for social observation would, however, have been fed not only by the range of Titian's contacts in the international arena but also by developments in Venice which by 1530 – and following a general exodus from Rome – had led the city deliberately (under the guidance of the Doge Andrea Gritti) to pursue the role of an intellectual capital. Certainly the artists of Venice, building on achievements by the Bellini family and Giorgione, could pursue their own particular preoccupations, responding as much to Flemish and German as to Florentine suggestions. It was Venice, far more than Florence, that affected the subsequent course of art in the age of Rembrandt, Rubens and Van Dyck – to be resisted only in the eighteenth century by William Blake's furious preference for Michelangelo's *disegno*.

Titian throughout his life displayed an ability to assimilate not only social insights but also stylistic and thematic motifs, and likewise to reject all forms of cliché in favour of relentless experimentation. In this respect there is something Shakespearian about the workings of his genius; and when John Keats ascribes the virtue of 'negative capability' to Shakespeare, he provides a term of equal usefulness in discussing Titian. For Keats negative capability stands in contrast to the 'egotistical sublime'. A genius of the egotistical kind will pit himself against transcendent goals. But the genius of negative capability ensures that one should remain 'in doubts and uncertainties without any irritable reaching after fact or reason' thus allowing (as Keats himself did) the 'feel of the thing' to guide the imagination. This corresponds exactly to Titian's own technique of composition. As the remote but definite descendant of Van Eyck and immediate heir of Giorgione, Titian creates a unity in his canvases not by linear perspective but rather by a slow, symphonic diffusion of colour and texture. He would work over his canvases (sometimes thought to be prepared with a darkish or creamy primer) for as long as ten years, adding wet oil to layers which had already dried, allowing in some cases the texture of canvas to remain visible, in others adding glaze to glaze. The imaginative feel for a narrative or a face could easily over time develop a corresponding narrative of its own in the artist's treatment, involving a chain of deepening decisions and intuitions. It is not perhaps surprising that Titian's nudes (as in his Venuses or the *Danaë* in the Prado) are profoundly erotic, regardless of any narrative or allegorical reason. But the same processes could also produce effects of intense meditation or burning violence. At no point is the viewer allowed to shelter behind predictable effects or facile sentiment.

An early illustration of this is the *Assumption of the Virgin* painted between 1516 and 1519. The Tridentine doctrine of the Assumption powerfully – and against increasing resistance – reasserted the Catholic devotion to the Blessed Virgin as the uniquely favoured mediatrix and archetype of the Church. Titian's huge altar-image is placed against the bright, airy traceries of a Gothic east window in Santa Maria Gloriosa dei Frari, and reasserts the ancient justification for church embellishment, which is that the Blessed Virgin is herself the exemplar of the Church, a justification for the value we place upon physical images. But the figures are heroic in stature; God's pleasure is expressed in a dynamic foreshortened glide towards the viewer; and light, in contrast to the natural illumination of the windows, is represented (as Alberti would have wished) by an incandescent cloud of golden pigment, embossed with angelic faces. Some of these features develop suggestions to be found in Raphael's later style. Initially, the Franciscan brothers who had commissioned the work found all this too innovatory but were finally convinced of its merit when aristocratic connoisseurs offered to buy the work-in-progress.

In the *Assumption* colour creates great surges of energy, comparable to the linear dynamics of a Michelangelo – as the Venetian Tintoretto (Fig. 64) would recognize in seeking in his own work to unify the two modes of composition. But the same powers could appear in a small square portrait as well as in a towering rectangle – and in this case could offend even the most worldly and sophisticated connoisseur. When Titian painted the portrait of his friend and propagandist Aretino (Fig. 59), Aretino objected that he had not been presented in the conventional terms which would emphasize his social dignity. Titian apologized with a portrait that brings medallions, furs, aquiline brows and (almost) saintly eyes into satisfying prominence. Yet the original is not only a depiction of taurine libido, but a profound investigation of power – both painterly and personal – emerging from the dark and becoming 'more like the individual than the individual himself'. (Aretino himself praised Titian for creating 'a second nature'.) The eye here is not like St Matthew's eye, nor the eyes of Dürer's Pirckheimer. It emerges from, but conspires with, its own lustreless surround; eyebrow and beard are creatures of the dark, directed upwards but rather to challenge than to receive inspiration. The gold chain is dull and unimportant but a vivid lightning flash accentuates the paunch; and the massive body turns away in heavy *contrapposto* from the slightly tilted head. Light falls from the left on sumptuous silken lapels and crinkled sleeves but also on a domed forehead, unquestionably there and present. Steady attention – and negative capability – reveal the lecher as a hero; and Titian proves no more judgemental in his revelations than Shakespeare does in portraying Iago or Iachimo. But the same attention could work in many different tempers and keys. Titian's *Man with a Blue Sleeve* – or *Ariosto* – (National Gallery, London) is as unified – and tame – as Aretino is not. Isabella Gonzaga could declare that Titian's portrait of her erred only in making her too beautiful – though a later portrait captures the aplomb of middle age.

Similar qualities and a similar range of responses expand again into the horizontal panels of Titian's mythic and narrative paintings. And in these an intuitive philosophy – embodied in the suggestions of technique – begins to declare itself. Venuses appear in heroic lineaments that are drawn from both Michelangelo and Leonardo. But the responsiveness of their bodies could only come from a brush that replicated the interpentration of light, gold and flesh (see *Danaë*, Naples, Capodimonte), of blushes and mirror reflections (see *Venus at her Toilet*, Washington, National Gallery

Figure 59   Titian, *Pietro Aretino*, 1545. Canvas 98 × 78 cm. Pitti Palace, Palatina Gallery, Florence. With permission from Scala.

of Art) or naked forms and the surreptitious peekings of fully clothed male musicians (see *Venus with Organist and Cupid*, The Prado). These are works for purely secular, even pornographic use. Yet they also evoke the spirit of Ovid, who in turn draws upon Lucretius for his view of a world that is constantly in flux and constantly able to produce new *frissons* of sexual surprise, of touch, sight and sensation in unprecedented conjunctions.

It is processes such as these – both metamorphic and chemical – that Titian replicates in the tactile flow and diffusion of his oil paint. The effect can be terrifying. In several portrayals of Diana and Actaeon, Titian shows how the eye of the hunter Actaeon falls, by the purest accident, on the naked flesh of Diana who, in turn, hunts the hunter through a shifting and immaterial landscape in which the man is himself metamorphosed into a hunted stag and finally struck down by the arrows of the goddess. Or else transformation can be ecstatic, as in the *Bacchus and Ariadne* or even comic as in *The Rape of Europa* (Fig. 60), where Jove in the form of a bull ploughs his way through the waves, urged on by mocking Cupids, with the massive figure of his loved one (reminiscent, parodically, of Michelangelo's *Dawn*: see p. 196) plump on his back, teetering between her human distress and deified lust.

In the end, however, the same sense of violence, of change and of quantum shifts can also be put to the service of Christian truths. In *The Annunciation* of 1559 to 1562 in the Church of San Salvatore at Venice (Plate VII), the subtlest unities of colour reveal the agitation of a material universe invaded by divinity; and the narrative itself confounds all the expectations of graceful compliance that are commonplace in treatments of the same episode by artists from Donatello to Leonardo. The background, as though in Michelangelo's *Last Judgement*, is rent by forces that, instead of encouraging control or promising redemption, collapse perspective inward on the viewer. The angel is almost a stable presence. Yet its iridescent wings are painted in the broken brush-strokes that characterize the composition throughout, transforming the texture of the plumage into slashes of vigorous motion. The Madonna rises on a diagonal that parallels the axis of the angel's pose, but also draws her into a column of turbulent light. The action is graceful but the grace is animated by joy and surprise; and the dance that she seems about to perform will be Orphic, embracing an inspiration that disintegrates the known world in order to create it anew.

The key to this Annunciation is fire. Fire, as an expression of process and a stimulus to technical experiment is the theme for many of Titian's later works, as in the tragic *Martyrdom of St Lawrence* or in the flambeau that illuminates his unfinished *Pietà*. But here beneath the pedestal of the picture Titian inscribes a verse from *Exodus* 3:2 referring to the burning bush which is not consumed, *Ignis ardens et non comburens*. Freedom from slavery comes through association with the providential actions that have always been expressed in images of fire, whether in the bush on Mount Sinai or the tongues of flame that fall on the Apostles. This is Titian's equivalent of the

Figure 60   Titian, *Europa*, 1559–62. Canvas, 108 × 75.6 cm., 73 × 81″. Isabella Stewart Gardner Museum, Boston.

penitential understanding expressed in the Medici Chapel, but it is an understanding that reconciles Christianity and Titian's interest in Ovidian philosophy. Nor need one doubt that Titian was independent enough to have conceived this theme without reference to patrons or philosophical advisors. And the artist carries his intentions through even to such details as the tiny glass vase by the Virgin's chair. This vase draws directly on the Flemish tradition in its delicate transparency and sheen. But the flowers it contains translate cool light itself into fire. These are no wilting lilies but rather an allusion to the bush of *Exodus*, a flourishing efflorescence of flame. Fire is again the shifting element that destroys and sustains us and brings us into union with the burning light of revelation.

MOVEMENTS IN MANNERISM

Artists in the middle and later years of the sixteenth century could hardly ignore the examples laid before them by Leonardo, Michelangelo, Dürer and Titian and (to a lesser degree) Raphael; and, while many subsequent artists developed an imprint of their own, the styles that characterized this period have often been described, globally, as 'Manneristic'. The notion of 'Mannerism' has itself proved to be a remarkably popular one among cultural historians, suggesting a sophistication of formal design which may produce effects of conscious grace but also of deliberate paradox and irrationality; and the term is sometimes taken to express the agitations of a declining cultural epoch. John Webster's revenge plays, on this view, might be described as Manneristic, as could Shakespeare's *Hamlet*.

In regard to the visual arts the term 'Mannerism' needs to be employed with caution. There was indeed a period when, in response to the celebrated 'divinities' of art, less divine artists adapted their achievements in a deliberately stylish style. The cultivation of 'manner' – of style and skill for its own sake – became a marketable, even an international vogue – as for instance with Rosso Fiorentino at Fontainebleau.

Figure 61 Angelo Bronzino, *Portrait of the poet Laura Battiferri*, 1555–1560. Panel, 83 × 118 cm. Uffizi, Florence. With permission from Scala.

The elongations and elegances of line which the fashion favoured resuscitated memories of the International Gothic as did a certain abandonment of perspectival rigidity and the cultivation in sculpture especially of multiple points of view. More immediately they developed motifs such as the *figura serpentinata* that appears in the Medici Chapel along with a certain illogicality of architectural construction, or else drew upon the swirling volumes of Leonardo's *Leda and the Swan*. Only rarely were these motifs associated with the intensity and symbolic implication that led, when first conceived, to that deep relationship between form, technique and meaning which has been exemplified in the works of Michelangelo, Dürer and Titian. A piquant pleasure in wit and technical expertise – as in Cellini's Salt Cellar (Fig. 20) – was one prevailing feature of this art. But a certain cool attention to the frozen gestures of a passing age can be observed in Bronzino's great portraits (Fig. 61) while frissons and agitations may sometimes have been cultivated (as sometimes they are in the present postmodern age) as the conscious reflection of a decadent culture.

A comparison of Raphael's frescos from the *Heliodorus* Rooms of the Vatican with the work of his most gifted pupil (and the only artist to be mentioned by Shakespeare), Giulio Romano, indicates something of what it means to cultivate style for its own sake (Figs 62 and 63). Raphael's own career is itself an indication of how a native facility, responding to the experimental genius of artists such as Leonardo or Michelangelo, could then produce a genius of its own. Raphael does not deeply concern himself with the philosophical and scientific issues that animate the searching minds of his older contemporaries. But he understands *disegno* to the point of creating a sculptural balance of masses even in portraits such as his *Castiglione* (Fig. 1), where mass does not exclude *brio* in the curve and cut of Castiglione's hat. With the simplest of colours he can also create a harmonious orchestration of whites, greys and blacks – or else in the pinks and golds of his many *Madonnas* or the exhilarating swirls of red, skin-tones and washes of green-blue in the fresco *Galatea* in the Villa Farnese (1513). Line and colour can also combine (as in *The School of Athens*) to produce a remarkably classical evocation of the classical world. They can, however, also take flight towards a baroque future in paintings such the *Expulsion of Attila*, where – in effects that point forward from Leonardo towards Rubens – Attila's horse bucks and rears at the sight of the advancing Cross, while elongated angels advance from the vault with firm swords and agitated vestments.

It is a similar movement that Giulio Romano illustrates in *The Circumcision*. Giulio is if anything more notable as an architect than a painter – and among his works includes the pleasure palace at Mantua – the Palazzo del Tè – where a whole room, the so-called *Salon of the Giants* is given over to *trompe l'oeil* effects suggesting that the room itself is about to be dragged into ruins by labouring Titans. In *The Circumcision* the columns of the temple buck and cavort in a sinuous upward motion that recalls the pillars of the *baldacchino* in St Peter's, Rome, and also those that Raphael drew in his cartoon, *The Healing of the Lame Man*. Perspective matters less here than the swirl of the human dance in sympathy with these columns.

It would be possible to argue that a certain genetic connection exists between Giulio's work – where elongation, elegance and invention all combine – and Parmigianino's *Madonna with the Long Neck*, Bronzino's *Laura Battiferri* (Fig. 61) and on through Fontainebleau to Isaac Oliver's *Petrarchan Lover* (see cover), or even to the architecture of Hardwick Hall in Derbyshire ('more glass than wall') where vertical sheets of windows turn stone into light. Yet, if one applied these formulae prescriptively to all artists of the later sixteenth century, one would extinguish all sense of the originality and diversity that such freedom of manner could itself encourage. Three examples – drawn from Tintoretto, Holbein and El Greco – must here suffice to suggest – how great that range might be.

Figure 62 Raphael, *Expulsion of Attila*, 1513–14. Fresco, Stanza d'Eliodor, Vatican, Rome. With permission from Scala.

Figure 63 Giulio Romano, *The Circumcision*, 1520's. Panel, 111 × 122 cm. The Louvre, Paris. © photograph RMN – RG Ojeda.

In Tintoretto, we see a profound and on the whole successful desire to synthesize the achievements of Michelangelo and Titian while putting their example to wholly new use. Tintoretto ran a busy, even frenetic workshop which ensured an endless stream of productions often rough in finish but always experimental in form and vision. *The Last Supper* (one of many by Tintoretto) here illustrates (Fig. 64) a profound concern with the Eucharist – a matter of obsession in the Counter-Reformation period – while also displaying an attention to the lives of the servants who attend the miraculous event. There is an element of genre-painting and realism here. But the supposedly real world is shattered and suffused by the institution of the Sacrament and, correspondingly, by the stunning perspective in the representation of table and lozenged floor, by the effects of *chiaroscuro* and blinding light (round the lamp and Christ's head), by the rarefied painting of the angels in the right-hand corner. Estrangement – which is also recognition of a religious truth beyond any secular observation – is the emotion that Tintoretto here seeks to unleash; illusionistic painting here attempts to transform the world into a holy illusion.

Unlike Tintoretto, Holbein (born in Augsburg in 1497 or 1498; died in England in 1543) was perforce a traveller. Seeking profitable employment, he had been elected Chamber Master of the Painters' Guild of Basle in 1520, but had fled the city when it succumbed to the Protestant Reformation. He had by that time acquired a remarkable virtuosity which was to be demonstrated in all manner of visual arts, from the design of jewels to architecture for theatre and court. He had also a wide variety of styles at his command and a coolly searching eye for the many types of human dignity or folly. He is capable, for instance in his *Dead Christ* (Basle, 1521), of producing an image that showed acquaintance with the works of Grünewald – and was powerful enough attract the attention of Dostoevsky. Yet his colourism in the *Noli me Tangere* at Hampton Court has Venetian qualities reminiscent of Titian's painting of the same scene in 1512, while the Adam and Eve whom he depicted in *The Old Law and the New* (1535, National Gallery of Scotland) are clearly akin to Dürer's representation of these figures.

All of these qualities and affiliations proved their importance when in 1532, having unsuccessfully sought employment in Antwerp, Holbein returned to England, where he would work for the rest of his life. He arrived with letters of recommendation, addressed to Sir Thomas More, from Erasmus – for whose *Praise of Folly* he had provided marginal illustrations in 1515. Henceforth, Holbein was to pursue his career in the intensely urban environment of London; and his first paintings tended to be of German merchants at work there, as for instance in the portrait of *Georg Gisze* of Danzig of 1532 (Berlin, Staatliche Museum). But, in this peculiarly agitated period of English history, Holbein was soon to find himself at the centre of the circle of civil servants or royal advisors who were the main actors in this drama and developed a peculiarly observant but also detached way of representing its implications. He depicted Thomas More and his family, but also Robert Southwell who played an

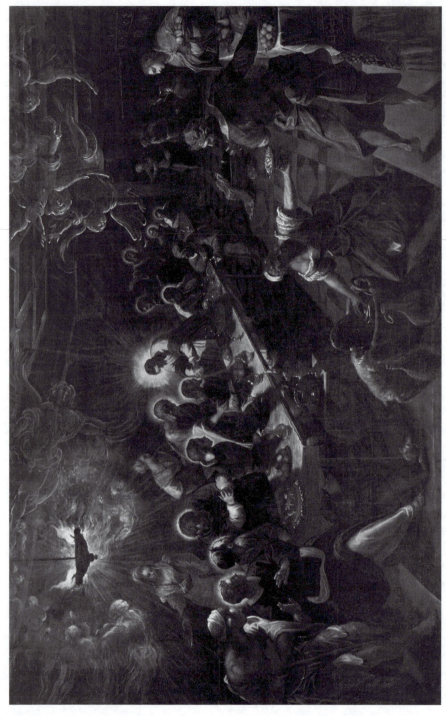

Figure 64   Tintoretto, *The Last Supper*, 1592–94. Canvas, 366 × 569 cm. Chancel. San Giorgio Maggiore, Venice. With permission from Scala.

important role in More's downfall. In *The Ambassadors* he shows two figures who coolly observe the onlooker in the seeming security of their social standing. Yet these figures are themselves observed with an equal coolness by the painter – and also by Death; for it is here that the painter introduces in a tour de force of perspectival illusionism a skull which can only be seen by those who know the secret that will reveal it. If Mannerism is style, then the stylishness of the courtiers is met with the dextrous stylishness of the artist who here introduces a *memento mori* as chilling as any of Grünewald's effects and as wittily melancholic as Hamlet's sense of the 'too, too sullied flesh'.

Somewhat ironically, it was on the strength of *The Ambassadors* that Holbein came to the notice of Henry VIII who recognized in it a talent that might allow him to vie in his own terms with the distinctly Mannerist court of Francis I. This brought Holbein into the vortex of the very Reformation that he had sought to avoid in leaving Basle. One result is the depiction of Henry as Solomon receiving the Queen of Sheba, which symbolizes the new subservience of the Church to the Crown (Fig. 18). Manneristic features are evident in the elegant treatment of architectural swirls and swags. But there is also a responsiveness to motifs of Tudor Gothic such as might also have been visible at Nonsuch where Holbein was employed on the design of Henry's now-lost palace. (Francis I of France would not have approved of so much gilding). The elegant and yet voluminous figures – with bright touches of fruit against the *grisaille* and muted gold – are also Manneristic. But the dominant figure is that of Henry himself who in an almost cartoon-like anticipation of later portraits combines power and eroticism in the swagger of the pose that Holbein has given him.

A series of royal portraits are associated with this phase of Holbein's career: the ill-fated depiction of Anne of Cleves; Prince Edward depicted as a child with a monkey but also with a very regal demeanour; the cold, pinched features of Jane Seymour posed against a background which accentuates her finery. But the underlying principles of Holbein's portraiture may be observed in his portrayal of the French envoy to London, Charles de Solier, Sire de Morette (Fig. 65) that echoes the familiar full frontal depictions of Henry VIII. The figure is cast against an unusual green background but wholly fills the frame. The skill in oil-painting is displayed by the glitter of daggers and the sheen along the kid-gloved left-hand. The coloration of the slashed sleeves with delicate stitches of gold has something in common with Bronzino's style, as does the overall effect of *gravitas*. But the originality that Holbein displays may best be seen by comparing his treatment of head and eye with Titian's handling of Aretino's pose in Figure 59. Titian's dynamism is here replaced by a solid human object that the viewer is compelled to encounter directly. There are no surges of energy within the picture frame. But between sitter and painter – as also between sitter, painter and viewer – there is an optical battle of wills, as if the one were called to outstare the other.

Figure 65 Hans Holbein, *Charles de Solier, Sire de Morette*, c.1534. Oil on wood 92.7 × 75.2 cm. Gemaldegalerie, Alte Meister, Dresden. AKG, London.

In this respect, too, Holbein's vision is wholly different from El Greco's, where serpentine lines spiral upwards – in frames which are usually narrow verticals – to the point of dissolving all fixity of viewpoint or any material sense of volume. Born Domenikos Theotokopoulos (he always signed himself in this way, in Greek characters) in Candia, Crete, El Greco (1541–1619) along with other Greek artists was drawn first to practise his art in Venice – at one time in the circle of Titian and Tintoretto – where he remained for ten years before moving to Rome and thence to Toledo in 1576. Manneristic qualities are immediately apparent in the elongation of line, the flouting of perspective; and in the great *Laocoön* of 1610–14 (Fig. 66), it is possible to measure how far El Greco has moved – even when his frame is horizontal

Figure 66   El Greco, *The Laocoon*, c.1610–1614. Oil on canvas, 138 × 172 cm. Samuel H Kress Collection, © 2002, Board of Trustees, National Gallery of Art, Washington.

and his subject classical – from the fundamental principles of Florentine classicism. The famous Hellenistic sculpture depicting the destruction of the sooth-sayer, Laocoön, and his sons is here transformed into a nervous Manneristic ballet. Toledo (representing the Troy of the legend) appears in the background, but is no part of any narrative or perspectival landscape. Coherence here comes from the idiosyncratic choreography of sinuous and discrete figures; the interest lies entirely in their sway and reptilian twist.

Though El Greco has here taken a pagan theme, the *Laocoön* parallels many works in which his Christian vision (very far from Alberti's cult of rational self-possession) is represented in a similar way. The early *Martyrdom of St Maurice* and the *Burial of Count Orgaz* (1586) may represent among the crowd illustrious men of Toledo. But their faces so far from showing any simple or recognizable grief are faces in a trance

Figure 67   El Greco, *The Holy Face*, c.1600. Oil on Canvas 71.2 × 55.3 cm. Prado, Madrid. With permission from Scala.

– dignified, receptive to forces beyond themselves. Likewise the colours that surround these black-robed figures are the brilliant, even virulent colours of a vision. So too in El Greco's portraits there are dangerous tensions, ranging from those expressed in the bespectacled Grand Inquisitor, Don Fernando Niño de Guevara, to the tilted yet composed energy of the Dominican Friar Hortensio Felix de Paravicino (1610 – who wrote an epitaph for El Greco's tomb (1600)) and is here seen as a composition in white and grey. In these portraits it is the eye that dominates, along with the 'winged hands' of which Unamuno speaks, both seeking something beyond material form, as if to dissolve the human outline.

In Toledo, it seems, El Greco discovered a repertoire of figure types which elicited from him a response which might have lain undeveloped in Venice and led him to envisage a hieratic but dynamic mode of spiritual theatre. In this respect, he responds to his time. For these images, in common with so many Catholic images in the Tridentine period, require from their viewer the same sort of devotional intensity as their subjects themselves display, as for instance in the representation of the Spanish *St Dominic Kneeling Before the Crucifix* (1595–1600) (Fig. 33), where against the striations of a lowering sky, the whole figure is animated by the contrasts that arise between glinting swathes of white and the matt-black of the cloak. But the Greek origins of El Greco are also alive in him. So, where we began this chapter with the iconic image of *Christ in Judgement* from the Baptistery in Florence, we may conclude with El Greco's portrayal of *The Holy Face* (*c*.1600). Here (Fig. 67) the features of Christ recall traditions more ancient than those of Florence or Venice and reveal a deep sensitivity to the iconic style of Byzantine art. Yet the insubstantial flutterings of the cloth on which the face is imprinted generate an impression of volume and movement which speaks equally of an apprenticeship to the whole development of Renais-sance art.

NOTES

Excellent and well-illustrated general introductions to Renaissance Art in Italy are to be found in Frederick H. Hartt, *A History of Italian Renaissance Art* (London, 1970), A. Chastel, *The Golden Age of the Renaissance* (London, 1965), George Holmes, *Renaissance* (London, 1996). For **Venetian Art**, see David Rosand, *Painting in Sixteenth-Century Venice* (Cambridge, 1997) and Johannes Wilde, *Venetian Art from*

Bellini to Titian (Oxford, 1974); Peter Humfrey, *Painting in Renaissance Venice* (London, 1994); Norbert Huse and Wolfgang Walters, *The Art of Renaissance Venice: Architecture, Sculpture and Painting 1460–1590* (London, 1990); Salvatore Settis, *Giorgione's Tempest: interpreting the hidden subject*, trans. Ellen Bianchin (London, 1991). For **Flemish Art**, see J. Białostocki, *Il Quattrocento nell'Europa settentrionale* (Turin, 1989) (from whom I quote Melancthon) and throughout Erwin Panofsky's great *Early Netherlandish Painting* (London, 1953); also James Snyder, *Northern Renaissance Art from 1350 to 1575* (New York, 1985). For issues raised in sections one, two and three, see John White, *The Birth and Rebirth of Pictorial Space* (London, 1957); M. Baxendall, *Painting and Experience* (Oxford, 1972); David Summers, *Michelangelo and the Language of Art* (Princeton, 1981) and *The Judgement of Sense* (Cambridge, 1987); John Gage, *Colour and Culture* (London, 1993). Above all, for questions both of history and of mimesis, see the incomparable studies of Ernst Gombrich, particularly in *Norm and Form: Studies in the Art of the Renaissance* (London, 1966) and in *Art and Illusion*; for a good defence of representational mimesis, see A.D. Nuttall, *The New Mimesis* (London and New York, 1983). For the philosophical arguments see Hilary Putnam, 'Fact and Value' in *Reason, Truth and History* (Cambridge, 1981), esp. p. 128 and 'The Craving for Objectivity' in *Realism with a Human Face*, ed. and introduced by James Conant (Cambridge MA and London, 1990). For **Alberti's On Painting**, see ed. by John R. Spencer (New Haven and London, 1956) from which I quote. Vasari is quoted here from *Vasari on Technique*, trans. Louisa S. Maclehose (New York, 1960): see also Leonardo da Vinci, *Treatises on Painting*, ed. A.P. McMahon (Princeton, 1956), 2 vols. For **Ghiberti** see R. Krautheimer, *Lorenzo Ghiberti* (Princeton, 1970). For **Donatello**, see the exceptional Bonnie A. Bennett and David G. Wilkins, *Donatello* (Oxford, 1984) and Charles Avery, *Donatello: An Introduction* (London, 1994). For **Rogier van der Weyden**, see Panofsky *op. cit.*, also Robert Genaille, trans. Leslie Schenk, *Flemish Painting from Van Eyck to Breughel* (Paris, 1954) and Martin Davies, *Rogier van der Weyden* (London, 1972). For **Michelangelo**, quotations are taken from Christopher Ryan (trans.), *Michelangelo: The Poems* (London, 1996); see also his *The Poetry of Michelangelo* (London, 1998); for biography see A. Condivi, *The Life of Michelangelo*, ed. H. Wohl (Baton Rouge, 1976) and Herbert von Einem, *Michelangelo*, trans. Robert Taylor (London, 1959) and Joachim Poeschke, *Michelangelo and his World* (trans. Russell Stockman) (Munich, 1992 and New York, 1996). For **Dürer**, see Jane Campbell Hutchison, *Albrecht Dürer: A Biography* (Princeton, 1990); Jan Białostocki, *Dürer and his Critics* (Baden-Baden, 1986). Peter Strieder, *Albrecht Dürer: Paintings, Prints and Drawings* (trans. Nancy M. Gordon and Walter L. Strauss) (New York, 1982); E. Panofsky, *The Life and Art of Albrecht Dürer* (Princeton, 1943) and Walter L. Strauss (ed.), *The Complete Engravings, Etchings and Drypoints of Albrecht Dürer* (Toronto, 1972). For **Titian** see D. Rosand, *Painting in Sixteenth-Century Venice* (Cambridge, 1997). For **Mannerism** see John Shearman, *Mannerism* (London, 1977), Linda Murray, *The Late Renaissance and Mannerism* (London, 1967), who speaks well of Holbein and of Spanish artists, and Franklin W. Robinson and Stephen G. Nichols Jr (eds), *The Meaning of Mannerism* (Hanover, New Hampshire, 1972). For **Raphael**, see Loren Partridge, *The Renaissance in Rome* (London, 1996); James Beck, *Raphael* (New York, 1976), R. Jones and N. Penny, *Raphael* (London, 1983). For **Giulio Romano**, see M. Tafuri (ed.), *Giulio Romano* (Cambridge, 1998). For **Tintoretto**, see Eric Newton, *Tintoretto* (London, 1952). For **Holbein**, see John Rowlands, *Holbein: the Paintings of Hans Holbein the Younger* (London, 1985).

chapter six

LYRIC, EPIC AND
PASTORAL

PETRARCHAN POSSIBILITIES

A notable effect of Renaissance humanism, with its enthusiastic emphasis on the acquisition of classical languages, was that, for almost a century, the energies of European poets were diverted away from the use of their native tongues. Dante's *Commedia* – which most twentieth-century poets considered the greatest poem of the modern era – had been written (between 1305 and 1321) in Florentine Italian; and Dante's *De Vulgari Eloquentia*, though written in Latin, had argued the case for the use of the vernacular in poetry. Chaucer (inspired not least by Dante's example) had produced at the end of the fourteenth century a massive, various and ambitious body of writing that drew upon the narrative traditions of France, Italy and the English regions while also employing a metropolitan form of English that formed the basis of the national language. France – North and South – had cultivated not only the great subtleties of Occitan literature but also a wealth of prose-poetry in the Romance tradition, as had the German writings of Gottfried of Strasbourg and Wolfgang von Eschenbach. Yet it was only at the end of the fourteenth century with Boiardo and Ariosto – writing between 1480 and 1530 – that the Italian vernacular began to revive and to display a renewed confidence. As for Spain, France and England, renewal begins only in the second and third decades of the sixteenth century, gathering momentum in a wave of experimentation that eventually produces Garcilaso de la Vega in Spain, the *Pléiade* in France and Shakespeare in England.

None of this need suggest that the period of humanist hegemony was altogether an impediment to vernacular aspiration. For one thing, just as visual artists learned a good deal about pose and drapery from classical sources, so acquaintance with an ever-widening range of classical texts opened the eyes of Renaissance poets to new stylistic and rhetorical possibilities and led them to expand the rhetorical resources of their native tongue. In literature as in the visual arts, imitation (or 'innurition') was a source of creative originality. Equally, a good deal of excellent – even original – verse was written by humanists in neo-Latin or sometimes in Greek, often in conjunction with vernacular experiments and sometimes in macaronic mixtures of Latin and vernacular. An example of macaronic verse is offered by Teofilo Folengo (1491–1544) whose *Baldus* was to influence Rabelais and Cervantes: An old man's clothes all fall off and the results are expressed in a mixture of dog-Latin and Mantuan dialect: *Concurrunt nudum vecchium guardare vilani. 'Day, day' cridabant, 'hay, hay, che cosa da rider!' Foeminae fazzae partem voltantur in altram.* (The bumpkins all rushed up to see the old man naked, yelling 'Di, Di, Hi, Hi, what a laugh!' The women turned their faces elsewhere.)

For all that, Latin (while remaining the language of science until the mid-sixteenth century and beyond) did not become the literary language of modern Europe. Some humanists expected that it would, as an elegant improvement on the Latin of the Medieval schoolmen. However, in resisting that expectation, vernacular poets claimed a certain independence from the humanist programme and even in some cases (Marot and Spenser are examples) married their humanist concerns to a vivid interest in the Medieval past. On the other hand, vernacular poets could not now simply re-attach themselves to the Medieval roots of their native cultures. They set themselves rather to explore a hinterland between the ever-more visible peaks of classical achievement and the oceans of Medieval mystery – finding ore in the former and flotsam in the latter – and forging for themselves in all the genres a new range of forms and styles.

In epic, for instance, a form developed, largely under the influence of Ariosto, in which Homeric and Virgilian models were fused with narratives of quest and adventure drawn from Medieval Romance. The invention of the Epic Romance aroused a certain resistance, particularly in the sixteenth century when humanist critics began to emphasize anew the canons of Aristotelian poetics – and thus prepare the way for seventeenth-century classicism. It was this development, as will be seen, that led Tasso to argue against the influence of Ariosto. But the epic romance – with all its Medieval connotations – remained, for Tasso as for others, the form in which ambitious poets now chose to work, responding to cultural and political changes that early humanists could never have anticipated. In Ariosto's hands, the genre may have expressed above all else the *sprezzatura* on which the courtly culture depended. But Tasso – exiled from court and confined for fourteen years in the Hospital of Sant' Anna as a suspected lunatic – could transform quest into crusade. His *Gerusalemme Liberata* describes the liberation of Jerusalem from Muslim dominion in the First Crusade. Simultaneously the poem explores and attempts to vindicate the inward agitations of his own overwrought personality. Similarly, the Portuguese poet Luis de Camões turns colonial enterprise into heroic and also missionary adventure when in *Os Lusiadas* he describes the journey of Vasco da Gama to Goa on the west coast of India. Edmund Spenser – choosing the same genre in *The Faerie Queene* – combines the national epic of the 'English gentleman' with an analysis of the moral psychology of the heroic mind.

A similar process, in which imitation leads to a transgression of classical norms and an investigation of contemporary concerns, emerges in the history of the pastoral. Pastoral writing – which often occurs as an interlude in the epic romance or as an expansion of the lyric form – looked back to the eclogues of Theocritus and Virgil and found in the classical representation of the Golden World a repertoire of myths that articulated some of the deepest concerns of the Renaissance mind. The great forward movements of Renaissance culture all derive their vigour from looking backwards; and the exploration of a Golden World satisfied that desire to discover archetypal origins that originally impelled the humanists to consolidate their relationship with the world of antiquity and to assert their command of origins – expanding in some cases beyond the familiar fields of nymphs and shepherds – to include, for instance, piscatorial pastorals. Whether concerned with sheep or fish, the pastoral reflects the interest in myth displayed by Renaissance philosophers such as Ficino. Yet the Golden World could also reveal the deficiencies of the present, and offer either an escape into another, imaginary world (as in the writings of Sannazaro and Guarini or in Francesco Colonna's *Hypnerotomachia*), or else provide a laboratory in which (as in the case of Sidney's *Arcadia*) the imagination could investigate philosophical, political and sometimes satirical possibilities.

It is, however, in the lyric that the issues at stake in the advance of vernacular literature were initially and most acutely articulated. Though, eventually, poets such

Figure 68   Piero di Cosimo, *Mythological Scene*, c.1510. Panel, 65.5 × 55.3 cm. National Gallery, London.

as Ronsard would draw directly on a wide range of classical lyrics, the earliest vernacular writings were poems in the lyric love traditions of Provence that by the late Middle Ages had penetrated to Northern France, Sicily, Catalonia and Germany. The theme that runs through all European literature from the twelfth century onwards to the twenty-first – distinguishing it from its classical antecedents – is the theme of love. Certainly in the poetry of the Renaissance, erotic love, love of God, love of glory and sometimes the desire to escape from the entanglement of all such desires are endlessly in contention, whether it be epic, pastoral or lyric. Ariosto's *Orlando Furioso* has already suggested as much. It is, however, in the poetry of Francesco Petrarca that the strands of this variegated fabric are first spun out.

In Chapter Two, Petrarch appeared as the founder of the philological interests of Renaissance humanism and a moral philosopher whose work anticipated those Augustinian questions concerning the inner self that were brought to their conclusion in the Protestant Reformation. It is consistent with Petrarch's humanist ambitions (though at odds with any Augustinian counsel of humility) that he should have expected his epic poem *Africa* to win him the laurel crown as the continuator of the classical tradition. He was indeed chosen as laureate by the Roman people in 1341. Yet the *Africa* (which Petrarch never finished) has remained largely unread, whereas his collection of lyric poems in Italian – concerned with the poet's unrequited love for Laura – was to become a model of theme, style and diction for all European poets in whatever genre throughout the fourteenth and fifteenth centuries.

Petrarch described his vernacular poems as *rime sparse* – 'scattered verses' – and the term is both self-disparaging and disingenuous. On the one hand (as compared with his *Africa*), these poems are offered merely as trifles, especially since the greater number of them are written in sonnet-form. Under Petrarch's influence the sonnet became the seemingly natural medium for the expression of amorous sentiment. Originally, however, the form had been devised at the beginning of the thirteenth century by poets at the Sicilian court of the Emperor Frederick II, where it was used as an epistolary channel through which poets could exchange brief thoughts – sometimes scientific in character – about the curious phenomenon that we now call love. Dante, though he wrote fifty or so sonnets, preferred the *canzone*, which was more complex than the sonnet in rhyme-scheme and rhetorical texture and could be used to address elevated themes of public interest, in politics, philosophy and ethics. Petrarch can write *canzoni* and often does. Yet in deliberately concentrating on the confessedly humble sonnet, he transforms what had once been a medium for debate within the Sicilian coterie into an instrument of intensely inward (and Augustinian) investigation, where sentiments, moral choices and the state of his own being are unceasingly at issue: 'If Love does not exist, then what is this I feel?' (*Rime Sparse*, CXXXII). Here – in a sonnet first translated into English by Chaucer – Petrarch defines his inner existence in terms of a phenomenon to which he can ascribe only hypothetical reality.

On the other hand, Petrarch's vernacular poetry is, in its own way (and almost by stealth) no less ambitious than the *Africa*. The evidence of manuscript drafts suggests that Petrarch returned repeatedly to these poems, refining the choice of word and the melodic flow, exploring simultaneously the nuances of word and of conscience. These poems, moreover, are not really 'scattered' at all but constitute rather a finely wrought collection in which image-patterns, verbal echoes and tonal contrasts are at every point brought to attention by the positioning of particular compositions. The architectonic aspect of the *Rime Sparse* was eventually to attract as much attention from Petrarch's most ambitious successors as did the poet's linguistic craft or his powers of intimate self-expression; and in the most obvious instances, the sonnet-sequence would become a form of sequential narrative. Narrative, however, is not for Petrarch as great a consideration as number symbolism and kaleidoscopic cross-reference. There are 365 poems in the *Rime Sparse*, with one further poem standing as an introduction. These poems, therefore, constitute a Poetic Year and – though they allude very distantly to events that took place over a period of some fifteen natural years – their ambition is to incorporate a fifteen-year span of moral and emotional experience within the frame of masterly artifice. Time is here arrested and transformed by art. So is it too in the liturgical year of the Church. Petrarch (a cleric) is aware of this. He is also aware – sometimes triumphantly, sometimes guiltily – that his own collection of poems, focusing on the heart-searchings of an earthly lover, provides a profane alternative to the Holy Days that the Church administers. His first encounter with Laura occurred at Passion-tide (*RS*, III): Was that providential? Or does it obscure the true workings of Providence?

There are many contradictions here – between the claims of the classics and those of the vernacular, between unremitting craft and emotional spontaneity, between the forms of love both sacred and human, between the sequences of time, natural, liturgical and artistic. Indeed contradiction itself is one of the central features of Petrarch's poetry. These verses, as a result of craft and technique, present an invariably melodious surface yet move in their depths continually between the affirmation and excoriation of self-hood. And nowhere does Petrarch show himself more conscious of this than in the sonnet he wrote, retrospectively, to appear as an introduction to the *Rime Sparse* – a poem that might equally stand as a prologue to all the poetry of Renaissance Europe:

Voi ch'ascoltate in rime sparse il suono

di quei sospiri ond'io nudriva il core

in sul mio primo giovenile errore

quand'era in parte altr'uom da quel ch'i' sono,

del vario stile in ch'io piango e ragiono,

fra le vane speranze e 'l van dolore,

ove sia chi per prova 'intender amore,

spero trovar pietà non che perdono.

Ma ben veggio or sì come al popol tutto

favola fui gran tempo onde sovente

di me medesmo meco mi vergogno

e del mio vaneggiar vergogna e 'l frutto,

e 'l pentersi, e 'l conoscer chiaramanete

che quanto piace al mondo è breve sogno.

(You who hear in scattered rhymes the sound of those sighs with which I nourished my heart during my first youthful error, when I was in part another man from what I am now: for the varied style in which I weep and speak between vain hopes and vain sorrow, where there is anyone who understands love through experience, I hope to find pity, not only pardon. But now I see well how for a long time I was the talk of the crowd, for which I am ashamed of myself often within, and of my raving, shame is the fruit and repentance and the clear knowledge that whatever pleases the world is a brief dream.)

Here a long sentence, sustained throughout the whole of the octet, displays a mind that has nourished itself on the periodic syntax of classical Latin. Likewise, the opening apostrophe, *Voi ch[e]* ... (though significantly addressed to an indeterminate audience) is drawn from the repertoire of classical rhetoric, as are the balanced but subtly varied adjectival constructions *vane speranze . . . van dolore*. Through innumerable instances of such 'innurition', Petrarch generates a sonority in his own vernacular that is Latinate but still entirely at one with the fluency of his native tongue. Petrarch's followers, feeding on such examples, will be encouraged to develop similar qualities in their own vernacular style. So too they will learn from Petrarch how the fourteen lines of a sonnet may be subdivided by rhyme and by the division of octet and sestet, to produce significant effects of sequence and contrast: the *Ma* (But) that opens Petrarch's sestet marks a shift from the epic grandeur of the opening line to a ruminative, inward perception – stressed by an obsessive emphasis on the first person pronoun, *di me medesmo meco mi vergogno* – that echoes with apprehensions of guilt and delusion.

In this introspective opening, no mention is made of Laura; and when she is mentioned in the *Rime Sparse*, there are only rarely references to her physical or historical being. Characteristically, Laura dissolves into a figment of the poet's own linguistic refinement. Petrarch puns endlessly on Laura's name as meaning 'breeze' (*l'aura*) or 'gold' (*l'oro*) or 'dawn' (*l'aurora*); and he is followed in this by all those Petrarchans who speak of their ladies as Light or Stars or, in Scève's case, as the 'Idea' that derives from the anagram *Délie–L'idée* (see pp. 239–40). For Petrarch, Laura is supremely the Laurel, the everlasting emblem of poetic triumph; and his thoughts – by virtue of the pun that her name invites – are as much about the love of literary 'laurels' as they are about his Lady. Notably in his *Secretum* Petrarch utters a scathing self-criticism that incriminates both his poetic aspirations and his own linguistic practices, confessing that the height of his delirium is that there is not one of his poems that does not include some allusion to 'Laura', now in one sense and now in another. Likewise, in the introductory sonnet – which casts its disconcerting implications over the whole of the coming sequence – Petrarch represents the poetic enterprise itself as a source not only of glory but also of guilt. By virtue of the very reputation that his *rime sparse* have won for him, the poet had become a *favola* – a fiction, a fable, a source of gossip. If 'Laura' is merely a delusive word, then the poet's own selfhood, despite his desire for utter sincerity of expression, is always marginal to and dependent upon the linguistic character of human existence – and words which are never contemporaneous with the sentiments they express are always likely to outpace him. In the twentieth century, we have come to understand how far human selfhood is a verbal construct, and recognize – at the risk of cliché – the extent to which 'we write ourselves'. Petrarch in his own Augustinian way acknowledges as much – offering his *Rime Sparse* not as a biography but rather as an instance of confessional practice, in which the self is observed in a process of constant adjustment towards the words it utters.

Petrarch on this understanding inaugurates a cultural movement in which words are the very element through which human nature pursues its true existence. The exhilarations and anxieties that Montaigne pursues in his *Essais* are already implicit in the opening sonnet of Petrarch's collection. Others poets too – such as Marot and Wyatt – will discover not only the pleasure of 'textual living' but also the reflexive need to write confessionally – as in the translations of the *Penitential Psalms* that punctuate their careers. In a similar way, when Sir Philip Sidney, introducing his own sonnet-sequence *Astrophil and Stella*, exclaims, ' "Fool," said my pen: "look in thy heart and write" ', he declares both a profound debt to Petrarch and also some of the resistance that Petrarch's example would stimulate, especially at the end of the sixteenth century. With Petrarch, the notion (or myth) of the heart as the centre of emotional identity begins to acquire particular importance; and the *Rime Sparse* encouraged Petrarch's followers not only to think of identity as an inward location but also to view the vernacular – precisely because of its marginality in respect to the public voice of Latin – as the natural language of the private self, akin to the language of sighs and, appropriately, the food of love. At the same time, the rhetorical conventions that Petrarch first formulates – often on the model of Latinate usage – themselves come to seem, through long habituation, an impediment to spontaneous utterance. If Petrarch delivered the vernacular from the bondage of Latin, who will deliver the vernacular from Petrarchism?

For the most part, however, the profound contradictions in the Petrarchan project are veiled beneath an elegance of diction that contributed to the growth of a distinctively Renaissance sensibility and directly assisted the advance of national vernaculars. When, for instance, an anonymous English poet translates the opening line of the *Rime Sparse* as 'You that in play peruse the plaint and read in rhyme the smart . . .', it is evident that early Renaissance vernaculars had much need of Petrarch's melodic example if they were ever to be released from the effects of crude alliterations and overemphatic metres. As to rhetoric, among the most familiar bequests of Petrarch to the European world is the oxymoron 'icy fire', expressing the contradictory passions of love, which rages 'like an epidemic' over Europe. A subtle example of this device is line 2, where the audience is asked to respond to insubstantial sighs that nonetheless 'nourish' the heart. Even if they rarely achieve a comparable finesse, musicians and madrigalists were no less impressed by such locutions than fellow-poets (see pp. 301). As to theme, Petrarch reveals not only an interest in Love but also in Fame, Time, Art and Beauty. The titles of Petrarch's vernacular *Trionfi* confirms this catalogue; and painters as well as poets were to follow his lead.

If in all these ways Petrarch establishes the thematic and stylistic registers of Renaissance poetry, so too he decisively marks himself off from the Medieval past. It was Petrarch who declared that he did not 'adore Aristotle' (see pp. 82–8). In a similar spirit, he recoils from the work of his great Florentine predecessor, Dante Alighieri. There can be no mistaking the debt that Petrarch owes to Dante's love-poetry. Yet Petrarch refuses to allow a copy of the *Commedia* on to his bookshelf, for fear, he says, that it might play on his mind. This is a clear case of what now would called the 'anxiety of influence'; and a full analysis of the differences between Dante's mentality and Petrarch's would include discussion of their attitudes to authorship, to Love and even to religious belief. But nowhere are these differences more apparent than in Petrarch's dissatisfaction with the stylistic models that Dante (along with other Medieval poets) has laid before him.

Words in Dante are used in utmost variety and with the utmost precision as if to leave a palpable mark on the political, moral and even physical universe: when Dante wishes to reveal how morally disgusting flattery must always be, he does not hesitate to depict a group of flatterers sunk in the *merda* or 'shit' of Hell. He is equally likely to describe the blesssed in Paradise as being like mill-wheels of light, grinding out the extremes of joy. It was this concreteness of reference – along with the wiry and argumentative intelligence that Dante displays in his three-line verses – that led twentieth-century poets, such as Pound and Eliot, to favour the Dantean rather than the Petrarchan model. For Petrarch certainly could not tolerate any such abrasiveness of word or phrase. (Nor would he have appreciated the words of Chaucer's feisty Alisoun: '"Tee hee," quod she and clapped the window to', or the passionate sensuality of the Occitan poet, Arnaut Daniel who wishes to be close to his mistress 'as finger is to finger nail'.) In his attempts to refine the Italian language and reveal its melodic possibilities, Petrarch seeks to evade any contact with the taste and textures of the physical world or of words that relate to that world. The result is a style dominated by abstractions or conventional formulae, by lists rather than specific description, by rhythmic rather than argumentative impulse.

A case in point is the sonnet which more than any other was to impress both the poets and the musicians of the High Renaissance:

> Solo e pensoso i più deserti campi
>
> vo mesurando a passi tardi e lenti
>
> et gli occhi porto per fuggire intenti
>
> ove vestigio uman la rena stampi.
>
> . . .
>
> sì ch'io mi credo omai che monti e piagge
>
> et fiumi et selve sappian di che tempre
>
> sia la mia vita, ch'è celata altrui;
>
> ma per sì aspre vie né sì selvagge
>
> cercar non so ch'Amor non venga sempre
>
> ragionando con meco, et io con lui.

> (Alone and deep in thought, I go measuring the most deserted fields with steps delaying and slow, and keep my eyes alert so as to flee from where any human footprint marks the sand. . . . So that I believe by now that mountains and shores and rivers and woods know the temper of my life, which is hidden from other persons; but still I cannot seeks paths so harsh or so savage that Love does not always come along discoursing with me and I with him.)

Here the self traverses a landscape with the heroic *gravitas* of an epic hero impelled also by the appetite for solitude that will characterize many a pastoral swain. Yet the journey does not lead home to Rome or Ithaca, nor do Petrarch's words engage, as Dante's narrative invariably does, with the particulars and details that are encountered on the way to a better world. The fields are denoted by an undifferentiated plural, as are mountains, shores, rivers and woods. People themselves appear as unspecified 'others' rather than as named individuals. Yet in all these respects, Petrarch's 'evasive' diction is an exact reflection of his sensibility and of the poetic temper he would instil into his Renaissance successors. His journey is one that takes him away from community and into the self – and also absorbs him into *melancholia*. Petrarch's world is one in which the mind must enter ever and again – sometimes with the utmost grace and triumphal success – a region designated by its own verbal creations and its own devotion to the cultivation of linguistic finesse.

When Shakespeare writes: 'My mistress' eyes are nothing like the sun . . .' (Sonnet 130) he displays something of the anti-Petrarchan tendency that by the late sixteenth century had come to demand a greater attention to the realities of human features and the recognizable or communicable effects of voice that had been dissipated by the diffusing veil of Petrarchan convention. These, of course, are tendencies that Shakespeare can pursue with particular intensity in his dramatic writing. Yet overall Shakespeare's *Sonnets*, as the last great example of the Renaissance lyric tradition, continue to display an unmistakably Petrarchan repertoire of themes. Time threatens our affections and values. But Art may provide in the 'monuments' it creates a miraculous salvation, so that 'in black ink my love may still shine bright' (Sonnet 65). On the other hand, a world of art may prove to be a weary world, trapped between the inevitability of linguistic conventions and the lover's need to make things new: 'Why is my verse so barren of new pride' (Sonnet 76). And a self constituted only of human words may know itself only in its own disintegration, as Shakespeare does when his baptismal name – 'Will' – becomes a flurry of puns, veering between moral and lubricious acceptations, denoting both moral freedom and sexual urge: 'Think all but one, and me in that one Will' (Sonnet 135).

Even in his plays (especially perhaps *Troilus and Cressida*; see pp. 360–3) Shakespeare is far from abandoning the Petrarchan realization that a human existence is lived between aspirations to private sincerity and the often-exhilarating but also melancholic exercise of public rhetoric. Indeed if (as this volume has suggested throughout) there are profoundly countervailing forces at work in the culture of the Renaissance, then this is in part because the national languages of Renaissance states – developing first in the lyric, epics and pastorals of the period – tended to replicate in the public forum the contradictions that are first perceptible in the private poetry of the *Rime Sparse*. Poetic achievements came to be regarded as significant indications of national glory and cultural prestige. At the same time, such affirmations were subject no less than Petrarch's poetry to anxieties of influence and effects of marginalization: Latin makes the vernacular feel small but is edged out by it; Italian literature casts a brilliant shadow over Spain, France and England until each nation in turn finds a language in which to enunciate its own characteristic claims.

Thus on the one hand, the skilful cultivation of the myths of personal identity, with all the conventions that support these myths, could produce an apparently confident affirmation of national pride. The Hungarian poet Balossi fights against the

Turk on the furthest borders of European territory (carrying with him an admiration for the work of the Scottish humanist, George Buchanan) as does the Spanish poet Garcilaso in his involvement in the military crusades of the Castilians or, in further fields still, the Portuguese Camões; and each is subsequently canonized by his nation as if war and writing could be viewed as comparable modes of patriotic endeavour at a point of intersection (and reciprocal corroboration) between person and nation.

On the other hand, poetry is always likely to rediscover and voice its own marginality. It is for this reason that some of the most impressive poets of the Renaissance are women. Some write within the conventions constructed by their male counterparts. Others turn the gender margin into a place of profound and original insight. We have already seen this, considering the case of Marguerite of Navarre (pp. 132–4). And Marguerite is not alone. Others such as Vittoria Colonna work in a similar region of courtly evangelism with a freedom of understanding that, in Colonna's case, won the admiration of Michelangelo. Members of the Lyonnaise coterie such as Pernette du Guillet and Louise Labé stood alongside their male counterparts. The courtesan Veronica Franca was unquestionably a poet, and the Jewish literary patron Sara Copio Sullam managed to run a salon in the Venetian ghetto in defiance of all the sumptuary laws that circumscribed her activities.

Turning now to examples, we shall discover, even in the male poets who provide these examples, that the very act of writing will often uncover inclinations and strains that their public fame might encourage readers to ignore.

THE LYRIC: PASSION AND PENITENCE

Petrarchism, a hundred years after Petrarch's death, became an important factor in courtly culture, exerting an influence over artistic ambition and taste while contributing particularly (as Chapter Eight will show) to the development of the madrigal. In Florence, Lorenzo de' Medici himself wrote verses, in one case declaring that 'shaded woods, rocks, the mountains, dark caves' and the odd wandering nymph are all much to be preferred to 'pomp and high honours'. 'Il Magnifico' here creates for himself the *persona* of a would-be shepherd; and linguistically – in its list of unspecified locations – the poem displays the Petrarchan inclination to evasion, opening a 'wish-space' that stands as a rhetorical and imaginative alternative to the world of political reality. Others in his court – such as the humanist Poliziano in the *Caccia* and the *Orfeo* – provided similarly magical mirrors for the courtly mind, anticipating the elegant pastoralism that flourishes, for example, at Fontainebleau.

At court, the esteem that poets enjoyed stood as a plausible alternative to the immortal laurels that Petrarch longed for. The Ferrarese poet Antonio Tebaldeo (1463–1537) may – like Petrarch – have thought most highly of his own Latin works, as for instance his *Orphei Trageodie*, composed in the wake of Poliziano's *Orfeo*. But Lucrezia Borgia was his patron at Ferrara, as was the Medici Pope Leo X in Rome; and Ariosto eulogistically proclaims that Tebaldeo – who composed some 283 sonnets – has eclipsed Petrarch himself (*OF*, XLII, 83).

In Tebaldeo's vernacular works, antithesis and oxymoron are already familiar features of the lover's rhetoric: *In ghiaccio cerco fiamma in foco gielo*: 'In ice I seek flame; in fire the frozen'. But replacing the subtle articulations and qualifications that are generated in Petrarch's own sonnets by metrical divisions and the interplay of octet and sestet, Tebaldeo prefers a linear crescendo of effects. Simultaneously, he simplifies the nuances of Petrarch's moral concern, to produce (in one of his most influential poems) a resonant and teasing statement of the *carpe diem* theme – 'gather ye rose-buds' – which Petrarch himself would never have countenanced:

> Tu puoi quel ben, che mai non se ristora,
>
> Goder, e donar vita a un corpo morto

(You can enjoy the good that never will return and give back life to a dead body.)

Similar comments apply to the work of Serafino d'Aquila whose death at the age of thirty-four in 1500, aroused public demonstrations of emotion at the loss of a 'seraphic' genius. (It was in this period that painters such as Raphael and Michelangelo were also being celebrated as 'angelic' and 'divine'.) Serafino elicits from Petrarch's example an exquisite playfulness – or conceited preciosity – which, as with Tebaldeo, substitutes a surface brilliance for a reflexive awareness of authorial process. In Sonnet XLIII, Serafino chides his Lady's fan for making her cooler towards him than she already was. In Sonnet LXXXI, Cupid has made the mouth of the Lady a prison for her lovers; but when she loses a tooth this is a mercy, allowing a little light to fall on those who are imprisoned within.

In the visual arts, Petrarchan 'grace' comes to be associated with the virtuoso display of *sprezzatura*. So too in verse, where the artistic *persona* is applauded as a true courtly identity displayed in the melody or brilliance of word-play – the more so when it answers to a taste for a 'stylish style' that Mannerism encourages (see pp. 210–13); as will appear, the madrigalist Gesualdo writes a ballad, if not to his mistress's eyebrow, then to the mole that marks her lip.

In certain of the greatest writers of the Sixteenth Century – Tasso in Italy, Donne in England – the increasingly precious tendencies of lyrical rhetoric reveal their own exploratory possibilities in the cultivation of new forms (or fashions) of sensibility. An example is Michelangelo's investigation of the melancholic possibilities of shadow, in a poem that is clearly connected to his lines concerning the Medici Chapel (see p. 196): night in one poem may be seen as 'more sacred than day'; in another its fragile powers can be threatened by the light from a single glow worm: *vedova scura in tanta gelosia/c'una lucciola sol gli può far guerra*: desolate, dark so fragile that a single firefly can wage war on it (Ryan, *op. cit.*, 103 and 101).

At the same time, lyric poetry demonstrated the subtlety of which vernacular rhetoric was capable and in Italy, as later in all European countries, generated confidence in the development of national languages. The Italian case is most influentially represented by Cardinal Bembo (1470–1547).

In his own lyric poetry, conscious of Petrarch's original example and of the tenets of good taste, Bembo (who appears as a character in Castiglione's *Il Cortegiano*) seeks to restrain some of the shriller effects of manneristic Petrarchism. Brilliance displayed through clarity is the hallmark of his style. The familiar notions of amorous bondage are rendered with syntactical and metrical fluency and a harmonious attention to the synaesthetics of sound and light:

Quel dolce suono, per cui chiaro s'intende

Quanto raggio del ciel in voi riluce.

(That sweet sound through which, in all clearness, is understood how great is the heavenly ray that shines forth in you.)

There is scarcely a word in Bembo's writing that could not be found in Petrarch's; indeed, Bembo's diction displays an even higher degree of 'evasiveness' than Petrarch's own. These, however, are now the qualities that Bembo establishes as a norm for all Italian writers. Bembo himself surpassed most of the humanists of his day in his command of Latin and Greek. He also gave considerable attention to the early manifestations of vernacular writing in the Medieval Occitan poetry of Provence. Nonetheless, in his dialogues, the *Asolani*, he takes up a project that Dante had begun in the *De Vulgari Eloquentia* to define a form of the Italian tongue that will be 'purer and better ordered than even the language of the Provencals'. Lyric poets are themselves to be the national leaders. Petrarch in verse and Boccaccio in prose have established the prestige of literary Florentine. Italian writers should now be as confident in imitating them as in imitating the classics.

Bembo's writings remotely anticipate those interests in the regularization of the vernacular that will re-emerge in the French *Pléiade* and eventually in such academies pledged to the defence of the vernacular as the *Académie Française* and the Florentine *Della Crusca*. Resistance to uniformity was also displayed by comic poets such as the Francesco Berni (?1497–1535) – who displayed a propensity for lewd puns on the subject of eels. However, at a time when national identities were in the process of being formed, academicism – and even Petrarchan ideals of refinement and evasiveness – acquired a political implication in addition to the ethical significance that the cultivation of a courtly *persona* at its most Petrarchan could imply.

This is nowhere more apparent than in the development of Spanish literature. Spain, galvanized by its contest with Moorish overlords, had developed a national and linguistic identity far earlier than France, England or even Italy (which ultimately had to return to the issue during its Reunification in the nineteenth century). Thus, Catalan or Portuguese authors (such as the great dramatist and lyricist, Gil Vicente) could write by choice in the language of Castilian Spain. Moreover, while Imperial Spain proved to be triumphant in the sixteenth-century invasions of Italy, its very acquaintance, as military victor, with the cultural achievements of the Italian courts appears to have induced a brooding sense of inferiority into its cultural make-up. This sentiment persisted for centuries and may account, in a European perspective, for many of the subtlest features of Spanish literature, always European but always on the margins, always aware of, yet always suspicious of its own greatness. By the 1530s, however, Spain had found the opportunity to celebrate a cultural hero in the figure of Garcilaso de la Vega (1503–36), who spent most of his life as a soldier in Spanish Naples, sometimes venturing forth to fight against the French or the Turks. In Naples, Garcilaso developed a close relationship with the founding father of Italian pastoral poetry, Jacopo Sannazaro (1457–1530); and (as will be seen in the concluding section of this chapter) some of Garcilaso's greatest poetry was written in the pastoral genre. Yet when Garcilaso (like Sir Philip Sidney) died an early death, on a military campaign against the French, he was quickly elevated to the position of a cultural emblem. Applauded as the cynosure of the courtly arts that Italians such as Castiglione could teach, he was at the same seen to exemplify a perfect union of military and literary endeavour in the interests of Hispanic glory. Henceforth (in a crescendo that eventually produces the comedy of Cervantes's *Don Quixote*) the possible combination of Literature and Arms was to be one of the great preoccupations of Spanish poetry.

Garcilaso's standing also stimulated literary critical reaction, particularly from Fernando de Herrera (1534–97), who – while providing a peculiarly attentive commentary on Garcilaso's lyrics – was also concerned to designate a place for his own poetic style in the developing canon of the Spanish tradition. Garcilaso and Herrera both admit a debt to Petrarch. But each draws from Petrarch's poetry his own distinct nuance. Garcilaso strengthens the suggestion that lyric poetry can invoke a personal voice and presence – frequently sounding an erotic note that Petrarch himself would never have allowed. Herrera, by contrast, tends to cultivate rhetorical richness, intensifying both voice and visual effect in a manner that leads him away from Garcilaso's sphere of sensation and private voice towards the stage of heroic public affairs (as, for instance, in his *Lament for the Defeat of the Portuguese at Alcazarquivir*). Thus Garcilaso in his sonnet '*Estoy en lagrimas banado . . .*' subtly combines a reading of both '*Voi ch'ascoltate . . .*' and '*Solo e pensoso . . .*' (as well as '*Una candida cerva . . .*') to produce a poem in which the poet explores his own dependence on the emotional atmosphere that arises from the attention – or lack of attention – shown to him by his mistress. The loneliness of Garcilaso's landscape seeks to be filled by lights and airs that emanate from her and from her alone; and his sighs appeal not to an audience of poetic connoisseurs but directly to the Lady who has plunged him into this obscure region by her utter lack of concern:

> Y sobre todo, fáltame la lumbre
>
> de la esperenza, con que andar solia
>
> per lo oscura región de vuestro olivido.

> (Above all, the light of hope fails me, by which I used to travel through the dark region
>
> of your oblivious disregard.)

In contrast to the delicate modulations that characterize Garcilaso's verse, Herrera looks for an elevation in his poetry, sometimes adopting the gestures of Neoplatonic ecstasy, sometimes concentrating on the richly embellished images that in the later sixteenth century became characteristic of the Catholic Reformation. His sonnets can speak to a lady who illuminates the mind of the lover with divine love: *Serena Luz, en quien presente espira/divino amor* . . . : 'Serene Light, in whose presence divine light breathes'. Or else he strives to deepen the mental perception with rich adjectival embossments and rhetorical tropes, as in the second quatrain of the same sonnet:

> ricos cercos dorados, do se mira
>
> tesoro celestial d'eterna vena:
>
> armonia d'angelica Sirena,
>
> qu'entre las perlas i el coral respira.

> (Rich, golden tresses where one sees celestial treasure from an eternal source; harmonies
>
> of an angelic Siren which breathes amid pearls and coral.)

Garcilaso maintains the courtly moderation recommended by Castiglione and Bembo; Herrera points forward to the linguistic amplitudes and excesses that characterize the Baroque poetry of Góngora. It is, however, a third, earlier and less celebrated poet, Juan Boscán (1487/92–1542) who illustrates most clearly the linguistic and moral issues that are involved in the dissemination of the Petrarchan tradition.

Boscán was a close friend of Garcilaso and responsible (along with his own wife) for the publication of Garcilaso's poetry, accompanying it with a theoretical account of how, by accepting the example of Italian lyric poetry, Spanish poetry could itself achieve greater refinement, particularly in regard to metrical form – where an Italianate lightness of stress (foreshadowing Garcilaso's interest in Italian verse-forms) outraged those who remained faithful to the 'manly' emphases of earlier Spanish metrics. But Boscán himself was a Catalan, much influenced by the Catalan poet, Ausias March – and hence by a tradition that had remained peculiarly open to the language of the Medieval lyric, as represented by the troubadours and the Florentine *stil novo*. In this perspective, Boscán's poetry reveals a marked sensitivity to the problematic relationship between identity and writing that Petrarch had bequeathed to his Renaissance successors. Notably in his *canzoni* – a form that enjoyed especial prestige in the eyes of the troubadours and Dante – Boscán can regularly conclude (as Dante does, but Petrarch rarely will) with a formal *envoi* in which the poem itself is counselled to go out into the world, as though it were rhetorically and linguistically independent of the poet's personal presence. But, as it goes, the poem leaves the poet, now that he has delivered himself of words, in a state of empty being. The self, glorying in words, is also at the mercy of words.

On the other hand, Boscán realizes, as few early Petrarchans do, that Petrarch's *Rime Sparse* need to be read as a collection, and attempts ambitiously to write a sequence of his own, as if no single sonnet could ever be complete in its own self but always formed (intertextually) the beginning of another. The outcome is a series of poems which – concentrating less upon visual impact than upon rhythmic line and verbal restraint – displays a constant sensitivity to the problematics of conclusions and new beginnings; here, the poet's identity resides as much in the gaps between his poems as in the cadences of emphatic closure. So in a *canzone* which shows an awareness of Petrarch's '*Nel dolce tempo . . .*' and also of his '*Lasso non so in qual parte mi pieghi . . .*', Boscán, realizing how far from 'quiet' a writer must always be, writes: '*Hablare, por no starne como stoy . . . .*' making speech synonymous with restlessness of being.

Any rebirth – any renaissance – requires a certain rending and division. Later poets may disguise that truth. But Boscán insists that the lacerations should be visible: *Las llagas que de amor son invisibiles,/Quiero como visibiles se presenten* (Sonnet II). The condition of readership (in Boscán's version of Petrarch's opening sonnet) is that the reader must wander among these written wounds, seeking to establish their depth and significance: *O! vosotros que andais tras mis escritos/Gustando leer tormentos tristes . . .* (Sonnet I).

Turning to France, the characteristic factors of Renaissance poetry – linguistic and moral self-consciousness, cultural patriotism and an acute awareness of the strains that arise between tradition and innovation, convention and personal affirmation – come into play once again. Here, though, they are formulated according to a particularly confident theoretical programme. In 1549, Joachim du Bellay (1522–60), collaborating with Pierre de Ronsard (1524–85), published his *Défence et illustration de la langue françoyse* in which he makes a set of proposals for the renewal of the French literary language. Du Bellay (anticipating Sidney's *Defence of Poetry*) ascribes to poetry a patriotic function and develops an elevated conception of the poet himself as a philosopher or prophetic seer. This manifesto led to the formation of the *Pléiade*, the first of many avant-garde movements that were subsequently to enliven French culture. Ronsard in particular (endowed with a high sense of his own prestige) draws as much upon the sophisticated Neoplatonic conceptions of art developed in fifteenth-century Italy as upon Petrarchan models; and in practice (as will appear) he directly appeals to a wide variety of classical models. Yet, in pursuing such a renewal, Ronsard also distances himself with some aggression from an earlier moment in the French Renaissance represented by the court poetry of the age of Francis I and particularly by the writings of Francis's court poet, Clément Marot. For where Ronsard (living through the Wars of Religion) combined cultural chauvinism with a fervently political Catholicism, the earlier phase of the French Renaissance not only maintained a linguistic and cultural relationship with the Medieval past but also began to explore the intellectual possibilities of the Protestant Reformation. Notably Marot took a particular interest in the writings of the fifteenth-century poet, Villon.

Marot was closely associated with the circle of Marguerite of Navarre (see pp. 132–4); and a sensibility akin to Marguerite's displays itself in a mind that combines religious conscience with an extraordinarily wide range of vernacular experimentations. Like Juan Boscán, Marot came from the margins of the national culture – from Cahors where Occitan traditions still retained some currency. Indeed in his biographical prison-poem, *L'Enfer* (lines 395–6), Marot describes how, at the age of ten he was transported to 'France', and – forgetting his 'maternal language' – learned the 'paternal' language that was esteemed at Court.

His success at the court encouraged his vigorously original forays into panegyric, satire, epigram, nonsense-poetry, *coq-à-l'âne* and soft pornography. Yet, in his association with the courtly evangelism of Marguerite's circle, Marot also learned the meaning of exile and imprisonment; and his own religious writings, particularly his translation of the *Psalms*, not only impressed Calvin and added a significant dimension to the development of French vernacular style but also expressed a continuing understanding of his own marginality.

Marot was inclined to pun on his own name, drawing attention to himself as a French descendant of Virgilius *Maro*. Compared with the *Pléiade*, Marot may not have cultivated the programmatic concern with classical literature that supposedly characterizes the Renaissance mind. But classical influences are registered as easily in his poetry as those that flow from Medieval or vernacular origins. At the same time, Marot's pun alerts one to questions of conscience and identity that traverse all his writing and connect him to the Petrarchan tradition. So in '*De Soy mesme*' he writes:

Plus ne suis ce que j'ay esté,

Et ne le sçarois jamais estre;

Mon beau printemps et mon esté

Ont fait le saut par la fenestre.

(I am no longer that which I have been and do not know how I ever shall be. My lovely

springtime and summer too have both leapt out of the window.)

As with Boscán and Petrarch himself, these lines acknowledge and contemplate the fissures that arise in any supposedly unitary being when it begins to contemplate the dependencies of Love, the effects of Time and the problems inherent in Writing itself – though the ruefully comic or colloquial bathos in line 4 would probably not have appealed to Petrarch. Moreover, 'De Soy mesme' stands merely as the first of three epigrams in which the poet re-adjusts his attitudes to time and division over the temporal divisions of the sequence itself. Similarly, Marot can attack the question of whether he is a Lutheran or not – or whether he has eaten pork in Lent – without any real sense that verbal definitions will ever finally decide the matter, and indeed with an ironic understanding of how shiftingly ambiguous words and rhetoric must always be. (The result is that scholars are still debating, to little purpose, whether Marot did or did not have a taste for bacon or whether he was or was not a fully accredited Lutheran.)

Marot (especially when compared to the poets who belong to the ambitious and sophisticated *Pléiade*) is in many ways an easy, even transparent poet, shifting from one rhetorical level to another, and always ready to engage with the classics even while favouring the lower registers of poetic diction. Yet to speak only of ease and transparency would be to underestimate the extent to which Marot (in common with Dante and Chaucer) embodies a certain suspicion of rhetoric and would equally lead one to ignore the subtle play between accomplished utterance and the silences that speak in the margins of any written text. Marot's nonsense-poems reverberate with abundant rhythms that all but evacuate the closures that literal meaning apparently imposes. Epigrams stimulate a silent but risky suggestiveness beyond the confines of conventional expectation: if the eyes of Shakespeare's mistress are 'nothing like the sun', then Marot – claiming Marguerite of Navarre as his mistress – can declare epigrammatically that he is the servant of the strangest of 'monsters', an androgyne with 'a woman's body, the heart of a man and head of an angel':

Que je suis serf d'un monstre fort estrange:

Monstre je dy, car pour tout vray, elle a

Corps feminin, cueur d'homme et teste d'ange.

A similar play of verbal abundance and attentiveness to linguistic limit appears in Marot's most subtle responses to Petrarch and also in his vernacular versions of the *Psalms*. Though Marot translates a series of Petrarchan sonnets (1539), the following verses are in *rondeau* form and also display a continued adhesion to the repetitions and phonetic parallelisms of the 'Great Rhetoricians' of the age of Marot-*père*:

> En espérant, espoir me desespére
>
> Tant que la mort m'est vie très prospere;
>
> Me tormentant de ce qui me content
>
> Me contenant de ce qui me tourmente
>
> Pour la douleur du solas que j'espére.

> (In hoping hope takes hope away from me so that to die is pure prosperity. Tormenting myself with that which gives me happiness, happy at what torments me still, in pain for the solace I hope for still.)

Marot-*fils* – drawing directly on such influential examples of 'contradiction' as Petrarch's '*Pace non trovo e non ho da far guerra . . .*' – creates here a form of aural prison: bars are constituted out of lexical repetition and the internal rhyming of participles (which themselves designate unrelievedly continuing conditions); and hope lies beyond language in the silences of death that only religious awe can contemplate. It is this same understanding that Marot pursues in his translation of the *Psalms*. These poems are introduced by an address (extraordinarily free of moral bombast) to the Ladies of France, whose bodies, being the temples of love, may now echo to 'a love that does not torment the heart'. Beyond the inevitable conventions of love-poetry there may, it seems, be a language – which is no language at all – where in the freedom of undetermined presence we encounter the truly infinite. Petrarch had begun to realize this in concluding the *Rime Sparse* with a hymn to the Virgin Mary. Marot – displaying a more fully developed Protestant sensibility – abandons himself in the act of translation to the inspired yet almost anonymous words of the psalmic tradition. With all the *gravitas* of his plain style – Marot evokes a landscape that is re-made in the eye of its original Creator and illuminated by the abandonment of all hopes save a single hope in an utterly single God. In this perspective the mountains skip like lambs (as if in a religious version of the familiar 'world-turned-upside-down' motif). But beyond all contradictions there is the surety that only a leap into the insecurities of religious sentiment can reveal:

> Car Seigneur, ta bonté l'ordonne
>
> et elle seule espoir me donne
>
> Que seur et seul regnant seray.
>
> (*Psalm* IV)

> (Lord your goodness ordains it, and that alone gives me hope that reigns certain and alone for ever.)

In terms of purely religious poetry, France will eventually produce Guillaume du Bartas (1544–90) and his Huguenot epic on the Days of Creation which influenced Tasso in *Il mondo creato* and John Milton's *Paradise Lost*. However, on the way, to works such as these and also to the Catholic *Pléiade* is the poetry of Maurice Scève (1500?–60), an author who has the reputation of being as recondite and difficult as Marot is easy.

Working in Lyons – a southern city peculiarly open to Italian influence – Scève's writing displays a high degree of philosophical ambition, especially in his own account of Creation, *Microcosme*, inspired by an acquaintance with Italian Platonism and Sperone Speroni's dialogues. He also writes within a Lyonnaise coterie that includes a notable number of women intellectuals, among them Scève's poetic Lady Pernette du Guillet (1520?–45) and Louise Labé (1524–66). Within this circle, Petrarchism thrived, as did a remarkably strong sense of the visual culture of Italy. It was Scève who supposed that he had discovered the tomb of Petrarch's Laura in Avignon and who orchestrated an architecturally sumptuous Entry into Lyons for Henri II. The result of such Italophilia in Scève's lyric sequence *Délie* (written in *dixaines*, not sonnet-form) that involves a haunting cultivation of enigma, atmospheric mysteries and visual suggestion, and displays a similarity to Michelangelo's poems in its attention to the antitheses of darkness and light and appealing to the heightened taste of an intellectual coterie. For example, only an educated and knowingly sophisticated sensibility could be expected to appreciate the dream-like swing in the following lines between a crouching hare and a backdrop of Egyptian mysteries:

> Car dès le poinct, que partie tu fus,
>
> Comme le Lievre accroppy en son giste,
>
> Je tendz l'oreille, oyant un bruyt confus,
>
> Tous esperdu aux ténèbres d'Egypte.
>
> (For from the time you left me like the hare crouching in its hide, I sharpen my ears hear-
>
> ing a confused sound, all lost in the shadows of Egypt.)

or else to respond to the rich evocations of myth and exotic reference that allows Scève to represent his Lady as a 'Cedar-tree', which alone can remedy the 'poison' that she herself, as a Serpent, has instilled in the lover:

> Tu m'es le Cèdre encontre le venin
>
> De ce Serpent en moy intention.

Marot may be said have brought to fruition many of the possibilities inherent in the language of fifteenth-century French and employed them all to generous effect, without any inclination to purify or regularize their character. Scève seeks a language verging on the hermetic – and may indeed have organized *Délie* on the principles of mystic numerology. Correspondingly, the *Pléiade* proposes that poetry in its learned character – as the child of humanism, possessed of secret, even magical powers – should commit itself to the salvation of national culture.

Du Bellay, less learned than Ronsard, also registers an understanding which he may share with Spenser (who imitates his French predecessor in *The Ruines of Rome*) and even with Shakespeare that at the very moment in which we create an artistic monument we expose all we value to erosive currents of Time, Envy and Fortune. In the *Regretz* IV, Du Bellay declares how little he himself wishes to follow the examples of the Greeks or Horace, still less to 'imitate the grace of Petrarch' or even the voice of Ronsard. Moved by no other argument than passion, he has not undertaken to imitate in this book

> Ceulx qui par leurs escripts se vantent de revivre
>
> Et se tirer tous vifs dehors des monuments.

> (Those who boast of how through their writings they will live anew and draw themselves
>
> living from their tombs.)

Du Bellay may allude here to Horace's enduring work (*Odes*, III, 30). But he abdicates on his own account the ambition to be any sort of literary monument beyond the point of his own death. Anxieties, even embarrassments, such as these became increasingly visible in all the arts as the Renaissance in the late sixteenth century entered the melancholic shadow-phase of its existence. Rome itself – which Du Bellay visited in 1533 – may inspire the newcomer to emulate the ancient example but also reminds us that culture itself is little more than a verbal re-duplication echoing in the cavernous ruins of its own monumental past. In the following lines one notes the rhetorical duplications of the very word 'Rome' and a sonorous yet dying rhyme, that gradually evaporates from *nomme* to *comme* to *consomme*:

> Nouveau venu, qui cherches Rome en Rome
>
> et rien de Rome en Rome n'aperçois,
>
> Ces vieux palais, ces vieux arcz que tu vois
>
> Et ses vieux murs, c'est ce que Rome on nomme.
>
> Voy quel orgueil, quelle ruine: et comme
>
> Celle qui mist le monde sous les loix,
>
> Pour donter tout, se donta quelquefois,
>
> Et devint proye au temps, qui tout consomme.

> (Newcomer seeking Rome in Rome, in Rome seeing nothing of Rome, these ancient
>
> palaces, these ancient arches that you see, these old walls, that is what is known as Rome.

Look at the pride, the ruin; and how the One – who set the world beneath her laws in power over all – falls to power and becomes the prey of time that all consumes.)

In Ronsard's extraordinarily varied and fluent writings, there is rarely any comparable sense that the artistic enterprise may itself be complicit with the flux of time – despite an interest in the poetic evocation of cloudy shiftings. One reason is that Ronsard displays a profound affinity with the essentially theatrical world of cultural politics that underlies, as we have seen, a court such as that of Fontainebleau. A second is that he perseveres in the confident claim that poetry can be an instrument of philosophic or magical insight into truths that transcend the mutabilities of the temporal world.

Thus, on the one hand, his work (in common with Herrera's) is marked by a vividly visual illusionism in which words histrionically claim to evoke the real presences of the historical figures that he is privileged (or is the privilege theirs?) to meet in imaginative space. When asked to write an epic on the history of France – governed by fact and historical sequence – Ronsard proved no more successful in his *Françiade* than Petrarch in his *Africa*. Nonetheless, he could still put the skills of lyrical rhetoric to courtly and political purpose. So Mary Stuart, Queen of the Scots may leave the shores of France. She may indeed be 'beyond the power of the Muses, let alone of poets to describe' but Ronsard offers to spin around the very moment of her departure an evocation of her presence (as if her image could hear it) spun from the rhetorical strands of adjectival accumulation: the 'white ivory' of her breast, a hand, 'long, fine and delicate', a lovely waist, that seems to be the portrait of an angelic image: *Qui ressemble au portrait d'une celeste image* ... (29–32). A similar command of rhetorical resources allows Ronsard (at the behest of Catherine de' Medici) to write a sequence of his most adroit verses to the ill-favoured Hélène, who – while sitting by the fire in Sonnet XXIV – will sing Ronsard's verses, marvelling that he should ever have lauded her in the years of her supposed beauty. Here love becomes, as Sonnet XXX declares, a *beau ballet* and Ronsard's own poetic dance is, self-confessedly, designed to reveal the elegance of his own courtly ankle. Even when he descends into the depths of his own dying or insomniac self, it is as if he had entered the grottoes of Fontainebleau, to reveal with a manneristic urbanity the interestingly gruesome hollows of the Renaissance ego, as in Sonnet I of his posthumous verses:

Je n'ay plus les os, un squelette je semble,
Decharné, denervé, demusclé, depoulpé.

(I have bones no longer, I resemble a skeleton, unfleshed, unnerved, unmuscled all pulp gone.)

or in Sonnet II

> Meschantes Nuict d'hyver, Nuicts, filles de Cocyte,
>
> Que la Terre engendra, d'Encelade le soeurs . . .
>
> J'appelle en vain le Jour, et la Mort je supplie,
>
> Mais elle fait la sourde et ne veut pas venir.

> (Vicious Nights of winter, Nights daughters of Cocytus engendered by the Earth, sisters
>
> of Encelades . . . I call upon Day in vain and plead with Death, but she acts as if deaf and
>
> will not choose to come.)

Notably, when Ronsard takes up Petrarch's 'Solo e pensoso . . .' he relegates the sombre beginning of the authorial self-examination to a merely elegant conclusion (LIV: Pl, I, 69–70)

On the other hand, Ronsard's courtly and existential spaces can be filled with an abundant sense of the poet's function as seer and myth-maker. In La Promesse (L. 10) he writes, apostrophizing himself: La parolle, Ronsard, est la seule magie: 'The word, Ronsard, is the only magic'; the association of word with personal identity and with magic could stand as an epitome of Renaissance thought, especially in its Neoplatonic phase. In Ronsard's Hymne de la Philosophie, the Word, as the 'only' Magic, displaces the false and lying enchantments or the magique murmure of those false sorcerers who wish to bind the world to their own devices (ll. 44–50). Nonetheless, there is no aspect of the created world that Philosophy cannot translate to the written page: Il n'y a bois, mont, fleuve ne cité/Qu'en un papier elle n'ait limité. Within the borders of a page the word can contemplate the whole – hierarchy of being – which Ronsard in common with others describes as a dance (ibid., ll. 83–4) – while the poet stands as a prophetically inspired spirit, at one with the gods: he foretold all things before they were made; he knows the secrets of the skies and raises himself in tumultuous spirit to the gods.

Poetry here becomes a place of animated solitude; and so far from such solitude revealing – as it would in Petrarch – the agitations of the authorial alter ego, it is in this region that Ronsard is most assured of his own unembarrassedly integral being: Mais courage, Ronsard, he proclaims in the Hymn to Autumn (line 65), les plus doctes Poëtes,/Les Sibylles, Devins, Augures & Prophetes,/Huez, siflez, moquez des peuples ont esté. But they still speak truths which tyrants and villains will never understand:

> Car Dieu ne communique aux hommes ses mysteres
>
> S'ils ne sont vertueux, devots & solitaires,

> (For God tells his mysteries only to those who are virtuous, devout and solitary.)

This is already a pastoral world – and plainly the philosophy that is born here is not the systematic philosophy that Petrarch deplored or that scientific thinking would shortly encourage. It is a philosophy of secret wisdom, arising out of rhetoric and myth. This form of wisdom, however, is one that allows Ronsard to give full vent to what has been called his *élan imaginatif* – for a poetry that constantly and confidently generates myths, expanding all experience and observation in a way that accepts and fructifies the shifting visual fields of fact and fiction. In the resonant hollows of Ronsard's own ego, there is something of the Shakespearian Prospero who conjures up spirits in his pastoral island (cf. *The Tempest*, Act V, scene i: 'Ye elves of hills, brooks . . .') – though little of that sense of self-estrangement that Prospero always carries with him:

Je n'avois pas quinze ans que les monts & et les bois

Et le eaux me plaisoyent plus que les Courts des Rois.

Et les noires forests en fueillage voutées,

Et du bec des oiseaux les roches picotées:

Une valée, un antre en horreur obscurci,

Un desert effroyable estoit tout mon souci:

A fin de voir au soir les Nymphes & les Fées,

Danser dessous la Lune en cotte par les prées,

Fantastique d'esprit: e de voir les Sylvains

Estre boucs par les pieds & hommes par les mains,

Et porter sur le front des cornes en la sorte

Qu'un petit aignelet de quatre mois les porte.

Hymne de l'Autumne (31–42)

(And when I was no more than fifteen years of age, the mountains and the woods were more pleasing to me than the courts of Kings, and the black forests with their vaulted foliage and the rocks pecked at by the beaks of birds: A valley, a cave hidden in horror, a fearful desert was all that I sought. So that in the end I saw the Nymphs and the fairies dancing beneath the moon in their flimsy skirts in the meadows, brilliant, fantastic in spirit and I saw the woodland beings, with goats-feet and the hands of men, bearing horns on their heads in the way they are borne by a little lamb of four months old.)

Ronsard and Du Bellay were to impress those English writers such as Sidney and Spenser who (along with critics like George Puttenham in *The Art of English Poesie* (1589)) deliberately attempted in *The Apology for Poetry* and *The Faerie Queene* to reform

English letters and to celebrate the achievement of their national culture. In common with their Spanish counterparts, English poets recognized that their country lay on the margins of Europe, and that their entry into the Renaissance tradition was relatively belated. Many, however, also understood that English, as a language, possessed characteristics that were very different from those of the Romance languages (including Spanish); and, as the Protestant Reformation took a hold on the English mind, so too did a need to insist upon the ways in which the cultural identity of the English differed from that which had developed in Renaissance Europe. Indeed from the first English authors, while eagerly assimilating the achievements of Italy and France, were far more critical in their attitudes than most Spanish authors tended to be, to the point, sometimes, of belligerence and idiosyncrasy.

This is apparent even in Chaucer's approach to continental Europe. In his early *Troilus and Criseyde*, Chaucer – taking as his unacknowledged source Boccaccio's *Il Filostrato* – had also offered a dramatization of one of Petrarch's most anguished sonnets, which he uses with a hint of parody to express the first melodramatic outpourings of the lovelorn Troilus ('Canticus Troili', *Troilus and Criseyde*, Book I). He shows a similarly guarded (and Anglo-Saxon) response in *The Clerk's Tale*. Through the Clerk in his Prologue, Chaucer acknowledges that Petrarch has 'illuminated Italy with his eloquence', yet he also allows the muscular voice of the Host to call eloquence – and Petrarch himself – into question with his forthright conclusion: 'Petrarch he is buried and dead'.

Evidence of attractions and resistances such as Chaucer displays grows more striking as – during the Tudor sixteenth century – courtly influences and national ambitions begin to penetrate the English imagination. During Henry VII's reign, Skelton (1470/80–1529) who was tutor to the future Henry VIII could speak out in the skeltonic verses of *Speke Parrot* against the corrupt machinations of the English Renaissance court, declaring in a language that draws its energies from Chaucer and Langland – that Wolsey is 'so fatte a maggot bred of a flesshe flye' (*SP*, 609). He can also deride the exquisite tapestries of Wolsey's Hampton Court with their 'nakyde boyes strydynge/With wanton wenches wynking' (*ibid.*, 967–8) and vigorously oppose the Cardinal's humanist ambitions to promote the study of Greek (145–7). Fifty years later figures such as Ascham, Queen Elizabeth's tutor, registers explicit and patriotic antipathy to the fashion for Italian learning. Shakespeare, too (as will appear in Chapter Eight) has his own delicately nuanced response to make to such sentiments. On the other hand, Petrarch's poem in opposition to papal corruption (*RS*, CXXXVI) could be adapted by Protestants such as Sir John Harington (the elder) to produce: 'Vengeance must fall on thee, thou filthy whore of Babylon'; and, in the Elizabethan period, forms of political petrarchism developed in which conventional references to white and red roses – perfectly blended in Elizabeth's own complexion – were seen to represent the final reconciliation of the Lancastrian and Yorkist parties.

It was Wyatt, however, who in the mid-century engaged most subtly with the Petrarchan tradition. His close contemporary Surrey had attempted to increase the rhetorical and stylistic resources of English by introducing features drawn from the Latin repertoire – which he had explored in his translation of the *Aeneid*. Wyatt follows suit in his translation and adaptation of vernacular Italian. His work shows a remarkable breadth of interests, ranging from the *Penitential Psalms* on the model of Aretino's version to verse epistles in the style of the exiled Florentine libertarian, Luigi Alamanni (1495–1556). But Wyatt is particularly responsive in his treatment of Petrarch's poetry, sometimes offering direct translation, sometimes testing himself against the moral and emotional issues that Petrarch raises (allowing himself as it were, to be 'read' by Petrarch), sometimes producing wholly independent versions of the Petrarchan original. A sonnet such as 'My galley charged with forgetfulness . . .' (*RS*, CLXXXIX) is sometimes taken to display a peculiarly muscular reading of a delicate original yet might also be seen as an indication of how much, in technical terms, English poets had still to learn from the Italian. On other occasions, a deeply introspective, even obsessive, tendency in Wyatt's mind leads him to intensify and particularize the moral issues raised by Petrarch's work, while in other cases – displaying what Spearing has called a predatory instinct – he wholly transforms the Italian text to his own ends. Thus, in 'Whoso list to hunt . . .', Wyatt takes complete possession of the original, and creates a bitter, almost parodic text of his own, shot through with the half-suppressed anxieties of courtly life under Henry VIII's regime. Petrarch had evoked a moment of contemplation realized in the flux of his own moral agitations by the visionary perception of a doe 'shining white with horns of gold' seen 'between two streams in the shadow of a laurel'. For a moment, the claims of beauty, poetic aspirations to the laurel and moral harmony all seem to be reconciled. But Wyatt writes:

Whoso list to hunt I know where is an hind.

But as for me, alas, I may no more.

The vain travaile hath wearied me so sore,

I am of them that farthest come behind.

Yet may I by no means my wearied mind

Draw from the dear, but as she fleeth afore,

Fainting I follow. I leave off therefore

Sithens in a net I seek to hold the wind.

Who list her hunt, I put him out of doubt,

As well as I may spend his time in vain.

And graven with diamonds in letters plain

> There is written her fair neck round about:
>
> *Noli me tangere* for Caesar's I am,
>
> And wild for to hold though I seem tame.
>
> (XI)

Here the authorial voice struggles not only with the strains of erotic distraction but also with the fear of naked power. When Petrarch's doe declares its allegiance to 'Caesar', the poet introduces references to Christ's appearance in the Garden on the morning of the Resurrection and momentarily contemplates the freedom that comes in devotion to the Christian truth. Wyatt's version turns Caesar into an autocrat, bestowing gifts that are also brands of ownership, and speaking in a Latin that dissolves all liturgical implication into an atmosphere of political danger. Surrey – who was executed at the command of Henry VIII – had already shown in his verse what it meant to possess a free spirit in a Renaissance court:

> Thus I alone, where all my fredome grew,
>
> In pryson pyne with bondage and restraynt.
>
> (27, 51–4)

Wyatt was not executed; but he was imprisoned under suspicion of guilty relations with Ann Boleyn. In 'whoso list to hunt . . .' he pictures a situation in which love itself as the well-spring of human personality can expose the lover not only to familiar pains of love but also to the jealous misapprehensions of the Monarch himself.

The first phase of English Petrarchism led to the many translations of single poems that are collected, as Wyatt's versions were in Tottel's *Miscellany* of 1557. The next three decades witnessed a certain shift away from Petrarch's own example – and even the beginnings of a certain inclination to anti-Petrarchan sentiment – towards the elegant wit of a Serafino or the dark conceits of Tasso's poetry. In the 1580s, however, the fashion shifted again when, with Thomas Watson in his *Hecatompathia* (1582), followed by Lodge, Constable and Daniel, English poets began to attempt to compose ambitiously extended sonnet sequences. This argues an increasing confidence in the capacities of English as a literary language along with a willingness to modify or oppose the Petrarchan conventions. It is in this spirit, for instance, that Edmund Spenser in the *Amoretti* is able to take married love as his theme (as in his own allusions to Petrarch's 'Una candida cerva . . .' and Wyatt's 'Whoso list to hunt . . .'). It is, however in Sir Philip Sidney's *Astrophil and Stella* that the issues arising in the Petrarchan tradition are explored most critically. Like Chaucer, Sidney can recognize that Petrarch is long since dead – despite the attentions of his eager followers – and speak of those 'apes of Petrarch' that 'poor Petrarch's long-deceased woes/With new-born sighs and denizened wit do sing' (*AS*, 100, 5–8). He can also produce his own very unpetrarchan phrases, as when he evokes – in a series of erotic suggestions and blunt English locutions – the 'honied sighs' that rise from his mistress's breast, causing 'unspilling cream to flow' and refreshing 'the hell where my soul fries' (*AS*, 100, 5–8). Yet this does not imply a rejection of Petrarch's themes. Indeed there are times when Sidney in his religious poems expresses the need to leap beyond words and realize (in a Protestant vein) the true demands of the heart.

Central to this conflict is Sidney's concern to develop a poetics of spontaneity: '"Fool," said my pen: "look in thy heart and write"' (*AS*, 1). Yet the heart of Renaissance self is not that of Romantic self. This self thrives upon and is supported by the very conventions that seem to imprison it. In his historical existence, Sidney – whose family had pretensions to the Crown – lived and defined himself through the paraphernalia of conventions that the Tudor court encouraged: he probably did wear an armour decorated with stars to declare the devotion of the star-loving 'Philisides' for Stella; and on his death his great state funeral was used by Elizabeth to divert attention away from the execution of Mary, Queen of Scots. Correspondingly, his search for sincerity involves an intense desire to reconcile the conventions of naming to the realization of an ever-fleeting presence. When Sidney speaks of 'Astrophil' or 'Stella', he verges on territory that Petrarch surveys with his multiple punnings on 'Laura'. But he is equally concerned to recognize that the self is a text that might best be understood through close attention to the artifice of its metaphors and tropes. Thus in Sonnet 67 the presence of the lady is read as that of a flickering book: 'Look on again, the faire text better trie/What blushing notes doest thou in margine see?'

Or else Sidney will attempt to make the name of his lady itself evoke her presence, as if a name could be a peculiar word of power and privilege:

> Muses, I oft invoked your ayde,
>
> With choicest flowers my speech to engarland so:
>
> That it, despisede in true and naked showe,
>
> Might winne some grace in your sweet grace arraid.
>
> And oft whole troupes of saddest words I staid,
>
> Striving abroad a foraging to go
>
> Until by your inspiring I might know,
>
> How their black banner might be best displaid.
>
> But now I mean no more your helpe to trie,
>
> Nor other surging of my speech to prove

But on her name incessantly to crie:

For let me but name her whom I do love,

   So sweete sounds straight mine eare and heart do hit,

That I well find no eloquence like it.

(Sonnet 53)

'What's in a name': this question at the end of the Renaissance emerges as the final form of the questions that from the first have haunted the writings of the lyric poets. Shakespeare confirms this. In his work, these considerations can be ludic as in *Twelfth Night* – a play much concerned with twinnings and family bonds, that also produces an anagrammatic pun on the names Olivia and Viola. *Romeo and Juliet* provides a tragic counterpart where disaster arises from the insistent demand of the lovers that there must be some way of touching and preserving the presence of another human being which can transcend the roles that are projected upon them by family names and social structures. (But is there?)

In social terms and political terms, one may recall that even at the end of the seventeenth century 'individuals' were not yet fully endowed with the property rights and bureaucratic descriptions that would eventually define the modern identity. At the same time, there was a sharp recognition – especially perhaps in England, where idiosyncrasy had already come to be associated especially strongly with the nature of individuality – that the singularity of human existences lay tantalizingly beyond the competence of language to circumscribe. Shakespeare as dramatist practised in a literary form where this was especially evident – where dramatic immediacy of voice was accompanied by an abiding sense of the two-in-oneness that acting always depends upon. In lyric verse – leaving aside Shakespeare's own – the clearest indication of how this issue develops is to be seen in the witty and famously 'metaphysical' poetry of John Donne.

Donne is not only an eccentric but also in many ways an uneven poet and by Petrarchan standards little concerned with refinement of phrase. No Petrarchan would have attempted the brutal equivocation of Donne's epigrammatic '"I am unable," yonder beggar cries, "To stand or move": if he say true he lies.' Nor would Petrarch have ever begun a love poem with the dramatic gestures of Donne's 'For God's sake hold your tongue and let me love . . .'. Donne here rides on the great wave of linguistic enthusiasm and experimentation that swept through England in the late sixteenth century. France – in the poetry of Marot and also (as will appear) in the prose of Rabelais – generated a somewhat similar energy. But only in the poetry of Dante had there been anything like the linguistic daring, in register and diction, that was to be displayed in England in the Elizabethan period, culminating in the works of Shakespeare.

In another sense, too, the majority of Donne's most characteristic poems depart from the preceding tradition by preferring to depict the happy fulfilment of sexual affection rather than the sublimated torments of spiritual agony. This is not of course to suggest (as once might have been said) that Donne is writing biographically about his relationship with his own wife, Ann. Perhaps he is: on their daring elopement, he certainly does write the epigrammatic, 'John Donne; Ann Donne; Undone'. Be that as it may, his poetry at its best is remarkable for being scored for two voices, allowing – as might a good dramatic script – room for the reader to imagine gesture, the movement of bodies and the play of reciprocating responses, as for example in the first stanza of the two-stanza 'The Expiration':

So, so, break off this last lamenting kisse,
   Which sucks two soules and vapours Both away,
Turne thou ghost that way, and let mee turn this,
   and let our selves benight our happiest day,
We ask'd none leave to love; nor will we owe
   Any so cheape a death, as saying, Goe.

It is in this regard that the Shakespearian concern with the metaphysics of identity takes on its particular force in Donne. In the 'Valediction: of my name in the window', Donne engraves his own skeletal name with a diamond on a casement window pane, as a valedictory remembrance for his mistress; and, asking his mistress to contemplate the name, writes a poem that represents his own contemplation of true nature. By turns, this name denotes his fidelity at the moment of departure and adds 'firmness' to the fragile glass; it is also – like the glass that bears it – 'through-shine' and thus a token of transparent sincerity. At the same time, this 'ragged bony name' is a *memento mori*, a 'ruinous Anatomie' – as much an indication of how insubstantial, in fact, the human person is as the coffin in which Donne slept when he was Dean of St Paul's. But this is not all. For the name will be read by his mistress too. Sometimes she will fling open the window 'with inconsiderate hand' and cause the name to tremble on its glassy page. But she too, as the reader of this name, is the power that will raise it – in all its boniness and fragility – to a paradise comparable to that which the Resurrected Body will enjoy on the Day of Judgement. And if in infidelity she should write another name over his, then that 'superscribing' will bring his own name back into her memory: 'So, in forgetting thou rememberest right'.

Two or three of Donne's greatest poems depict a self plunged into a world where there is no other person to speak his name and assure him of his own being: in 'Twicknam Garden' the lover is 'blasted with sighs and surrounded with teares' to the extent that he wishes to poison all other lovers with the invidious truth that – in being true to the perversity characteristic of her sex – 'her truth kills mee'. Yet this is unusual. Much more characteristically, the self abandons itself to the erotic and yet ontological paradoxes of sexual love in which no self is ever one self – or oneself. Fleas jump between the bodies of lovers (as mosquitos will in the madrigals of Gesualdo: see pp. 310–13); lovers are a pair of compasses, simultaneously stiff and mobile, travelling and still. Or else lovers are ecstatic in the fullest sense of the word, standing outside of their single identities. 'The Ecstasie' is as alert to the paradoxical nature of love as any Neoplatonist could be: 'When love, with one another so/interinanimates two soules,/That abler soule, which thence doth flow,/Defects of loneliness controules.' Yet this solemn discourse – as in 'The Expiration' in its meditation on 'ghosts' – is a piece of wit, a conceit passing between lovers whose far-from-solemn and wholly unplatonic bodies are shortly to benefit from the seductive exchange.

The reader too, like any lover, will read the poem as one which counsels the abandonment of all crudely unitary views of the self and participate in the communality that sexual intelligence generously fosters:

And if some lover, such as wee,

    Have heard this dialogue of one,

Let him still marke us, he shalle see

    Small change, when we'are to bodies gone.

THE EPIC IMAGINATION: TASSO, CAMÕES AND SPENSER

To the German Romantic philosopher Friedrich Schlegel, epic poetry is the expression of the history and spirit of the Nation. Epic poems, describing the wars that tribes have fought, the journeys they have undertaken, the cities they have destroyed or founded, embody the ethical principles that were implicit in such endeavours; and for Schlegel the supreme example of epic poetry is Luis de Camões's *Os Lusiadas* (1572). This poem relates the story of Vasco da Gama's exploratory journey to India, and celebrates the heroic history of the Portuguese people. The Portuguese (with English assistance) had driven out the Moors two centuries before the Spanish did so, and could henceforth look forward – as the poem prophesies – to a flourishing colonial future in the Orient, ranging from Japan which 'yields the finest silver mines' (*Os Lusiadas*, X, 131) to the Banda Isles 'to take their tribute of the Nutmeg plant' and to Borneo 'for its Camphor-trees' (*ibid.*, 133).

Schlegel is not alone in regarding Camões's epic as the summation of Renaissance culture and the most clear-sighted anticipation of the principles on which the modern world will depend. Here, a historical and contemporary figure takes up the destiny of legendary wanderers such as Aeneas and Ulysses. Voltaire describes Camões as the Portuguese Virgil – anticipating a culture in which journeying itself will become a manifestation of virtue – while Hermann Melville in *White-Jacket* makes his young sailor cry enthusiastically 'Hear Camões, boys!' Impelled by Christian belief and a Christian understanding of an orderly universe, Vasco becomes the modern equivalent of classical refugees and adventurers. But the goal he sets himself is not simply the re-establishment of an older and threatened order but rather a command of resources – both intellectual and material – that will make possible an ever-wider and ever-more luxuriant realization of the Portuguese destiny. The course that Vasco charts is one in which all the technological skills that the Renaissance has developed are brought into play, and where botanical and mineralogical curiosity help him to ensure survival and commercial success. Above all, he is a hero of practical rather than speculative understanding, a mariner 'who hath no mistress but experience' (Canto V, 16).

Thus Camões presents a hero wholly assured in his own national identity (though remarkably unassuming on his own account) who finds a home in the very heart of oceanic movement and flux, a hero who is able confidently to orient and recreate himself in the face of all the alien cultures that he encounters, and finally to promote an Empire which is likewise regenerated in its opulence by its own imaginative and material capital.

Or is it opulence? Could it be that all the luxury of intellectual and maritime adventure that Camões cultivates in *Os Lusiadas* is an illusion, an effect merely of desire and wishful thinking that glosses over the realties of oppression, slavery and exploitation that began when Genoese merchants in the fourteenth century first travelled down the African coast on slaving missions? In the abundant diction of his epic (as also of his lyric) poetry, Camões seems confident that words can invoke and deliver up the presences of the world, even at their most foreign and exotic, to the powerful grip of the European imagination; and there is little indication in Camões's own authorial position that he wished to acknowledge the fissures that always exist between words and thing or between imaginative and political realities. Indeed, one of the most notable (and, in the perspective of modern criticism, most suspect) features of Camões's narrative is his insistence that all the tribes that his seafarers meet – especially if they are Muslims – speak with a forked tongue, inspired by their affiliation with the luxurious gods of the pagan world: 'But the Moor well instructed in deceit (To whom his lesson spiteful Bacchus gave) . . .' (*Os Lusiadas*, Canto I, 97). Europeans on the other hand are justifiably confident not only of the rightness of their own commercial enterprises but also of the divine providence that creates and sustains this world. The pagan creates an empty and idolatrous world (VII, 47), 'carv'd in cold stone, in dull and stupid wood'. The European surveys an order that is rational, divine and true:

In all these Planets motions different

Thou mayest perceive, some speedy, and some slow:

Now climbing nearer to the Firmament,

Now stooping closer to the Earth below,

As seemed best to the Omnipotent,

Who made the Fire and Ayre, the Wind and Snow. . . .

Upon this Center is the seat of Man:

Who, not content in his presumptuous pride

T'expose to all Earth's Mischiefs his life's span,

Trusts it to the unconstant Ocean wide. . . .

See Christian Europe, higher by the head

In Arms and civil Arts then all the rest!

(Canto, X, 92ff. in the translation of 1655 by Sir Richard Fanshawe)

Plainly, there is little sense here of the generous curiosity that Montaigne displays towards other cultures and other races. Yet the very richness of Camões's word and imagination, along with his desire (and ability) to attempt an extraordinarily wide range of literary exploits, produce at times surges of uncontrollable counter-suggestion. As Vasco's fleet sails out of Lisbon, a venerable old man denounces the vain pursuit of glory, and vividly calls to mind the deaths and horrors that must follow under pretence of spreading true religion (IV, 95–7). Camões here speaks eloquently in the tones of an Old Testament prophet or a Savanarola; yet he allows these words to be drowned by the gathering of the ocean wind and the enthusiastic shouts of mariners. Then again, in one of the most influential episodes of the poem (which finds resonances in the South African poet Roy Campbell's *Rounding the Cape* of 1930), Camões invents the myth of Adamastor, which has since been taken to express 'the white man's anxieties about Africa'. Here as Vasco encounters the terrible storms around the Cape of Good Hope, Camões devises a massive vision of incomprehensible enmity, emerging from the storm like some irreducible Caliban:

I had not ended, when a humane Feature

Appeared to us I' th'Ayre, robustious, ralli'd

Of heterogeneal parts, of boundless Stature,

A Cloud in's Face, a Bear prolix and squalid:

Cave-Eyes, a gesture that betray'd ill nature,

And a worse mood, a clay complexion pallid:

His crispedt *Hair* fill'd with earth, and thick as Wire,

A mouth coal black, of Teeth two yellow Tyre.

This figure declares that the Cape it guards will always oppose Christian voyages: 'This point their enemy for ever' (*ibid.*, 43). To which Vasco can only reply ('the black Cloud melting with a hideous yell') with prayers, beseeching 'the Lord to shield his Heritage/From all that Adamastor did presage' (*ibid.*, 60).

Beyond the margins drawn by the European mind, Camões acknowledges that there are turbulences that it cannot shape to its own design, save in the imagination. So finally *Os Lusiadas* offers us two conclusions. One is a return to Portugal – which itself is seen, in a piece of imaginative geography, as the true crown of Europe: if we view the continent from East to West, then Portugal stands like a diadem illuminated by the setting sun on its outer limit (III, 20). Another conclusion, however, commits us to a continual digression in search of excitements and satisfactions that only the imagination can encompass. Unlike Ariosto's romance – which is constantly digressive yet constantly attached to a courtly centre, Camões's poem is in some sense all digression, never ceasing to explore beyond the centre; and just when it is coming to its conclusion, a final digression in the penultimate canto offers an alternative to the unified resolution of Vasco's journey in which he is shown the workings of Divine Providence. The alternative is located in the pastoral Garden of Delights that Venus has prepared for Vasco's mariners. This, however, is no moment of Circean distraction (though no doubt it is intended as an analogue to such episodes in Homer and Virgil). Throughout the poem, Venus has been the supporter of the Portuguese against the claims of Bacchus who hitherto has been ruler of the Orient. Such appeals to the apparatus of Pagan Gods – necessary for the full imitation of classical epic – had caused heart-searching among the poets themselves and had been disturbing to the Churches of the Reformation in their rigorous concern with the truths of Christian orthodoxy. Here, without compunction, Camões imagines how Venus creates a whole island of pleasure as the backdrop to an explicit erotic ballet in which the very desire to test whether the nymphs are true beings or false adds piquancy to the chase:

Sigamos estas Deusas, vejamos

Se fantasticas sao, se verdadeiras . . .

De hua os cabelos de ouro o vento leva

Correndo, e de outra as fralds delicadas:

Acende-se o desjo, que se ceva

Nas alvas carnes, subito mostradas.

Hua de indústria cai e já releva,

Com mostras mais macias que indinadas

Que sobre ela, empecendo, também caia

Quem a seguiu pela arenosa praia.

(IX, 27–8).

(One's golden tresses up the wind did blow,

The light coats of another as she fled:

The desire, kindled by the naked snow,

Upon the dainty Prospect greedy fed.

This falls on purpose and whilst she doth go

To rise with kindness more than Anger red.

He that pursues, falls over her; like one

That rubs the Mistress when his Bowl is gone.)

Petrarchan motifs are here employed to a far-from Petrarchan purpose. It is true that at one point these nymphs are viewed allegorically as figures representing Glory and Fame. At the same time, in a daring turn of thought, the generous impulsions of love, sensuous beauty and the excitements of the aesthetic imagination are seen as the remedy for all the meanness and perversion that arises in our attempts merely to control and rule the world in which we live.

The concern that Camões displays with heroism, ambition, love and the actions of the imagination is repeated in all the major epics of the sixteenth century. But all display in some measure a realization of the pressures

Figure 69   Kesu Das, *Crucifixion*, (after European engravings) around 1600. Gouache and Ink on Paper, 19.5 × 17.8cm. An anonymous eye-witness account of Vasco's journey shows that Christian strictly only distinguished themselves from Moors ('Anyone who is not a Moor may be termed a Christian.' Once in India (expecting to find Syrian Christians) they mistook Hindu temples for churches dedicated to the Virgin Mary. Other miniatures delicately satirize the inebriation of European travellers. British Museum, London.

that lie beneath the surface of the national myth or else of the difficulties that the poet himself ex-periences in sustaining or controlling the implications of such myths. In common with Ariosto, Trissino (1478–1550) in *La Italia liberata dai Gothi* (1547–8) writes of the so-called Dark Ages with an awareness of how dark the foreign invasions of contemporary Italy had now made the peninsula itself. Ronsard in *La Françiade* (1572) attempts to link the history of France to the history of Troy but seems to have been too depressed by the death of Charles IX in 1574 to complete the work. In *Araucana*, the Spanish poet Alonso de Ercilla (1535–94) pictures the overthrow of the native tribes of Chile but is drawn to display something of the generosity that Ariosto exhibits towards the Muslim world in his depiction of the melancholic love stories of aristocratic Araucanians. However, it is in Tasso's *Gerusalemme Liberata* that such conflicts – involving the sensibility of the lyric poet as much as the ambitions of the epic poet – produce their most complex result. Writing itself becomes, for Tasso, an act of heroic competition – in which, as he declares, the only rival he fears is Camões. But the greater contest is with his own ambitions and his own highly charged – even disturbed – imagination.

This is apparent even in the opening lines of the *Gerusalemme Liberata*. In his invocation, Tasso painfully denies any appeal to the pagan muse – who in Helicon surrounds the brow with 'fading laurels'. Rather – anticipating the opening of Milton's *Paradise Lost* – he seeks to invoke the Holy Ghost. Yet he knows irrepressibly and guiltily that there will be 'fringes' or exotic decorations that, as a poet, he is bound to include in the texture of his poem.

> tu perdona
> s'intesso fregi al ver, s'adorno in parte
> d'altri diletti, che de' tuoi, le carte.

> (*Gerusalemme Liberata*, Canto I, stanza 2)

(Pardon me if I weave fringes into the truth and adorn in part my pages with other delights than Yours.)

In the course of the *Gerusalemme Liberata*, the Christian crusaders will constantly be distracted from their military purposes by love affairs and enchantments. It is, however, the poet himself who invents these romantic distractions; and he no less than the crusaders will have to struggle to impose order and purpose upon his own disruptive invention.

In large part the opening of the *Gersualemme Liberata* reflects the theoretical considerations that Tasso had developed in his *Discourses* on the epic poem. Here he attempts to distinguish his own conception of the epic romance – written at the height of the Counter-Reformation – from that which Ariosto had pursued at the beginning of the sixteenth century. (See pp. 5–10.) With Ariosto, Tasso recognizes that epic poetry must satisfy the imagination by introducing marvels and miraculous events. Yet where Ariosto is happy to adopt a whole catalogue of flying horses, magic rings and enchanted castles from the romance tradition, Tasso insists (in theory at least) that the miracles he depicts should be the true miracles that display the workings of Divine Providence. Similarly, Tasso demands that the subject of the poem ought to possess the gravity of historical truth, even though the historical subject that the epic poet chooses should be sufficiently remote for both the poet and his audience to enjoy the freedom and pleasure of imaginative reconstruction. As to the form of an epic poem, here, in parallel with his Counter-Reformation desire for religious orthodoxy, Tasso seeks to establish critical correctness, by resuscitating an authentically Aristotelian understanding of the epic genre. Ariosto had created, on his own understanding, a 'tapestry' in which multiple story lines were dextrously interlaced and where the authorial tone could slip within a matter of lines from tragic to elegiac, from comic to burlesque. In this respect he anticipates the subtle modifications of genre and tone that are characteristic of Shakespeare's writing; and in Ariosto's own time there were some who defended his practice as evidence of the chameleon-like originality of a truly poetic imagination. Tasso himself, from his earliest writings as a child prodigy, displays a capacity for vigorous invention and rhetorical display. Yet the theoretician insists (as will his neo-classical followers in the seventeenth century) that the epic should pursue a single unified action. The whole purpose of the nominal hero of the *Gerusalemme Liberata*, Geoffrey of Bouillon, is to attempt at least to direct the energies of his errant companions towards a single goal, the defeat of the Muslims in Jerusalem. Correspondingly, Tasso as author abandons the tapestry woven by Ariosto in favour of a structure of highly concentrated episodes in which each canto for the most part does indeed trace the unrolling of a single psychological, military or amorous situation, sometimes bringing episodes into significant juxtaposition. Yet in each case there is – in the poet's text as in the Christian armies – a centrifugal pressure which leads the imagination not only into the 'fringes' of romantic or erotic indulgence but also into the depiction of magical and cabbalistic scenes and even to a horrified fascination with the glamour, guile and often-heroic dignity of the Muslim enemy. At all times, too, Tasso, along with his devotion to 'truth', also realizes that an appetite for 'fiction' is (in fact) an undeniable component of the human mind.

It is an indication of how closely the tensions registered in the action of the *Gerusalemme Liberata* reflect those of the poet's own mentality that Tasso should have wholly rewritten his original version of *Gerusalemme Liberata*, excising supposedly dangerous or divergent episodes and retitling the work *Gerusalemme Conquistata* so as to emphasize unambiguously the victory that the Christian forces accomplished over their pagan enemies. Tasso's paranoid attempts to reconcile himself with the hierarchical authorities of Church and Court are recorded painfully in his letters from the hospital of Sant'Anna. They are directly comparable to the negotiations that lyric poets such as Wyatt and Surrey were obliged to enter upon in forming their own identities within an institutional framework – a framework that often provided its own definitions of political identity while simultaneously claiming authority over the selves that it had thus defined. The *Gersualemme Liberata* derives a great deal of its melancholic energy from a similar source.

For instance, the great Christian hero Tancredi falls in love with the Muslim woman-warrior, Clorinda. Encountering her at night in a skirmish, he fails to recognize who she is and (in a scene later rendered into operatic form by Monteverdi) slays her, only realizing what he has done when he raises her helmet to offer her baptism. At which, he begins a descent into violent madness, and in a subsequent canto finds himself wandering in a wood that has been enchanted by a Muslim magician. Every tree, it seems, shrieks out at Tancred in the voice of the woman he has unwittingly murdered. The climax is prepared by two stanzas that emphasize the confusion of signals and signs – *segni ignoti*; *sensi occulti* – that Tancred (and the author, it seems) experience here. The Renaissance mind had sought to write itself on the world as clearly as it could. But here the world proves wholly foreign. Tasso's word-painting is exact, as the wind soughs through the ghastly foliage – *fremere intanto udìa continuo il vento*. But all that this amounts to is a mystery – or worse – expressed in the phrase *un non so che* – 'an I-know-not-what' – that is one of the *leitmotifs* Tasso's poetry. Here it registers appalling apprehension of what will be experienced when the voice of Clorinda speaks from a place that is simultaneously nature, grave and a dreadful parody of eternal rest and resurrection:

> Pur tragge al fin la spada, e con gran forza
>
> percote l'alta pianta. Oh meraviglia!
>
> manda fuor sangue la recisa scorza.
>
> e fa la terra intorno a sè vermiglia.
>
> Tutto si raccapriccia e pur rinforza
>
> il colpo e 'l fin vederne ei si consiglia.
>
> Allor, quasi di tomba, uscir ne sente
>
> un indistinto gemito dolente.
>
> (*GL*, XIII, 41)

He drew his sword at last, and gave the tree

   A mighty blow that made a gaping wound;

Out of the rift red streams he trickling see

   That all be-bled the verdant plain around;

His hair start up; yet once again struck he,

   (He nould give over till the end he found

Of this adventure) when with plaint and moan

As from some hollow grave, he heard one groan –

(trans. Edward Fairfax (1600) XIII, 41)

In the darkness of the night – which by the middle of the sixteenth century had come to be the appropriate setting for particularly dignified actions – Tancredi's very skill in reading the signs made by other cultures betrays him tragically into a nightmare. The external world, so far from being supported by Divine Providence, has been possessed by pagan magic. Even the voice of the dead Clorinda – newly converted to Christianity – is conjured back into the pagan cause to act as a peculiar torment to the mind of the Christian hero. The marvels here are the marvels of the wholly unknown. Nor is it only Tancredi's mind that suffers in this scene. Where Adamastor in *Os Lusiadas* remains a threatening manifestation of alterity, otherness here enters the very fibre of the text. The mind is driven to contemplate a death that is not a death, trees that are not trees, words that are foreign and yet all too vivid in their implication. But Tasso's own verse calls at every point upon verbal echoes of a Dantean Hell – where in *Inferno* Canto XIII, suicides, transformed into trees, bleed and speak simultaneously. The culture, to which in other parts of his work Tasso looks back in his pursuit of doctrinal firmness, here produces a recession of vistas in which images of self-division themselves are the food of the poet's frenzied virtuosity.

The inherent instabilities of the Renaissance epic are confronted by Edmund Spenser in his (probably unfinished) *The Faerie Queene*. This work is intended, as Spenser makes clear in an introductory letter to Sir Walter Ralegh, to outdo Ariosto in the handling of *entrelacement*; and, to that extent, the work is part of the deliberate cultivation of an English response to the achievements of Italian literature. Equally, Spenser, in a firmly puritan perspective, clearly feels that he can impose a moral order on the dangerous vortices of Tasso's poem. Already in the late sixteenth century Ariosto's poem had begun to appear with moralizing and allegorical comments intended to demonstrate the serious implications of this frivolous courtly narrative. Spenser adopts this device. He also subtly rewrites episodes that he has taken from Tasso's work to ensure, for instance, that the eroticism of the Bower of Blisse in Book Two should unequivocally be read as a representation of the mechanics of sensual corruption and pornographic artifice.

In choosing an Arthurian theme at all, Spenser had entered dangerous territory. For while, to the Tudors, such themes were of course part of their propaganda to assert an affinity with the ancient order of pre-Conquest Britain, humanists such as Ascham (in common with Erasmus) had begun to deride the taste for blood-thirsty adventure displayed by works such as Malory's *Morte d'Arthur*. But Spenser boldly allegorizes these stories to provide a running analysis of the Renaissance mentality, particularly in its heroic dimension. The heroism of military adventures is a figure for a spiritual heroism that must constantly be aware that fallibility and distraction are internal dangers from which we can protect ourselves only by self-knowledge and penitential self-awareness. Glory is promised to us. But glory comes to those who confidently acknowledge that we live our earthly lives as a quest, constantly seeking new lands in which our prowess might be put to the test and new definitions achieved of the virtues that 'fashion an English gentleman'.

It is in this spirit that Spenser, in the last complete book of *The Faerie Queene* concerning the virtue of Courtesy, reformulates the understanding of courtesy that originated among the courts and courtiers of Castiglione's Italy. Spenser fully recognizes how easily the fluency of talk and behaviour as displayed in the *sprezzatura* of courtiers such as Ariosto can slip into gossip, backbiting and the envious slaughter of reputations. These possibilities are vividly realized in his allegorical depiction of the Blatant Beast, with its teeth of festering iron. But true courtesy remains for Spenser a possibility, provided that it derives from the cosmic (rather than the social) order that is discernible in both the spiritual and natural realms of human existence. The value of courtesy in this perspective depends upon the prior establishment of the virtues of holiness, temperance, chastity, friendship and justice; and, when it is achieved, it will serve as the means to make these virtues an attractive or 'charming' part of our everyday conduct. On this view, courtesy becomes a form of spiritual or ethical *sprezzatura*. Consequently, it is not in the political court that Spenser finds the highest expression of that virtue but rather in the pastoral setting of Mount Acidale – where indeed he depicts a vision he sees of the Graces dancing in celebration of the shepherd girl Pastorella, accompanied by his own literary *alter ego*, Colin Clout, on his rustic pipe:

> Those were the Graces, daughters of delight,
>> Handmaides of *Venus*, which were wont to haunt
>> Upon this hill, and daunce there day and night:
>> Those three to men all gifts of grace do graunt,
>> And all, that *Venus* in her selfe doth vaunt,
>> Is borrowed of them. But that faire one,
>> That in the midst was placed paraunt,
>> Was she to whom that shepheard piped alone,
> That made him pipe so merrily, as never none.
>
> She was to weete that iolly Shepheards lasse,
>> Which piped thereunto that merry rout,
>> That jolly shepherd, which there piped, was

> Poore *Colin Clout* (who knowes not *Colin Clout?*)
>
> He piped apace, whilest they him daunst about.
>
> Pipe jolly shepheard, pipe thou now apace
>
> Unto thy love, that made thee low to lout:
>
> Thy love is present there with thee in place,
>
> Thy love is there advanced to be another Grace.
>
> (FQ, VI, x, 15–16)

Thus the epic resolves into a dynamic order responsive to the subtleties and delicacies of human behaviour and generous in its confidence that the quest can produce constantly new manifestation of life.

Yet here too there is a problem. It is hard now to forget that Spenser's own quest took him to Ireland on the first of many colonial adventures. It is also significant that *The Faerie Queene* – which, throughout, displays a nostalgic appetite for the Medieval world – should conclude with a return to the great theme of Mutability that characteristically had been explored by the poets and moralists of the late Middle Ages. (Spenser's pseudonym, 'Colin Clout', derives probably from Skelton.) With the confidence of a Tudor patriot, Spenser could provide his own remedy for the dangers that other Renaissance epics had encountered. Yet a realization of how flimsy the highest flights of civilization may be is expressed in the ultimate distintegration of Spenser's project. All things pass into the hands of Mutability:

> Then gin I think on that which Nature sayd,
>
> Of that same time when no more *Change* shall be,
>
> But steedfast rest of all things firmely stayd
>
> Upon the pillours of Eternity,
>
> That is contrayre to *Mutabilitee:*
>
> For, all that moveth, doth in *Change* delight:
>
> But thence-forth all shall rest eternally
>
> With Him that is the God of Sabbaoth hight:
>
> O that great Sabbaoth God, graunt me that Sabbaoth's sight.

PASTORAL EXPERIMENTATION

The pastoral idiom pervades all other forms of poetry in the Renaissance and exerts a considerable influence over the experimental theatre that developed in the second half of the sixteenth century. Pastoral, indeed, is perhaps the genre most characteristic of the Renaissance mentality. In lyric poetry, personal and authorial identity are put to the test, as is national and cultural identity in the epic. But the Golden Worlds evoked in pastoral fiction express a desire to shape the world beyond us to our own design – to the extent of avoiding historical and moral realities; the pastoral offers a return to origins not only in the classical past but also in Eden. It presumes that – as in Eden – our words may produce an immediate engagement with objective reality and that selves and social constructs are directly in harmony with the natural order.

Of course, Renaissance authors perfectly understood that the pastoral world was a fiction, a genre with its own conventions, a place for the connoisseur as much as the shepherd. In some cases, the longing for Arcadian origins is intertwined with an exquisitely melancholic appreciation of how far our Utopian dreams must always fall short of realization. Equally, in pastoral as in Utopian literature, authors could experiment with alternative political worlds sometimes sharpened to a satirical or polemical edge – as in Sidney's account of a decidedly troubled Arcadia – or else the pastoral in a world of religious conflict could be a way of imagining alternative forms of religious practice. This is particularly evident in the pastoral drama, which realizes to the full the dramaturgical interest of ritual theatre; scenes of sacrifice are common in these plays, as are priestly figures with names such as Tirenio (recalling Sophocles's Tiresias) – all pointing forward to Prospero in Shakespeare's *The Tempest*. Above all, however, the pastoral imagination – freed from the claims of supposed reality – could either explore the possibilities of aesthetic and even sensual freedom or even of licence. Thus in Tasso's *Aminta*, 'whatever is pleasurable is legitimate' (compare Rabelais, p. 331). Teasing out a vertiginous confection of illicit pleasure and endless desire, humanism here could often discompose the self-possession that humanist education sought to encourage, revealing in its fantastic and imaginary perspectives a hypnotic recession of possible starting points. Such countervailing considerations took on particular force in the Counter-Reformation where pastoral played an often titillating game with the canons of official censorship. And the genre proved to be one of the most enduring of European forms: its nymphs and shepherds would constantly re-emerge in the shape of Dresden shepherdesses, Marie Antoinette's cottages, or the soft-focus camera-work of the modern shampoo advertisement.

The extreme possibilities of the pastoral in its own time are marked on the one hand by a Petrarchan desire for introspective solitude and on the other by claims such as Ronsard made to adopt a confidently magical view of our relationships to the world around us. Between these two poles, the subtlest variations are revealed by the relationship between Sannazaro – in some ways the inventor of the Renaissance pastoral – and the founder of the Spanish lyric tradition, Garcilaso de la Vega, who knew Sannazaro while on military service in Naples.

Naples – once the Angevin court at which Boccaccio had served his literary apprenticeship – had come in the course of the sixteenth century to be the agitated centre
of Spanish rule in Italy. Sannazaro – whose own forebears were Spanish – knew of
these agitations at first hand; he had himself for a short time gone into voluntary exile
from the city and in *Prosa* VII of the *Arcadia* offers a nostalgic account of Neapolitan
history. Yet this is merely an interlude in an otherwise almost plotless and a-historic
work, where landscape is woven from a tissue of literary reminiscences and time
moves to the particularly hypnotic rhythms of Sannazaro's text, shifting as it constantly does from prose to formal verse. There is a hint of biographical reference, in
that the principal shepherd in the work is one Sincero; and Sannazaro's own nick-
name in the intellectual academy for which his work was originally destined was itself
Sincero, a translation of the Hebrew *nazaro* meaning 'pure'. Any reference more
specific than this (and any pretence of emotional sincerity) is hidden by a diffusing
filter through which Sannazaro projects a constantly shifting glimmer of elegy, mystery, terror and ritualistic awe. The archetypes he refers to in evoking the Arcadian
world are the archetypes of primary emotional states, unconstrained by the details of
personality or setting. When, for instance, Sincero speaks of his own unhappy love
the vocabulary he uses is Dantean, drawn from both the *Vita nuova* and the *Inferno*.
But he replaces the clear incisive rhythms that Dante employs in his search for
emotional and religious significance with an emphasis on indulgent intensity and
psychosomatic thrill:

> Elli mi venne una tristezza di mente incurabile, con una compassione grandissima di me
>
> stesso mossa da le intime medolle, la quale non mi lascia pelo veruno ne la *persona* che
>
> non mi arricccii.

> (There comes upon me a sadness of mind beyond all remedy, with perturbations of feel-
>
> ing deep within myself which arise from the very marrow of my being, so that there is
>
> not a hair on my head that does not bristle.)

In place, too, of Petrarch's moral interrogations of the lover's motives, we have here
a new mode of feeling that was certainly to harmonize with the sensibility of the late
sixteenth century – much given to the exploration of receding perspectives of melancholia – as exemplified in figures such as the Jacques of Shakespeare's Arcadian *As You
Like It*.

In a similar way, Arcadia in Sannazaro's treatment is a location designed to
heighten effects of sensation and narrative suprise but also to translate them into
melodic form Thus in *Prosa* III, the shepherds are described passing along a silent path
lit by moonlight as bright as the sun where the only sound is the hoarse cry of pheas-
ants – and these brittle interruptions themselves are a source of delight to the trav-

ellers. But then the dream can become impressively disturbed as the shepherds enter a landscape so dominated by caves and lakes that the earth seems to have lost all its natural solidity: 'O wonderful artifice of God that the earth which I thought to be so firm should so enclose in its bosom so great a hollowness' (*Prosa* XII).

Notably, the moment of horror is here turned into one of religious awe; and that emotion too is one that Sannazaro's *Arcadia* consistently encourages. Not that there is any explicitly Christian programme to the work. There is, however, a clear recognition of the imaginative appeal that arises from the evocation of religious moods and the fictional reconstruction of religious practices. So in *Prosa* X, Sannazaro offers a history of the pastoral and reveals that the pastoral world is the realm of Pan into which every Shepherd must be initiated; and at the centre of the initiatory ritual is the great figure of Pan himself leaning on a stick as a great as an olive tree: the neophyte will be bathed nine times in the sacred water; a new altar will be built where the priest

> will take with his left hand a black lamb by the horns, holding a sharp knife in the right, and in a loud voice, utter the three hundred names of the unknown gods . . . He will slit the throat of the lamb . . . and pour the blood mixed with oil and milk into a trench . . . so that Mother earth may drink it. (*Prosa* X).

The theatrical possibilities of such passages will be taken up by the pastoral dramatist Guarini, as will its novelistic implications by the Portuguese Montemayor and ultimately by Cervantes. In Sidney's hands, pastoral reveals its epic possibilities when the Knight of the Tombs – a woman dressed entirely in the emblems of mortal decay – enters the lists to avenge unsuccessfully her fallen husband: the origins that Sidney here lays bare, against the endless cycles of human vengeance, are those of the tomb and love – and short of the tomb, love can never now be requited.

It is, however, the Spanish poet Garcilaso who most immediately draws on Sannazaro's example and develops most fully the implications of the verse-pastoral. In his three great eclogues – each several hundred lines in length – Garcilaso intensifies the aura of gentle melancholy that had characterized Sannazaro's *Arcadia*, to produce a profound concentration on wished-for but never realizable presences. Pastoral here is a form of Adamic dream. Adam (as John Keats put it) dreamed and awoke to found his dream was true. So here, as also, in his sonnets, Garcilaso, along with later pastoralists such as Guarini and Tasso – and remotely Keats himself – opens a rich vein of erotic choreography. An example is to be found in *Eclogue* III where nymphs move effortlessly through waves and shadows that are arranged in the imagination to enrich and display their seductive lineaments: one nymph 'combing her hair of finest gold' draws her head from her dwelling place in the waves, and suddenly the shore is seen full of shadows and flowers:

> Peinando sus cabellos d'oro fino,
>
> una nympha del agua do moraba
>
> la cabeza sacó, y el prado ameno
>
> vido de flores y de sombras lleno.
>
> *Eclogue* III, 69–72

Such moments of dreamlike intensity are further enriched by the suggestion of mythic and archetypal perspectives in which elemental images of light, heat and movement intersect with the psychological and sensational narrative of the melancholy lovers at the rising of the sun and with the onset of night. The movements of the mind are echoed and shaped by the movements of the natural world itself. And the poem ends in delicate shade with sudden shadows rushing down the mountainside while the shepherds, with Petrarchan 'step by step' – *paso a paso* – withdraw with their flocks.

Or else as in a famous episode from *Eclogue* III, lines 105–12, nymphs are seen weaving tapestries from leaves and river gold:

> Las telas eran nechas y tejidas
>
> del oro que el felice Tajo envia,
>
> apurando después de ben cernidas
>
> las menudas arenas do se cría,
>
> y de las verdes hojas, reducidas
>
> en estambre sotil cual convenia
>
> para seguir el delicado estilo
>
> del oro, ya tirado en rico hilo.

> (The web and woof were drawn and knitted of the Gold that the Tagus bears down puri-
> fying then with its fine siftings the tiny sand grains from which it is made, and from the
> green leaves, drawn out in subtle fabric fittingly to follow the delicate fashion of the gold
> now drawn out in rich thread.)

The scenes depicted in these tapestries contain mythological episodes of love such as the tragic instances of Venus and Adonis or Eurydice:

> la hermosa
>
> Eurídice, en el blanco pie mordida
>
> del la pequeña sierpe ponzoñosa,
>
> entre la hierba y flores escondida.
>
> (*ibid.*, 129–32)

(The lovely Eurydice bitten on her white foot by the tiny venomous serpent hidden among the grass and flowers.)

This exercise in *ecphrasis* – responding equally to the sensuous possibilities inherent in natural objects and to the refinements of art – stands as an emblem of Garcilaso's own pastoral achievement and suggests a contrast with the achievements of Ariosto in his closely contemporary *Orlando Furioso*. Ariosto (see pp. 5–9) had compared his own authorial skills to those of the maker of tapestries; and at every point it is clear that he means his poetic work to be displayed to courtly view, to an audience that understood the role that he was adopting and the conventions that governed his activities. Garcilaso is himself a courtly artist; at the same time, he commits himself to the uncertain fluxes and breezes of the natural world as if he half-believed that by his art he could derive from them some guarantee of quintessential presence.

A certain melancholia is the very condition under which this belief (or half-belief) was bound to be sustained: art and nature are reconciled only in a pastoral dream. Thus in the First Eclogue Garcilaso produces a particularly delicate counterpoint of lamenting voices, each in its own way impelled, by the loss of a nymph, to a realization of a lack which in each case is made the more exquisite by conjunction and contrast. The Shepherd Salicio is driven by jealousy, Nemoroso by grief at the death of his beloved. Salicio attempts incomprehendingly to realize why he should suffer; and he summons up the richest images available to him in the pastoral world, so as to endow himself once more with the value that infidelity has deprived him of: 'My dairies always with new milk abound: summer and winter all my vats run over with richest creams and my superfluous store of cheese and butter is afar renowned'; why, then, should the nymph have deserted him? Nemoroso correspondingly sharpens his own misery by an erotic attention to the few traces of his mistress that still remain to him: a few ringlets of her hair will always be preserved in a fold of white linen: (357–8). *Tengo una parte aquí de tus cabellos,/Elisa envueltos in un blanco paño*. Yet each voice in the end is only the haunting echo of the other, resounding in a hollow that represents the only reality that the natural or the artistic worlds can offer. This is an art of constantly shifting *entrelacement*, itself at its most responsive when it recognizes how far from substantial the world in which it works must be.

Queriendo el monte al grave sentimiento

de aquel dolor en algo ser propicio,

con la pasada voz retumba y suena.

La blanca Filomena,

casi como dolida

y a compasión movida,

dulcemente responde al son lloroso.

(ibid., 228–34)

(The mountains, moved by the deep feeling of that grief, echoed and with the voice gone by. The lovely Filomena, almost as if she were pained and moved to compassion, responded gently to the tearful sound.)

Echo-scenes are a regular feature of pastoral theatre; and pastoral theatre itself becomes in the last decades of the sixteenth century a medium in which Renaissance culture can contemplate – in dream-like form, resonating with the echoes of ancient art – a vision of its own immunity to the claims of nature.

Of the innumerable examples of this fashionable form, the most influential was undoubtedly Guarini's *Il Pastor Fido*. Though this is the only play that Guarini wrote, it was some ten years in the making and aroused a controversy when it was published that led Guarini to develop an extended theory of the pastoral form – or, as he would put it, of the *'tragedia da lieto fine'*: tragedy with a happy ending. For Guarini, indeed, this form is the most sophisticated of all literary genres. It surpasses comedy in being able to introduce an air of solemnity through the refinement of its lyrical arts, producing a refreshing 'breeze' of exhilaration rather than the roar of the belly-laugh. But it also surpasses tragedy in being able to contemplate with due gravity all the most serious issues of human existence and yet avoid the crudity and violence that undoubtedly did characterize some of the earlier examples of Senecan tragedy in the late sixteenth century. Death is always an impending possibility in a pastoral tragi-comedy. Yet in such, 'tragedies with a happy ending', as the plot reaches its conclusion, some priestly figure or seer will always enter to ensure that Arcady returns to a state of harmony, usually asserting that the new order is a manifestation of the overarching power of God's inscrutable Providence. In this respect, too, by virtue of its ability to change imaginative and moral temper, the pastoral can be regarded as a more advanced form of literature than tragedy. In its comic aspect a play such as Guarini's *Pastor Fido* does not hesitate – any more than did the Mannerist artists of Fontainebleau – to appeal in its depiction of amorous nymphs and shepherds to a taste for soft pornography. At the same time, in asserting the ultimate power of providence, the same play will confess its Counter-Reformation origins and allow the greater mysteries of the divine to resolve the admitted fragilities of the human condition.

Il Pastor Fido is a play of great length, made all the longer, in performance, by the introduction of erotic ballets depicting mythological scenes and, on the page, by authorial notes and commentaries. Nor does Guarini ever hesitate to point out how superior he himself as author is in his handling of plot to both Terence and Sophocles. It must here be enough to say that the plot begins with Arcady in peril: as a result of offences done to a long dead swain, the Arcadians are obliged to offer to Diana a yearly sacrifice of their fairest and best. This harsh imposition will be lifted – so the oracles say – only when two descendants of the God Hercules can be brought to marry. The problem is that the only male Arcadian descended from Hercules – Silvio by name – prefers hunting to love. As to the sleights that reverse this situation – and the long-lost brothers who emerge in the course of it – the play must speak for itself. But it only reaches its climax on the steps of the sacrificial altar when the seer Tirenio steps forward to unravel all with the words:

> Vain men, how can you boast of knowledge so?
>
> That part of us by which we see and know
>
> Is not our virtue but derived from Heaven.

The pastoral, as the final word in Renaissance literary sophistication, allows us to contemplate our own vulnerability and weakness – though always at a safe distance. But the subtleties of form that Guarini encourages continue to resonate in the imaginations of Shakespeare, Fletcher and of many others down to the time of Rousseau.

NOTES

For **Petrarch**, see Peter Hainsworth, *Petrarch the Poet* (London, 1988) and Kenelm Foster, *Petrarch, Poet and Humanist* (Edinburgh, 1984). For **European Petrarchism**, Leonard Forster, *The Icy Fire* (London, 1969). For **Spanish**, Paul Julian Smith, *Writing in the Margin: Spanish Literature of the Golden Age* (Oxford, 1988); Ignacio Navarrete, *Orphans of Petrarch* (London, 1994); Elias L. Rivers, *Garcilaso: Poems, A Critical Guide* (London, 1980); For **French**, Terence Cave, *The Cornucopian Text: Problems of Writing in the French Renaissance* (Oxford, 1979); P.M. Smith, *Clément Marot: Poet of the French Renaissance* (London, 1970); M.A. Screech, *A Renaissance Poet Discovers the Gospels* (Leiden and New York, 1994); *Joachim du Bellay, Poems*, ed. Kathleen M. Hall and Margaret B. Wells (London, 1985); Hugo Tucker, *The Poet's Odyssey and Joachim du Bellay and the Antiquitez de Rome* (Oxford, 1990); Terence Cave (ed.), *Ronsard the Poet* (London, 1973); M. McGowan, *Ideal Forms in the Age of Ronsard* (Berkeley, 1985). For **English**, A.C. Spearing, *Medieval to Renaissance in English Poetry* (Cambridge, 1985); Thomas M. Greene, *The Light in Troy* (New Haven, 1982). For **Wyatt**, Patricia Thomson, *Sir Thomas Wyatt and his Background* (London, 1964). For **Donne**, George Parfitt, *John Donne: A Literary Life* (Basingstoke, 1989); Wilbur Sanders, *John Donne's Poetry* (London, 1971). Richard Fanshawe's seventeenth-century translation of **Os Lusiadas**, ed. G. Bullough (London, 1963). For **Camões**, *The Lusiads*, trans., intro and notes, Landeg White (Oxford, 1997); G. Monteiro, *The Presence of Camões: Influence in the Literature of England, America and Southern Africa* (Lexington, KY, 1996); Sanjay Subramnyam, *The Career and Life of*

Vasco da Gama (Cambridge, 1997). For **Tasso**, Fairfax's translation, ed. Kathleen M. Lea and T.M. Gang (Oxford, 1981); C.P. Brand, *Torquato Tasso* (Cambridge, 1965). For **Pastorals**, *Sannazaro's Arcadia*, ed. Carol Kidwell (London, 1993); W.J. Kennedy, *Sannazaro and The Uses of the Pastoral* (Hanover, NH, 1983); Elizabeth Story Donno, *Three Renaissance Pastorals* (Binghampton, NY, 1993); Thomas Sheridan trans. of Guarini's *Il Pastor Fido* (London, 1989).

chapter seven

MUSIC

In 1497, the Flemish composer Johannes Ockeghem – chaplain and chapelmaster to three successive French kings – died in Tours at the age of 77. Laments in verse were written by colleagues throughout France and Burgundian Flanders while Erasmus, the greatest of the Northern humanist, composed a *Naenia* for the occasion.

The piece, however, that has since become most famously associated with Ockeghem's death is the *Déploration* written – to the French verses of Jean Molinet – by Josquin Desprez, who having been a pupil of Ockeghem's in Flanders had spent twenty-eight years in the service of the courts of Milan and Ferrara. Josquin writes:

In common with most of the musical examples that will appear in the present chapter, these measures – while in many ways foreign to the modern ear – possess a distinctive logic in regard to the treatment of human passions, of the words uttered by human voices and also of musical form. There can, for instance, be no doubt of the concern that

Figure 70 Josquin Desprez, *Les Nymphes du bois*. Biblioteca Laurenziana Medicea, Florence. Microphoto srl.

Josquin has to express and evoke a profound emotion: his title itself, the *Déploration*, declares that intention, as does its invocation to the 'Nymphs of the woods' and 'singers of every nation' to come and share in his grief. Yet the range of emotion that Josquin evokes includes not only the personal grief that might now easily be recognized but also a contemplative understanding of death, specific to Josquin's own culture, that interweaves references to the Catholic ritual with delicate allusions to classical elegy. As in a portrait by Van der Weiden or else a sculpture by Claus Sluter (Figs. 71–72), formality in the *Déploration* intensifies feeling, adding to the simple cry of passion those levels of response that are consciously articulated by liturgy and meditation.

This eloquent formality even extends to the visual properties of Josquin's score; as a sign of mourning he adopts here the antique style of black notation which was replaced in the course of the sixteenth century by a use of modern white notes. But in text and music also the *Déploration* sets out to symbolize both the gulf and the unity that exists between past and present. Ockeghem in his own lament for the Burgundian Court composer Gilles Binchois (*c*.1400–60) had written – over a continuing repetition of the words of the *Dies Irae* – of 'how death had wounded us'. Now, less portentously, Josquin takes a text which is itself vernacular in form but classical in its allusions and sets it over the liturgical Latin, *Requiescat in Pace*. So, four voices in the

Figure 71 Claus Sluter (and others), *Mourning figures from the Tomb of Duke Philip of Burgundy*, c.1345–1406. Sluter, working at Dijon, inspired a school of Burgundian sculptors in the International Gothic style which ranks in expressive power and technical subtlety with the works of many better-known Italians. The two figures illustrated here are from the sculpted cortège of mourning figures that surround the tombs of the Burgundian Dukes. Musée des Beaux-Arts, Dijon.

vernacular sing of the harm that music has suffered with Ockeghem's death: 'Atropos with cruel shears has taken away Music's very treasure and true master'. But the fifth voice (the 'tenor') offers 'Domine' – the Christian Saviour – as an alternative to 'Atropos', the classical Fate. Similarly, four voices sing 'the earth covers him' – *la terre couvre* – and step down a semitone to express the combined weight of earth and grief. Yet the tenor simultaneously is evoking eternal light with the Latin phrase: *luceat eis*.

In musical as well as textual conception, *Déploration* is correspondingly many-levelled. Indeed the piece allows not only that one voice should sing in a language quite different from the other three but also that each of the four voices should independently trace its own melodic and rhythmic line, only occasionally singing in unison and then to special effect. This is consistent with the principle of polyphony which (as will appear) was to dominate both the grandest and most intimate manifestations of European music throughout the fourteenth and fifteenth centuries. But this genre allows great freedom in both the composition of particular scores and in the shift from one composer to another. And Josquin is clearly aware of this. In homage to Ockeghem the opening nine lines of the fourteen-line poem are written in a slightly archaic style where the melodies, though multiple, are relatively close in their range, flowing densely together. However, in the last five lines, where Josquin names himself along with other contemporary musicians, the texture is lighter and more open – in a way which, as will be seen, is characteristic of Josquin himself:

Notably, the tenor is silent in this section until the final bars of the piece when it adds renewed weight as all five voices now move from the vernacular to Latin. The last words are *Requiescat in pace*. But even here there is a formal play – both witty and moving – which allows that the dead and silent Ockeghem should still be heard: by the principles of notational symbolism – or *gematria* – which ascribe alphabetical significance to note values, the last sixty-four notes may be taken to spell out the name of Ockeghem himself.

By the early years of the sixteenth century, Josquin had come to be as widely renowned as Ockeghem was in his own day, and not merely in the minds of his fel-

Figure 72   Claus Sluter (and others), *The Tomb of Duke Philip of Burgundy*, after 1404. Musée des Beaux-Arts, Dijon. With permission from Scala.

low musicians. Martin Luther – always deeply interested in music – praised Josquin as 'the master of notes' and also for the finch-like sweetness of his melodies. Figures as diverse as Castiglione and Rabelais's Pantagruel mention Josquin in similarly flattering terms, while the music publisher Petrucci devoted three volumes to Josquin's work, where one was the norm for other composers. Likewise in 1543 at precisely the time that Vasari had begun to promote the cause of Michelangelo, Cosimo Bartoli attempts a *paragone* or comparison – between art and music in which Ockeghem is compared to Donatello and Josquin to Michelangelo himself: Ockeghem and Josquin are both 'wonders of nature' who have brought their art to such a peak of perfection that they have no rivals.

Bartoli's comments suggest that in surveying the music of the period, there are parallels to be drawn and developments to be recorded no less significant than in any of the other arts. One might indeed go further than that. In characterizing the Renaissance, it has become usual for critics to point primarily (as this volume has so far done) to examples drawn from the figurative or literary arts; and nothing can take away from the importance of figurative and linguistic phenomena in the cultural experience of the period. Yet music was no less important in the period itself. Indeed there are indications that thinkers as influential as Ficino regarded aural experience as being superior to visual experience in point of subtlety and refinement; and in this light – granted that Renaissance music has until recently been less accessible than the other arts – it is worth asking what the Renaissance would look like if its musical culture were taken as a defining feature. There are undoubtedly certain common-places that would still hold good. In Bartoli's terms – as in Vasari's – art might here reveal a progressive concentration of intelligence in the development both of tech-nique and of the natural passions that characterize the lives of human individuals. Josquin's *Déploration* might indeed exemplify this in the interest it takes in named individuals, in its sensitivity to human grief and in its critical attention to the unfold-ing possibilities of musical style. Yet certain other assumptions would not find such ready support. For one thing music, as a performing art, is essentially a social activ-ity – and one that, to judge from Josquin's deeply affecting appeal to tradition and to his contemporaries, might be thought to unite its practitioners more closely than many other arts did. One looks in vain here for the individualism that stirred ani-mosities in Leonardo, Michelangelo and Dürer. Music, as Renaissance mythology itself suggests, can master the barbaric overreacher and generate (as modern studies of the Renaissance might lead one to expect) its own peculiar reciprocation of indi-vidual and group. In the second place, the musical group itself – as Josquin again makes clear – was constituted at least in the early part of the period almost entirely of Northerners rather than Italians: Josquin names Ockeghem, Brumel, Pieron and Compere – to which one might add, among many others, northern appellations such as Dufay, Binchois and John Dunstable. England is said by contemporaries to be 'full of song' at this time. Nor is it clear that these Northerners – although most of them went to Italy and thrived there – ever thought that they were breaking as decisively with the medieval past, as say Dürer did in pursuing his Italian journeys. Music dis-plays more clearly than other arts the historical continuities that underlay the devel-opment of the Renaissance.

In both social and individual terms, there can be little doubt that, beyond the cir-cles of intellectual literati and the walls of private art galleries, the Renaissance mind must to a notable degree have defined itself through its music. Festal Masses – per-formed by trained choristers – punctuated the Catholic year; indeed in the period of Popes and Anti-Popes musical life seems to have been stimulated by the deliberate declaration of new festivals by competing Pontiffs – who were also quick to censor any songs that expressed satirical intention. In the Lutheran Reformation the contin-uing power of music was recognized; and Luther's vernacular hymns were intended to involve his congregations directly in the act of worship and offer as much oppor-tunity for communal singing as possible. But the liturgy and its music could also serve or collude with secular purposes. In this osmotic relationship, Josquin could dedicate to Duke Ercole of Ferrara a Mass built around symbolic notations of the Duke's own name; and it was familiar practice – condemned during the Counter-Reformation – to base a Mass around variations on popular tunes. One such was a tune known as 'I do not eat pork'; another – set in turn by Ockeghem, Dufay, Josquin and Palestrina – was the bluff, belligerent war-song, *L'homme armé*:

L'hom - me, l'hom - me, l'homme ar - me, l'homme ar-me, L'homme ar - me doibt on doub -

Fine

ter doibt an doub - ter. On a fait par - out cri -

D.C. al Fine

er viegne ar - mer D'un hau - bre - gon de fer.

O, the man the man at arms

Fills the folk with dread alarms.

Everywhere I hear them wail.

'Find, if you would breast the gale,

A good stout coat of mail'

O the man, the man at arms

Fills the folk with dread alarms.

It has been estimated that a Renaissance ruler could spend up to 6 per cent of his annual revenue on music and musicians. Moreover, composition was a pastime even for some of the most reputedly despotic rulers such as the Sforza and Malatesta. Professional composers could themselves expect a reasonable income from these affiliations. Most began life as boy choristers; and that early and continuing experience may account for a remarkable sense of – and willingness to test – what was possible in performance. But in terms of social prestige fine voices were prized to the extent that kidnappings – as in the case of Lassus – were far from unknown; and subsequently a musician such as Ockeghem could acquire a considerable fortune or end with a high position in the Church. Certainly Josquin was able to haggle imperiously – as Bach and Mozart could not – over the conditions of his employment. Likewise, by the end of the period, Tallis would be granted royalties for all music published in England; and the same privilege was extended to William Byrd, in spite of the fact that Byrd was a Catholic recusant living in a Protestant country. (Elizabeth I seemed to favour Catholic Latin motets.) In the case of music as of other genres, an alliance of power, money and art produced lavish public results. Organs might be built ostentatiously out of gold or alabaster; and initially at least money was likely to be spent on drummers, trumpeters, trombonists, shawm and sackbutt-players who could fill the piazza with an appropriate din. But composers learned to extend their range, writing for public events to mark dynastic marriages, or disasters such as the Fall of Constantinople or else victories such as Lepanto. The best composers, too, along with the best humanists, would be drawn to provide material for events such as Carnival. By the end of the period great public works such as Palladio's San Giorgio in Venice could be built with due attention to the acoustic and musical possibilities.

Yet music responded not only to public purposes but also – and with increasing finesse – to the shifting sensibilities that were cultivated in the courtly, aesthetic and devotional life. Isabella d'Este, Duchess of Mantua, had a low opinion of 'clowns and trumpeters' but was herself a courtly musician of the highest order and extended enlightened patronage to musical experimentalists and to the makers of fine key-boards and stringed instruments. Castiglione, as the arbiter of courtly taste, approved of music, provided that the aristocratic practitioner did not distort his features by blowing on wind instruments, or annoy others by humming too ostentatiously. Dance music and chamber music for singers, lutenists and keyboard players flourished in this atmosphere and was performed both by aristocratic amateurs and professional virtuosi such as the lutenist, Pietrobono. Extemporization was at times a feature of this cultivated interest, as when Serafino (see p. 231) would learn a Petrarch poem by heart and then produce appropriate music to accompany it. So too from the 1520s onward was the rage for highly complex madrigal singing, which thrived on the rapid diffusion of printed copy, spreading from Italy to England in a matter of decades. Music and Petrarchism form a strong alliance to define the character of courtly sensi-bility, increasingly providing the 'food of love' and nutriment for fine feelings that would otherwise remain beyond expression. But private music could serve deeply devotional as well as social ends. Luther wished that music should be taught in schools as an aid to spiritual and intellectual discipline. Calvin believed that one should 'constantly be singing in one's heart' and encouraged the great passion for the *Psalms* that run through the period. The secular sphere, by the end of the period, re-absorbed some of this devotional intensity; and John Dowland writing his *Lachrymae*, in dance-form for the lute, seeks to voice feelings that mix the tears of joy and tears of sadness in chords and cadences.

Music, then, could serve as a form of religious celebration, satisfy an appetite for conspicuous consumption, act as decoration for courtly life and be taken as a language of the interior self. In all of these respects, its developments and achievements inter-sect with those of other arts and practices. In two ways, however, music – at least in its polyphonic character – is notably distinct, firstly because it develops most fruitfully in the North and secondly because it cannot, until very late in the period, draw its models from classical texts or monuments.

Polyphonic music (of which the *Déploration* is an example) originated in the great wave of cultural activity that surrounded the building of Gothic cathedrals in Paris and Northern France during the twelfth and thirteenth centuries. This early manifestation of Renaissance impulses was encouraged to a high degree by a cult of the Virgin Mary, with all that that implies in terms of an interest in human grace, delicacy of feeling and form or, subsequently, with the pathos and pity of human emotion (see p. 21). Music in the period responds with particular warmth to these demands and came eventually to be cultivated in lay communities that often made choral singing a central feature of their worship. Throughout Europe, choral communities were founded – as in the *Laudesi* companies of Florence – to meet and develop forms of devotion, usually in the vernacular, beyond the regular confines of the liturgical Ordinary. Such developments could be connected also with the courtly and chivalric cultures of Burgundy producing songs that combined the language of secular love with that of divine veneration. An example is Binchois's *Je ne vis onques la pareille* where the second verse declares: 'Seeing you I marvel/and say you are like Our Lady. I never saw your equal/my courteous

Figure 73 Donatello, *The Cavalcanti Madonna*, c.1443. Limestone with gilt (terra *cotta putti*) 414 × 274 cm. Santa Croce, Florence. With permission from Scala.

Lady.' This was sung by a child of about twelve, seated between the horns of a stag, the child singing the uppper register, the stag singing the lower.

The consequences in terms of musical organization can be seen in the Confraternity of Our Lady in Antwerp, founded in 1482 by businessmen, bankers and artisans which funded twelve choirboys, as well as organs and carillons and seems to have encouraged the participation of a wide range of musical instruments, including wind instruments.

Unique among the arts, Renaissance music, then, was impelled in its early stages almost wholly by vernacular and Christian impulses. This is not to say that it did not progressively acquire colour from a humanist interest in the classics. By the late fifteenth century, the humanist Vittorino could include music in his educational programme; and by 1507 music from composers such as the German Tritonius was employed in schools to assist in the teaching of metres of the Latin poetry; Josquin himself not only composes to a text that includes references to 'Nymphs' and 'Atropos' but also sets verses from Dido's lament in Virgil's *Aeneid*. Moreover, by the mid-sixteenth century the figure of Orpheus had come to be of central importance in the mythology invoked by discussions of music; and in 1585 Andrea Gabrieli produced choruses for a presentation of Sophocles's *Oedipus Rex* at Vicenza. Yet a proper understanding of Greek notation was only achieved in the last decades of the sixteenth century. Until that time artists, especially in the early part of the period, seem largely to have derived their stimulus from close association one with another (as witnessed, again by the *Déploration*). Later, as contact with the wider culture of humanism increases, the source of stimulation shifts. Certain tensions – which themselves prove to be a spur to new thought – come to be apparent between the programmatic demands of intellectuals and the fund of musical intelligence that had developed in the rapid advance of polyphony over the first part of the period.

As will be seen in sections three and four, the debate precipitated by musical humanism concerned in particular the range of passions that music might be expected to evoke, along with a consideration of the technical means that might be employed to reconcile the sometimes competing demands of music and words. Yet none of this would have been necessary – or possible – if vocal polyphony had not been the prevailing form of Renaissance music. It is also polyphony that accounts – in terms of modern listening habits – for the aural strangeness of much Renaissance music. For a number of the formal features that best characterize the mainstream of modern musical experience are absent from polyphony and form no part of its own aesthetic nature.

Rhythm, for instance, is cultivated in polyphonic writing less for any insistent regularity than for the variety of metrical patterns that can be derived from a basic motif. Melody, likewise, is for the polyphonist not a matter of tune – circling around a few memorable and often repeated notes – but rather an evolution or efflorescence of musical phrases, again constantly varying and exploring new lyrical possibilities. As for harmony, the chordal conventions of the modern key system only began to develop in the seventeenth century, along with devices such as the ground-bass, which could act as a point of harmonic reference beneath the upper voices of an ensemble. Polyphony is modal in its harmonic structure, but also, in avoiding the insistent use of a ground-bass – with its own emphatic rhythms – it resists the inclination to resolve in familiar cadences. Polyphonic music could never have been conducted with the hefty staff employed later by Baroque directors.

Though polyphonic composition has its own highly sophisticated conventions, these conventions themselves favour an aesthetic of liberation and abundance rather than one of control, encouraging (as in the *Déploration*) an attention on the part of composer, performer and listener alike, to multiple lines of interweaving melody and text, listening always for the unexpected change of pace, for expressive turns, symbolic gestures and skilful unresolutions. This is an art that grew directly out of monodic Gregorian plainchant – which has itself been described as the purest form of song. Polyphony never abandoned this tradition. Most polyphonic Masses take as their starting-point a piece of plainsong; the daily services with which composers would have been familiar from their daily experience as choristers would have been monodic – polyphonic Masses were reserved for great occasions. Composers as original as Dufay continued to write monodic plainchants.

On this foundation, however, musicians such as Pérotin at Notre-Dame in Paris had began as early as 1200 to superimpose voice upon voice, melody upon melody – or even text upon text – allowing increasingly, over the following three hundred years, a high degree of independence to each voice in the musical whole. Some of these developments depended upon and demanded the development of notational techniques in which the composer could simultaneously attend to the development of three or more melodic or rhythmic lines; and as these techniques developed so did the notion of counterpoint itself as a principle of musical organization: a voice would enter with a musical 'point' to make and then be 'countered' or else imitated, sometimes in terms of tune but just as often in terms of rhythm, by the other voices in the ensemble. Choral unison – later developed by Luther – was a rarity, reserved for moments of particular emphasis.

There were early objections to this style, some of them moral – many of which would re-emerge in different forms during the controversies of the sixteenth century. The musical exuberance of polyphony can – unless skilfully controlled, as by a Josquin or Palestrina – distract from the words of the text. Certain popes therefore objected to the use of notes of short duration in that they detracted from the solemnity of liturgical utterance. So too the trills that short notes produced led John of Salisbury to fulminate against: 'the lewdness of lascivious singing voices and the foppish manner that spell-binds all little followers with their girlish ways'. Some composers certainly refused to take the demands for contemplative stillness in the liturgy with proper seriousness. At the same time, developments in polyphonic writing revealed a whole spectrum of purely musical considerations – in regard particularly to harmonic organization – which might at first have been experienced as technical difficulties but which also pointed to opportunities for formal development. As the horizontal melodies of polyphony came to increase in number so too the need was revealed to achieve a vertical correspondence between simultaneous notes. Dissonance, for instance, became a danger. And, while dissonance itself would eventually be put to expressive purposes, the early part of the period sees a marked sensitivity to questions of chordal structure. Indeed in this regard the foundation of fifteenth-century music may be traced – as it was in the comments of Johannes Tinctoris in 1477 – to England where composers such as Lionel Power (d. 1445) and John Dunstable (c.1380/90–1453) began to organize the vertical axis around triadic chords and produce a readily comprehensible lyricism of effect, as, for instance, in his *Beata Mater*:

It is music such as this that in a French poem of 1410 is said to represent the 'English countenance "joyous and bright"' and be capable of making a *frisque concord* of loud and soft, of sharps and flats, of rests and modulations. Along with such evidence of technical expertise, other forms of experimentation were progressively pursued. One such was the development of the cyclical *cantus firmus* Mass, in which a single motif – often taken from plainchant, though frequently from secular song – would be adopted as the point of reference in all five movements of the Mass, producing a unified and yet varied structure and a genre which in its formal complexity bears comparison with later genres such as the sonata or symphonic variations. The composer thus claimed architectonic control over his own material – to the extent that Josquin in the *Illibita Mass* could take the symbolic notation of his own name and sign himself into his own work as a painter such as Van Eyck might in the *Arnolfini Marriage*. Similar evidence of artistic independence is provided also by the history of the motet. This – like early forms of drama – began as an addition to the formal words of the Mass, sung at intervals in the liturgy as the priest, for instance, prepared to deliver his homily. Texts were originally scriptural but they invited a freer musical treatment than did the Mass itself, offering opportunities for experimentation in musical form and also in the treatment of narrative or expressive possibilities. Before long, the motet was the medium in which a composer could respond, beyond the walls of the Church, to the secular demands of feasting and political occasion.

The development of polyphonic music has sometimes been compared to the development of linear perspective. This comparison may reasonably suggest the extent to which polyphonic compositions allow – as in the groupings of a Masaccio painting – an organized attention to many and various points of interest. Beyond that, however, the comparison is misleading. For one thing, perspective undoubtedly does conform, roughly, to the way we see the world and certainly remains part of the conventions that currently allow painters and persons-in-the street to orientate themselves. Yet music can never stand in any such simple mimetic relationship with common-sense reality, nor – in spite of certain attempts at musical word-painting in the madrigals of the sixteenth century – do composers themselves seemed to have to wished to do so. Even in technical terms, polyphonic music begins and ends with the Renaissance, a symbol and expression of Renaissance alterity. It is true that even in the nineteenth century there were composers such as Liszt who aspired to become the Palestrina of their day; and some of the expertise that had been developed in the period may indirectly have been influential in contributing to the contrapuntalism of the eight-eenth century. But if anything, the spirit and conception of Renaissance music points backward rather than forwards. Thus one of its greatest theorists, Pietro Aaron (1480–1550), can stress the extent to which music conforms to the rational nature of human beings and analyse polyphony in terms of plainchant. Certainly, the intel-lectual complexity and symbolic richness of polyphonic music – along with its sym-pathetic understanding of religious sentiment – points back rather to scholastic argumentation than to any supposedly realistic representation of the natural world. And some humanists in the sixteenth century were known to resist this music pre-cisely for that reason.

Yet in one respect polyphonic music is unmistakably a product of Renaissance culture, in being very firmly embodied in and encouraged by the practices of a courtly culture. Thus when Bartoli compares Josquin to Michelangelo, the point of compar-ison must in part be that courtly virtue of *sprezzatura* that wins applause through-out the Renaissance whenever an artist confronts the difficulties of a subject and overcomes them with grace and freedom (see p. 44). Polyphony is as demanding in this respect as any Sistine ceiling; and it is *sprezzatura* that in the first instance promised Flemish polyphonists a hearing in Italy. Josquin is one example, another even earlier case is Guillaume Dufay. We may now consider in more detail the work which these two Northern artists were able to bring to fruition in the ambience of musical Italy.

DUFAY AND JOSQUIN IN ITALY

By the time that Josquin arrived in Italy, the Italian courts had recognized for many decades the value and prestige of Northern musicians, most notably in the recep-tion they had given to Guillaume Dufay (1400–74) and to many lesser composers.

Indeed for fifty years or so – at precisely the point when Donatello and Masaccio were at their most vigorous – Italian composers fell temporarily silent before returning to the centre of the stage – particularly in Venice – in the later part of the sixteenth century. This is not to say that there was no native Italian tradition nor that the styles of Northern composers failed to respond to those of their hosts. Carnival music – though often written by Flemish professionals – demanded attention to the versification and rhyming schemes of a lyric tradition which, with Dante and Petrarch, proved more sophisticated than any other in Europe. There were also communities of lay singers that had developed since the time of St Francis who sang words concerning Death, Judgement and the Virgin Mary to monophonic melodies with strong rhythms and firm chordal emphases as for example in Demophon's *Volgi gli occhi* and Landini's *O cieco Mondo*. Such music rose to the surface at the time of Savanarola in Florence. Above all, there was the *frottola* – a generic name for a number of formal types, deriving ultimately from the songs of improvisatory artists. Though popular in origin, the *frottola* cultivated at court, notably at Mantua by the great musical patron Isabella d'Este and came to be available in Petrucci's printed versions as music – often though not always trivial in character – suited for all occasions, emotional and social. Again, as with the *Lauda*, chordal considerations were here more significant than was common in Northern music of the time; and most importantly these songs retained a directness of expression that was eventually to link with Northern sophistication and contribute to the rise of the madrigal. Tromboncino (who murdered his wife, thus anticipating the great madrigalist Gesualdo, who also murdered his) writes: *Io son l'uccello che non può volare/non me essendo rimasta penna aduna*: I am a bird who cannot fly; there remains for me no feather:

One cannot speak of Italian music at this time as providing a direct influence on Flemish composers. Dufay himself clearly absorbed musical suggestions from France and Burgundy as well as from Italy. In any case he brought to Italy a *chanson*-style that overtly refers to his own country of origin as, most famously, in the early song *Adieu ces bons vins de Lannoys*, with its plangent sonorities and carefully graded descents in the top voice. So, too, in pieces such as *Flos florum* Dufay brought to fruition many of the qualities that had characterized the *contenance anglaise*. This is written as a *cantilena* in courtly celebration of the Virgin Mary allowing – as did the motet – discretion and freedom to the composer himself. Dufay responds with a piece that is both highly decorated and yet controlled in rhythm, which seeks for a certain openness of texture in the three voices:

Particularly at its conclusion the music shows a remarkable sense of tonal colour in its relation to the word from *Pasce*.

For all that, *Flos florum* was written in Italy and hints occasionally at Italian analogues. Nor can there be any doubt that Dufay's Italian experience would have alerted him to certain factors that were of central importance in the developing idiom of polyphony and would become controversial in the theoretical debates of the sixteenth century. These include the claim made by the words of a text for sufficient attention; the possibility of chordal and harmonic emphasis and an interest in the ways in which music might reflect mental states and experiences. Indeed the piece that Dufay asked to be played at his own funeral is a setting of the antiphon *Ave regina celorum* which while being one of Dufay's most powerful works is comparable to the *lauda* in displaying an interest in clear declamation and simplicity of texture.

Equally important were the influences that flowed from the cultural atmosphere of the Italian Renaissance court; and it is because of his responsiveness to these influences that Dufay deserves to be called a composer of the Renaissance. Dufay first arrived in Italy around 1420. He had probably been present at the great Council of Constance where were to be found humanists and philosophers such as Poggio Bracciolini and Nicholas Cusanus (see p. 76 and p. 96). Here he seems to have made contact with the Malatesta family of Rimini and his first Italian work is a luxurious ballade – *Resveillés vous* – written to celebrate a dynastic marriage, in which bracing chords awakening the married pair combine with rhythms and melodies that shift through a whole gamut of suggestions from languor, to stately procession to flirtatious liveliness.

From this point on Dufay was to visit Bologna; and he became a member of the papal chapel of Martin V when the papacy returned to Rome. This was a highly lucrative post, ensuring that Dufay, in common with many other composers, enjoyed the benefits of chaplaincies in his native Flanders; and Dufay continued to travel North into Flanders, Burgundy and Savoy. But he also began to play a full part in the religious and ceremonial life of humanist and courtly Italy.

One indication of this is the setting of *Vergine bella*, taken from Petrarch's *Rime Sparse*. A hundred years later the whole of Italy would be setting Petrarch's poems to music; and significantly Dufay restricts his choice to one of Petrarch's religious poems, not yet venturing into the more secular areas of his sensibility. However, the response to Petrarch's poem – somewhat in the style of *Flos florum* – is a clear indication of Dufay's literary intelligence. More significant still is the visit that Dufay made to Florence in 1436. By now, he had begun to compose great ceremonial pieces, as for instance on the entry of King Sigismund into Rome. But his task in Florence was to write a piece for the inauguration of the cathedral. Already Dufay was known to the Florentines – in the words of Lorenzo de' Medici's father – as 'the most important ornament of our age'; Dufay responded in kind with *Nuper rosarum*. This work was first performed within and in honour of Brunelleschi's great dome on 25 March 1436; and the composition is planned in almost literally architectural terms to reproduce the spatial proportions that governed the cathedral in the temporal divisions of its own musical form. There is every likelihood that this reflects discussion with Brunelleschi himself. For both architect and composer seem to have recognized in the numerical sequence 6:4:2:3 a reference to the dimension of Solomon's Temple (in 1 *Kings* 6). Symbolism, both mathematical and scriptural, musical and architectural, here combine in a public celebration of humanist achievement.

Among the most important characteristics of Dufay's work is an ability to discover and sustain orderly structures which were consistent with the melodic variety of polyphonic writing. It is Dufay who consolidates the technique of the cyclic *cantus firmus* Mass that had first developed in England. In this form the fundamental motive is pursued in each part of the five parts of the Mass, making for compositional unity and also for subtleties and concealments in the variations that are woven around this identifiable unit. (Writing on the powerful and easily recognizable *homme armé* motif Dufay seems particularly interested in how far he could hide the structural sinew beneath an elegant play of surface texturing.) Yet even without the *cantus firmus*, an exhilarating interplay of control and risk in architectonic as well in lyric detail is the prevailing characteristic of Dufay's style, as it is – to some degree – of all polyphonic writing.

Nowhere is this more evident than in the motet *Ecclesie militantis* of 1431, written to mark the Coronation of Pope Eugenius IV. The least of its complexities is that the five levels of polyphonic voice are all given different texts to sing – sometimes at the same time – and yet also construct a totality in which one voice celebrates Eugenius's life while others allude to the problems and possibilities that will face him in his Papal rule. To quote Weinberg: 'The elegiac distich of the Contratenor attempts to encourage Eugenius to deal with the more pressing issues of the time: saving the Eastern Empire from imminent Turkish subjugation, unifying Eastern and Western Churches and reforming and democratizing the papacy.' The Superius sings: 'Let Rome now the militant/and triumphant Church's seat/send with voice at last set free/up to the Father above the stars/the song of her priesthood offering/praise for pope resoundingly'; the Motet voice sings: 'Surely by will of saints, a breed/of clergy, balanced just in deed,/their own hearts' choice weighing,/enter now the conclave court'; the Countertenor sings: 'Wars the heathens sing;/best of Fathers, our time we lament; but if you will it one day/shall set multitudes free'; the Tenor sings: 'Behold the name of the Lord./Gabriel'.

This is an example of how the isorhythmic motet – sometimes regarded as a medieval form – could be put to the great ceremonial uses of the Renaissance era. This form depended upon a subtle relation between two distinct elements: a set of intervals (known as the *color*) and the pattern of rhythm (called the *talea*). These two elements could be joined in various ways – for example, if the two were of the same length, the *color* might be repeated with the *talea* in halved (or otherwise diminished) note values; or else the *color* and the *talea* might be of such differing lengths that their endings did not coincide, so that some repetitions of the *color* would begin in the midst of a *talea*. Isorhythm in this way produced a particular form of organization that could be extended coherently over long stretches of music. The interlocked repetitions of *color* and *talea* would not always be obvious to the ear; and in the Late Middle Ages this might have suggested an interest in the realm of abstraction and contemplation. The same inner coherence in Renaissance versions of the isorhythmic form might be employed, as here, to sustain a structure of the utmost magnificence, but (in common with the esoteric paintings of the period) would also have offered, as numerical symbolism also did, a sustained line of secret interest, audible only to the initiate.

At the end of his career Dufay returned to his birthplace, Cambrai. He seems during his final years to have kept in contact with the court of Savoy and was certainly approached by the Medici with an invitation to return to Florence. He remained, however, in Flanders and seems to have become acquainted there with Ockeghem, even allowing the younger composer's work to influence his own.

By this time, Ockeghem was already Chaplain to the King of France and never travelled to Italy. There is, however, an intensity of invention in his writing, even an idiosyncrasy, which have led some critics to associate his 'renunciation of rational organization' with the devotional and mystic currents that were beginning to run through the Low Countries. These same qualities, however, could just as easily be explained as the workings of an extraordinarily inventive and single-minded musical intelligence, which leads to the abandonment of certain of the stylistic features that had characterized Dufay's compositions. Dufay had tended to keep voices relatively apart from one another and assign different functions to each, the one providing decoration, another adding sonority. In Ockeghem each voice fulfils a similar function in providing the other with new material thus ensuring a constantly varied stream of musical ideas. Even repetition or the imitation of voice by voice – which Josquin was shortly to emphasize as a principle of formal clarification – are absent here or deliberately avoided. Thus, while Ockeghem does write *cantus firmus* Masses, his most characteristic works are those like the *Mass Mi-Mi* where such restraints are abandoned in favour of a concentrated abundance of musical ideas.

To Josquin, variety seems to have meant something different, an ability to clarify his own invention, to make it effortlessly simple and always to combine inventiveness with poise. None of which, however, should be taken to suggest that his music, any more than Raphael's painting, is bland. Rather, working as he did for a certain time at Ferrara, he might reasonably be compared to Ariosto who also shows an ability to control – and enjoy controlling – the widest possible range of artistic effects available within the tradition he had inherited.

Born in Picardy around 1445, Josquin came to Milan as a singer in the cathedral in 1459 and remained for fourteen years, moving briefly to Florence then to employment under Duke Hercules I in Ferrara. After a period at the French court of Louis XII, he returned to Flanders, dying there in 1521. Josquin, it seems, enjoyed sufficient prestige to live and compose relatively freely in accordance with his own musical purposes; and there is evidence to suggest that he consciously placed some value upon artistic independence and talent. By the turn of the century a body of musical theory had begun to develop, notably in the work of Tinctoris and Aaron, regularizing and codifying polyphonic practice. Josquin himself wrote no theoretical treatises. But an account of his teaching methods suggest something of what his interests must have been:

> If he discovered pupils with an ingenious mind and a promising disposition, then he would teach these in a few words the rules [of polyphonic writing] . . . always providing them with examples to imitate. Josquin did not consider all suited to learn composition; he judged that only those should be taught who were drawn to this delightful art by a special natural impulse.

In Josquin's own compositions, his most significant formal innovations are designed to liberate an elegant rapidity of melodic flow. In the first place, the possibilities of rhythmic imitation in the counterpoint of voices are here carried further than in earlier composers, so that an identifiable (though constantly) shifting accentual pattern can underlie and sustain variations of pitch. There is in fact a certain use of canon-form in Josquin's writing which, along with a harmonic sense that at times anticipates subsequent key tonalities, makes the writing more accessible to the modern ear than much Renaissance music. In addition, Josquin is notably sensitive to aural texture. Following Dufay his voices tend to be well separated and, while each voice claims equality of attention in melodic terms, the ensemble can produce many-skeined textures of dark and light.

In his very long life, Josquin composed in all available forms from the *chanson* to the great *cantus firmus* Masses; and his particular characteristics are as visible in detail as they are in architectonic design. On the other hand, Josquin can move as easily in his *chanson* as in the *Déploration* (or to tonalities of dignified passion as in *Mille Regrets*). This could lead to music of great passion and dignity. But equally it could produce a *chanson* in the French style such as *Petite camusette* which (with its canon-like structure around rhythmic imitation) invites dynamic contrasts between loud and soft as well producing unexpected and lightly stressed harmonic points of interest. Similarly *El grillo* ('The cricket is a fine singer who holds a good long note') does not descend (as later, and less inventively, some madrigals can) to mere onomatopoeia but it does capture and sustain an extraordinary vibrancy of effect.

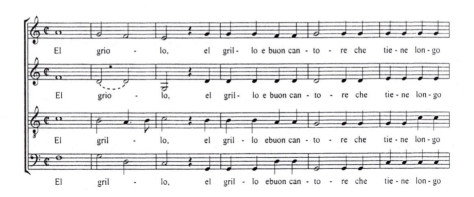

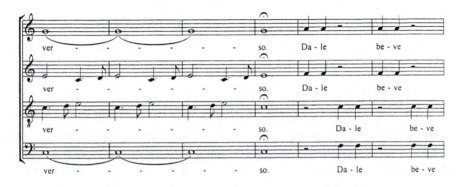

Here Josquin interests himself wittily in the cricket's natural sense of antiphony, composing a joke on the very notion of imitation: art imitates nature while imitation becomes the formal basis of art. The tightly percussive nature of Josquin's miniature antiphons and echoes, and the quick-fire homorhythmic patter-singing of the ensemble, may owe something to the native Italian *frottola* but equally reveals the limitations of that form when matched against the resources available to the Northern polyphonist.

Josquin's Masses expand such qualities into great cyclical structures. Even without the aid of the *cantus firmus* – which was beginning to become dated in Josquin's day – these works can develop great unity of effect. Yet strikingly one of the most original of these Masses – the *Missa La sol fa re mi* – takes the five notes of its title and, so far from hiding them, makes this motif audible in different note-lengths and different pitches throughout the five movements of the Mass.

The Masses, then – even within the disciplined form of liturgical words and inherited musical forms – still yields a high degree of freedom to Josquin. The motet, however, which began as a form in which polyphonic composers claimed the right to exercise their own initiative, reveals Josquin at his most graceful and most intense. The *Ave Maria*, for instance, could stand alongside Raphael's *Madonnas* or Michelangelo's *Pietà* as an example of the clarity that Marian devotion could contribute to Renaissance culture; and, while its chordal structures are easily assimilable to modern listening habits, it is also the sort of work that may well have led the theorist Zarlino to speak of Josquin's work (as Vasari might of Michelangelo) as a 'perfected art' to which nothing could be added in future times without corruption. Here (following Howard E. Brown) one observes a notable lucidity of musical design. A clear development of melodic interest is sustained as voice imitates voice, often in duet pairings and sometimes in antiphonal replies between the voices which anticipate the later development of double-choir construction (as for example in Lassus's *Missa della Bell'Amitrata Altera*: see below p. 307). But variety and a constant flowering of melodic invention is ensured by refreshing moments of non-imitation. So the fifth line, at *Ave cuius conceptio*, is set as non-imitative duets with a third voice added in the answer; and, along with such considerations of 'horizontal' lyricism, the 'vertical' considerations of chordal sonority are satisfied by the matching, for instance, of high notes in one voice pitched against low notes in another, to ensure a certain spaciousness of effect. It is characteristic of the polyphonic style that no single voice should ever establish itself as dominant in pursuit of the melody; each voice sings only enough of a motif to introduce another voice, and entries overlap. But the text is also allowed to contribute to the structural shaping of the motet, not so much by any emotive emphasis upon single words but rather by an attention to strophic paragraphs of couplets and quatrains.

Indications of what 'expressiveness' and attention to word might mean in Josquin's polyphony are offered by his great *Miserere*, written probably by the commission of Duke Hercules of Ferrara and yet profoundly responsive to the penitential preachings of Savanarola. Words matter here as well as melodies. In merely technical terms, this means that Josquin avoids the confusion that can arise through polyphonic exuberance, or else through an over-emphatic loading of any single word. But the result of this is that the music, so far from insisting upon a preconceived emotional posture, induces a state of attention in which one is free to meditate upon and investigate anew the meaning of sentences which otherwise would have followed by rote. One notes (following Macey) that the word *Miserere* ('Lord have mercy') is repeated no less than twenty-one times and the phrase *non delectabaris* five times. However, this does not mean that vocal or dramatic gesture is allowed to overcome a musical meditation on the meaning of such phrases. Textual repetitions occur at different points on the musical scale; tonal considerations govern the initial invocation to God and, again, the melodic profile responds continually to considerations of variety and forward movement.

Freedom of musical imagination is the prevailing characteristic of Josquin's compositions. And there is no clearer example than the *Agnus* of his '*Homme armé*' Mass *a sexti toni* (the second of two Masses that he composed on this theme) which may stand as a final example. Built around the most familiar motif of polyphonic *cantus firmus* musical investigation here leads into areas that cannot be defined either in Renaissance terms or those of subsequent musical history. Initially, Josquin makes some reference to Dufay's style, in his command of great melodic sweeps (once more sustained by contributions from each of the voices) that rise and fall effortlessly through the octave. However, impetus remains the characteristic of this work. And here as elsewhere this is achieved not by rhythmic beat or by the observance of bar lines as it would be in later music, but rather by the careful planning of the whole, in regard to the interrelation of melodic lines and the control of cadence. In themselves the points of imitation are short, often coming in irregular units of two or three beats each. But between them (given the assurance of Josquin's overall design) these units generate melodic lines that float free of the constraints that would later be imposed by key disciplines into tonal areas of the utmost originality and strangeness. Throughout the three movements of the *Agnus Dei*, the characteristic intervals of the *L'homme armé* theme (bars 1–4) are progressively developed in an increasingly lyrical and florid melody. In the first movement, the motif of the falling minor returning by steps (and ultimately rising to the melodic apex) is based on the second six bars of the second section of the *chanson*, and is in turn the basis of lyrically antiphonal scale passages – at first falling then rising – that are progressively extended both in range and in rhythm. These progressively develop into a free-flowing set of cadences in the final section (see p. 29x), answered in canon by shorter motifs, tightly based once again on the intervals and their inversions of the original *chanson*. Even the surprising octave leap in the superius (bar 11) which is echoed in the altus (bar 51) is that of the mid-section of the *chanson*. The *Homme armé* theme cannot be said to exert formal control over the melodic freedom and rhythmic vitality of the *Agnus Dei*. Nonetheless, the close relationship of the germs of Josquin's melodic motifs to the original tune demonstrate his constant inventiveness and the extreme economy of means.

Josquin *Missa L'Homme Armé* Agnus Dei II

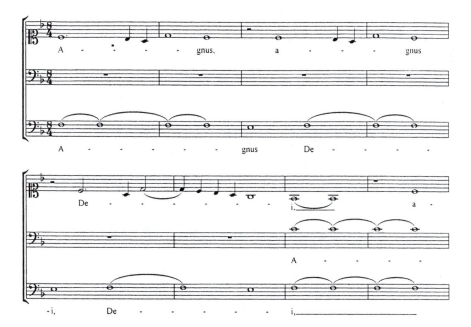

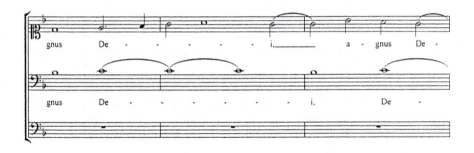

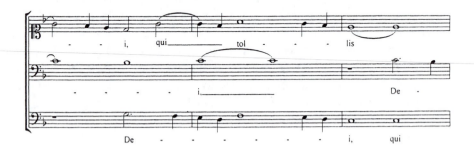

Agnus Dei III

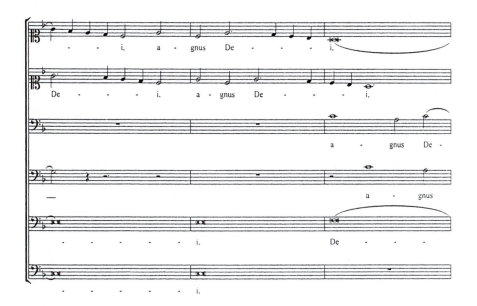

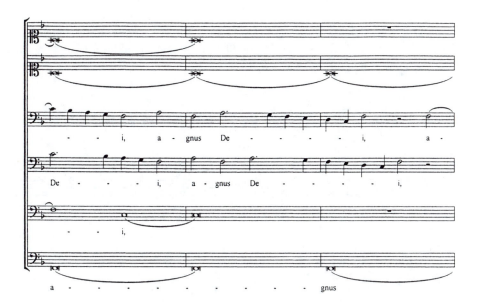

THEORY, SYMBOL AND PASSION

In the mid-1550s, Orlando di Lasso (Lassus) (1532–94) – Director of the Papal Choir and therefore directly acquainted with the Sistine Chapel – could write the very early and highly experimental *Prophetiae Sibyllarum*:

Here as in Michelangelo's depiction of the Sibyls (see Plate III), the oracles of the Greeks are presented as foreshadowings of Christian truth; and, if Michelangelo draws on the sculptural examples of the classical world, so Lassus – though writing elsewhere in the polyphonic tradition – here attempts to create a version of Greek musical style in the highly chromatic texture of his composition. Chromaticism explores the aural possibilities of intervals hidden within the accepted range of possibilities; and, just as oil painting could be regarded as an alchemical art, so chromatic composition has been thought of as secret music, exploring the colorations of half- and quarter-tones that are hidden by conventional conceptions of the interval. Nicola Vicentino (author of *L'antica musica ridotta alla moderna prattica* of 1555) constructed an *archicembalo* – a harpsichord with six manuals – that divided every tone into five, so that an octave contained not twelve but thirty-one tones. So, too, by the last quarter of the sixteenth century, élite academies had been founded, particularly in Florence and Paris that were concerned to recover Greek musical notation and to reproduce in vernacular form the quantities of Latin metre.

Such developments exerted, as will appear, a considerable influence on the development of vocal and instrumental styles, especially in madrigal writing. But they also expressed a shifting conception of music itself, cultivated in the symbolism as well as the theory of the period, which sought in music a more direct and passionately expressive medium than polyphony could provide. To some humanists, such as Erasmus, polyphony risked being as over-complicated as scholastic argumentation; Erasmus looked askance at the artificialities of the Eton Songbook. On the other hand, Ficino (see pp. 90–4) had envisaged for music an elevated role as the point of connection between magic, mathematics and medicine; and this notion pointed not only to the cosmic but also to the psychosomatic effects of music; it was music of all the arts that could work most directly on the nervous system as well as on the mind.

For Ficino, then, the musician is a new Orpheus able, with the few strings of a simple lyre, to move rocks, sway the moods of beasts and transform the passions of human beings. But there are wide implications to this mythic fantasy. For one thing, the suggestion must be that the power of music is fundamental to the human psyche and need not be constrained by the particular demands of a Christian culture; it is no accident that Monteverdi's first opera is the *Favola d'Orfeo* of 1607 (nor that his last is the scandalously immoral *L'incoronazione di Poppea* of 1642). In this respect, the Orphic myth encourages a conception of music in which the ecstasies and rapture of a musician would speak spontaneously to the passions of the listener and temper them accordingly. Music theory at this stage constantly appeals to examples of musicians who changed the mood of heroes or tyrants from anger to sadness or tranquility:

> It was with two songs in the Phrygian and Sub-Phrygian modes that Timotheus gave proof of his power on the person of Alexander, whom, with a Phrygian tune, he caused to rush to his arms when at table, immediately afterwards causing him to return to his former tranquility with a Sub-Phrygian tune. (Originally, in Dio Chrystostum *De regno I.*)

To this extent, music – in common with humanism at large – possesses an ethical function; and much of the interest that theorists took in Greek music was related to the ways in which the Greek modalities might be thought to correspond to certain states of mind – the Phrygian is warlike, the Dorian is magnificent, the Mixolydian is plaintive. Gregorian plainchant had always been modal, but its concentration had been on the contemplative frame of mind in which Christian texts might be received in an appropriate spirit. Theorists such as Glareanus now extended the number of modes from eight to twelve; and the Greek modes took one deep into the history of the Greek temperament, apparently liberating a whole spectrum of possible passions. Such interests also affected conceptions of musical performance, encouraging above all a rhapsodic virtuosity in the solo singer or instrumentalist that was wholly at odds with choral polyphony.

Music, then, was close at this point to declaring ethical and aesthetic independence in the hierarchy of the arts. Yet any notion that music might be the 'pure' form that later ages have made it would have been wholly out of keeping with the profound if increasingly tense relationship that existed in the humanist mind between music and rhetoric. It is true that as in the Middle Ages, so in the Renaissance, musical human-ists such as Gafori, Glareanus and Zarlino continued to investigate the relationship between mathematics and music. All were concerned with pure relationships and proportions that might indeed be thought to reflect the harmonious structure of the cosmos itself. Yet there were shifts even here that began to suggest, for example, that there was no such thing as a dissonance; all harmonic intervals had a function if properly understood. So dissonance – along with chromaticism – became a resource that composers might use for expressive purposes. Increasingly, theoreticians and composers agreed that the ear itself should decide what was fitting to a musical composition. Simultaneously, Michelangelo would claim to possess 'compasses in the eye itself'; and clearly such developments are consistent with an interest in the fluctuations and appropriate expression of the inner self.

Yet, in music as in the visual arts, rhetoric remained the measure of humanist achievement, particularly in the musical academies of Florence and France. In Florence, Vincenzo Galilei – a lutenist and theorist as well as being father of the sci-entist, eloquently invokes Greek authority – during a discussion of the enharmonic to demonstrate the persuasive power of even the simplest musical devices: and writes in his *Discorso intorno all'uso dell'enharmonico*:

Witness the compositions of Olympus and Terpander, and of all other musicians and poets of their sort. These compositions, although reduced to three strings and to simple means, so completely surpassed those varied and multi-stringed that no one could rival them.

Here music is seen as synonymous with poetry; and musical simplicity meant, among other things, the possibility of greater clarity in expressing the power of a text. Nor did Galilei simply mean by this a superficially mimetic or onomatopoeic illustration of single words. He was in fact strongly opposed to the over-detailed effects of this sort that had begun to emerge in madrigalism. His own concern was with the underlying rhythm of a narrative that might be generated by its passionate words. Declamation – and ultimately recitative – was to be as important as decoration.

In a similar vein the aristocratic leader of the Florentine *Camerata*, Giovanni Bardi, insists that words are the soul of a song and music its body, and points to Ariosto (a poet, as we have seen, of constantly changing moods) as one whose verbal musicality invited the attention of the composer. Bardi's own compositions reflects a concern to suppress both polyphonic and madrigalist tendencies in favour of a pseudomonodic top line. Such concerns were linked with arguments concerning the nature of Greek drama where certain theorists argued that all Greek theatre was musical theatre; and numerous experiments were under way which led in the early seventeenth century to the development of opera. So too in France at the academy which existed between 1571 and 1576 under Jean-Antoine Baïf (1532–89). Here in his inaugural document, Baïf claims an ethical, even political, power for music:

It is of great importance for the morals of the citizens of a town that the music current in the country should be retained under certain laws for . . . where music is disordered, there morals are also depraved and where it is well ordered, there men are well tutored.

The Academy was for a short time remarkably true to its own precepts. It operated at the height of the Wars of Religion, and its members included Huguenot composers such as Claude Le Jeune as well as Catholics such as Jacques Mauduit; Le Jeune is said to have saved the *Psalms* of his Catholic colleague from destruction in the Massacre of St Bartholomew's Day. *Psalms* – especially when translated into the vernacular – were here as elsewhere at this point in the Renaissance a genre of the utmost importance to the Academy. For these too were a form of ancient music, which – through the example of David – and of Christ himself – could be reconciled with the Orphic myth.

Stylistically, however, the Academy was again concerned to recover the purity and power of ancient metrical declamation. Its members included poets from the *Pléiade* such as Ronsard who, as we have seen, was notably experimental in his interest in classical metrics. Now, the Academy set itself to discover a form of music that would allow the vernacular to be 'measured' by quantitative rather than accentual considerations:

> Le Jeune who was the first to be bold enough to draw poor Rhythm out of the tomb to join here to Harmony. For harmony alone with its agreeable consonances may well arrest the admiration of the most subtle spirits. But rhythm coming to animate these consonances may also animate, move and draw whither it wishes by gentle violence of its regulated movements all souls however gross and rude they may be.

The music produced by this theory was not monodic; but it did provide for parts to be arranged so that each syllable was sung simultaneously by all the voices, producing a marked and discernible rhythmic pulse in the ensemble. To this the academicians sought to add measured movements in the writing of dance steps, so that if the Florentine academy favours recitative Baïf's academy contributes something to the development of Baroque court theatre.

WORDS AND MUSIC IN THE SIXTEENTH CENTURY

The theoreticians of the sixteenth century display an increasing appetite for the forms that would lead, in the seventeenth century, to the development of opera. The Florentine emphasis upon the passions and monodic recitative influenced Striggio and Peri in the staging of musical narratives from the 1570s onward; Baïf's Academy encouraged styles of declamation and dance that similarly affected music at court in the early Baroque. It was Monteverdi, however, in a career spanning the turn of the century, who provided the theory as well as the practical foundations for the new form. It is he in the preface to the fifth book of *Madrigals* (expanded by his brother in 1605) who distinguishes the *prima prattica* of music from the *seconda*. The first practice – which Monteverdi does not disparage – is represented by masters of polyphony such as Ockeghem and Josquin. The second, which included Cipriano da Rore, Gesualdo and Monteverdi himself, is concerned with the power of words, with the passions and (as in Tasso's theory of the epic) with historical subjects and their moral example. There is also a clear distinction in Monteverdi's mind between his own practice and that of the dominant figure of late Seicento religious music, Palestrina.

Even before works such as *Orfeo*, *Il Ritorno di Ulisse* and *Arianna*, Monteverdi in his madrigals had begun to explore the implications of the *seconda prattica* where, like many other madrigalists, he seeks to make music evoke the emotions and sensations of a human scene, as in *Ecco mormorar* (*Madrigals*, Book II), where rhythms picture the languorous breezes and the rippling of pastoral streams. But Monteverdi's preoccupation with the complexities of the human psyche and the comparable complexities of the poetic word intensifies when he encounters Tasso's poetry, with its own charge of sensuality, spiritual ambition, historical themes and high linguistic colour. Tasso himself in his dialogue *La Cavaletta* (published in 1587) had called upon Alessandro Striggio and others to generate a new seriousness in music. Similarly, his pastoral drama *Aminta* along with Guarini's *Il Pastor Fido* (see pp. 266–7) sets itself to explore the turbulent and titillating possibilities of total theatre. Monteverdi, in the Third book of the *Madrigals*, engages deeply with the heroic pathos of *Gerusalemme Liberata*, where, for instance, frail heroines dress in ill-fitting armour to pursue their heedless lovers and tombs dominate the nocturnal landscape. These madrigals anticipate Monteverdi's great account of the *Combattimento di Tancredi e Clorinda* – the battle that forms, in Tasso's poem, the catastrophe in a story that ends in the haunted wood (see pp. 257–8). But, as Monteverdi recognizes, certain radical changes will be necessary in musical organization before opera can begin flourish. Most important, perhaps, is the invention of the *basso continuo*; in polyphony a value is placed upon the interweaving of melodic lines, and, structurally, upon imitation and reciprocation between these lines. In contrast, the ground-bass will provide a continuing and persistent point of harmonic and rhythmic reference. Similarly, the convention that allows that many voices should sing in terms of the first person pronoun, confessing in chorus to the torments, passions and palpitations of the lonely heart, will also need to be replaced by another convention that favours confident flights of monody.

With hindsight – or else with long familiarity – developments such as these may seem to be entirely logical or even natural. Yet vocal polyphony remains the dominant form of sixteenth-century music; and it would be reductive in terms of both musical and cultural significance to suppose that polyphonists were merely marking time until the advent of opera. Consider, for instance, the cultural significance of the choric first person. As was suggested in an earlier chapter, Renaissance thinkers may up to a point be taken to celebrate the achievements of the heroic individual. Yet they also acknowledge how many surfaces there are in the communal world that echo and augment – or sometimes refract and fracture – the voice of any single self. Orpheus himself – the archetypal musician – was torn apart by the Maenads; and we have only to consider the case Don Carlo Gesualdo, Prince of Venosa and madrigalist – who, in murdering his wife, responded to the lacerating claims of the honour code – to see that composers might have understood this Orphic truth. Similarly, the demands of the Counter-Reformation insisted that selves should resist any claim to absolute self-sufficiency. Tasso was driven to the point of madness not least by his desire to find favour in the eyes of courtly and religious institutions; and Tasso not only provides a stimulus for Monteverdi's innovations but is also the friend – and companion in neurosis – of Carlo Gesualdo. It is equally true that Tasso's appetite for orthodoxy was shared by one of the most balanced and productive polyphonists of the late sixteenth century, Giovanni Pierluigi da Palestrina.

Seicento music may, then, reveal moments of both difficulty and grace which are not to be found in later music. Indeed Monteverdi himself unwittingly suggests an area in which his own operatic style might lead to oversimplification when in his prefaces he suggests an interest in representing certain definable states of anger and love, as if these could ever have fixed and conventional musical equivalents. The danger of formulaic assumptions as to the nature of our emotions or heroic and histrionic posturing is not far away. So, too, there is the possibility that music – seeking to emulate the descriptive power of the visual arts – might yield all too easily to the clichés of aural word-painting. G.B. Doni reprimands this tendency when in 1635 he writes in his *Trattato della musica scenica*:

> The error consists in this: that instead of expressing or imitating the whole concept, given in an appropriate melody, they set about to express the separate words and in this they believe consists the true imitation of the word, as they call it, even if it be an extremely clumsy method of imitation and much too affected. . . . If they wish to set such words as denote height or speak of the sky, the stars and like things they will suddenly search out high notes and sink when they mention Hell.

These of course are dangers that also exist especially in the madrigalism of the sixteenth century; and there are moments in the music of all periods when word painting can produce effects of considerable charm (as, for instance, in Jannequin's *La Guerre*). But Seicento music – driven by theoretical interests and cultural pressures – reflectively confronted its own nature. One factor in this regard was the very determination to assert the relationship between music and rhetoric. For, as we have seen, language itself was fired by enormous and centrifugal energies throughout the century, particularly in vernacular poetry. These would come to a climax in the rich ambiguities and driving rhythms of Elizabethan, and supremely Shakespearian, poetic language. The earliest madrigalists tended to set texts by Petrarch; and indeed to reduce Petrarch's linguistic complexity to relatively simple formulae. But Tasso, Sannazaro and Guarini in the richness (and often erotic or sophisticatedly decadent) charge of their style put extreme pressure on their musical admirers. To which in some cases, composers responded with great sensitivity. When Gesualdo writes the *Ardita zanzaretta* (*Madrigals*, VI, 13), he comes close to Donne's famous conceit of the flea that unifies the blood of two lovers in its bite: 'My lady takes the mosquito and squeezes it . . . O happy end . . . I shall bite you myself . . . and if you take me and squeeze me, Oh! I shall faint from tasting the sweet poison in that beautiful breast.' Gesualdo's musical response to this goes beyond the merely onomatopoeic reproduction of mosquito buzzings to the creation of those chromatic stresses that led Aldous Huxley to speak of this madrigal as an anticipation in miniature of Wagner's *Tristan und Isolde*. The daring of the composer's invention becomes the greater when one notes (with Glenn Watkins) that the music intensely recalls Gesualdo's treatment in his *Responsoria* of the death cries of the Saviour on the Cross.

At the same time, composers must have been increasingly aware that music itself, even without words, possessed in its own terms uniquely expressive possibilities. It is a small but significant indication of the character of the madrigal form that instrumental settings of madrigals were made where subtleties of effect beyond the range of the human voice could be registered on the instrumental string (in, for instance, the writing of extremely rapid rhythms). Such developments might lead – as in many of the lyric poems of the period – to a relatively superficial treatment of the moral implications of Petrarchan love poetry, and to a certain narcissism in the display of emotional posture and narrative word painting. But the same developments also encouraged the development of melodic instruments such as the viol da gamba. Examples could be found in the writings of the English madrigalist John Wilbye of Hengrave Hall in Suffolk or in the madrigals – 'reduced' for instrumental performance – by Orazio Bassano.

In the frenzy of madrigalism that overtook Europe in the late sixteenth century, musical virtuosity led to the development of techniques that are easily comparable to those that characterized the 'stylish style' or Mannerism of the period. Where Michelangelo might cultivate a structurally illogical style of architecture in the Laurenzian Library, so musicians came to see the expressive value of unprepared dissonances, of broken and intensely crystallized phrasing, of chromaticism and falsetto or *sotto voce* effects of voice, all employed in pursuit of narrative or psychological intensifications of the expressive moment.

Yet to speak of the madrigal is to speak only of one strand in musical fabric of the Seicento. Religious music continued its own exploration of the possibilities of polyphony; and some of these in Lutheran Germany themselves pointed forward to the independent power of music or of the congregational chorale which in the seventeenth century was to form the basis of a particularly great tradition. Likewise in Reformation England, composers – often caught between the contending and rapidly shifting claims of Protestant and Catholic rulers – were perforce required to deal with

experimental forms of the liturgy and eventually with the demands of the great vernacular versions of prayer book and bible. The result was works such as Tallis in
Salvator Mundi or Munday's *Magnificat*.

It was, however, in the Italy of the Counter-Reformation that religious music –
running in parallel with the madrigal fashion – developed polyphonic music to its final
manifestation, and displayed at times not only the profound melancholia that characterizes the Counter-Reformation period but also a remarkable sense of jubilation
at the appearance of newly reformed Christianity. In the early 1500s Venice, in particular, became a new centre of experiment, anticipating the role that the city would
play in history of early seventeenth-century music. The Flemish Adrian Willaert
(1490–1562) worked in Venice for thirty-five years, establishing a school that included da Rore, and winning praise from Zerlino as the 'new Pythagoras'. Combining
a career as an early madrigalist with his religious compositions, Willaert was particularly concerned with the power of clear declamation and, in developing – from
Josquin – techniques of the double choir, could produce antiphonal compositions
which greatly enhanced the dramatic power of the words of liturgy and scripture. In
Psalm 109 *Dixit Domine* – where composition alternates from verse to verse between
Willaert and his colleague Jachet – heads are shattered (*conquissabit capita*) and wrath
descends on the nations. But this – unlike some Monteverdian battle-scene – is more
inclined to evoke awe at the power of God rather than to indulge any frisson in the
face of human violence. At Rome, meanwhile, Northern musicians were for a time
still dominant, notably in the figure of Orlando di Lasso, who directed the Papal choir
between but, as will be seen, was responsible for some 1,300 compositions in the
widest possible range of genres and moods. Lassu's successor was the Italian
Palestrina who, along with the Spanish composer Tomás Luis de Victoria (1548–
1611), restricted himself almost entirely to the writing of sacred music and avoided
even the example of Willaerts in bringing polyphony to a form that is still taught as
the model of the genre.

In some respects, both musically and morally, Palestrina may well be seen as a
conservative. Like Josquin, he was concerned with the graceful control of dissonance
and the pursuit of bright and elegant aural textures. Moreover, it was Palestrina who
responded most enthusiastically to the demands of Counter-Reformation popes
that the sacred words should be audible without the fripperies of musical decoration.
Yet the clarity of organization that Palestrina achieved in his imitative technique
impressed Wagner, who may have been encouraged in the development of musical
leitmotifs by Palestrina's practice; and Debussy, on hearing the Mass *Papae Marcelli*
declares that 'This is what music should be'. Debussy seems to have been comparing Palestrina's work with the emotive religious music of nineteenth-century
France: 'Wherein does the *Kyrie* of the *Missa Papae Marcelli* express supplication?

Here there is nothing else but form' (*Outspoken Essays*). In this regard, Debussy identifies a willingness on Palestrina's part to accept formal limitation as a liberation rather than a restriction, as the means to a certain purity of expression that can be devoted to the service of religious truth. In the *Missa Papae Marcelli*, even the *Kyrie*, as a cry for mercy, is heard in a perspective – opened up by the contemplative power of music – that reveals confidently and joyously that mercy will unfailingly be offered.

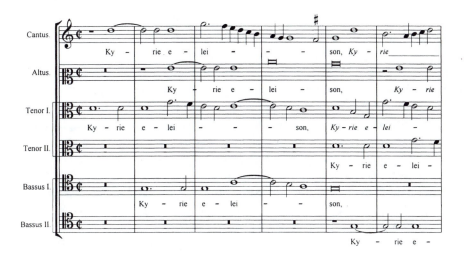

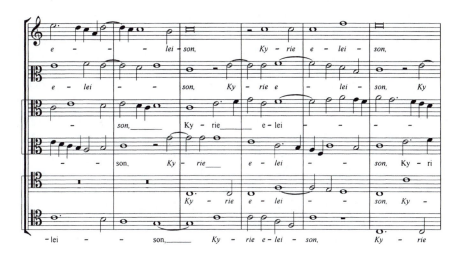

This is not a matter of mere conformity to papal *diktat*. Rather, revivifying the traditions of plainchant, Palestrina makes clear his own commitment to the programme in his account of his setting of the *Song of Songs*:

> There exists a vast mass of love-songs of the poets, written in a way that is entirely foreign to the profession and name of a Christian. They are the songs of men ruled by passion and a great number of musicians, corrupters of youth, make them the concern of their art and their industry. I blush and grieve to think that once I was one of their number. But since I cannot change the past I have mended my ways. Therefore I have already laboured on those songs that have been written in praise of Our Lord Jesus Christ and his Most Holy Virgin Mother Mary; and now I have produced a work that treats of the divine love of Christ and His Spouse the Soul, the *Canticle of Solomon*.

In his setting of verses from the *Canticus*, Palestrina comes closest to the madrigal tradition; and in *Nigra Sum*, for instance, he is capable of producing a certain oriental colour in his composition. But even in a text that is as full of erotic suggestion as the *Canticus*, the music remains remote and meditative. Reflecting the use made of the canticle in the mystic writings of the Middle Ages, Palestrina here invites one to contemplate those allegorical and figural suggestions of the text that point forward to the mystical union of the soul and its creator or the Church and its God. Words in this text are released by the music to fulfil once more a role in approaching transcendent rather than merely psychological states.

Something of the same can be said of the great Litany of the Virgin Mary, where hypnotic repetitions and variations upon the phrase *Ora pro nobis* intensify and refresh the supplication at every turn. So, too, in the *Missa Assumpta est Maria*, the assumption of the Virgin is celebrated with a triumphant orthodoxy that produces in the *Kyrie* an especially clear texture of soprano and tenor voices, while resolving, in the *Sanctus* and *Hosanna*, into a sustained expression of religious celebration.

A similar depth and freedom of religious composition is to be found in Victoria's work. Victoria belongs to a tradition of Spanish and Portuguese composers that deserves more attention than it has until recently received. (King John of Portugal, himself a composer, declares that Victoria. . . .) But Victoria also comes from a background deeply affected by the chivalric, mystic and exhilaratingly ecstatic traditions of St Teresa, St Ignatius and St Philip Neri. Born near Avila, he became a priest of the order of St Philip Neri and brought with him something of the spirit of that order – a lightness of spiritual touch and clarity of musical and religious design (as for example in the *Agnus* of the *Pro Victoria Mass*).

Orlando di Lasso (Lassus), though mainly writing in the polyphonic tradition, presents in a number of ways a marked contrast to both of these composers. As we have seen, he is among the first composers to experiment, if only briefly, with classicizing chromaticism in the *Prophetiae Sibyllarum*. But his vast output ranges from bawdy ditties and drinking songs (on the model of the Greek Anacreon) to great Masses for double choirs, while also encompassing, in various *chanson*-forms, poems by Petrarch, Ronsard and Du Bellay, settings for *commedia dell'arte* characters and versions of the *Penitential Psalms*. Moreover, Lassus (kidnapped at an early age) was a traveller. His time in Rome as Director of the Papal Chapel was followed by employment in Munich at the court of the Duke of Bavaria. There is a corresponding variety in the traits of his personality: wit, vitality and intellectual daring are part of it; and so is a profound religious sense, though this verges more towards an introspective melancholia than towards the orthodox public rhetoric of a Palestrina or Victoria.

Throughout his career, words are of abiding importance to Lassus, in a sense that is consistent with madrigalism but which also derives from its polyphonic origins, a powerful narrative and musical pulse in where rhythmic imitation is more significant than pitch identity. *Pour courir en poste a la ville* (a setting of a poem by Clémont Marot: see pp. 236–7) pictures Brother Lubin (who is wholly incapable 'of performing any generous act') running to town 'post-haste' if there is the chance of 'seducing in a smooth manner some girl of good breeding'. On the other hand, his setting of Du Bellay's *La nuict froide et sombre* traces the rhythms of an ordered (but scarcely Christian) cosmos from nightfall, 'when the earth and heavens let sleep flow down like honey on the eyes', to the renewed variety of daybreak and finally to a contemplation of how all is 'composed' in the 'tapestry' of this 'great universe':

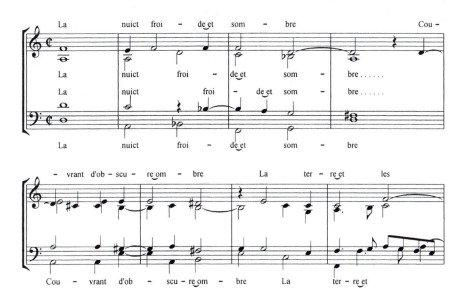

Running through all of Lassus's music, there is a skein of penitential devotion which shows itself in works that turn madrigalism to spiritual ends such as the *Lagrime di San Pietro* or his great setting of the *Penitential Psalms*. This work was commissioned by his patron Duke Albert of Bavaria and appears in a particularly luxuriant edition. Yet musically there is a profoundly personal ring to the rich yet sometimes painfully strained melodic lines that Lassus here composes. On the other hand, Lassus, like Dufay and Josquin, can also produce works of the greatest public stature, as, for instance, in the Mass *Bell'Amfitrata Altera* written for double choir that combines a remarkably unified and sonorous setting of the liturgy with a celebration of the civic splendour of Venice itself and brings together the resources of two answering choirs that had been developing since Josquin began internal dialogues within his motets as in the *Kyrie* and *Agnus* of this mass:

Kyrie

Agnus

In Shakespeare's *Henry IV*, Part II (V, iii), there occurs an allusion to 'Samingo' in Silence's tippling-song which is drawn from a song set by Lassus. Musical culture was spreading; and it would shortly join forces with the theatrical forms that will be discussed in the following chapter. But until that time the madrigal – which was the most widely disseminated of Italian musical forms in the later sixteenth century – attempted to keep within its own private and aristocratic limits the possibilities of theatrical and narrative display. In origin, the madrigal of the fourteenth century owed something to the relatively free songs of the improvisers and street musicians. But even then it drew on the lessons of the *canzone* form – which allowed great latitude to the poet in the construction of rhyme schemes and stanza lengths. This form, on Dante's understanding, had been the most elevated of all, not because of its association with court life but emphatically because it gave the artist the opportunity to stamp his own craft and intelligence on his composition. The madrigal claims similar rights, and in musical terms relies on through-composition rather than the repetition of strophic units. It is, however, a form distinctly cultivated in courtly circles sometimes with a sense (developed, for example, at the French court of Louis XII) of aristocratic indulgence of pastoral scenes or scenes of day-to-day life, imitating for instance the stuttering of gossip-women or the plod of an old man's stick.

The earliest sixteenth-century madrigals, by Wert and Cipriano da Rore, tended to be setting of texts by Petrarch, and to respond to the emotional or colouristic aspects of Petrarch's work rather than to its moral drama. But these works already qualified to be considered by Monteverdi as examples of the *seconda prattica;* and advancing further in the period, the complexities of musical expression available through the development of musical humanism allowed madrigalists to explore, if not the moral questions that Petrarch raised, then at least the refinements of word and sensibility that had come to be expressed in the works of Sannazaro, Tasso and Guarini (see Chapter Six).

Notable in this respect is Luca Marenzio (1553–99) whose work was largely responsible for the popularity of the madrigal in England. Born near Brescia, Marenzio developed a reputation that allowed him to be responsible for such courtly and proto-theatrical displays as the 1593 *intermedi* for the Florentine wedding of the Grand Duke Ferdinand and Christine of Lorraine in 1589. But the most notable qualities of Marenzio's work, accounting for his great influence in England, are those – in the words of the Elizabethan composer, Thomas Morley – of 'good air and fine invention'. Thus Marenzio's own setting of Peterarch's *Solo e pensoso* introduces a traditional *cantus firmus* yet one that is marked, unconventionally, by chromatic qualities and the readiness to indulge in long leaps over the octave. His bass lines too – as in his setting of Tasso's *Giunto alla tomba* – show an exceptionally wide and expressive range. Yet Marenzio's most characteristic works are those in which – under the influence of Sannazaro and Guarini – the Petrarchan search for moral solitude is turned into an artificially pastoral scene – where the musical word painting can invoke landscape and indulge in the expression of stylized emotion. One such case is his setting of Petrarch's *Zefiro torna;* in another, drawn from Sannazaro, he displays a three-fold quarrel between shepherds and nymphs (one of whom is suggestively named 'Ophelia'). Here the scene setting is especially vigorous and the voices sharply distinguished in their character features in which – after passages of word painting on words such as 'dance' and *gelosia* – the fragile sadness of the pastoral world, is evoked by the two male voices singing single notes, entering dramatically to dispel too easy an indulgence in the pastoral idyll – as Mercadé might at the end of *Love's Labour's Lost*. As elsewhere in this very prolific composer madrigalism, for all its polyphonic origins, requires that short intense units of text and musical phrase should be 'loaded with ore' to the benefit of textual intensity but the detriment of melodic flow.

In Marenzio, despite the lightness, there are moments of erotic depth and melancholy. Death can mean death; but also it can mean, in the conceits of the age, a sexual as well as a physical expiration. Indeed, Thomas Morley, though a broad-minded devotee of the madrigal, still speaks of the danger of obscenities and blasphemies represented by the indulgence of phrases such as 'I wish no other God than you'. And Marenzio's setting of Guarini's unambiguously erotic *Tirsi morir volea* – 'Do not die yet,' pleads the Lady 'I wish to die along with you': *Deh Deh! Non morire ancora/che teco bramo di morire anch'io* – does not hesitate to enhance the sensual charge.

The same poem is treated more concisely and yet more intensely by Gesualdo. There can be little question that Gesualdo takes the madrigal form, in terms of both music and text, to its utmost extreme. This is a matter of musical originality – and not simply a reflection of the dark personality that he undoubtedly possessed. Gesualdo is a skilled polyphonist and includes religious music in his repertoire – even if one of his most impressive works in this regard is a setting of the *Tenebrae*, a ceremony in Holy Week in which liturgical candles are extinguished one by one as the Passion approaches. Nonetheless, extreme and conflictual states are as much a part of Gesualdo's musical mentality as they are of Tasso's poetic imagination. Tasso wrote verses that recounted the pathos and horror of Gesualdo's murderous deed – which involved the death of wife, lover and also an infant of suspect origins in a particularly sadistic and ritualistic fashion – though he also writes an epithalamium for Gesualdo's second marriage. No less a figure than Stravinsky can identify Gesualdo as a devotee of 'the English vice' and speaks of the 'lashing syncopations' that are to be found in *Candido e verde fiore*. Stravinsky, too, recognizes the exquisite detail and yet overall unity of Gesualdo's art, in which twenty-seven songs will each provide a passionate *vignette* while also being cyclically connected to its context – 'twenty-seven dishes of caviare unlikely to please a dumpling eater'.

It was at Ferrara that Gesualdo brought his madrigals to their highest pitch. The city was a particular centre of *virtuoso* music, featuring (between 1583 and 1589) the famous four sopranos of its chamber choir. And writing in this ambience, Gesualdo develops a style that favours short, concentrated compositions tending to promote a certain fragmentation of musical and textual phrase. Textual implications are treated with a sensitivity that draws out something of the ambiguity and nuance of psychological and linguistic implications. But purely musical ideas, too, are pursued, to the extent, for instance, of allowing repetition and transposition of phrases even against the dictates of textual logic. An extreme chromaticism, likewise, can produce moments that float free of musical and textual structure. Gesualdo's music displays at times a marked disregard for both melodic progression (which had been emphasized by Josquin's polyphony) and of narrative progression (which had been emphasized in the development of declamatory style). This very feature itself becomes a point of imaginative interest, as, for instance in the famous *Beltà* . . . – where the idea of 'absence' in the first line *t'assenti* produces a chord which itself evaporates into absence.

Yet finally one of the simplest of Gesualdo's compositions is also one of the subtlest. *Io tacerò* plays as love lyrics did from their origins in Occitan and Sicilian poetry on the margins of silence where the silence of death will itself utter the most eloquent cry:

Io tacerò, ma nel silenzio mio

Le lacrime e i sospiri

Diranno i miei martiri

Ma se avverrà ch'io mora

Griderà per me la morte ancora.

(I shall be silent, but in my silence/My tears and my sighs/Shall speak of my torments./But if I should die/Then death shall yet cry for me.)

Here the *io* – the 'I' of the first person – resolves continually into a condition that is haunted by sexual complicity, even tenderness, yet also by the knowledge that our deaths mark the point when others alone can speak for us. Gesualdo is sometimes rightly characterized as a composer of angular, even 'violent' music. But the beautifully shaped sensuality of *Io tacerò* witnesses not only to Gesualdo's versatility, but yet more notably to his skill in marrying text to harmonic sequence. The madrigal moves suggestively through a progress of suspensions that operate as a powerfully sensual attempt to delay, cling to and hold back the harmonic resolution. The opening melodic motif is restated at bars 21/22 in inversion of the initial melodic motif (a

falling minor third) while a transposition of the bass line echoes the falling or weeping of the treble entry in bar 6, which opens out into a sustained canonical development of suspensions urged on by the syllabic treatment of *diranno i miei martiri*. The brief chromatic resolution of bars 47/48 moves the music on to the homorhythmic almost-resolution of bars 55–9, with its heightened chromaticism leading to the final canonical imitation on *griderà per me*, where the individual voices cry out to each other in short plangent bursts, resolving languorously in bar 65 on the sustained 6-bar cadence. Musically, Gesualdo's compositions seem in no way to have led forward nor did they produce any subsequent school – at least until the cult of Gesualdo established itself in the twentieth century. As a coda, however, one may turn to one of the greatest composers of this later period, William Byrd.

In common with Monteverdi's, Byrd's extremely long career spanned the turn of the century. Yet he chose to resist both madrigalism and any move towards monodic declamation. His originality derives from an ability to look back and turn the polyphonic style, in his vocal as also in his instrumental music, to ends that speak both to the private sensibility and to public occasion. Byrd for all his public success remained a Catholic, and some of his most powerful music is to be found in the simplicity of the Mass. One recalls how important music was to the recusant Pastons; and notes of clandestine meditation run through much of Byrd's simplest and most restrained music, as in the opening of his *Mass for Three Voices*:

Yet Byrd too could write movingly for the death of the Puritan Sir Philip Sidney, while some of his finest consort music blends forms of dance and song with structures that still recall the *cantus firmus* and even plainchant. These rich, dense textures for viols may be said to have encouraged the great wave of instrumental composers that England produced in the early seventeenth century, passing on the spirit of polyphony to a future that would scarcely realize where the endless trust in the flowering of melodic form had come from.

NOTES

For **contemporary documents**, Gary Tomlinson (ed.), *Strunk's The Renaissance* (new ed., New York and London, 1998). **General introductions** include Reinhard Strohm, *The Rise of European Music 1380–1500* (Cambridge, 1993), the excellent Howard E. Brown, *Music in the Renaissance* (Englewood Cliffs, NJ, 1976), and Gustave Reese, *Music in the Renaissance* (London, 1954); also Edward E. Lowinsky, 'Music in Renaissance Culture' in *Renaissance Essays*, ed., Paul O. Kristeller and Philip P. Weiner (New York, 1968), Willi Apel, *The Notation of Polyphonic Music 900–1600* (Cambridge, MA, 1944), and Nino Pirotta, *Music and Culture in Italy from the Middle Ages to the Baroque* (Cambridge, 1984) and James Haar, *Essays on Italian Poetry and Music in the Renaissance* (Berkeley, 1986). For **social context**, see esp. Iain Fenlon (ed.), *Music in Medieval and Early Modern Europe* (Cambridge, 1981) and Iain Fenlon (ed.), *The Renaissance* (London, 1989). For **music theory**, Claude V. Palisca, *Humanism in Italian Reniassance Musical Thought* (New Haven and London, 1985). For the **connection between music and Neoplatonism**, Gary Tomlinson, *Music in Renaissance Magic* (Chicago and London, 1993); and *Monteverdi and the End of the Renaissance* (Oxford, 1990); also Ingrid Brainard, *The Art of Courtly Dancing in the Early Renaissance* (West Newton, MA, 1981). For **Josquin**, Sydney R. Charles, *Josquin des Prez: A Guide to Research* (New York, 1983); Wilhelm Elders (ed.), *Proceedings of the International Josquin Symposium* (Utrecht, 1991); Edward E. Lowinsky (ed.), *Josquin des Prez. Proceedings of the International Josquin Festival-Conference, New York 1971* (Oxford, 1976); Helmuth Osthoff, *Josquin Desprez* (Tutzing, 1962–5), 2 vols; P. Macey 'Savanarola and the sixteenth-century motet', *Journal of the American Music Society* 36 (1983), 422–52, also an excellent account of Josquin in Elders, *op. cit.*, and Alec Robertson, *Music of Mourning and Consolation* (London, 1967). For **Dufay**, D. Fallows, *Dufay* (rev. ed., London, 1987). For **French music**, Francis Yates, *The French Academies of the Sixteenth Century* (London, 1947); Howard M. Brown, *Music in the French Secular Theater 1400–1500* (Cambridge, MA, 1963). For **Lassus**, James Erb, *Orlando di Lasso: A Guide to Research* (New York, 1990); P. Berquist (ed.), *Orlando di Lasso Studies* (Cambridge, 1999). For **Palestrina**, see Coates. For the **madrigal**, Alfred Einstein, *The Italian Madrigal*. For **Gesualdo**, Glenn Watkins, *Gesualdo: The Man and his Music*, with Preface by Stravinsky (Oxford, 1991). For **Byrd**, Richard Turbet, *William Byrd: A Guide to Research* (New York, 1987); John Harley, *William Byrd, Gentleman of the Chapel Royal* (Aldershot, 1997).

Most of the musical pieces referred to in the foregoing pages can be found in the following recordings: **J. Dunstable**, *Music of the Renaissance*, Ulsamer Collegium (Deutsche Grammophon); *Medici Carnival Songs*, Doulce Mémoire (Astrée); **G. Dufay**, *Chants and Motets: The Virgin and the Temple* (Archiv) and *Chansons*, Ensemble Unicorn (Naxos); **Ockeghem**, *Missa Mi-Mi*, The Clerks Group

(ASV); **Josquin des Prez**, *Motets and Chansons*, Hilliard Ensemble (Veritas), *L'Homme armé*, The Tallis Scholars (Gimell); **Lassus**, *Prophetiae Sibyllarum*, Cantus Coln (Harmonia Mundi), *Penitential Psalms*, Hilliard Ensemble (Veritas) and *Missa della ll'Amfitrata altera*, Choir of St John's College, Cambridge (EMI); **Palestrina**, *Missa Papa Marcelli*, Westminster Cathedral Choir (Hyperion) and *Missa Assumpta Est Maria*, Tallis Scholars (Gimell); Gesualdo, *I tormenti d'Amore*, Claritas (Etcetera) and *Tenebrae*, Taverner Consort (Sony Classical); *Voyage en Italie: A collection of Madrigals* (Harmonia Mundi); **William Byrd**, *3 Masses*, King's College, Cambridge (Decca); **Adrian Willaert**, *Vespro della Beata Vergine*, Collegio Vocale (Stradivarius), *Chansons and Madrigals 'da sonare': Io Canterei d'Amor*, Schola Cantorum Basiliensis (Harmonia Mundi).

chapter eight

PROSE FICTION AND
THEATRE

THE POPULAR VOICE: CARNIVAL AND BOCCACCIO

At some point around the year 1600 Shakespeare's Hamlet, Prince of Denmark speaks
to (the dead) Yorick in the company of a grave-digger, and Shakespeare invites his
audience to ask whether the Prince possesses any greater understanding than a stolid
peasant or the empty-eyed skull of a court jester.

The culture of the Renaissance was the culture of a social and intellectual aristocracy; and most of the works of art that have been considered in previous chapters
articulate the codes by which a courtly or political *élite* sustained its identity. This is
not to say that the period produced no popular or countervailing voices; and modern
studies of the Renaissance have rightly been eager to liberate the long-silent tongues
of defeated tribes and oppressed minorities. Yet even here Renaissance culture often
proves to have been peculiarly subtle in its ability to accommodate these voices and
to channel their energies into its own service.

A case in point is Carnival. This great festival in, for instance, Venice or Florence
could run between 26 December and Shrove Tuesday. Sex and feasting were central
features of the festival; phallic and scatological humour prevailed in public displays
that were characterized by protuberant noses, codpieces, and pig-bladders. In the
language of carnival songs, innuendo and *double-entendre* were *de rigueur*: the 'tools'
of normal trade took on a wholly different meaning in these lyrics. Masks ensured
a degree of social anonymity; and anarchic violence was sanctioned to the point at
which deaths among the revellers were a frequent occurrence.

In all these respects, Carnival asserted impulses that not only stood against the
darkness of the winter months but also – and especially during the period of the Black

Death – may be said to have represented a resistance on the part of human beings to the senseless waves of destruction that had assailed them. Likewise Carnival may be seen – up to a point, at least – as an expression of the popular voice. The celebrations frequently involved parodic up-turnings of the institutional order, in which, for a season, lords would agree to act as servants and boy-choristers would be dressed as bishops and popes. Yet plainly such inversions were only possible with the consent and complicity of institutional power; and while Carnival festivities may subsequently have provided an outline for revolutionary action, the Renaissance Carnival could well be regarded as subtle instrument of psychological and social control. The magnates of Florence and Venice certainly participated as vigorously as the people themselves in these events and availed themselves just as enthusiastically of the licence they afforded. But the great entertainments orchestrated, for instance, by the Medici could easily be seen as a feature of their political and social programme of management. Savanarola may have objected to the immorality of the Carnival season; he also objected to the insidious dictatorship that the Medici imposed on the erstwhile Republic of Florence by its provision of bread and circuses.

Similar ambiguities traverse the two literary forms that draw most directly on the freedoms of the popular voice – which is to say, drama and prose fiction. Both forms remain largely under the control of authors who by virtue of rank or intellectual formation belong to the Renaissance *élite*. But Renaissance comedy – which is the dominant form of secular drama in the early part of the period – relishes, if only in a spirit of aristocratic superiority, the doings of servants – whores, pimps or bawds – and can even deride certain figures, such as schoolmasters, scholars and medics, who occupied a central place in the official culture of the period. Prose, too – in the form of risqué anecdote, piquant gossip and sensational disclosure – drew its material knowingly from the margins of the social order. In addition, prose was less regulated by rules or traditional generic categories than lyric or epic verse or even comedy; and this itself was significant in an age when connections might be drawn in terms of literary decorum between social considerations and considerations of literary genre. To a theoretician such as Castelvetro, tragedy could only successfully be attempted in democratic states where the fall of princes might be viewed with equanimity. Comedy, on the other hand, was appropriate in despotic regimes insofar as it fostered a certain confidence in a happy order that underlay the comic confusions of the surface. As will appear, it was only in the hands of certain highly original practitioners that comedy came to realize to the full its own subversive possibilities. In Shakespeare, as also in the two greatest writers of prose fiction in the period, Rabelais and Cervantes, a carnivalesque imagination combines with the utmost literary intelligence to call into question many of the social preconceptions that inspired Renaissance culture and also the conventions of perception that were embodied in the theories of the genre and decorous language. Rabelais, even when he is addressing Erasmus in a letter of grati-tude and praise, speaks of the fastidious humanist in irrepressibly carnivalesque terms as a 'mother' or 'androgyne' at whose breasts Rabelais himself has sucked. In Cervantes's work, some of the most important principles of the Renaissance vision – its concern with books, with epic journeys, with the supposed realities that the imagination can deliver – are exposed to ironic inspection. As for Shakespeare, tragedy and comedy come together in his depiction of Hamlet and Yorick, as in many of his most characteristic scenes, to reveal the echoing hollow of a death's head, in which our notions of status, moral order and even the nature of persons are constantly called into question.

To Rabelais, Cervantes and Shakespeare one will return in the concluding sections of this chapter, where more will be said about the countervailing energies that may be generated in formal and linguistic experimentation. But Rabelais, Cervantes and Shakespeare do not stand alone. Behind them (as will be seen in section two) there runs a tradition of writings in the form of the *novella* and theatrical comedy which progressively develops the range of vernacular registers available for literary usage. And to a considerable degree these developments are inspired by the achievements of a fourteenth-century author – Giovanni Boccaccio – who in the area of prose fiction and of drama exerts an influence as great as the influence of Petrarch in the sphere of lyric poetry. As well as the many Italian followers of the *Decameron*, such as Cinthio and Bandello, Marguerite of Navarre translates the work, as do many others such as George Painter, Geoffrey Fenton and George Pettie in the English sixteenth century. The last story of the *Decameron* is translated into a Dutch version for the stage. Rojas's work which is now usually known as *La Celestina* is an extended prose *novella* written in dialogue-form with clear Boccaccian affinities. Italian comedy – which was the most influential form of drama in the sixteenth century – openly acknowledges its debt to Boccaccio. As for Shakespeare, Boccaccio, who provides the ultimate source for plots in *All's Well That Ends Well* and *Cymbeline*, has been described (by Leo Salingar) as the only author who can stand comparison with Shakespeare in the range of experience that he depicts.

Bocaccio's *Decameron* takes as its setting the worst natural disaster that has ever afflicted the human race: the Black Death, travelling along the increasingly active trade routes of fourteenth-century commerce, is known to have destroyed up to two-thirds of some populations in the Mediterranean basin. Yet the response that Boccaccio invokes in the hundred stories of his collection calls directly upon the carnival energies of sex, feasting and exuberant guile; and particular prominence is given to the appetite for fiction – or even the propensity to lying – that Boccaccio recognizes as natural in human intelligence.

Ten young Florentines, gathering at the Church of Santa Maria Novella at the height of the plague, convince themselves that there is no point in staying in Florence simply to die, and indeed argue – in a spirit of witty casuistry – that it would be blasphemous to remain, since this would presume that they were immortal and immune to disaster. This brigade – or *brigata* – of ten storytellers consequently leaves for their country villas. A frame is thus established for all the stories that follow, in which the Florentines conduct themselves with both playfulness and elegant decorum, making little or no reference to the horrors that beset the disease-ridden city.

At first sight, this frame seems to represent a device for evading the implications of the plague; and it is true that the atmosphere reflects something of the aristocratic ethos that Boccaccio absorbed during his formative years at the proto-Renaissance court of Naples. Yet, following the argument that the *brigata* have given to themselves – this apparent indulgence in illusion is itself the affirmation of an appetite for survival, and storytelling, along with the laughter it generally provokes, comes to be seen as a regenerative even therapeutic resource, reasserting the bonds of fellowship that the plague itself had threatened. There are tragic stories in the collection and, subsequently, tragedians such as Cinthio could draw directly on such tales from the *Decameron* as that of Tancred and Ghismonda (Day IV, story 4). However, whenever the mood swings too dangerously towards melancholia, the *brigata* themselves react, to re-adjust the balance. The youngest member of the *brigata* – Dioneo, whose name is associated elsewhere in Boccaccio's work with the wine-god, Dionysus – claims the right to speak last on each of the ten days of storytelling, and in doing so generally ensures that each day ends on an outrageously risqué cadence.

Wit itself is seen to be as much the property of otherwise oppressed and marginalized members of the social order, of women pursuing illicit love affairs, of cooks, grooms and craftsmen. A cook steals a leg from the stork he is preparing for his master's table. The master complains; the cook replies that storks only have one leg. The master, to sustain his argument, insists on going to the local pond to prove that storks have two legs. 'Look, they don't,' says the cook – pointing to them standing on a single limb. The master claps his hands, the storks fly up, displaying two legs; and the master thinks he has made his point, till the cook replies: 'But you didn't clap your hands when you saw the one-legged stork on your table.' A duel of wits has run its course; and, whatever their social differences, the two protagonists have proved themselves equals in humour and intelligence.

A similar but more serious story (VI, 7) suggests the extent to which readiness of wit may serve to liberate the voices of women from oppression. In Prato, an ancient law dictates that women who are taken in adultery should be burned at the stake. Madonna Filippa – described as a woman of great dignity and firmness of purpose – is surprised in the company of a lover by her husband who drags her before the court. The judge is moved by her beauty and seeks to offer her a legal way of escape from the capital charge. She rejects his advice and openly acknowledges her adultery. She does, however, claim the right to interrogate her husband, and proceeds to ask the indecorous question: 'Did I ever fail to satisfy your sexual demands?' The husband confesses in some confusion that this side of things was always very satisfactory. To which, his wife 'rapidly' answers: 'Then what should I do with my excess of passion? Throw it to the dogs?' The reply is not on the surface a brilliant piece of repartee. But the court, taken aback by its unexpectedness, breaks into laughter, and not only insists that Madonna Filippa should be exonerated but that the cruel law that condemns adultery in noble women should be rescinded. In effect, laughter here has allowed the court to realize, firstly that passion is a human attribute (not to be wasted on dogs) and secondly that morality consists not in the fearful restraint of such passions but in the preservation of those who are capable of generous feeling. What is more, laughter itself implies a freedom to look – laterally, as it were – at the established law and realize that human beings need not be bound by a superstitious preservation of existing edicts. Laws are tissues of words; words can, however, be rapid, unexpected and charged with suggestion; it is a mark of civilization that Law – as a form of words – should recognize its ability to change.

Though there is at times a discernibly misogynistic strain in Boccaccio's rhetoric, there is also a sustained attention in the *Decameron* to a disconcerting brilliance in the feminine mind that anticipates Shakespeare's characterization of Portia and Beatrice. There is too a realization that fiction – which henceforth is to have a long history in European civilization – must itself be a medium in which we can pursue a liberating inventiveness and indeed generosity of mind. In Day I, story 3, a Muslim Sultan – short of cash – seeks to put pressure on a Jewish moneylender by asking him the embarrassing question: which of the three great religions of the ancient world – Christianity, Islam or Judaism – is the true religion. The Jew, chary of committing himself, answers with a fable: A father loved his three sons equally but had only one precious ring to bequeath as an heirloom. So, he has two counterfeit rings made; and without divulging which ring is true and which are false bequeaths them to his sons, who subsequently fight over them but ought to have realized the truth, which is that they are all equally loved. There is no moral offered to this story. But the Muslim is so beguiled by its dexterity that he abandons his desire to pressurize the moneylender – who in their newly established friendship proceeds to lend the sum that he had originally required. The sharing of an interest in fiction here replaces the settled and dangerous ideologies that hitherto had kept the two men apart. Moreover, the story itself with its broad-minded implication that all great cultures may live in harmony anticipates much that will be most conspicuously liberal – and open to the relativities of cultural myth – in the subsequent culture of the Renaissance.

John Dryden in the seventeenth century makes several translations from Boccaccio's tales, among them the tragic story of Tancredi and Ghismonda. Here a widowed princess insists on taking a lover against the inclinations of her royal father. The King discovers the affair, murders the lover, presents his heart in a golden chalice to his daughter, who promptly fills the cup with poison and drinks the lethal draft.

In concluding his version, Dryden cannot restrain an impulse to settle all accounts in a moralizing summary of the preceding events:

> Thus she for Disobedience justly dy'd;
>
> The Sire was justly punish'd for his Pride.
>
> The Youth, least guilty, suffer'd for th'Offence
>
> Of Duty violated to his Prince.

('Sigismundo and Guiscardo', from Fables Ancient and Modern, 750–3)

This is precisely what Boccaccio would never do. So far from attempting to enforce stable judgements or decorous postures of supposed comprehension, Boccaccio's stories, once concluded, are the subject of discussion and varying response among the *brigata*. And in the *novella* tradition and the comic theatre Boccaccio's own stories are themselves regularly treated as a source of suggestion rather than definition. In this regard his procedures anticipate the often-subversive poetics which govern the writings of Rabelais, Cervantes and Shakespeare, but which may also be discerned in many of the lesser writers who, drawing on Boccaccio, contribute to the development of prose fiction and drama.

NOVELLE AND PLAYS: FRAMING GOSSIP

One of the most significant works of the early sixteenth century is *The Comedy* (later designated *The Tragi-Comedy*) *of Calisto and Melibea*, a work of prose-narrative which is notably divided into twenty-one dramatic acts, written at the age of 24 by the Spanish Jew, Fernando de Rojas (who seems subsequently to have written nothing else). On publication in 1499, the work achieved immediate popularity, indicating (as will works by Rabelais and Cervantes) the ways in which the press could generate new tastes and could lead to developments and adjustments of emphasis within the original conception of a work. Later editions appeared in 1500 and 1502 (possibly with additions by other hands); and translations into French, Italian and Latin quickly followed, as well as an anonymous English version that emerged from the humanist circle of Sir Thomas More.

It is an indication of one shift in taste that Rojas's work quickly came to be known as *La Celestina*, after the name of the central character, a bawd, a go-between and, probably, a witch. It is Celestina who makes it possible (conceivably by witchcraft) for the lover Calisto to overcome the reluctance of his mistress Melibea – who is unwilling to yield to his advances in the face of opposition from her family. The affair, however, is violently ill-fated. Celestina is suspected by her low-life accomplices of double-crossing them. They murder her in – a scene strident with Dostoyevskyan resonances – and are themselves killed when they attempt to escape from the scene of the crime. Thus, significantly enough, the aristocratic Calisto is deprived of his disreputable but very effective allies. Thrown back on his own effete resources, he bungles an assignation with Melibea and dies falling from a ladder. Melibea imitates him, in an heroic leap – sometimes compared to the suicide of Shakespeare's Juliet – from a high tower in her parents' garden.

In his depiction of Celestina herself, Rojas creates a figure who might well be compared to Breughel's *Dulle Griete* (Plate III). This is a woman from the margins of society, from the murky suburbs of the city, surrounded by an aura of dangerous energy. She is old now, remembering with affectionate nostalgia those from whom she first learned her trade of repairing maidenheads with needle and thread. She speaks with practical concern for the whores under her control. But she also exhibits a voyeuristic appetite in watching the games played by her employees and their customers; and she takes a vigorous pride in her own skills. Indeed, her involvement in the affairs of Calisto and Melibea is motivated as much by a desire to prove her undiminished acumen as by simple greed. Thus she can at times summon up precisely that combination of cunning and impetuosity that Machiavelli, twenty years later, was to designate as 'manly' *virtù*: 'The wise man changes his mind. Only fools are obstinate. When a situation changes, new plans are necessary. I never thought that I was going to strike such luck.' A good ambassador does what opportunity suggests. And as things are at present no time must be lost. To which practical wisdom Celestina adds a necromantic dimension, admiring the eerie bravado of an old associate who 'could take seven teeth from a hanged man with a pair of eyebrow tweezers in the time it took me to pull off his boots' and relating how 'she frightened the devil to death with her blood-curdling spells'. For her part, she clearly believes that her success in wooing Melibea depends not only upon *virtù* but upon demonic assistance: 'I am indeed grateful too you, Devil! You tamed that female fury.'

On evidence such as this, it is not surprising that La Celestina should have been compared to such great immoralists as Shakespeare's Falstaff or Rabelais's Panurge. She has also something in common with the vigorous low-lifes and rogues that, especially in Spain, are to be encountered in picaresque novels such as the anonymous *Lazarillo de Tormes*. Yet it would be a mistake to suppose that the interest of *The Tragi-Comedy* – and in the works that it foreshadows by Rabelais, Cervantes or Shakespeare – lay only in character, or at least 'character' in this sense that has developed in the wake of nineteenth- and twentieth-century representations of the human personality. Undoubtedly Rojas's work contributes something to the development of such representations. Yet here as in Boccaccio's *Decameron* the figure is seen less in terms of an inward biography than in her public or theatrical role as the epicentre of an action in which all around her are inevitably swept up:

> If a dog sees her, he barks 'Old bawd!' Birds sing it, sheep bleat it and donkeys bray as
> she goes by. . . . And if she enters a smithy the hammers beat it out too. Carpenters,
> armourers, farriers, tinkers and fullers, all make the air ring with her name. (*La Celestina*,
> trans. J.M. Cohen. p. 36)

In this respect *La Celestina* demonstrates a peculiarly subversive power, releasing
erratic even anarchic forces that, for the most part, Renaissance culture assiduously
kept at bay – and from which, even now, readers seek to defend themselves by constructing coherent explanations of a psychometric kind. Similarly, the very originality
of the form that Rojas devises – veering between drama and narrative, between a
comedic indulgence of detail and the heroic postures of tragic death – itself prevents
any easy assumption of a single point of view. Thus on the one hand Rojas is capable
of generating high flights of rhetoric, consciously inspired by classical analogues. On
the other hand, his words themselves are likely to be invigorated by dramatic gesture
and graphic details that insist upon visualization: 'Damn these long, cumbersome
skirts!' says Celestina. 'How they hamper me when I'm in a hurry to tell my news.'

The result is that the play cannot be supposed to offer any definable moral perspective. It is true that the theoretical justification for comic writing in the Renaissance was often that it should expose folly to public derision; and it may well be that
Rojas himself had some such justification in mind. Yet it is notable that Rojas himself – who was after all of Jewish lineage – makes little reference to Christian moral
principles in the course of the work; and, while he refers confidently to classical texts,
these are applied to a situation fresh and raw from the stream of a vivid imagination.
It is entirely appropriate that the play should end not with some choric overview but
with questions posed by Melibea's grief-stricken father who hitherto has had no part
in the play:

> O world full of evils, that Anaxagoras and I were alike in our grief and loss, and that I
> could repeat of my beloved daughter what he said of his only son: 'Being mortal, I knew
> that whatever I engendered must die.' . . . Why did you behave so cruelly to your old
> father? Why did you leave me in torment? Why did you leave me sad and alone in this
> vale of tears? (*ibid.*)

Considerations of 'character', 'realistic' detail and linguistic and physical energy
resonate throughout the *novelle* and comic writing of the sixteenth century. And so
too does the question of how (if at all) observation and energy should themselves
be framed. Are there moral codes that can unequivocally respond to these questions? Or are the available frames inadequate to that purpose? These are particularly
pertinent questions in regard to comic drama. Comedy begins as a form of courtly

entertainment, often intended to corroborate (as Carnival might) the preconceptions of an aristocratic audience. Yet it ends on the margins of metatheatre with a series of Shakespearian plays-within-plays that tax our very conception of what a frame might be. But the same question, which has already arisen in regard to Boccaccio's *Decameron*, can also be asked in regard to the *novella* where – particularly in the sixteenth century – there is a strong recurrent concern with the gossip, corruption and often the sexual violence that might – to the titillated imagination – be observed in the courtly behaviour of the period.

Boccaccio, in setting his stories in country villas against the background of the plague, had combined, in an effortlessly tragi-comic style, suggestions both of disaster and of festivity. The author of the *Heptaméron* (presumably Marguerite of Navarre) continues this tradition, choosing as the setting for her stories a spa-town in the Pyrenees, and thus reiterating (in a way that the physician Rabelais would have understood) that entertainment and laughter may, themselves, be regarded as a medicinal response to distress. But here a certain nervousness over the claims of imaginative freedom and the interest of moral ambiguity is already visible: in Marguerite's opinion, Boccaccio deserves to be praised to the skies; yet, in contrast to the *Decameron*, the *Heptaméron* is intended to contain only stories that are ascertainably true. There are, to be sure, some Renaissance collections that adopt a purely ludic frame, as for example that of George Pettie (1548–89) who imagines his storytellers gathering at winter parties, choosing their themes in the high spirits of a snowball fight. But this implies a certain oversimplification of the Boccaccian mix of tragic and comic suggestions and may be set against those stories where the the frame is unambiguously catastrophic. A particularly notable example of the latter is the *Hecatommithi* of Giambattista Giraldi – surnamed Cinzio (Cinthio) – from which Shakespeare was to draw material, possibly, for *Measure for Measure* and certainly for *Othello*. Cinthio begins his work with a harrowing account of the Sack of Rome (see p. 9) and proceeds, in a spirit that exactly reflects the grimmer realities of the Counter-Reformation, to imagine a far-from-ludic frame: aristocratic fugitives from Rome set out to sea under the patriarchal leadership of the elderly Lord Fabio and (having chosen as companions ladies of a certain age) console themselves with stories intended to reflect the ethos of married and philoprogenitive love. This does not prohibit a taste for horrors, fed by such classical exponents of the art as Lucan and the same concerns led Cinthio in his plays to experiment with violent Senecan tragedy. But the attempt to create a frame that insists upon an orthodox moral structure is evident and can be seen to affect the tenor of some of Cinthio's stories. Thus in the tale that provided Shakespeare with his source for *Othello* Cinthio envisages a conclusion in which the Moor, having been exiled for his crimes, is murdered in an act of revenge by Desdemona's relatives. But this act is also seen as the final working through of a providential plan which throughout has secretly opposed the guile, stratagems and violence that the human protagonists of the drama have been guilty of. Shakespeare himself envisages a far more troubling conclusion in which the very powers of human mind and hand that breed violence and murder are themselves the powers that are called upon to produce a solution to the mayhem they have wrought. Human beings in Shakespeare's play destroy and recreate themselves beneath an unresponsive 'marble heaven'.

If Shakespeare had found the *Othello* story (as is possible) in a French intermediary version, then the moralizing tone that he set himself to resist and reformulate in his play would have been all the stronger. For it is characteristic of French *novella* at this time to insist upon both a frame and an ethical vocabulary that act as moral chorus to the vivid events that such stories usually depict. But another of Shakespeare's sources – and the most prolific of all the *novella*-writers – makes his own peculiarly interesting attempt to elude the grip of the moral frame. This is Matteo Bandello (1485–1561) who chooses to do altogether without a frame of corporate narrators – replacing it by a scandalous version of the *Heptaméron*'s insistence on the supposed virtues of verifiable truth. Thus, Bandello will only tell stories that have been authenticated by eyewitnesses. He himself as a count – eventually a cardinal – stands at the centre of an international social circle; and it is to the chatter of such a circle that he regularly appeals, to supply authority for the often-scurrilous tales he has to tell. The consequence is that truth here is accepted – in a familiar modern sense – as reportage; and 'gossip' becomes the mode of storytelling in which author and reader are complicit. Bandello himself repeatedly speaks of his stories unashamedly as tittle-tattle. Notably, his accounts of the court of Henry VIII pay lip-service to Catholic detestation of the King's divorces, but, much more emphatically, interest themselves in the salacious details of perverse and brutal behaviour among the English. (According to Bandello, Henry VIII continued to visit Anne of Cleves, even after his marriage to his last wife.)

To many of the firmer moralists of the period, the malicious use of words was itself a peculiar danger of the courtly life. Spenser pictures its effects in his representation of the blatant Beast in Book Six of *The Faerie Queene*; Shakespeare follows suit (taking Spenser as his intermediary) in *Much Ado About Nothing* – and indeed in *Othello* itself. Yet in their own way, Bandello's stories – written in a style that is deliberately plain, even 'non-existent' – enact the consequences of a world in which codes are not only disintegrating but are now so well – or so deviously – understood that the only point of interest must be the 'marvels' that moral corruption itself can generate. To be sure the chatter can often produce the highly decadent story – supposedly true – that eventually leads, *via* Painter and Belleforest to Webster's *The Duchess of Malfi*; and in the original version of the *Romeo and Juliet* story, florid pathos and sentiment are the keynotes (allowing one to recognize how much more incisive is Shakespeare's version, in both technique and moral vision). But Bandello's work is the register of a culture decaying into marsh lights and foggy phantoms; and gossip is its gaseous fuel. One is in no longer concerned (as in Ariosto) with fantastic flights of the imagination and certainly not (as in Tasso) with the miracles of faith. Driven only by an appetite for scandal, one is led, rather to inquire: How is it – suspending any Oedipal gravity – that a man came to marry a woman who was also his own sister and daughter (II, 35)? What is the story behind the case of a girl who ate the testicles of a castrated priest (III, 30)?

The *novella* then tends to cultivate an unresolved tension between content and frame in which content frequently threatens to become transgressive while frames express the institutional and moral norms that, nominally at least, might be expected to contain the disruptive factors of the narrative itself. Such tensions are felt, if anything, still more acutely in the dramatic comedies of the period, where the social settings in which the plays were performed, along with the formulaic nature of many of the plots that comedy depended upon, produced – initially at least – a certain conservative bias. The actors of early comedies are likely to have been themselves amateurs from the courtly or educational coterie. It is true that by the middle of the sixteenth century, groups of professional actors had begun to form for the performance of the *commedia dell'arte*. In this genre, improvisation was encouraged and plots and characters came to display certain recognizably carnivalesque inclinations, and to cultivate a marked interest in the gross stupidities of such type-figures as ageing lovers and fatuous physicians or else in the brilliant sleights of Harlequins and 'Zannis' – whose familar lozenged outfit was a conventionalized form of the tattered clothing of the lower orders. From this form of comedy, there derives a powerful set of images that subsequently were to influence Goldoni, Molière, Mozart and even Picasso. Yet in the period from 1400 to 1600 the prevalent form of comedy remained the *commedia erudita*. And where the term *arte* signifies the professional or 'trade' character of the *commedia dell'arte*, 'erudite' comedy was closely linked with the educational practices of Renaissance humanists in schoolroom and court.

The *commedia erudita*, originally written in Latin, attempted on the one hand to resuscitate the themes and forms of classical comedy and to employ in the schoolroom performances as a pedagogical device to encourage interest in ancient culture and – not least – to inculcate a confidence in public delivery. Petrarch is said to have written at least one such comedy (now lost) on the model of Terence; Terence's plays were thought to be so morally reliable that they could be performed by nuns, while later in the period the Jesuits gave a central position to comedy in their school syllabuses. In 1448, comedy was accorded a new lease of life with the scholarly discovery by Nicholas Cusanus (see pp. 96–7) of the manuscript of twelve plays by Plautus; and these provided the example of a racier comic style than Terence had displayed. At the same time, vernacular plays began to be written on classical models by authors as

Figure 74 Sebastiano Serlio, *Ideal Set for Comedy. The Five Books of Architecture*, 1569. Venice. This figure is reproduced by kind permission of the Syndics of the Cambridge University Library.

eminent as Ariosto and Machiavelli. But the link between comedy and schoolroom remained strong throughout the period, as for instance in *Ralph Roister Doister* by Nicholas Udall and *Gammer Gurton's Needle* by 'Mr S., Master of Arts'. Even a writer as profoundly original as Ben Jonson could view the comedy in terms of neo-classical decorum as a means for moral improvement, exposing the follies of human behaviour to medicinal derision.

As comedy moved from schoolroom to court, so its affiliations with the established social order grew the stronger; indeed the very setting of the stage on which the comedy was performed symbolizes many of its underlying characteristics.

This example is taken significantly from the architectural treatises of Sebastiano Serlio as a concluding illustration of perspectival construction. Here, as Serlio's own notes make clear, the set designer could take the opportunity of displaying his skill or *sprezzatura* in the command both of rules and of structural fantasies; and indeed, while Serlio's model is simply a theoretical prototype, artists as renowned as Raphael and

Holbein are known to have contributed to the construction of such entertainments. To that extent, display and sophisticated courtly taste were an inherent part of the theatrical performance itself. At the same time, a high degree of social and political control is implied by such a setting. The set – in common with the text of the play – might make flattering allusions to the topography of the city in which the play itself was performed. But, in doing so, it tended to celebrate the underlying orderliness that the prince of that city – usually present in the audience – had benevolently cultivated. For a couple of hours, an audience would be invited to watch a play in which characters – usually from the middle and lower classes – ran through a gamut of ludicrous errors and mishaps. But the set remained, unchangingly present as a constant reminder that order and control would eventually be restored.

An example of what such court comedy could produce is *La Calandria* written by Cardinal Bibbiena – one of the participants in the conversations recorded in Castiglione's *Il Cortegiano* – and first performed in Urbino in 1515. Notably, Castiglione's eyewitness account of this performance says next to nothing about the play itself (merely, 'It went well') while describing in great deal the furnishings of the auditorium, and the festoons that spelled out the words 'Delights to the people' across its ceiling. But Castiglione's sense of elegant social occasion is entirely at one with the character of Bibbiena's play. Here, Bibbiena adopts one of the standard themes of classical comedy – that of the confusion wrought when identical twins, unknown to each other, are on the loose simultaneously in the same small city – and weds it to the representation of a character drawn from Boccaccio's *Decameron*, the same Calandrino (now named Calandro) from whom the play takes its title. But the variations that Bibbiena spins around these adopted themes are themselves evidence of his own *sprezzatura*. To render the events of the play that much more intriguing, Bibbiena makes one of his twins a boy, the other a girl (separated at birth); and then, for good measure, he devises a plot in which the twins are obliged to cross-dress – the girl for safety in a foreign land, the boy so as to pursue, under this disguise, a love-affair with Calandro wife. Of the many problems (and sexual innuendoes) that this situation produces, the central one is that Calandrino should set out to seduce the transvestite visitor who frequents his house. Eventually suspecting what is afoot, Calandro is about to expose his wife's infidelity in dramatic fashion. Too late, however; for by this time the twins have been reunited; the girl twin has taken her brother's place and Calandro 's furious accusations are palpably proved to have no substance.

In the midst of this extremely witty turmoil stands the witless character of Calandro himself. In Boccaccio's original conception – developed in no less than four stories of *Decameron* – Calandrino had been a Florentine painter notable for his literalness of mind and for the ease with which he allowed himself to be bamboozled by his more intelligent colleagues. Socially, he belongs to the lower ranks of Florentine society. But the repetition of Calandrino-stories suggests a degree of civic solidarity which unites the Florentine storytellers with their ludicrous subject: repeatedly they insist that they are telling the Calandrino-stories to *far festa*, to generate a spirit of Carnival. But Bibbiena has rather reduced the opportunities for entertainment of this sort in his own version of the character. His Calandro is a man of some standing in the bourgeois ranks, and is indeed married to an aristocratic wife. Yet the humour that Bibbiena generates at his expense is largely designed to keep the upstart in his place. Duped by his wife and by the twins, he is also emphatically at the mercy of his intelligent servant, Fessenio. So far from allowing any breath of social disruption or overreaching, the play concludes with Calandro firmly returned to a social ambience that is markedly distinct from that which is occupied by the original audience of the play.

There is then a conservative strand in the comic drama of the period. This is not to say, however, that the forms and motifs established in the comic writing of the period had no power to test or question the prevailing order. A case in point (considered earlier at pp. 152–3) is Bruno's *Il Candelaio* – a play that is as subversive in its intellectual as in its political implications. So, too, there is Machiavelli's *La Mandragola*, where Machiavelli elicits from an essentially Boccaccian scenario a troubling demonstration of how dangerous (but delicious) the pursuit of *virtù* might become when translated to the sphere of domestic politics. Wit here produces a stratagem which requires that a jealous husband be persuaded knowingly to consent to his own wife's adultery. The husband longs for an heir. His (as yet wholly innocent) wife will provide one. But first she must be made to drink a potion of mandrake root provided by the servant of her would-be lover. The difficulty is that the first man to sleep with her after this draught is quite likely to die. So her husband is persuaded to allow a random beggar (actually her aspiring lover in disguise) to risk the lethal consequences. All of this goes according to plan. Indeed in the process, the wife – bearing, ironically enough, the name of the paragon of Roman wifely virtue, Lucretia – develops a hitherto undiscovered taste for adultery.

If order is re-asserted in *La Mandragola*, it rests upon a perilously mercurial cynicism. But moving beyond the formal comedy, a comparably imaginative (if usually more generous) vision of fictional and comedic possibilities is to be found in three of the greatest writers of the period, Rabelais, Cervantes and Shakespeare. In Shakespeare, as will be seen, motifs (or as they have been called, by Louise George Clubb, 'theatregrams') such as that of twinning can be associated, as in the carnivalesque *Twelfth Night*, with explorations that run deep into the emotional structures of identity. In Cervantes, an ability to offer in prose a burlesque version of most of the genres that were central in the Renaissance canon – epic, romance, lyric, pastoral – leads the author to a profoundly humane understanding of the motives and unexpected consequences that often lie hidden beneath the codes of his native culture. It is, however, Rabelais who, in language and narrative, engages most directly and most subtly with the traditions of Carnival, folly and misrule.

RABELAIS, CERVANTES AND TEXTUAL RIOT

In Book Four, chapter 30 of the *Heroic Deeds and Sayings of Pantagruel*, Rabelais personifies the season of Lent, and provides a point-by-point description of its meagre constitution:

> His vermiform excrescences like a tennis-racket . . . his pineal gland like a bagpipe . . . his uvula like a pea-shooter . . . his bum-gut like a monk's leather bottle. . . . His abdomen like an Albanian's tall hat. His peritoneum like an armlet. His sperm like a hundred carpenter's nails . . . His discretion like an empty glove . . . His reason as hollow as a little drum.

Here the meanness of Lenten austerity is subjected to that exhilarating exposure of secret hollows and ridiculous excrescences which is regularly a feature of Carnival festivity. The unembarrassed gusto of the passage clearly strikes a popular note, and is consistent with the popular (and by no means unjustified) association of Rabelais's name with scatological excess. Rabelais's book concerns a brood of giants, Gargantua and Pantagruel, who had originally made their appearance in the popular chap-books of the period. Each of these giants – according to the logic of his physique – is able to produce gallons of urine to irrigate the humour of the work. But as the author's vision unfolds in successive volumes, Gargantua and particularly Pantagruel display many unexpected delicacies of tone and personality. It is equally characteristic of Rabelais's own style that in describing the internal anatomy of King Lent, he should write with a crazy precision of line and detail. This reminds one that Rabelais was a practising physician (and so not only that he could command a technical vocabulary but also that he had daily acquaintance with human excreta). The passage also justifies the familiar comparison between Rabelais's work and that of Hieronymus Bosch (and also with Breughel's painting of Carnival). Here, ordinary, day-to-day objects (gloves, bottles, nails, bagpipes) are endowed with a life of their own (as in Bosch's kitchen knives, shoes, lanterns, spoons and sinister vegetables) and rise up as if to take their revenge on minds that sought to keep them safely in their functional place (Fig. 75). At the same time, it needs to be emphasized that, just as the paintings of Breughel and Bosch had a devoted following among the connoisseurs of the period, so the learning and learned vocabulary that Rabelais displays in such passages won him a greater audience among the *élite* than among the readers of the chap-books from which he takes the original suggestions of his story. His writing stands at a point of

Figure 75 Hieronymus Bosch, *The Garden of Earthly Delights* (detail), 1516. Oil on Wood, 220 × 97 cm. Madrid, Prado. With permission from Scala.

confluence, revelling in both the popular and learned manifestations of Renaissance culture and revealing the vertiginous idiocies as well as the subtleties that its clashing currents were always likely to produce.

Born in Chinon at some point between 1490 and 1494, the son of a lawyer and landowner, Rabelais was educated at the Benedictine monastery of Seuilly. Subsequently, he joined the Order of Observant Franciscans. But he returned later to the more relaxed rule of the Benedictine Order and finally left the monastery to become a secular priest. These shifts of affiliation suggest that Rabelais was sensitive to the same pressures that led both and Erasmus and Luther to question the dependency of the Church upon monastic institutions; and some of the circles that he frequented in France itself were Protestant in their sympathies. But Rabelais remained a Catholic throughout his life. As to his secular life, Rabelais was trained as a lawyer and also as a physician at the University of Montpellier, and developed a profound interest in questions of academic and educational procedure that he was to display itself on every page of his writing. By 1532, he had begun to practise medicine in Lyon and was publishing translations of medical treatises. Simultaneously, however, (around the age of forty) he had begun to write a sequel to the popular chronicles of Gargantua, which he entitled *The Terrible Deeds and Acts of Prowess of Pantagruel*, under the anagramatic pseudonym of 'Alcofribas Nasier'. This volume – already satirizing the logic-chopping of Sorbonne theology – was viewed with extreme disapproval by the theologians of the University of Paris, as it was later by Calvin. But Rabelais found protection in the person of Cardinal Jean du Bellay,

Bishop of Paris. When the outrage precipitated by Rabelais's writing was at its height, du Bellay took the author with him, to act as his physician, on an embassy to Rome – on matters concerning King Henry VIII's divorce proceedings.

Against this variegated background – moving from cloister to university to court, experiencing Italian influences in Rome itself and in the southern city of Lyon – Rabelais can produce passages which celebrate with enthusiasm and in a prose style of remarkable eloquence the advances that the new learning of Renaissance now promised at the beginning of the sixteenth century. Here in the midst of a story that has already begun to produce a riot of carnivalesque motifs and effusions, Rabelais composes the letter of Gargantua to his son Pantagruel which, in prose of the utmost elegance, celebrates the liberties of thought and taste that had been introduced by the development of humanist education:

> Now every method of teaching has been restored, and the study of languages has been revived: of Greek, without which it is disgraceful for a man to call himself a scholar, and of Hebrew, Chaldean and Latin. The elegant and accurate art of printing, which is now in use, was invented in my time by divine inspiration; as, by contrast, artillery was inspired by diabolical suggestion. The whole world is full of learned men, of erudite tutors and of most extensive libraries. . . .
>
> Therefore, my son, I beg you to devote your youth to the fit pursuit of your studies and to the attainment of virtue. . . . All the birds of the air, all the trees, shrubs, and bushes of the forest, all the herbs of the field, all the metals deep in the bowels of the earth, the precious stones of the whole East and the South – let none of them be unknown to you. (*Gargantua and Pantagruel* II, 8 trans. J.M. Cohen p. 195).

In a similar way with a characteristic combination of gusto and precision, Rabelais imagines the Abbey of Thélème (*ibid.*, p. 155):

> In the middle of the said main building, was an internal stair, the steps of which were some of porphyry, some of Numidian marble and some of serpentine but all twenty-two feet broad, three inches thick and twelve in number between each landing. In the middle of the first court was a magnificent fountain of fine alabaster, on the top of which were the Three Graces with horns of abundance, spouting water from their breasts, mouths, ears, eyes and other physical orifices.

Over the entrance of the Abbey, 'banishing hypocrisy and discord', are words declaring that 'Our Holy Writ and Word for ever shall be heard'. But the one rule of the place is: 'DO WHAT YOU WILL' (*ibid.*, p. 159). Here then in passages that could stand as ideal descriptions of Urbino or Fontainebleau, Rabelais directly associates himself with the architectural as well as the educational humanism that owed its origins to men like Alberti and Guarino (see pp. 36–8 and 78–9). Equally, the liberation from guilt that he promulgates rings with the robust enthusiasms of the redeemed Luther.

At the same time, Rabelais is capable of mocking even this elevated and heartfelt understanding. In Book Four, chapter 13, Epistemon speaks of how he found himself in the shadow of Brunelleschi's Dome, 'contemplating the position and beauties of Florence . . . the magnificence of its churches and grand palaces' (see Fig. 12). But then Brother Lardon breaks in, to declare a vigorous preference for the cook-shops of Amiens. Contemplating the Strozzi palace in Florence he declares: 'I'd rather see a good fat gosling on a spit. All this porphyry and marble is very beautiful. . . . But our cheesecakes at Amiens are more to my taste' (ibid., pp. 473–4).

If there is a constant in Rabelais's humanism then it derives from an unfailing commitment to the example of Erasmus. In Erasmus's writings, he would have discovered that profound interest in education and in language which not only inspires his own style but also provides the points of constant reference in the otherwise wholly episodic stories of Gargantua and Pantagruel. In Erasmus, too, Rabelais would have discovered a 'praise of folly', in which folly itself becomes a redemptive power, revealing the shortcomings of even our most august institutions and unleashing energies and an appetite that would otherwise be stifled (see pp. 114–16). To which Rabelais, in a spirit of Carnival, adds his own very literal understanding of the Neoplatonic cult of blind and drunken fury.

In the opening lines of the book the author invites his readership to become fellow tipplers at a textual feast: 'Most noble boozers, and you my very esteemed and poxy friends'. Correspondingly, the volume ends with an extended celebration of the Oracle of the Bottle. This conclusion may be spurious. But if it is, then that in itself suggests that Rabelais's earliest readers were aware of how reading and the acquisition of wisdom, too, can be regarded as bibulous activities. 'Innurition' is as much a part of Rabelais's literary composition as it is of every other great artist in the Renaissance. But 'intoxication' expresses something of the particular appetite with which he appropriates new-found knowledge or responds to the various promptings of all types of literary genre and all types of language. His story is in part a burlesque epic, influenced by student drama but capable of rising to something like true epic in, for instance, the famous description of the storm in Book Four: 'Believe me, we felt that ancient Chaos had come again; that fire, earth, sea and air and all the elements were in rebellious confusion' (ibid., p. 491). Linguistically, too, the text ranges from nonsense riddles to the subtlest forms of thought-experiments, from brilliantly parodic versions of scholastic argumentation to prose that stands as the most elevated example of Renaissance eloquence. Most significantly of all, the gigantic figures that Rabelais imagines, who might in other works of the period (including Edmund

Spenser's) have been allegorized into the sober counters of some moral or conceptual game, are here presented with an unambiguous emphasis upon their disruptive corporeality.

Ariosto commands a range of stylistic sensitivities and comic skills as great as that of Rabelais, but he also invents an authorial *persona* that stands at the centre of the work, claiming to guide its narrative and always providing an ironically sophisticated semblance of control in its appeal to the courtly audience (see pp. 5–9). Rabelais creates no such *persona*. Rather, he plunges himself and his reader into a stream of linguistic and narrative extemporization which – so far from attaching itself to any such principle of courtly taste as Ariosto invokes – constantly veers between the ridiculous and the sublime. There is no theme to this book, no single narrative action or unifying tonality. Indeed, Rabelais himself seems to have allowed his initial conception to develop from episode to episode and from volume to volume, responding in part (as Luther did and Cervantes will) to the popular success that the printing of his books had brought him. The press rather than the court is Rabelais's arena; and in his hands the printed page produces its own form of Carnival.

Yet Rabelais's ability to move so dextrously and inventively from one episode or style to another itself represents a display of *sprezzatura*. In his prose there is an unprejudiced lightness of touch, which proves in the narrative itself to be central to Rabelais's investigation of both education and folly. But in the narrative of the book the very incarnation of such qualities is the giant Pantagruel. In Rabelais's sources, Pantagruel had in fact been a dwarf; and, while he becomes for Rabelais himself the gigantic son of Gargantua, the reader's perception of him constantly changes focus to represent this little big man at certain points in terms of his overwhelming corporeality, at others in terms of his penetrating subtlety of intelligence and humanity of feeling. 'Pantagruelism', as Rabelais describes it, in the Prologue to Book Four, 'means a certain lightness of spirit compounded of contempt for the chances of fate' – to which Rabelais adds, 'I am sound and supple, and ready to drink if you will' (*ibid.*, p. 438). So, too, in Book III, chapter 51, Rabelais rhapsodizes on the properties of the miraculous herb, Pantagruelion – now identified as hemp – without which every table would be 'repellent, even though it was covered with every exquisite food', and every bed pleasureless 'though adorned with gold, silver, ivory and amber' (*ibid.*, p. 427). Like Pantagruel himself, Pantagruelion is the embodiment of a vital spirit that enables millers to carry wheat to the mill but also inspires the 'Arctic people, in full sight of the Antarctic people, to pass the twin Tropics, go down beneath the torrid zone, measure the entire zodiac and disport themselves on the Equinoctial Line' (*ibid.*, p. 428).

It is one indication of Pantagruel's own lightness of intelligence that, like Erasmus, he should be concerned to bring the world of discourse (or of *sermo*) into life by acts of interpretation which represent, simultaneously, readings of texts and readings of persons. A particularly notable instance is Pantagruel's interpretation of the myth of Pan (in Book Four, chapter 28) where in common with other humanists since Boccaccio, Pantagruel demonstrates that myths may yield truths of the highest order. In this light, Pan may be understood as a figure for the crucified Christ. For he can rightly be called, in the Greek tongue, Pan 'seeing that he is our All. All that we are, all that we live by, all that we have, all that we hope for is from him, in him and by him. He is the good Pan, the great Shepherd' (ibid., p. 511). Reading the legend of Pan we read more deeply into the person of Christ. In this spirit, Rabelais's page is punctuated by innumerable lesser instances – of prophecies and riddles which elicit and respond to a similarly generous style of hermeneutics that at times produces not merely word-play but a richly poetic texturing of suggestion. In Book Two, chapter 24, Pantagruel receives a letter which contains no writing but only a gold ring with a flat-cut diamond. All known methods are used to test whether the letter is written in invisible script. It is rubbed with walnut oil and bullfrog's blood, bat's grease and even fresh water. But only when it is realized that the diamond is false does its message declare itself: Pantagruel has proved himself a false lover by leaving his Lady without bidding her farewell. Characteristically, Pantagruel is 'depressed' at the thought of his own discourteous omission (ibid., p. 247).

The hardest tests, however, that Pantagruel faces are posed by his constant companion Panurge – who is as necessary a part of this story as Sancho Panza is of Don Quixote's.

Panurge – a sly, voluble, immoral parasite of noble appearance – clearly belongs to the same tradition that produces La Celestina and Falstaff; and it is he who initiates most of the tricks that have since come to be regarded as characteristically Rabelaisian: a lady whom he is attempting to seduce spurns him; he skilfully arranges for all the dogs of Paris to piss on her and rut after her. Or else, at the height of a storm described in Book Four, chapter 8, Panurge employs his knowledge of the behaviour of sheep to destroy a whole flock: flinging a single sheep that he is holding into the waves, he causes a stampede in which all obediently follow – with the strongest ram tugging the owner overboard: 'in much the same way as the sheep of Polyphemus, the one-eyed Cyclops, carried Ulysses out of the cave. Dingdong was drowned, as were the rest of the shepherds and drovers who seized the sheep.'

Where Pantagruel constantly seeks to interpret the world and reveal in it possibilities that can comfort or enliven human existence, Panurge is determined to command the forces or urges – mechanical, biological, economic and intellectual – that might seem to account for the workings of the universe. A debate is implied – which will by no means be settled in the Renaissance period itself – between a Panurgical view in which our knowledge (or cunning) leads us to control our environment and another in which we value and take delight in all conceivable manifestations of human activity.

Pantagruel does not always find it easy to defeat the rampant energy of Panurge's thinking. At one point, for instance, Panurge delivers a great oration on the orderliness of the cosmic system:

O what harmony there will be in the regular motion of the heavens! I believe that I can hear them just as clearly as Plato did. What sympathy there will between the elements! Oh, how nature will delight in her works and productions! (*ibid.*, p. 299)

For a moment one might suppose that this was some celebration of universal order as might appear in Pico della Mirandola or else in the speech from Shakespeare's *Troilus and Cressida* on 'Degree' (see p. 360) that might seem to express a confidence in an orderly world picture. Yet in fact the sustaining force of such an order, on Panurge's understanding, is the principle of Debt, which maintains the whole universe in a state of tense reciprocation. (One recalls that in Shakespeare's *Timon of Athens* Theft is represented as the sustaining force of Nature: 'The sun's a thief', stealing from the ocean and initiating a whole process of consequent misappropriation.)

This world in which nothing is lent will be no better than a dogfight, a more disorderly wrangle than the election of a Rector in Paris, an interlude more confused than the devil's play at the Mysteries of Doué. . . . In short Faith, Hope and Charity will be banished from that world, for men are born to aid and succour one another. (*ibid.*, p. 299)

Pantagruel has more success in the thought-experiment conducted in Book Three, chapters 39–43, where he encounters the ageing Judge Bridoye who decides his cases quite accurately by the throw of a dice. Bridoye's decisions have never been challenged by appeal courts and he is even capable of pursuing such justice effectively when his eyesight begins to fail. Bridoye himself offers his own unembarrassed explanation of his methods, allowing that ritual, the passing of time and the thumbing of papers are as necessary a part of legal process as forensic argument and that, in the course of such processes, cases mature to a point at which they make themselves and can be decided by the throw of a dice. Wise passiveness here replaces any arrogant attempt to impose an order upon a chancy but beneficent world; and Pantagruel enthusiastically welcomes this, in defending Bridoye from one of his few *faux pas*:

I recognize in Bridlegoose [*bridoye*] several qualities which make him, in my opinion, deserving of pardon in this case under judgement. In the first place his old age, in the second his simplicity under judgement. . . . For God, as you know, often wishes his glory to be manifested in the confounding of the wise and the raising up of the simple and humble. (*ibid.*, p. 408)

Erasmian folly here displays its salvific potentiality. But throughout the episode, folly is also related to the great appetite that Rabelais displays for the very flow of words and narrative, even if the words are legal terms. For him as for Pantagruel (for Boccaccio, too, and any other true humanist) the human world is one in which words are triumphant over rules and logical argumentation – since words are indeed the ultimate substance of both rules and argumentation. Rabelais's text invites us to move with this understanding into areas where linguistic pleasure is itself the source of liberation. In this respect, Rabelais anticipates Joyce; and in the Renaissance itself, the force of his example was realized, for example, by the German poet Johann Fischart (1547–90), who in his *Affentheurlich Naupengeheurliche Geschichtklitterun* produces, if anything, an even greater riot of language than Rabelais. It is left to Rabelais himself to combine irrepressible inventiveness with the utmost stylistic finesse. Reaching the Isle of Ennasin in Book Four Rabelais imagines a realm in which all relationships are dissolved into pure metaphorical play. 'The [inhabitants] were all so interrelated and intermarried one with another that we found none of them who was a father or mother to any other except for one tall, noseless old man whom I heard calling a little girl of three or four, Father, while the little girl called him Daughter' (*ibid.*, p. 468). The travellers seem too disconcerted by all this to find it amusing, especially when they are brought to witness the marriage of a 'pear' – 'a very luscious female, she seemed to us, though those who felt her said she was over-ripe' – and a 'young downy-haired cheese with a somewhat reddish complexion':

> As we went on I saw a lecherous fellow who greeted his female relative as 'My mattress', and she called him 'Eiderdown', and indeed he looked a downy old bird. One man called his girl 'Sweet doe', to which she answered; 'Old Crust', 'Shovel'. . . . Two similarly allied persons called one another 'Omelette' and 'My Egg' and 'Poker'.

Folly and compassion are as much a part of Cervantes's vision as they are of Rabelais's (or indeed of Shakespeare's); and Cervantes, like Rabelais, is greatly indebted to Erasmus: the world needs to be turned upside down if true lucidity – which is to say a true understanding of the relationship between person and person – is ever to be achieved. Yet Cervantes, in pursuing this understanding, plays rather on a lute than a Rabelaisian saxophone, devising in *Don Quixote*, a narrative instrument which is no less liberating (or subversive) than Rabelais's but which is more attentive to psychological nuance, to ironic resonance and to melancholic suggestion, to the interrogatives and quiet exhilarations of an infinitely extended and infinitely subtle game.

A knight – as lanky and lean as his own horse, living in reduced circumstances yet one of the many who possess an ancient shield and always have a lance in the rack – wishes to believe that every windmill is a giant so as to demonstrate his prowess by attacking it. His imagination is filled with the chivalric literature that in Italy had produced Ariosto's *Orlando Furioso* but in Spain had become a national obsession, affecting even the young St Teresa of Avila. So the whole landscape that Quixote traverses is subject to constant metamorphosis. For Quixote himself (as for the Cervantes who invents him) the dusty roads of Iberia are transformed into an endless field of chivalric and imaginative possibilities. Quixote's acquaintances watch his exploits with anxiety, irritation and solicitude.

Cervantes published the first account of his adventures in 1604. But the first volume proved so popular (within two years a Carnival masquerade on the Quixote-theme appeared in the Americas) that imitations began to be published and the original author was provoked into writing a second volume, which appeared in 1614. There can be no doubt that Cervantes responded to an appetite in the late Renaissance mind. Yet this itself suggests a number of questions about the relation of the work to its Renaissance background.

Is the chivalric ethos that Don Quixote absorbs from his voracious reading entirely ridiculous? If Don Quixote in his lunacy turns the world upside down, is the source of his popularity (and subsequent influence on the European imagination) simply amusement that Quixote's notable literal-mindedness should produce such incongruously fantastic consequences? And what relationship is there between the imagination of the knight errant and that of the author himself – who has after all read all the books that Quixote has read and pursued them in constructing his own narrative? What does it say about the human person and its motivations that it should not only be driven to delirious adventure by an involvement in reading but that even those who recognize delirium when they see it, should conceive an irrepressible appetite for more, demanding further volumes of these adventures?

In posing these questions, Cervantes concerns himself with the potentialities and conflicts within the literary and ethical culture of the Spanish Renaissance whose codes could include, variously, a commitment to rational clarity, a cult of personal integrity and a celebration of imaginative exuberance. With Rabelais, Cervantes recognizes that the words and texts on which his own culture depends can be seen as the cause as much of distraction and diversion as of lucid discourse. But more than Rabelais, Cervantes turns such considerations against his own authorial enterprise, and against some of the most central aspects of the culture he inhabited.

Cervantes himself – whose career spans the turn of the sixteenth century – stood at a point from which he was able to survey the whole achievement of the Renaissance. He does so, however, with a peculiarly Spanish sense of intellectual marginality, while simultaneously experiencing in his own personal history the critical pressures that European culture at this period had to encounter. Born in 1547, at Alcalá, son of a local surgeon, Cervantes studied in Madrid, wrote sonnets but also, it seems, became involved in a duel that led him to flee from Spain in 1569 and take up service in Rome. It was here that his story began to intersect not only with the cultural life of Italy but also with the military surges that brought the West into conflict with the Ottoman Empire. He fought, and was wounded, at the battle of Lepanto in 1571 where Christian forces, under Venice, won a great victory against the Turks. But in 1575, while returning from Naples to Spain, his ship was captured by Barbary corsairs and Cervantes himself was held captive as a slave for the next five years. Something of his experience informs a long digression in *Don Quixote*, Book I, 'The Captive's Tale' – which also offers a love story of a Christian prisoner and a Berber woman who, while praying to Allah, is also led by a devotion to the Virgin Mary to desire a Christian conversion. The tale registers close attention to the characteristics of Moorish architecture and military strategy, as well as to the supposed deviousness of the Islamic mind. As a Spaniard, these are considerations to which Cervantes was bound to be especially sensitive. But there is also a tendency – accompanied by emphatic references to the veracity of the tale – to suggest that the sea-adventures of the modern world provide continuing fuel for a spirit of romance which flickers, in apparently lunatic tongues, from the embers of Don Quixote's imagination. On his eventual return to Spain in 1580, Cervantes began his life as a more or less professional man of letters. He found himself from now on in an edgy and often contentious relationship with Lope de Vega. But he also discovered the impulse to write in the widest possible variety of genres, including theatrical comedies, pastorals with a strong Italian influence, 'exemplary novels' (1613) and eventually the romance epic *Persiles y Sigismunda* – which was left unfinished when he died (within a day of Shakespeare's death) in 1616 and which Cervantes himself seems to have considered his most serious work.

Though Cervantes never speaks disparagingly of the comic *Don Quixote*, it is clear from his secondary works that their author is a man of some intellectual ambition and one, moreover, whose thinking was as sensitive to the Counter-Reformation spirit as to that of the High Renaissance itself. (By 1609 Cervantes had joined a number of literary contemporaries as a member of the Congregation of Slaves of the Blessed Sacrament.) The *Galatea* written after Cervantes's return from captivity, enters the remote but intense world of pastoral. Drawing upon Sannazaro (see pp. 262–3) and also upon the *Diana* of Montemayor, the *Galatea* provides a richly rhetorical debate on the nature of love, influenced not least by the Neoplatonic notions of love as a divinely illuminating fury that had been developed by Leone Ebreo and Ficino (see pp. 91–3) – to whom Cervantes alludes in the opening pages of *Don Quixote*. The *Persiles* describes the travels and adventures of two lovers, on a quest which gradually becomes a pilgrimage, through the semi-darkness of a northern landscape.

Here Cervantes attempts to restore a spiritual significance to the epic romance (as Tasso and Spenser had also attempted to do in revising Ariosto's conception).

Medieval Romance had possessed such a significance in its original form where the adventures of knights were associated (as T.S. Eliot was to realize in *The Waste Land*) with a pursuit of inner purity that turned such objects as the Grail into symbols charged with the utmost spiritual force. *Persiles* seeks to recover something of such world. In that respect it may seem to be wholly at odds with *Don Quixote*. After all, it is a characteristic of the landscape that Don Quixote traverses that it should be one in which the purely mechanical operation of the world is emphasized – its windmills, the reflection on barber's bowls, its muscular Courtly Ladies. These constantly resist Don Quixote's own attempts to endow them with ulterior meaning. Yet Don Quixote persists in his desire to re-animate such a meaning – and of course in the imagination of author and reader each episode in turn does become signficant, if not in the way that Quixote himself had supposed it would.

Cervantes seems at times to have been engaged simultaneously in the writing of *Don Quixote* and the *Persiles*; and it is hardly likely that the interests of the one would be absent from the other. Indeed, on one view, the comedy of *Don Quixote* could itself be seen as a means of recommending a certain sobriety of mind. In the Prologue to Book I, for instance, Cervantes imagines an interlocutor who supposes that Cervantes's purpose was simply to destroy the exaggerated authority of books of chivalry, and (*ibid.*, p. 30) counsels him to write sentences that are 'plain but expressive, sober and well-ordered, harmonious and gay, expressing the purpose as well as possible and setting out ideas without intricacies and obscurities'. These words represent a far-from-inexact description of Cervantes's own prose style – especially when this is compared to Rabelais's. Similarly in Book I, chapter 48, a discussion takes place between Don Quixote and the Canon of Toledo in which the Canon enunciates a lucid conception of what a story should be and what a reader should expect from it: beauty is a matter of order and proportion; and there can be no beauty in stories that allow such disproportions as appear in the Romance genre, where a lad of sixteen stabs a giant as big as a tower and splits him in two as if he were made out of sugar. In any case, fictitious fables must be 'wedded to the intelligence of their reader'.

Indications of this sort correspond to a neo-classical conception of comedy which, in emphasizing balance and decorum, invites superior intelligence to take delight in the contemplation and control of human folly. This position certainly had a place in Renaissance literary theory. Nor is it out of keeping with the indulgent interest in universal foibles that marks the classicism of the eighteeenth century and led later readers of Cervantes's work to declare, for instance, that 'Every man has something of a Don Quixote in his Humour, some darling Dulcinea of his Thoughts that set very often upon mad Adventures.'

For all that, this apparently rationalistic atttitude to comedy represents only one strand among several that Cervantes pursues in *Don Quixote*; and the rational view is rarely uttered in the *persona* of the author himself. In common with most of Shakespeare's comedy, Don Quixote reveals the need for notions of comedy more complex than the Renaissance itself could muster. If it is legitimate to regard Cervantes as the forerunner of such novelists as Dickens, it is equally valid to see in his work a demand that will only be satisfied by those Romantics and Post-Romantics who stress the extent to which ironies and interrogatives are intrinsic to Cervantes's enterprise: 'Alone in the Manchegan plains, the lone figure of Don Quixote bends like an interrogation mark, like the guardian of the Spanish secret, of the ambiguity of Spanish culture' (Ortega y Gasset, *Meditations on the Quixote*). At the same time, the interrogative can be seen as reflecting backwards over the Renaissance itself. The very clarity and moderation of style that Cervantes undoubtedly derives from his own Renaissance education – and which probably recommends him as a classic to Europeans who might be otherwise be troubled by Hispanic exoticisms and excess – is itself here put to the service of a story that by its nature traces and records the disjunctions of rhetorical and psychological fantasy.

Something of how, in this sense, comedy may reveal the pressures within the codes of Renaissance thinking is implicit in the breach of comic decorum by which Cervantes takes a gentleman of rank – a would-be knight – as the butt of his humour. The *commedia erudita* (as exemplified by, say, Bibbiena's *La Calandria*) would never have countenanced such a move; and, while comedy of Bibbiena's kind is full of wily servants, it in no way anticipates the implications that arise when Cervantes makes Sancho Panza Don Quixote's closest accomplice.

As in the relationship between Panurge and Pantagruel, the pairing of Don Quixote and Sancho Panza represents a developing dialogue in which two contrasting world views are progressively explored and traced out in the details of character and response. But this dialogue is far less explicitly directed towards a conclusion than it is in Rabelais's work; Rabelais's conclusions may be outrageous but the target is frequently some recognizable problem in the academic or intellectual sphere. Cervantes's writing – with its episodic yet easy and generative flow – rarely assaults the reader but rather elaborates situations in which (again, as in a Shakespeare play) a work that concerns the power of imaginative suggestion itself builds up multiple strands of imaginative suggestion, far subtler than those of the original romances that it seeks to surpass. There is a correspondingly greater range of comic effect than one finds in Rabelais's work. Thus on the one hand, the narrative fully comprehends the implications of farce, where the human being is involved in the workings of a mechanical and repetitious universe and is always liable to encounter the celebrated banana skin (even when this is disguised as the vanes of a whirling windmill). On the other hand, intelligence or imagination is never submerged by the mechanism. In an expanded form of Boccaccian *ingegno*, Don Quixote constantly devises new and ever more extravagant explanations to extricate himself from the disasters that he suffers – despite the fact Sancho is always on hand stolidly to warn him against them. As for Cervantes himself, one of his own greatest gifts is to maintain variety of incident while revealing the essentially repetitive character both of the physical world and of Don Quixote's obsessions.

Then, too, there is a level of linguistic and literary humour in Cervantes's text, that in part involves parody and burlesque but also a significant advance upon early examples of these two genres. Since Pulci and Ariosto, the romance epic had lent itself to sophisticated comic treatment. Even neo-Latin writers such as Folengo – on whom both Rabelais and Cervantes drew – had begun to contribute to this development; and, whether in the vernacular or in Latin, parodic treatments implied a willingness to display – with courtly *sprezzatura* – the agility of mind to which 'innurition' could lead. Yet the fundamental joke of *Don Quixote* – and the fundamental alliance between the Knight and the Author – is directed against this central principle of Renaissance culture; it is precisely in taking the literature of the past to heart that Don Quixote becomes a mechanical figurine, caught on his own rhetoric as he is on the spokes of a turning world. Conversely, Cervantes demonstrates his own originality – and makes his own contribution to the literature of Folly – by calling into question, though never wholly rejecting, the cultural resources that all his predecessors had fed upon.

Here, as in the case of Rabelais, comparisons between Ariosto and the later author reveal the extent to which a shift in regard to authorial position has repercussions in regard to the conceptions of selfhood that each adopts. The courtly *persona* that Ariosto cultivates suggests a position that confidently draws upon the common interests and codes of the court and exerts complete control over the web of incident and shifting emphasis of generic play. Thus even when Ariosto contemplates – in one of the most tragic moments of his work – the descent into madness of the paladin Orlando in *Orlando Furioso*, Canto 23, the author skilfully pulls back, in concluding the canto, from any empathetic relation with the deranged hero, allowing a pastoral chorus of peasants to frame the scene and finally appealing, in terms of decorum, to his courtly audience whom the author is unwilling to fatigue with overextended attention to a single storyline. Yet Cervantes, like Rabelais, is a professional writer whose unexpected successes depend upon the chances of the press rather than courtly favour. This is particularly evident in the second volume of *Don Quixote*. Here, responding to the popularity of the first volume, Cervantes offers an extemporization that, so far from allowing any settled frame of reference to be established, is organized rather in a fugal pursuit of motifs and themes, developing according to an internal logic. Even in the first volume, Cervantes has already contrived to baffle any easy authorial orientation by relating how the story came to be beneath his hand. Where Rabelais writes under the vaguely Arabic pseudonym of Alcofribas Nasier, Cervantes attributes

the original story to one Cide Hamate. In other words not only is the work the product of a Moorish invention – and Moors are stereotypically devious to the Iberian
mind – it also purports to have been written by a man whose name in Moorish means
'Aubergine'. It is true of course that Ariosto's own work at times acknowledges playfully an unreliable source in the writings of Archbishop Turpin. But this is far from
allowing into the authorial chain a voice that comes from the very regions of alterity
that Cervantes experienced at first hand in his captivity. As Don Quixote has his
Sancho, so (in almost inverse relationship) the sane Christian author invents a potential liar as his *alter ego*.

In the *novella*, the narrative frame often reflected the codes and ethical postures
that the author wished to project upon his work. The authorial frame in *Don Quixote*
is as unstable – as much traversed by competing voices – as the hero's mind is comically fixed. And this interest in the conditions of fact and fiction, truth or falsehood
or imagination and lying – all of which have their counterpart in Shakespeare's
metatheatre – resonate throughout Cervantes's narrative.

Take, for instance, the 'tremendous' adventure of Book I, chapter 20. The night is
pitch-black. Tormented by thirst, Don Quixote and Sancho Panza come to a meadow
in a secluded valley and hear the refreshing sound of a nearby torrent. For a moment,
it seems that a pastoral scene is to be established in which the natural world feeds
and regenerates weary humanity. Cervantes's volume is, throughout, as much aware
of pastoral idiom as it is of romance epic; indeed at the conclusion of this same
episode Don Quixote declares that he was born in 'this iron age to revive the age of
gold' (*ibid.*, p. 158). But through the darkness, through the murmuring of leaves and
the roar of waters, another sound is heard, 'alarming, horrid and dread', an unremitting and never changing thumping. Don Quixote immediately transforms this into an
heroic fantasy: the waters 'seem to be hurled headlong from the mountains of the
moon', the inexplicable noise would 'infuse fear, terror and dread into the breast of
Mars himself' (*ibid.*, p. 150). Bidding Sancho, solemnly, to wait for three days, Don
Quixote prepares to ride towards the heart of the din. For once, the reader cannot
see ahead to the absurdity that the situation will reveal. Nor can Sancho, who now
displays a common humanity as great as Quixote's foolhardiness. Failing to dissuade
Quixote from his exploit, Sancho resorts to ingenuity and, unnoticed, ties Rocinante's
forelegs together with the halter of his ass, declaring – in a dextrous adaptation of
Quixote's own idiom: 'See, sir, the Heavens are moved by tears and prayers. They
have ordained that Rocinante shall be unable to stir' (*ibid.*, p. 151). Quixote deter-
mines to sit, as true knights must, in the saddle all night long. He does, however,
allow Sancho to divert him with an endless and impossibly incompetent tale – involving the transportation of goats across a river – which only concludes when Sancho is
obliged to answer a call of nature. Terrified by the din, Sancho does not wish to leave
his master's side; so, squirming, he undoes his breeches (which fall and hold him

as fast in fetters as Rocinante has been held all night) and 'baring a pair of ample buttocks to the air, he was so unfortunate as to make a little noise very different from the din which was causing him so much terror'.

Unlike most of Quixote's early adventures, which involve frenetic action, this episode depends upon stasis and suspense (shared by the reader) as they observe but also participate in the idiocies of each of the two protagonists. Unusually for Cervantes, the moment involves some Rabelaisian reference to the lower functions – Don Quixote conducts the latter part of the conversation with fingers pinching his nose. But it is characteristic of Cervantes alone that this moment should translate itself into one that registers a discreetly civilized recommendation to decency: 'pay more attention to your person in future and to the respect you owe me' (ibid., p. 156). But the suggestions of this episode are all magnified when, with the coming of dawn, Quixote advances to discover that the tremendous din was in fact the sound of the wool-processing hammers of a fulling-mill. For once, Don Quixote has to admit the error he has made – along with the fear he has felt and the distortions of mind to which knight-errantry is prone: 'Am I by chance, as being a knight, obliged to recognize and distinguish sounds and know whether they are fulling hammers or not?' The reader, too, may derive from the scene the mournful reflection that the world, so far from being a pastoral or chivalric arena, is a place where engineering and mechanics are soon to replace the pursuit of heroic value, to the point of rendering such pursuits ridiculous. But value has not been lost. The intensity of attention that the night (and the episode itself) has summoned up reveals anew the sensuous texture of a world of murmurs and odours, of physical motion and arrest. Don Quixote may declare that such things are beneath the attention of a knight errant. But the folly of that declaration is itself revealing, allowing the reader to concentrate anew upon the frailties and insufficiencies of even the best of human ambitions, and to find in humour and compassion an alternative to such ambition.

With the Second Book – written in response to popular demand – Cervantes's humour deepens, to inspect, with increasing virtuosity, the ways in which the reading of his own composition may lead to consequences comparable to those that are produced by the reading of chivalric literature. Though Cervantes himself seems to have preferred the episodic style of his earlier volume, he now produces a free flow of invention in which all his characters are impelled by a literary awareness of the success of the earlier work. In effect, the enthusiastic reader of Cervantes's work – driven by his own sort of literary mania – also becomes a character in this work and to some extent as much a puppet in the hands of the literary mind as Don Quixote originally was of the disenchanted world.

One consequence of this heightened awareness of literary considerations is that Don Quixote himself is given the opportunity to utter a defence of poetry as a proper part of the educational system – and thus to counter, in some measure, the sagacious words of the Canon of Toledo in Book I. Speaking to the Gentleman in Green – who may stand as a model of what, for Cervantes, a balanced and sober knight of Spain should have been – Don Quixote declares that 'Poetry is like a tender young and extremely beautiful maiden whom other maidens will toil to enrich, polish and adorn' (*ibid.*, p. 568); and the Gentleman in Green is much impressed by the sanity of his words. But against this educational background, the richest exploration of this new vein involves the introduction into the story of Sampson Carrasco, the scholar who eventually becomes the 'Knight of the Mirrors', and who deliberately provides a parallel to Don Quixote, as – in his own way – does the Gentleman.

It is Sampson who in the opening chapters of the second volume teases both Don Quixote and the reader with an account of how popular the first volume of adventures has now become: 'There are more than twelve thousand copies of this history in print today. . . . There is even a report that it is being printed in Antwerp' (*ibid.*, p. 486). There follows a lengthy discussion of the respective claims of historical and poetic writing, and much debate as to how accurately the original account has depicted the Knight and his Squire. Yet, so far from dissuading Don Quixote from further adventures, this discussion only adds a further literary impetus to the ambitions that had been inspired in the first place by the ancient tales of chivalry. Indeed, Sampson himself – though hardly as heroic as his name would imply – is himself drawn into the fantasy. Thinking that Quixote can only be prevented from further lunacies by defeat in chivalric battle, Sampson disguises himself as a knight errant and goes out by night to meet his deluded counterpart, adopting Don Quixote's own rhetoric and declaring that he has already overcome the famous paragon of La Mancha in a duel. In a constantly shifting perspective of truths, fiction and illusions, Sampson attempts to hold a mirror up to Don Quixote himself: 'a man of tall stature, withered of face, lanky and shrivelled of limb, grizzled, with an aquiline and rather crooked nose' (*ibid.*, p. 551). Then, as day breaks, Sampson is revealed to be the Knight of the Mirrors, wearing 'a surcoat that seemed to be of the finest gold, sprinkled with a great number of little disks of shining looking-glasses' (*ibid.*, p. 555). However, in the duel that ensues, it is Sampson who loses and Don Quixote who – albeit by accident – triumphs, taking renewed encouragement from what for once may be accounted an actual victory:

> Don Quixote found his adversary embarrassed by his horse and concerned with his lance which he either could not, or had not time, to put into its rest. Taking no heed of his embarrassments, however, Don Quixote attacked the Knight of the Mirrors in complete safety and without the slightest risk and with such force that almost unintentionally threw him over his horse's crupper to the ground, giving him such a fall that he moved neither hand nor foot but gave every appearance of being dead. (*ibid.*, p. 557).

The result is that Sampson now develops an urgent appetite for revenge: 'It would be folly to suppose that I shall go home till I have thrashed Don Quixote. . . . The pain in my ribs will not allow me to entertain a more charitable purpose' (*ibid.*, 561).

There is much in *Don Quixote* that anticipates the interest shown by twentieth-century writers such as Pirandello in themes of masks and masking – or by magical realists in the power of the imagination to expand our understanding of the forces that shape our human existence. Even Henry Fielding recognized that in adopting Cervantes's episodic style, the authorial presence that stood behind these episodes would itself need to be brought into question. Nor is it surprising that Flaubert should have acknowledged his great debt to Cervantes, even if, in *Madame Bovary*, an appetite for reading has tragic consequences – while correspondingly in his *Bouvard et Pécuchet* banality achieves an unambiguous victory over the powers of the imagination. But the significance of *Don Quixote* in its own time is to recognize how difficult many of the most characteristic features of Renaissance culture have made it to preserve a true responsiveness to the claims made upon us by the human person. The world we live in may become, the more we know of it, the more banal; the imagination may become paralysed in a fixed and ridiculous posture by the very act of reading. The remedy – urged finally by Don Antonio against the interfering and vengeful scholar, Sampson – is to hope that Don Quixote never will be cured; for if he did recover, the world would lose a vital source of pleasantry (*ibid.*, p. 892). This is the lightness of being that Rabelais defends so vigorously – as does Falstaff. Cervantes's work ends elegiacally with the slow advance of its hero towards both sanity and death: 'Don Quixote's end had come, after he had received all the sacraments and expressed his horror of books of chivalry in strong and moving terms.' Yet even here the books of chivalry reassert their claim, as a necessary way of conceiving the full significance of the moment. For it is the clerk attending this deathbed who declares that

> he had never read in any book of chivalries of a knight errant dying in his bed in so calm and Christian a manner as Don Quixote who amidst compassionate tears gave up the ghost.

A little later, on the final page of the volume the death of fiction is itself envisaged, as Cide Hamete also hangs up his pen, asserting: 'For me alone Don Quixote was born and I for him.' The Cervantian joke is evident; and the conclusion that 'Life is a dream' or that 'We are such stuff as dreams are made on' is not far away. At the same time, one begins to realize anew that these need not be melancholic observations. Could it be that human nature is simply at its truest when it is most fully involved in the playfulness of its own existence? To cultivate illusion – against an easy pretension to certainty – is an aim that Cervantes shares with Boccaccio, Erasmus and Rabelais, and also with Shakespeare.

SHAKESPEARE THE CRITIC

Was Shakespeare a Renaissance poet? It would be easy to think that he was not, or else to disregard in his case – as one cannot in reading, say, Ariosto, Ronsard or Spenser – the cultural character of the period in which he was active. In the seventeenth and eighteenth centuries, neo-classical readers such as Dryden and Johnson (drawing on principles that were first formulated in the Italian sixteenth century) identified the extent to which Shakespeare apparently transgressed the accepted rules of poetic procedure. Around the same time there also began a tendency to view Shakespeare's writings as a peculiarly English phenomenon, at its best in producing such specifically 'English' characters as Falstaff. Likewise, Shakespeare came to be seen as a purely natural genius, warbling (in Milton's phrase) his 'native wood notes wild'. Leonardo might, to some, appear the best example of a Renaissance man: the English Shakespeare, immune to learning especially as it flowed from a European Renaissance, is more likely to be represented as a 'universal' genius.

Shakespeare, as will be seen, does indeed have a strong sense of his own Englishness; and his language frequently testifies to an acute appreciation of the natural or rural world. Yet, arguably, there is not one of his plays that does not in some way demonstrate an interest in the central concerns of the European Renaissance. It is evidence of a profound cultural curiosity that Shakespeare should devote almost as many of his plays to classical history as he does to English history, while in no fewer than fifteen he turns to Italy for a setting or a literary source. Indeed it has recently been suggested that *The Merry Wives of Windsor* is Shakespeare's most Italianate play. If, moreover, as earlier chapters have suggested, one defining feature of the Renaissance is an interest in the formation of secular societies and another its concern with educational practice, then Shakespeare follows suit, constantly varying and reformulating these themes throughout his career.

For instance, in *Love's Labour's Lost* – which is one of his earliest and most conspicuously learned plays – Shakespeare examines the ways in which the humanist aspiration to form an *élite* intellectual academy (and to write sonnets) is tested against the claims of sexual instinct and, ultimately, sickness and death. The ambitions of a group of young aristocrats in pursuit both of erudition and courtly ladies are here compared not only with the country matters of yokel-lovers but also with the intellectual and dramatic aspirations of village schoolmasters and curates – themselves eager to perform a play of their own, *The Nine Worthies*. Shakespeare's play even finds time to satirize, in the figure of Don Armado, the supposedly Spanish propensity to excessive language and glorious gesture. Analogies with Cervantes would not be hard to find – nor indeed with Rabelais, considering that one of the lovers speaks of the 'Dread Prince of Plackets, King of Codpieces, Sole Imperator and great general of trotting parritors' (*LLL*, III, i, 5–7).

In a similar way, *The Tempest* – sometimes regarded as a summary both of Shakespeare's career and of the Renaissance project at large – envisages the quasi-pastoral setting of a remote island, and debates (as pastorals do) the possible conditions of an ideal social order. This play also registers, in the figure of Prospero, the relative claims of power and learning – to the point of admitting that both lead to forms of usurpation. Antonio – in a Machiavellian *coup d'état* – unseats the scholarly Prospero. Prospero himself discovers only belatedly – though Montaigne might have made him realize this – that European nurture was an impediment to the understanding of Caliban's alien nature.

Early and late, Shakespeare's work produces analogies in theme and stance to the work of his counterparts in Renaissance Europe. Does that, however, justify a description of Shakespeare as a critic of the Renaissance? The argument, henceforth, will be that (with some qualification) it does. Shakespeare has rightly been valued for the brilliance of his word play and his profundity in observing human character. At the same time, he also possesses a remarkable ability to diagnose with a critical eye the inner workings of social, political and cultural communities, including in his overview, not only the civilizations of Classical times, of Renaissance Europe and Tudor Britain, but even of the peculiarly transient groupings that gather as an audience in his own theatres. To associate Shakespeare with Montaigne and Machiavelli already suggests something of this. Montaigne and Machiavelli are critics in the true sense. Not only are they intelligent enough to recognize the inherent limitations of the culture they inhabit but also they train their intelligence to participate in and renew the modes of discourse from which they both had originated. A generous scepticism characterizes their thought, open to and willing to promote the questions that lesser minds might hide from. Shakespeare's art carries a similar impress, and points in its own Renaissance terms to questions that for centuries after have remained unanswered.

Shakespeare, probably, had read both Montaigne and Machiavelli. The *Essais* may well have been the volume that Hamlet carried as he asked 'To be or not be . . .'; and most critics would agree that Shakespeare's depiction of Caliban was influenced by Montaigne's essay on cannibals (see pp. 155–9). As for Machiavelli, *Richard III* makes it plain that Shakespeare shared with his contemporaries a fascination with the workings of an individualistic and amoral *virtù*; and the likelihood is that in writing *Coriolanus* – perhaps his fullest study of the relation between individual and community – Shakespeare consulted at first hand Machiavelli's *Discorsi*. (It is generally agreed that Shakespeare could read French; there is no reason to suppose that he could not read Italian, considering how easily many of his contemporaries acquired that language and how great Shakespeare's linguistic acumen self-evidently was.)

Yet even if Shakespeare had not read the French or Italian originals or else had encountered them only in translation, innurition, in his case as with Rabelais and

Cervantes, would have laid the foundations of a critical talent. The education he received at his late Renaissance grammar school in Stratford would have ensured not only a well-stocked memory but also an ability (once established on the London scene) to recreate and improvise as easily as he could imitate, in terms both of diction and of narrative orchestration. Moreover by Shakespeare's time, the 'domestication' of the Renaissance (see pp. 70–2) is likely to have carried the remote effects of an *élite* Italian original even to houses of ill-repute on the south bank of the Thames.

Shakespeare's early works are super-abundantly learned in both theme and language. Indeed one of the main developments that occurs in the course of Shakespeare's career is that, in responding to the demands and possibilities of specifically theatrical form, he came to realize the force that the simplest words could possess, especially in contrast to rhetorical extravagance: the murdered Desdemona, when asked who has done the deed replies: 'Nobody; I myself'; and (lying) dies. Yet this tension, which is itself an effect of innurition, is already implicit even in his early narrative poetry. In these poems, Shakespeare (in common with Petrarch and Titian) takes themes from Ovid and Livy but simultaneously emphasizes the claims of a vernacular idiom. In *Venus and Adonis* (to take only one instance out of hundreds) Venus – casting around herself seductive whisps of rhetoric and lyrical conceit – portrays her own body as an erotic landscape that offers to Adonis (the hunter) all possible variety of pleasing hillocks and dales to course over (ll. 230–41). The authorial voice, however, is quick to enter and – suggesting an analogy between the human protagonists and horses in heat – immediately descends to the demotic language of the auction-ring: the mare is 'A breeding jennet, lusty, young and proud' (l. 261), the stallion 'round-hoofed, short-jointed, fetlocks shag and long' (l. 296). This, however, does not imply a merely disparaging view of the more elevated forms of diction. It is true that in *Love's Labour's Lost*, Don Armado exclaims 'O base and obscure vulgar' (*LLL*, IV, i, 71) and goes on to produce the Latinate 'armipotent', 'juvenal' and 'volable'. Plainly Shakespeare was capable of scepticism towards pedantic disciplines and knew how magnificently ridiculous such terms could be. Yet it is the learned spirit itself that accounts for Othello's tragically strained 'anthrophagi' or 'exsufflicate' and 'the pride, pomp and circumstance' that intoxicate and also derange his spirit. Moreover the extraordinary rapidity of linguistic invention that Shakespeare shares with Donne and Sidney develops precisely from the play of these two forces: 'Ay, but to die, and go we know not where/to lie in cold obstruction, and to rot . . .', says Claudio in *Measure for Measure*, shuddering from Latinate obstruction to brute disintegration.

In linguistic texture, Shakespeare brings body and mind into collision as frequently as Don Quixote encounters windmills; and the effects can be as tragic as they are comic. In *Titus Andronicus*, an early work of great erudition and ambition, there is a terrible play between the over-abundant rhetoric of a father and the brute fact of a daughter's rape and mutilation. In terms, however, of dramatic structure, it is through his early comedies that Shakespeare – like Rabelais, Cervantes and his Italian predecessors in the *commedia erudita* – first discovers the theatrical possibilities of the learned tradition. *The Comedy of Errors* displays an ability to follow the classical models as exactly as Ariosto did. But even here one discerns a readiness to improvise on the established formulae; and this is particularly evident in the inventiveness that Shakespeare displays in constructing *The Taming of the Shrew*.

In this play, Shakespeare adopts a storyline from Ariosto's *I suppositi* (1509) – which had already been translated as *The Supposes* by George Gascoigne (1530–1577). A young scholar, aided by a wily servant, gains admittance, disguised as a tutor, to the house of his *inamorata* and wins her affection against the initial opposition of her father. There is a Boccaccian aspect to this plot, in the contrast it suggests between book-learning and the instinctual learning that love and sex may stimulate. There are, equally, possibilities for exposing the restrictions imposed by parental control, especially as these are expressed in the form of money-value and dowries. Finally – in the original version – the story establishes an unambiguously urban setting against which the comedy of 'supposes' and sleights of hand may all be played out to their harmonious resolution.

Yet for Shakespeare this is merely a subplot in a complex structure that not only depicts the disruptive, even brutal, wooing of Kate by Petruchio but also frames these love affairs with the story of Christopher Sly, a drunken peasant who – being deluded into thinking he is a nobleman at a courtly entertainment – observes the stories of both Bianca and Kate from a position of inebriated superiority. Two features of Shakespeare's mature style already make an appearance here – neither of which have any place in Italian theatre. Firstly, the play relies not only on a narrative that tells of twins and siblings but also on a dramaturgy of double-plotting. These double plots (reflecting each on each) then tend to produce what has come to be known as metatheatre. Parallels alert us to a subtext. 'Education' establishes itself as a theme, as the demure courtship of Bianca by her scholar is counterpointed against the taming that Kate (willingly or otherwise) undergoes at the hands of Petruchio. As Kate is dragged through the mire of the open country, her identity is tested and exposed in a way that would be wholly impossible in the urban and urbane twinnings of the *commedia erudita*. Nor would formal comedy of this type demand any such attention to questions concerning the personality and ambiguous sexual chemistry of Kate and Petruchio. At the same time – and metatheatrically – parallels arise between these central plots and the plot of Shakespeare's frame-story. Christopher Sly is no less put-upon, tamed, enriched (possibly) and fooled (certainly) than Kate. Watching Sly – as he watches the Italianate play – we are aware of the extent to which Sly the drunkard is much in need of the awakening that a sophisticated culture might bring to him, while being simultaneously in thrall to an educative system that is cruel and manipulative in its effects upon him. The audience itself, on this metatheatrical level, comes away less with a new understanding of order than with a dream that educates its members into the questions and vertiginous pleasures that metatheatre is always likely to stimulate.

Innurition – along with an appreciation of the civic forum in which innurition may be practised – has proved on the view that this volume offers to be a central factor in the mentality of Renaissance culture. The Stratford boy in theatrical London was shaped and formed by both. Yet already in *The Shrew* he had begun to demonstrate the limitations or complications of both. Kate receives her bitter education in the country. Innurition does not work smoothly in the case of rural Sly. Shakespeare's comedy would not be what it is if it did. This already suggests the extent to which Shakespeare may develop a consciously critical posture towards the themes and forms of the original text. And there are two ways in which this position is progressively confirmed in Shakespeare's writing. One is related to an inherent sense of Englishness, often associated with the claims of the natural countryside. The other is related to the playwright's understanding of what may be constructed theatrically in a community that gathers in the wooden 'O' of the Globe.

If Shakespeare shows a certain resistance to the main thrust of European humanism, he would not be the only English person of his time to do so. England stands on the margins of Europe and only belatedly comes to participate in its culture. Indeed for every Englishman who, like Sidney, enthusiastically accepted the Italian tradition, there was another, such as the puritan Ascham, who would maintain that 'an Englishman italianate is the devil incarnate'. Similarly, in a period when England, in religious and political matters, was establishing its identity through opposition to the mainly Catholic powers of Europe, there were many who defined the English version of the Renaissance in terms of a return not simply to the classical past but also of a recuperation of British history, coming to fruition anew in the Tudor dynasty.

Shakespeare cannot be associated unequivocally with either tendency. However, his English History plays, tracing the conflict between the Houses of York and Lancaster, display a degree of silent ambiguity that is itself significant. In these plays Shakespeare offers his own survey of the period from 1400 to the early 1500s that, in a European perspective, has come to be described as the High Renaissance. A dispassionate account of the fifteenth and sixteenth centuries in England would reveal no more disturbance than was suffered in the Franco-Spanish invasions of Italy or the French Wars of Religion. In England, as in Europe at large, these disturbances marked the final disintegration of the feudal system and in cultural terms were self-evidently productive. The coming of the Tudors marked a distinct openness to Italian courts such as Urbino (see pp. 40–4 and Pearsall, *Gothic Europe*, op. cit.). The Lancastrians, too, had been alert to European developments: Bolingbroke spent his exile at the despotic court of the Visconti and his brother Duke Humphrey established a humanist library at Oxford, the foundation stone of the Bodleian.

When Shakespeare reviews this period, the account he reveals no confident vision of rebirth but emphasizes rather the violence, division and disorder of dynastic and baronial strife – in which new-born children frequently suffer at the hands of new-born ambition: 'Enter a son that has killed his father. Enter a father that has killed his son' (*Henry VI*, Part III). In *Richard II*, a frail but divinely appointed monarch is deposed. The usurper Bolingbroke – once he is King – leads his life in the uncomfortable shadow of a hollow crown, sick in mind and body, aware always that, lacking divine warrant, he himself may easily fall victim to further usurpation. Under the charismatic (or, in the Machiavellian sense, 'virtuous') leadership of Henry V, the nation rallies briefly, only to descend on his unfortunate death into the Wars of the Roses. And when order is finally re-established, it comes – not as in Europe from the development in the city states, nor from the sophisticated display of courtly power nor even the exercise of Machiavellian *virtù* – but rather, on Shakespeare's view, from the Celtic fringes in the figure of the hallowed Welshman, Henry Tudor (who in fact proved to be an excellent businessman).

In all of this, there is a nostalgic strain, a conservative as well as a patriotic tendency. The extent, however, to which such attitudes can also produce a critical posture is demonstrated by the late play, *Cymbeline*. In this play (as in *Henry VIII or All is True*, which ends with a celebration of the promised reigns of Elizabeth and James I) Shakespeare shows himself entirely capable of courtly performance – and of employing theatrical machinery of courtly masque as a mask for despotic machinations. Yet *Cymbeline*, one of Shakespeare's most ambitious works, embodies his most explicit critique of Renaissance culture, especially in its Italian form. Here Shakespeare returns to ancient Britain, and depicts an alliance of high moral character between the natives of that realm and the noble Romans who have invaded it. The only impediments to this alliance arise from the machinations wrought by anachronistically Renaissance Italians, who are depicted with all the attributes – of sophisticated cunning, mercantile rapacity, duplicity and skill in the use of prohibited substances – that the Italophobes of Shakespeare's England regularly anathematized. Iachimo comes from Rome in the hope of perverting the honour of the famously chaste Imogen. His intentions mirror those of Tarquin in the ancient story of *The Rape of Lucrece*, but are the result of a bawdy and bourgeois gambling session in the company of assorted exiles. Meanwhile, Roman legions invade England, and in the battles that follow a bond of mutual respect is re-established between the heroic adversaries. The play ends with the exposure of Iachimo and (leaping over the Renaissance) celebrates a new-found alliance between the ancient powers of Rome and Britain: 'Let/A Roman and a British ensign wave/Friendly together' (Act V, v, 479–81).

For all that, it is in *Cymbeline* that one may gauge the extreme sophistication of Shakespeare's literary interests in Italian culture and begin to see that his critical

intelligence, so far from serving a merely conservative end, produces more disconcerting results in the very forms of drama that Shakespeare developed. For
Cymbeline not only draws its central plot from a Boccaccian *novella* (as does *All's Well*)
but also represents Shakespeare's response to the experiments in mixed genres such
as pastoral tragi-comedy that derived around 1600 from Guarini's *Pastor Fido*. We
have suggested in Chapter Five, as Ben Jonson recognized, how fashionable Guarini's
work had become. Indeed (to follow John Lever's reading) Shakespeare may have
been interested in Guarini's theories as early as *Measure for Measure*. Now Shakespeare
sets himself to reproduce in pastoral mode the variety of colours and tones that
Guarini deliberately cultivates. Yet the principle of Guarini's tragi-comedy has been
'the avoidance of deaths' (see pp. 266–7); and strikingly the most spectacular shift of
tones in *Cymbeline* occurs in Act IV between the gentle elegy, 'Fear no more the heat
of the sun . . .', and Imogen's terrible awakening to discover at her side a decapitated
corpse. Tragi-comedy even in Guarinian form offers a challenge to our settled expectations. The challenge that Shakespeare offers is taken to an inconceivably higher
degree.

When experiments such as these are conjoined with the disconcerting but exhilarating variety of Shakespeare's diction and his cultivation of metatheatrical effect,
there emerges an instrument of subversive action as potent as any employed in the
literary carnivals of Rabelais and Cervantes. And in Shakespeare's greatest plays it is
this instrument that he trains (sometimes satirically, sometimes in sceptical delight)
on the ethical, imaginative and political contradictions that shiver beneath the skin of
Renaissance culture. In the instance of three comedies – *The Merchant of Venice, Much
Ado About Nothing* and *A Midsummer Night's Dream* – he invites his audience, as will
shortly appear, to re-engage with the central themes of the Renaissance itself – the
city life and money, courtliness and scandal, learning and folly. In the highly problematical tragi-comedy *Troilus and Cressida* – with which this section will conclude –
Shakespeare's critique of both the classical and Renaissance worlds spills over into
something akin to self-loathing. First, however, there are two plays – *Julius Caesar* and
Antony and Cleopatra – where Shakespeare's eye falls directly, as the eyes of humanist
always did, on examples drawn from the classical world.

In *Julius Caesar* Shakespeare inspects a turning-point in Roman history, as Republic
begins to yield to Empire; and the play he constructs – through which to view the
inherent conflicts of this moment – is one where, almost uniquely in Shakespeare's
plays, explicit debate prevails over poetic suggestion. Antony's funeral oration is
symptomatic and already recalls the centrality of rhetoric in Renaissance education.
But Shakespeare's dramaturgy benefits here from that same tradition. Similarly, he
associates himself, in his sympathetic portrayal of Brutus, with one of the fundamental concerns of Renaissance historiography. Few things are more shocking to the

post-Renaissance mind than to discover, in Dante's Hell, that Brutus is condemned as a traitor against the Imperial cause. The Middle Ages, thinking of Rome, were primarily concerned with the period of Empire. The Empire was the institution under which Christ had come into the world and which subsequently – as the Holy Roman Empire – was divinely appointed to defend the Christian faith. Renaissance historians, however, were impelled by the Republican sympathies that characterized early Florence and Venice, and preferred to see the Republic as the most authentic period of Roman civilization. Shakespeare generally seems to resist the pro-Imperial tendencies of his primary source of classical history, North's *Plutarch*. But in his portrayal of Brutus, Shakespeare also identifies a point of complication in the perspective that the Renaissance itself had adopted. In Brutus (whose ancestors had driven King Tarquin from Rome), the humanist Michelangelo portrays an heroic but troubled figure – and leaves the bust unfinished, some say because the sculptor could not bring himself to contemplate the violence that flowed from Brutus's honourable convictions. Machiavelli, on the other hand, never baulked at violence and – for all his understanding of Republican principles – it is Caesar, the Imperial opponent of the ancient Republic whom he compares admiringly to that other new Prince of his own day, Pope Julius II (see pp. 17–18).

There can be no doubt Shakespeare shared with Machiavelli an interest in the dynamics of the *coup d'état* – in those moments at which *virtù* is tested and new princes and new forms of government emerge. Yet (with Michelangelo) Shakespeare, in portraying Brutus and Cassius, also pursues a critique of the Machiavellian position and of the interest in heroic acts of self-affirmation that Renaissance culture could at times encourage. It is Cassius who, in debating terms, summons up the best arguments on this score when vividly (and comically) he contrasts Caesar's impetuous attempt to swim the 'troubled Tiber' with the rescue of Caesar that he himself effected in the true spirit of the ancient Æneas – the original father of Rome who had attempted to save his afflicted compatriots from disaster (*JC*, I, ii, 111–16). It is Brutus, however, who in the silence of his suicide puts the question most eloquently to Shakespeare's

Figure 76 Michelangelo, *Brutus*, c.1540. Marble, height 64.8 cm. Bargello, Florence. With permission from Scala.

Renaissance audience: Is not vulnerability as true an expression of human nature as vaulting ambition? May not defeat be a moral victory?

Marlowe, in Machiavellian vein, had seen the ways in which *virtù* might produce the individualism, stupendous rhetoric and dramatic vigour of a Tamburlaine. Shakespeare in his tragedies never admits such vigorous simplicities into his ethical vision nor into his dramaturgical practice. At all points, he is aware that individuals exist in and through their participation in the public life of the social group; and his own theatrical art is as subtle in the representation of the workings of communities as it is in the presentation of individuals. Nor is the ethical vision ever more clearly allied to theatrical experimentation than in *Antony and Cleopatra*.

This play is as much a carnival as a tragedy. Corneille in the seventeenth century was to attempt a series of heroical comedies. Shakespeare in *Antony and Cleopatra* had already written a play that may start as a debate but ends, through the highest exercise of linguistic and dramatic suggestion, as a celebration of the relationships that are sustained by a full acceptance of our bodily and artistic natures. Here the Empire is about to establish itself under Octavius Caesar; and from the Imperial point of view (to quote the opening words of the play) 'the dotage' of Antony's eyes – declining into middle age – threatens to overthrow the measure that is needful for the upholding of the new military order. Yet all such prudential considerations are challenged by the influence of Cleopatra who (inclined always to her own forms of highly sophisticated carnival) causes the elements to be love-sick with the perfumes of the sails of her barge. There is here an aura, even a comedy – evoked by Shakespeare's own innuritional rendering of North's prose – that exceeds merely political calculation. Indeed the Machiavellian Caesar is uncomprehendingly offended when his sister Octavia creeps back to Rome unheralded by any such display – like 'a market-maid'. And the soldierly Enobarbus dies for a lack of charisma, sinking to the ground at the moment he abandons Antony's cause in regret over the generosity he has offended and the glamour he has forgone.

It is, however, in the deaths of Antony and Cleopatra themselves that vulnerability – along with comedy and carnival – arrive at their highest pitch. Antony attempts a noble Roman suicide. He ludicrously fails. The God, Hercules – so often, for the Renaissance, the symbol of an heroic power of human self-fashioning – has left him. But, in failing, he commits himself into the hands of Cleopatra, who after his death for the whole of the final act refashions him for the audience, as for herself, in a relationship that thrives wholly in the realm of imagination. Her language touches the heights of exotic oratory but also descends to the ungraspably simple yet paradoxical perception of a lethal asp as a suckling child: 'Peace, peace! Dost thou not see my baby at my breast'. The sheer theatricality of the gesture demands that the imaginations of the audience, likewise, should now abandon Hercules, all *virtù* and considered judgement, entering thus into the thrilling anarchy of the aesthetic moment.

Turning from Rome to Italy, and from tragedy to comedy, Shakespeare not only submits the great themes of the Renaissance world to searching scrutiny but in doing so, develops the art he had absorbed from his Renaissance forebears into wholly unexpected directions – none of which can be conveniently mapped within existing generic boundaries.

In regard to theme, *The Merchant of Venice* contemplates the workings of a civic culture built entirely on the artifice of money. To the eye of an Englishman – familiar with towns that were closely integrated with the surrounding countryside – Venice, even by report, would have seemed an unnatural manifestation of how a civilization could be constructed entirely by dint of human effort in the midst of the sea, fed and nurtured entirely by buying, selling and money. Boccaccio of course would have relished this 'as a celebration of human intelligence' and may even have seen how the intercourse fostered by mercantile exchange could (like the exchanges pursued in the narrative fiction of *The Three Rings* (see p. 319) foster a common understanding between the devotees of wholly inimical ideologies. Shakespeare views this position with some reserve. It is true that Portia resembles a number of Boccaccio's many witty women, skilfully modifying the apparently unchangeable terms of Shylock's legal title. It is also true that the fifth act of the play – set in Portia's Belmonte – attempts a festive conclusion, such as Boccaccio might seek in the courtly villas around a plague-stricken Florence. This, however, does not wholly dispel the Shakespearian recognition, expressed in his conception of the apparently 'merry bond' – that there are some aspects of human nature – above all its bodily integrity – that cannot be made the subject of exchange. At the same time, the play seems fully to recognize that an appetite for unchanging principles of law may itself be an unshiftable component in the moral psychology of certain individuals. If Shylock is a sympathetic as well as a comic figure, the reason must be that, beyond his compromise with the mercantile mentality of his Christian compatriots, there is an ancient insistence upon the value of the Old Law, and an equally ancient recoil from the offences that are done to the human being when the body is assaulted by derision or contempt: 'Hath not a Jew eyes?' Shylock may not observe the implications of this law in his own pursuit of Antonio. But Shakespeare here acknowledges as profoundly as did Rabelais the absurdities that arise when the gigantic significance of the human form are turned into mere commodity and poundage.

On another level, in *Much Ado about Nothing* – which draws, for the Claudio–Hero sub-plot, on Ariosto via Spenser – Shakespeare looks at the pleasures, fragilities and unexpected graces of a courtly society. Beatrice and Benedick display – with a more acidic edge than most Italian writers could muster – the qualities of courtly wit that would have been accounted *sprezzatura* by Castiglione. Yet these are played off against a darker stratagem that acknowledges the extent to which malicious gossip and melancholic envy are endemic in the life of the court. Shakespeare's Don John

– pointlessly besmirching Hero's reputation – is one version of Spenser's Blatant Beast in Book Six of *The Faerie Queen* and the kinsman of many a Bandellian courtier. (He is also, in this respect, the forebear of Iago.) But the resolution of the finely poised situation is one that requires that all settled habit – be it the witty and apparently clear-headed malice of Beatrice and Benedick or the 'motiveless malignity' of Don John – should be replaced by an educative understanding of the value of blind love. At the core of the play is the profound speech – attributed to a Christian Friar but shot through with suggestions drawn from the Neoplatonic cult of learned ignorance – which suggests that the swooning Hero should be proclaimed as dead, so that, when Claudio hears of this, 'Th'idea of her life shall sweetly creep/Into his study of imagination' (*Much Ado About Nothing*, IV, i, 124–5). A fiction – a play, a blinding to the coarse realities of merely physical perception – removes the actual Hero from Claudio's infected eye. And rightly so. For under Don John's influence it was his search for ocular proof – which is to say for some definite and apparently rational certitude as to Hero's fidelity – that led him to mistake a flirtatious maid for his mistress. It is, it seems, the elevated power of blind imagination that we need to employ in our pursuit of the highest truths; and the ruse works, not only in the case of Claudio and Hero, but also in the case of Beatrice and Benedick. Only when these two become the unwitting pawns in a game devised by their associates do they reconcile the contraries that they have hitherto sought to sharpen in the interchange of their barbed animadversions. Marriage concludes the play, reminding one that marriage itself – here as in other comedies – is one of the Neoplatonic emblems for the productive interrelation of opposing principles. One need only add that any so schematic a paraphrase of course contradicts the essentially Shakespearian addition to this formula: which is that the truths of the imagination are more fruitfully trained upon the complexities and ambiguities of human behaviour than upon those of transcendent mysteries.

Then finally there is *A Midsummer Night's Dream*. In Shakespeare's own canon, this relatively early play displays a dramaturgical command and an intensity of comic vision that is later to re-emerge in plays as different as *As You Like It*, *Macbeth*, *King Lear* and *The Tempest*. It is also the richest example of Shakespearian innurition and (paradoxically perhaps) of his interest in the Renaissance theme of Folly.

The *Dream* may well have been played at court. Yet so far from writing a masque or courtly interlude, Shakespeare here displays, in his authorial stance, a supreme quality of courtly *sprezzatura* in the handling both of sources and of complex strands of narrative. As to sources, Shakespeare in his depiction of the transformation of Bottom into an ass clearly draws upon the essential spirit of the Ovidian narrative and may even have somewhere in mind Apuleius's *Golden Ass* – which stood throughout the Renaissance as a tale of initiation and purification from the trammels of brute body. Yet the treatment of such suggestions is anything but subservient. As in Ariosto's *Orlando Furioso* or Spenser's *The Faerie Queene*, *entrelacement* here ensures an intertwining of stories concerning young lovers, mature lovers, fairy lovers and rude mechanical actors. The courtly entertainment that is, in fact, performed by the mechanicals is drawn from the hitherto deeply serious tragedy that Ovid offers, which is turned by Shakespeare into high farce. Yet he is no less able to parody throughout the *Dream* the themes of his own almost contemporary *Romeo and Juliet*.

Within this scheme, Shakespearian double-plotting – here as in *The Taming of the Shrew*, *Henry IV* and *King Lear* – ensures a clear emphasis on certain thematic pre-occupations. These include an interest in the contradistinctions to be observed across a spectrum of sexual behaviour ranging from the edgy maturity of the two erstwhile enemies, Theseus and Hippolyta, through the capricious choreography of teenage love and on to the canoodlings of a fairy queen and an ass. It also becomes evident that the play is concerned with questions of order and disorder in the civic and the metaphysical realm and, similarly, with education as the means of assimilation to that order. The civic (and patriarchal) dispensation is challenged by Hermia's defiance of both her father and of Duke Theseus, while Titania – in a speech as powerful as any in *Macbeth* – offers a picture of the chaos and misery wrought in nature by her tussle with Oberon over the Indian boy: 'the nine man's morris is filled up with mud' (*MND*, II, i, 89–93).

Not least, we are concerned once again with education and the nature of reason, with what can be learned from love, from plays, from apparent confusion, from poetry, from the popular voices of Bottom and the Mechanicals.

Familiar as all these themes have by now become, the variations that Shakespeare plays upon them are entirely his own. For it quickly becomes apparent that, if order is to be discovered in the midst of such 'melodious confusion' (*ibid.*, IV, i, 111), it will not come from the re-affirmation of the civic role nor the courtly strategies of a Theseus. Nor, for that matter, will it derive from any reference to a confident meta-physical system. Theseus himself in Shakespeare's version is brought, eventually, to speak as the champion of play-acting and its ignorant participants, even though it is he who earlier had declared contemptuously that 'The lunatic, the lover, and the poet/Are of imagination all compact' (*ibid.*, V, i, 7–8). And if there is any mean-ing to a play that unrolls in a progressive cultivation of unmeaning, then this mean-ing must be that – momentarily at least – we may well live most productively without the deliverances of high sentence, provided always that we are willing to understand and participate in the communities that form in the world of theatrical play.

Thus Shakespeare's play moves away from the city and the court into a recogniz-ably English countryside: 'I know a bank whereon the wild thyme grows . . .' But this is also a 'green world'; and so far from being a place of conventionally pastoral retreat, this world (anticipating Lear's heath) is one in which surprise and transformation are borne in upon its inhabitants, and where the contradictions and oppositions of love, whether human or fantastic (supposing there to be a difference), are acutely realized.

It is indeed appropriate, as lover shifts to lover, that Shakespeare should reiterate – in his own nuanced terms – the Ficinian precept that love, precisely in its blindness, perceives a higher truth than reason can muster: 'Love looks not with the eyes but with the mind,/And therefore is wing'd Cupid painted blind' (*MND*, I, i, 234–5).

Yet in Shakespeare's play, the most authoritative utterance of this doctrine is ascribed not to some courtly initiate but to that rude mechanical and irrepressibly enthusiastic thespian, Bottom. Bottom is in every sense the 'bottom' of the *Dream*, in terms not only of social and intellectual hierarchy but also in terms of the unintentional profundity of his *sententiae*. If he is in some ways a natural man, then nature in this case must be taken to encompass a wonderful appetite for art, for play and for all the contradictions that can be better realized in theatres and dreams than in rational argument: 'I will roar you as gently as any sucking dove'. Even when transformed into an ass, Bottom seeks no Apuleian delivery from brute body but enjoys with the utmost responsiveness of sensation the stimuli to his senses that Titania and the fairies excite in him: 'I could munch your good dry oats. Methinks I have a great desire to a bottle of hay' (IV, i, 33).

Finally, in a Renaissance perspective there is no more profound utterance in Shakespeare than Bottom's words, spoken as he awakes from his transforming dream, which reflect not only the rhythms of St Paul's prose but also Erasmus's in the closing pages of his *Praise of Folly*:

> The eye of man hath not heard, the ear of man hath not seen, man's hand is not able to taste, his tongue to conceive, nor his heart to report, what my dream was. I will get Peter Quince to write a ballad of this dream: it shall be called Bottom's Dream, because it hath not bottom: and I will sing it in the latter end of our play, before the duke.
>
> (*MND*, IV, ii, 206–20).

This is the sort of truthful folly that participation in a green world was always likely to produce. But, as the play returns to court, so too it summons its resources to teach a version of this lesson, through the medium of theatre, to the audience at Theseus's marriage-feast – and, of course, to the audience of *The Dream* itself, in presenting the great classical tragedy of Pyramus and Thisbe. For it is here – in an experience that transforms tragedy into utter comedy – that the play insists in its own way upon that acceptance (and enjoyment) of relativities that Boccaccio first encouraged in his often tragic-comic *novelle*. Indeed Theseus himself insists upon this, forbidding – in a last act of authority – Demetrius and Lysander to persist in their snobbish mockery of the rude mechanicals and recognize the appetite for play that is the unifying feature of all human beings. The folly that Shakespeare dramatizes in this play-within-a-play demands participation in a dance, defined as much by human limitation as by human possibility. The play of Pyramus and Thisbe – somewhat curtailed – ends in a distinctly carnivalesque morris dance. The love-narratives conclude in marriage, where contradiction is not so much resolved as brought into generative union. And so might many a Renaissance masque. But *A Midsummer Night's Dream* itself ends – as most of Shakespeare's comedies do – unresolvedly, with the teasing return of Puck and the suggestion of new and always unpredictable narratives yet to be pursued. There is here a theatrical equivalent of the essays and conversations that Montaigne offered.

The critical spirit, in its most productive aspect, is as likely to ensure a continuing participation in discourse as a censorious abdication. There are, however, certain plays in which Shakespeare's critical intelligence viciously threatens not only the foundations of Renaissance culture but also those of his own – and of his audience's – self-composure. The most notable instance of this is the black carnival, *Troilus and Cressida*. But there are important indications of this even in an almost contemporary sequence, the apparently assured *Henry IV*, Parts I and II. For in this play Shakespeare looks back – as he does in *Troilus* itself – to a world that seemed saner than the classical world or even the world of Elizabethan theatre ever could be, the world of Chaucer, which is, of course, the chronological setting of the *Henry* plays.

The Riccardian poet Chaucer had begun his *Canterbury Tales* with a supremely assured syntactical period – 'Whanne that Aprille with his shoures sote . . .' – that fluently associates the instincts and urges that are manifested in the English countryside with the longing of folk to undertake a pilgrimage to Canterbury. It was in *Richard II* that the dying John of Gaunt spoke of this sceptred isle. But when *Henry IV* envisages the countryside, it does so as a place of potential battle or at best as the sphere in which the ageing Shallow and Silence mutter their nostalgic *non sequiturs*. The usurper Henry longs to go on a pilgrimage – not however to Canterbury, a place of local sanctity – but to the far-off Holy Land. He never does; and his son Hal can do no more than to translate pilgrimage into territorial adventure. The two Henrys are as confined to the city as, largely, the audience of the play is itself. Nor is this city anything like the place of civilized order or even outrageous gusto that it would be for an Italian or for Ben Jonson. To be sure, London is the centre of the nation – or is attempting to become so. But it is also a place of brothels, taverns and skulduggery; and where, at the battle of Shrewsbury, kingly doubles miasmically multiply, so in London Falstaff possesses as much right to be the kingly father of Prince Hal as the erstwhile Bolingbroke. Meanwhile, Shakespeare's art measures its own incalculable distance from Chaucer's. Chaucer, in depicting the varied and often divergent voices of the pilgrim storytellers, maintained (rather as Ariosto was to do) a constantly varying and constantly ironic authorial presence. But dramatists have no authorial presence; and the brilliant symphony of double plots that Shakespeare here sustains artfully speaks of cacophony and stress. Indeed the opening of *Henry IV*, Part II – so far from producing any authoritative syntactical sweep, hands the play over to the chorus, 'Rumour, painted full of tongues', who speaks 'of peace while covert enmity/Under the smile of safety rules the world'. This is the world of gossip, of words run riot. The only authority here is the deeply ambiguous Sir John Falstaff – lawless, pathetic, mean and yet imaginatively generous, simultaneously a symptom of moral decay and an embodiment of Carnival. Likewise the only community is one that is constituted not by dying kings or suppurating cities but rather by the stage itself, by a willingness on the part of authors, actors and audiences to come together in realization of their temporary kinship.

Shakespeare had visited the Chaucerian realm in the *Dream* and will return in *Pericles* and *Two Noble Kinsmen*. So does he also in his own version of Chaucer's *Troilus* story. But in this play he calls into open dispute the whole literary legacy that Chaucer had (with some reservations) first identified and that Renaissance minds, including his own, had subsequently fed on to the full.

Shakespeare's theme in *Troilus and Cressida* is that of the Trojan War, a theme that the classical world itself had addressed – through the voices of Homer and Virgil – in defining its own understanding of its own characteristics. Correspondingly, *Troilus* is a play in which Shakespeare is sometimes thought to have enunciated explicitly the central principles of his (essentially conservative) philosophy, involving a conception of order and degree in which the microcosm of human actions is connected to the macrocosmic order of the universe itself:

> The heavens themselves, the planets, and this centre,
>
> Observe degree, priority, and place,
>
> Insisture, course, proportion, season, form,
>
> (Troilus and Cressida, I, iii, 85–94)

Behind this speech lies a late Medieval conception of universal order – visible in the account of the 'feyre cheyne of love' that Egeus provides in Chaucer's *Knight's Tale*. This Medieval system was rendered poetically available and imaginatively persuasive by thinkers such as Ficino and, in Tudor England, by Sir Thomas Elyot and Richard Hooker in his *Laws of Ecclesiastical Polity*; nor was such a system incompatible with the late Renaissance revival of absolutist ideas of Divine Right.

Yet to whom is this speech entrusted in *Troilus*? And to what purpose is it uttered? The speaker is Ulysses, who was the wiliest of the Greeks. And his purpose is to urge on, by appealing to this principle of collaborative harmony, the military action that will lead to the ultimate destruction of Troy. Shakespeare's play (in common with Chaucer's *Troilus and Criseyde*) is concerned with a lull in the military action of the Trojan War when indolence and lethargy reign, and when both heroes and lovers are shown to be the playthings of their own absurd instincts and pretensions. In this context Ulysses may employ the rhetoric of philosophical vision. But his only possible claim to virtue is Machiavellian in character, adapting even the most elevated sentiments to the call of occasion. This is not a claim that Shakespeare allows. Neither Ulysses – nor Shakespeare himself, in writing this speech for the Ulysses character – provides any philosophical or even Machiavellian remedy for the corruption that threatens to engulf both the Greek and the Trojan camps – and equally, on this view, late Renaissance England.

Troilus and Cressida, then, is a play in which all the foundations of ethical order that Renaissance culture had tended to cultivate are called into question. Heroes here are fools or tricksters. Achilles himself spends most of his time in the course of the play – in a sort of malignant metatheatre – enjoying scabrous imitations of the great Greek patriarchs, staged for him by his catamite, Patroclus. As for stories of heroic love, Troilus and Cressida themselves are undoubtedly moved by passion and by an obscure sense that their inward being might achieve some security if only they were able mutually to realize the full implications of their feelings. Yet there is no agreed discourse – between the two lovers themselves, or in their own relationship to the social order – which can support these feelings or articulate them as the sentiments of legitimate love. How could there be, in the circumstances of a war that is being fought over Helen of Troy, who is constantly represented as, at best, a token of exchange and, at worst, as a whore? In such a context, sexual values are bound to be confused with the values of mercantile appetite. Identity here depends less upon love than upon factual specification: 'This is and is not Cressid', Troilus exclaims (V, ii, 156) as he is brought by Ulysses to witness the evidence of Cressida's infidelity. The speech that follows is no less central to the play than Ulysses's 'Degree' oration; and the unresolvable doubt that it expresses turns the Renaissance mind from a posture of benign scepticism to one in which there are no grounds for any kind of order, micro- or macrocosmic.

Just as importantly, the dramatic form that Shakespeare devises in this play itself erodes the possibility of defining any stable orientation or reliable point of view. It is as if theatrical rhetoric, as the final product of the Renaissance tradition, were here turned against the tradition itself, to reveal (as early humanists would willingly have admitted) that its foundations were no more secure than rhetoric could make them. Troilus and Cressida may be the eponymous protagonists of the play. Yet the audience is never allowed (as it certainly is in *Romeo and Juliet*) to give undivided attention to the unfolding of their psychological action. On the contrary, the play constantly cuts away from intense moments of passion or emotional encounter to represent the longueurs of military or political debate or the fatuous bombast of pseudo-heroes such as Ajax. Likewise, the figures who move in the play between these disparate worlds of love and war – notably Thersites and Pandarus – are perceived more as peeping Toms than as moral authorities. Even the Prologue 'armed' is shown to be timorous of the audience's reaction, shifting from high-flown rhetoric to seedy prurience within the space of twenty lines in his opening speech:

> In Troy there lies the scene. From isles of Greece
>
> The princes orgulous, their high bloods chafed,
>
> Have to the port of Athens sent their ships . . .
>
> Now expectation, tickling skittish spirits
>
> On one and the other side, Trojan and Greek,
>
> Sets all on hazard.

> (*Troilus and Cressida*, Prologue 1–3; 20–2)

As in a Bandello *novella*, authority here resides in the area of gossip and voyeurism, recording without moral purpose the clash of competing aspirations, motives and points of view. In this perspective, it is entirely appropriate that the play should conclude with the words of Pandarus which seek to infect the audience of the play itself with the syphilitic diseases that he, as a fictional character, has now begun to suffer from: 'Till then I'll sweat and seek about for eases/And at that time bequeath you my diseases.'

In the end Shakespeare does not allow his own art to be immune to this scathing scrutiny. *Troilus and Cressida* shares with the *Sonnets* a deep interest in the Renaissance themes of Love, Art and Time. In the *Sonnets* (as also in *Romeo and Juliet*) the 'miracle' of love, once monumentalized in art (see p. 229), may overcome the depredations of Time. But *Troilus and Cressida* depicts a vicious subversion of that optimism. In Act III, scene ii, when Cressida comes forward to make a formal declaration of her fidelity, she declares that, if she proves false, then all false women must henceforth be known as 'Cressida':

> When waterdrops hath worn the stones of Troy,
>
> And blind oblivion swallowed cities up
>
> When they've said 'as false
>
> As air, as water, wind or sandy earth . . .
>
> Yea let them say, to stick the heart of falsehood,
>
> 'As false as Cressid'.

> (*ibid.*, III, ii, 187–95; 198–9)

Cressida's words are intended to ring as a confident challenge to the actions of Time (and indeed of gossip). Yet, of course, they do not. And the reason why they do not, finally, incriminates the audience in the moral debacle that Shakespeare has here so ingeniously devised. Because – like good humanists – we know the legends of the classical past, so we can know the future. But here the possession of such knowledge, so far from ensuring our control of the situation, generates a theatre of embarrassment. Too much knowledge – too much 'innurition' – prevents us from gaining any access to the tincture of compassion that – if we have also read Chaucer – we know that Cressida can invoke. So much for the world of classical tradition.

A TRAGIC AFTERWORD

In ancient Greece, tragedy was the form in which the Athenians, as their culture developed, confronted the contradictions that lay beneath surface of their current and apparently successful pursuit of wisdom, justice and order: the all-knowing Oedipus cannot hold at bay the unknown implications of his family origins; the claims of the Eumenides cannot be silenced entirely by the words of Pallas Athene. Shakespeare, too, stands at a point in European culture where success had been bought (as it must be in all civilizations) at the cost of many suppressions and half-answered questions, and where developments particularly in the sphere of science were shortly to provide a very different gloss. In his comedies, Shakespeare accepts – even if he radically modifies – the game that can be played within the formal conventions that he had received from the culture of Renaissance Europe. The same might be said of at least one of his tragedies, which is set in Italy and takes as its source the writings of a Counter-Reformation Italian, Giraldi Cinthio (pp. 11 and 323). This is *Othello*. Here Shakespeare perceives (as did the greatest of the humanists such as Montaigne) that the intrinsic excellence of human beings may inhere in figures as strange and unaccountable as the heroic Othello. He also sees in the Venetian and Machiavellian Iago that the very power of rational calculation which some – especially in later times – have come to see as the foundation of human excellence, is the mindless enemy of all that we understand when love reveals, as it does to Desdemona, what excellence truly is.

I have examined this dilemma at length in another volume, and shall say no more about *Othello* here. There are, however, three tragedies, located, significantly, on the margins of continental Europe that translate the Renaissance tragedy of *Othello* into terms that bequeath, with the utmost urgency, questions to future times that the Renaissance itself had the power to formulate but not the competence to answer. In *Macbeth*, *King Lear* and *Hamlet*, Shakespeare removes himself from the centre and prises open a number of issues, concerning, particularly, conceptions of personal identity and power, along with considerations of Folly, Violence and Love, in which the Renaissance centre seems unable to hold. No afterword to the Renaissance can ignore these plays.

In *Macbeth* Shakespeare takes up the question of political power – specifically in the forming of new principalities – that had first been raised by Machiavelli in *The Prince* and provides, arguably, a far subtler and more realistic account than Machiavelli himself had been able to offer. With Machiavelli, of course, one is bound to admit, as an essential feature of any effective statecraft, that the exercise of power and the pursuit of moral principle can – and in many cases must – be distinguished. It remains true, however, that moral sentiment is itself a real feature of the human psyche, an expression and a means to the achievement of human flourishing. Indeed, on a certain understanding, the virtues can themselves be defined as the very condition of human excellence. In that perspective, Macbeth is not merely a good man flawed by ambition, but a man who – once he has achieved his political ambitions – discovers in himself an irrepressible and now unquenchable urge to be at one with the forces that sustain his human existence. His political actions may be dictated by apparent certainties – uttered by witches. Yet his imagination remains alive with unformed thoughts of those children whom he will never have, or those will never come to succeed him, and likewise of the natural world – of temple-haunting martlets and Birnam woods – in which his actions make him an alien: 'Light thickens'. He is haunted and hunted down not by his crimes but by his own inherent goodness and by the same affiliations with sequences that go beyond any single acts of *virtù*. At the last, Macbeth will defy these sequences: 'Tomorrow, and tomorrow, and tomorrow/Creeps in this petty place from day to day'. But this wearily repetitive apprehension of mere sequence is itself a denial of that highly charged imagination that makes Macbeth the most intense and sensitive of Shakespeare's tragic heroes:

> And pity, like a naked new-born babe,
>
> Striding the blast, or heaven's cherubin, hors'd
>
> Upon the sightless couriers of the air,
>
> Shall blow the horrid deed in every eye.

(Macbeth, I, vii, 21–4)

Indeed even the simplest and most ordinary objects of existence – feasts, birds in the air, the knocking of guests at the gate – become in Macbeth's vivid apprehension the agents of a conscience that he cannot repress. *Virtù* in the Machiavellian sense is revealed to be a mere equivocation on a word that also points to the fundamental strengths that sustain us in our characteristically human way of living.

At the same time, there is another more disturbing reality to face. For if in acknowledging the moral power of the imagination (as he will also in the Romances) Shakespeare goes beyond Machiavelli, he also recognizes that the imagination will itself be complicit in the formulation of any political act. The energy of the

Machiavellian virtuoso will never strike with the clinical precision of a scalpel. It will always be a dagger with its hilt towards our own hands; and, by the time *Macbeth* is over, the audience themselves are aware of this. For their own imaginations have come to depend on a figure who, in his complexity and charisma, is no less compelling than the witches that he himself so willingly visits. Our fascination with the extraordinary is the ordinary source of evil. We love it as much as Macbeth loves Lady Macbeth; and the twentieth century – peopled by Machiavellian tyrants – was fated to realize in its own awful history what Shakespeare had already realized in *Macbeth*.

In *King Lear*, a ruler – so far from attempting any Machiavellian coup – seeks to abdicate all political authority so that he can 'crawl unburdened' towards his death. This story – set in ancient Britain against an indeterminate and shifting landscape – is something of a fable and, at times, in the Heath scenes, also verges on the dramaturgy of the Romances, evoking archetypal forces that lie beyond the lineaments of any particular culture. It is also, however, a tale of Folly in which, as a result of his own miscalculations, the King is driven into an anarchic pastoral of fools, madmen and outcasts. In their company, Lear comes to realize that power itself is always and inevitably a source of violent foolishness and finally recognizes, as Erasmus or Breughel might have taught him, that he stumbled when he saw.

Or this would be the story if Gloster were its main protagonist. Yet the case of Gloster reveals an appalling fragility in human nature that challenges all archetypal or pedagogical diagnoses. We witness a subjection to violence – 'Out vile jelly' – and an utterly incalculable capacity for endurance that cannot be contained within the frame of Erasmian conclusions or even the pacific words of Gloster himself: 'Ripeness is all'. There can be no order or educative process in a world where the eye – as the organ of perception and the mirror of love – is so painfully subject to attack. Nor does Shakespeare's play allow us finally to suppose that there is. It is true that Lear will say: 'I am a very foolish fond old man'; it is also true that in saying to Cordelia 'Come, let's away to prison/We two alone will sing like birds i'the cage' (*King Lear*, V, iii, 8–9), he momentarily enunciates a peculiarly delicate form of stoic resignation. Yet the last moments of the play demand that we should contemplate the same man who once wished to crawl unburdened towards his death still strong enough to carry the corpse of his daughter in his arms – away from the scene of an unripe death that expressed neither justice nor even the final desires of Cordelia's repentant enemies. It was this daughter, at the beginning of the play, who honestly but catastrophically had said 'Nothing' to her father; and it was Lear's violent reaction to the stubborn sincerity of this single word that precipitated a chain of capricious reactions, in which continually Lear himself was driven to contemplate the various ways in which the nothingness at the heart of human existence reveals itself. Now the dead Cordelia says nothing once again. And once again the King's reaction is more violent than one would have expected his frame to be able to bear. Yet violence itself – the very source of destruction – is now revealed as being the only conceivable source of creation. It is violence that voices the insane demand that Cordelia, somehow, should still be allowed to live against all possibility that she ever will – and against all kindness and reason, considering how cruel a world the child would now be re-born to: 'Why should a dog, a horse a rat have life/And thou no breath at all?' (*ibid.*, V, iv, 6–7). Earlier, King Lear has exclaimed:

> O reason not the need! Our basest beggars
>
> Are in poorest things superfluous.
>
> Allow not nature more than nature needs,
>
> Man's life is cheap as beast's.
>
> (ibid., II, iv, 262–5)

This speech undoubtedly marks the beginning of Lear's delirium. Yet in effect, as he now leans over Cordelia, Lear repeats the same demand, and reveals the folly of that demand to be the only expression of civilization, sanity and life. We are human in those very superfluities – and trivialities – that distinguish us from beasts. It is quite unnecessary for Regan to wear a low-cut dress. Yet it is, for good or ill, a sign of humanity that she should. It is unnecessary for Lear to have a retinue; but his demand that he should, deluded as it may be, is all that marks him off from nothingness. Now, in the final moments of the play, Lear sees that life itself is strictly unnecessary. Cordelia never had to live: it is a luxury that she ever did; it is a folly to suppose that she ever will again. But the demand that she might, against all reason, is the primal demand, uttered in the violence of love. When Lear cries out: 'Howl, howl, howl, howl', his apparently animal eloquence denies all that the Renaissance had ever stood for in its judicious cultivation of the word. But he also reveals the foundation of human civilization. Courts, fashions and emblems of power are all, after all, expressions of humanity. But they all rest upon the utterly gratuitous, utterly violent and utterly illusory demands that are voiced in love. Love, not justice, is the foundation of human existence.

In *Macbeth*, Shakespeare anticipates the awful appeal that is realized in the twentieth-century age of dictators, whose glamorous forebears were the political *virtuosi* of the Renaissance. *Lear*, likewise, has spoken more eloquently than any other Shakespearian play to a twentieth century that developed a profound suspicion of the Renaissance legacy, inspiring, for instance, in Samuel Beckett an absurd but loving sense of how, going on, we go on: 'I can't go on, I'll go on'. It was *Hamlet*, however, promoted so strongly by the Romantics, that first revealed how profoundly a Renaissance Shakespeare might question not only his own but also future time.

'What a piece of work is man! . . . how infinite in faculty! . . . in action how like an angel! in apprehension how like a god! the beauty of the world! the paragon of animals!' (*Hamlet*, II, ii, 312–16). Taken out of context, these words could be cited, as easily as Pico della Mirandola's *Oration on the Dignity of Man*, as the celebration of a familiar view of the achievements of Renaissance humanism. But the speech concludes: 'what is this quintessence of dust? Man delights not me; no, nor woman neither, though by your smiling you seem to say so.' Here, too, Hamlet speaks in the recognizable tones of the Renaissance; by the end of the sixteenth century the melancholic sentiments of the malcontent had become the height of fashion among Renaissance thinkers themselves. Tasso's madness was by now modish; and black was the colour of the season, particularly among those whose tastes inclined towards a Mannerist affirmation of their own idiosyncratic selfhoods. But Hamlet – and the play in which he appears – reopens the question implied by this incongruity on a level deeper than fashion can contain. Here the very consciousness that in Pico would have been the source of excellence, freedom and creative power becomes the cause of Hamlet's alienation from himself and from the world around him; and this is a possibility that always yawned beneath the Renaissance endeavour. As early as Petrarch – at its originary moment – the Renaissance had begun to understand how real this possibility might be, precisely in affirming its Petrarchan commitment to the word as the medium in which the excellence of human identity could display itself . The very words that claim attention for the shifts and subtleties of the inner being – recording the 'sighs that nourish the heart' – are words that we inherit from others and hope that others will remember. Hamlet's opening moments register that tension. In the second scene, Claudius offers Hamlet some stoic and sensitive advice as to how he might manage his grief. But already, there is an obscure sense that any such advice will betray or contaminate the character of the heart that hears it; and Hamlet at once increases the linguistic tension of the moment in a pun that threatens the control offered by logical polarities. He drives himself inward into his first miniature soliloquy; seeking an untouchable darkness in himself without relation to others, Hamlet mutters: 'A little more than kin, and less than kind . . . I am too much i' th' sun (*Hamlet*, I, ii, 65 and 67).

Shakespeare's play proceeds to place before its hero many of the scripts that the Renaissance culture had devised for human performance. At one extreme, Ophelia views Hamlet as the perfect courtier, 'the rose of the fair state'; and Hamlet's closest associate is the scholar and philosopher, Horatio. At the other extreme, Claudius is the Machiavellian 'new prince' and demonstrates a good deal of what a pragmatic ruler might need to do if the kingdom of Denmark – which has for generations been 'out of joint' – is to be secured from inward and outward menace. (There is every sign that Claudius is better fitted to be the King of a threatened realm than Hamlet, father or son.) Against this, Hamlet in his madness – and in his soliloquies – attempts to write a script of his own. Yet even in the darkness of his own self he cannot escape the claims of discourse; and the words that move at his agitated centre are the words of his dead progenitor, speaking of revenge and asserting claims that lie beyond the horizon of Renaissance discourse itself, mocking its pretensions to clarity and control. Hamlet's very name is a homonym of his father's. And the confusing imperatives – uttered by a ghost from some undetermined realm of the afterlife – imposes on his inner thoughts a demand for retributive action that forbids any further investigation of what a self in its creative freedom might yet become: all that matters is that the human being should be accounted for in some chain of appropriate vengeance. The Renaissance looked to the past as a creative resource, as if it could command and confidently feed upon its own origins. Hamlet's father opens a very different vista in which there can be no quest, no Romance, no exuberant display (as in *Titus Andronicus*) of the ritual of revenge. Worse still, once this perspective is opened, it leads into a darkness at the heart of the supposedly integral self-hood that teems with the proliferating growths of 'an unweeded garden', with questions that concern the biological origins of the individual, and lead back (to the disgust of the over-sophisticated mind) towards a contemplation of the 'nasty sty'. One recalls that the humanist Buchanan reminded his pupil James Stuart of the 'bloody nest' from whence he had come (see pp. 80–1). Hamlet's father unwittingly inserts the same thought into the mind of his overwrought offspring.

Already in *Troilus and Cressida* Shakespeare has turned his literary acumen against the foundations of that culture that gave it birth, revealing the dangerous insubstantiality of both heroism and literary art. The thought continues in *Hamlet* – which dates, of course, from the same period of Shakespeare's career. But beyond heroism and intellectual prowess, Hamlet finds that there can be no identity or certainty that is not a part of a cultural code; without such codes, there are only the gaping and derisive hollows of a father's grave, a mother's bed or Yorick's skull. Yet knowledge itself leads in the same direction. All that Hamlet's thirst for knowledge reveals is that all codes are liable to perversions and contaminations that drag one either to the crudity of revenge or the policy of Claudius. Ironically enough, Hamlet himself – in order to establish proof of Claudius's guilt – devises an instrument of his own, seeking to employ the delusive medium of a courtly entertainment, *The Mouse Trap*, to forensic ends; and the certainty that this experiment appears to provide leads only to a further and yet more elaborate desire to entrap Claudius in the trammels of eternal rather than temporal revenge. The only outcome of this certain proof is the murder of the lurking Polonius and the 'lugging' away of his guts into an adjoining chamber. Even self-knowledge – so far from producing the self-possession that an Horatio or the courtly diplomat Polonius might suppose it does – leads only to further words, flying up in Hamlet's case just as airily and just as emptily as they do from the lips of the praying Claudius.

It is not therefore surprising that the most intimate words that Hamlet speaks in his soliloquies should seek to extinguish the source of all words: 'O, that this too too solid flesh would melt' (*ibid.*, I, ii, 129). Existence itself – especially in its most ambitious and apparently sophisticated manifestations – has become a crime. Thus the conclusion of the play produces a manifold mockery, worthy of Yorick himself. Vengeance is finally enacted. Yet, so far from being the expression of purpose or resolve, it is the product of the clattering accident of mis-held rapiers. The bodies remain; and at once they are decorated with the plausible narratives of military prowess and personal loss that Fortinbras and Horatio attempt to spin around the scene. Yet nothing could be less appropriate than that Hamlet should be taken up into the ceremonies of a soldier's funeral. Nor are the heavens that he has opened likely to be peopled with the flights of angels that Horatio sentimentally hopes will sing the hero to his rest. The language of public men – or even of persons speaking in public – is as inappropriate here as when Claudius at the outset first attempted to moderate Hamlet's own grief. What remains is a scene of carnage. This is visible in overview only to the audience; and the audience itself must now stand in the same relation to this scene as Hamlet did initially to the 'unweeded garden' of Denmark. Our demand and expectation is that there will be, and must be, another and future Hamlet to question, however inconclusively, the meretricious order that the play itself – through the mouth of Fortinbras – has finally established.

Future centuries were to protect themselves from the implications of the play by emphasizing, in particular, the interest that Hamlet carries in terms of 'character' and psychological complexity. There is no denying that the play gives great impetus to the development of such categories. Nor can we now avoid thinking in these terms: it is part of our own code and part of our cultural fate that we should do so. Yet the very soliloquies that seem to encourage a belief in the workings of an inner self – subsequently inspiring, for instance, the development of streams of inner consciousness – are themselves studied exercises in public rhetoric. To be sure, the rhetoric is subtler than that which is displayed by the First Player in his eloquent evocation of Hecuba's grief. Yet even if these speeches are not meant to be overheard by Polonius or Ophelia, the audience overhears them. We are eavesdroppers. Indeed culture itself – a notion that certainly has its origins in the Renaissance – is close to being a matter of eavesdropping here, of listening to the past and to others for suggestions that we might assume into our own personae. Short of addressing our words to God, as the Protestant might, or revering, as a Catholic might, the images that humans have always used in approaching God or else of admitting, with Montaigne, that our words must always be subject to the gentle hermeneutics of friendship, this is what culture amounts to, a multiplication of tongues, a babel of conventions. Or finally we may determine that we shall tolerate the question, without any desire for conclusions or for certainty, or any of the shields that the Renaissance forges along with all its brilliant rapiers – or chisels or scalpels – of inquiry.

NOTES

For the general themes of this chapter, see J. Huizinga, *Homo Ludens: A Study of the Play Element in Culture* (London, 1998) and M.M. Bakhtin, *Rabelais and his World*, trans. H. Iswolsky (Bloomington, 1984); R. Andrews, *Scripts and Scenarios: the performance of comedies in Renaissance Italy* (Cambridge, 1993); L.G. Clubb, *Italian Drama in the Time of Shakespeare* (New Haven and London, 1989); Leo Salingar, *Shakespeare and the Traditions of Comedy* (Cambridge, 1974) On **Boccaccio**, D. Wallace, *Boccaccio* (Cambridge, 1990); V. Branca, trans. *Boccaccio: The Man and his Works* (New York, 1976); Pamela Joseph Benson, *Italian tales from the age of Shakespeare* (London, 1996); M. McKendrick, *Theatre in Spain* (Cambridge, 1989). For **Rabelais**, see translation of *The Histories of Gargantua and Pantagruel* (from which I quote) by J.M. Cohen (London, 1955); M.A. Screech, *Rabelais* (London, 1979); G. Josipovici, *The world and the book: a study of modern fiction* (Basingstoke, 1994). For **Cervantes**, see P.E. Russell, *Cervantes* (London, 1985); Edwin Williamson, *The Half-Way House of Fiction: Don Quixote and Arthurian Romance* (Oxford, 1984); Alban K. Forcione, *Cervantes and the Humanist Vision* (Princeton, 1982); A.J. Close, *Cervantes and the Comic Mind of his Age* (Oxford, 2000). For **Shakespeare**, the vast literature can be assessed from Stanley Wells (ed.), *Shakespeare: A Bibliographical Guide* (London, 1990). On the centrality of 'metatheatre' in Shakespeare's plays, see Anne Barton on *Shakespeare and the Idea of the Play* (Westport, CT, 1977), I refer in discussing *Measure for Measure* to John Lever's Arden ed. (London); for a close reading of Shakespeare's language, see F. Kermode, *Shakespeare's Language* (London, 2000). The study of *Othello* to which I refer is found in my *English and Italian Literature from Dante to Shakespeare* (London, 1995).

BIBLIOGRAPHY

ACKERMAN, J.S., *Palladio* (London, 1966).

AHLGREN, GILLIAN T.W., *Teresa of Avila and the Politics of Sanctity* (London, 1996).

ALLEN, MICHAEL J.B., *The Platonism of Marsilio Ficino* (London, 1984).

ASCOLI, A.R., *Ariosto's Bitter Harmony: Crisis and Evasion in the Italian Renaissance* (Princeton, 1987).

ATKINSON, JAMES, *Martin Luther and the Birth of Protestantism* (London, 1968).

AUERBACH, ERICH, *Mimesis: The Representation of Reality in Western Literature* (trans. W.R. Trask) (Princeton, 1953).

AVERY, CHARLES, *Donatello: An Introduction* (London, 1994).

BAKHTIN, M.M., *Rabelais and his World* (trans. H. Iswolsky) (Bloomington, 1984).

BARON, HANS, *The Crisis of the Early Italian Renaissance* (Princeton, 1955).

BARTON, ANNE, *Shakespeare and the Idea of the Play* (Westport, CT, 1977).

BAXENDALL, M., *Painting and Experience* (Oxford, 1972).

BECK, JAMES, *Raphael* (New York, 1976).

BENNETT, BONNIE A. and WILKINS, DAVID G., *Donatello* (Oxford, 1984).

BENSON, PAM, *The Invention of Renaissance Women* (Pennsylvania, 1992).

—— , *Tales from Shakespeare* (London, 1996).

BERQUIST, P. (ed.), *Orlando di Lasso Studies* (Cambridge, 1999).

BIAŁOSTOCKI, JAN, *Il Quattrocento nell'Europa settentrionale* (Turin, 1989).

—— , *Dürer and his Critics* (Baden-Baden, 1986).

BLUNT, ANTHONY, *Artistic Theory in the Italian Renaissance* (Oxford, 1962).

—— , *Art and Architecture in France 1500 to 1700* (London, 1953).

BOSSY, JOHN, *Christianity in the West 1400–1700* (Oxford, 1985).

BOUWSMA, W.J., *John Calvin: a Sixteenth-Century Portrait* (London, 1988).

BRANCA, V., *Boccaccio: The Man and his Works* (trans. R. Monges) (New York, 1976).

BRAND, C.P., *Ariosto* (Edinburgh, 1974).

BRATT, JOHN H. (ed.), *The Heritage of John Calvin* (Grand Rapids, 1973).

BRAUDEL, FERNAND, *Civilization and Capitalism* (trans. S. Reynolds), 3 vols (London, 1981–84).

BRENNER, ROBERT, *Merchants and Revolution* (Cambridge, 1993).

BURCKHARDT, J., *The Civilization of the Renaissance in Italy* (trans. S.G.C. Middlemore) (London, 1995).

BURKE, P., *The Renaissance* (Basingstoke, 1987).

—— , *The European Renaissance: Centres and Peripheries* (Oxford, 1998).

—— , *Italian Renaissance: Culture and Society in Italy* (Cambridge, 1999).

BURROW, COLIN, 'Literature and Politics under Henry VII and Henry VIII', in *The Cambridge History of Medieval Literature*, ed. David Wallace (Cambridge, 1999), pp. 793–820.

CASSIRER, E., *The Renaissance Philosophy of Man*, ed. P.O. Kristeller *et al.* (Chicago & London, 1945).

CASTOR, G., *Pléiade Poetics* (Cambridge, 1964).

CAVE, TERENCE, *The Cornucopian Text: Problems of Writing in the French Renaissance* (Oxford, 1979).

CHADWICK, OWEN, *The Reformation* (London, 1964).

CHARLES, SYDNEY R., *Josquin des Prez: A Guide to Research* (New York, 1983).

CHASTEL, A., *The Golden Age of the Renaissance* (London, 1965).

——, *Studios and Styles: 1450–1500* (London, 1965).

CLARK, KENNETH, *Leonardo da Vinci* (London, new edn, 1967).

——, *Piero della Franscesca* (London, 1951).

CLOSE, ANTHONY, *Don Quixote* (Cambridge, 1989).

——, *Cervantes and the Comic Mind of His Age* (Oxford, 2000).

CLOUGH, CECIL H., *The Duchy of Urbino in the Renaissance* (London, 1981).

COHEN, J.M. (trans.), *Don Quixote* (London, 1950).

——, *The Life of Saint Teresa of Avila by Herself* (London, 1957).

——, *Rojas's The Spanish Bawd* (London, 1964).

——, *The Histories of Gargantua and Pantagruel* (London, 1955).

COLEMAN, DOROTHY GABE, *Montaigne's Essays* (London, 1987).

COOPER, RICHARD (contributions by M. McGowan), *The Entry of Henri IV into Lyon, September 1548. A facsimile* (Tempe, Arizona, 1997).

COPE, CHRISTOPHER, *Phoenix Frustrated: The lost kingdom of Burgundy* (London, 1986).

CUMMINGS, BRIAN, 'Reformed Literature and Literature Reformed', in *The Cambridge History of Medieval English Literature*, ed. David Wallace (Cambridge, 1999), pp. 821–51.

DAVIES, MARTIN, *Rogier van der Weyden* (London, 1972).

DEFAUX, GÉRARD G., *Marot, Rabelais and Montaigne* (Paris, 1987).

DeMOLEN, RICHARD L., *Erasmus* (London, 1973).

DEMPSEY, P. (ed.), *Rome in the Renaissance: The City and the Myth* (Binghampton, NY, 1982).

EINEM, HERBERT VON, *Michelangelo* (trans. Robert Taylor) (London, 1959).

EINSTEIN, ALFRED, *The Italian Madrigal* (Princeton, 1949).

ELLRODT, R. (ed. & intro.), *Génèse de la conscience moderne* (Paris, 1983).

ELTON, G.R., *Reformation Europe 1517–1559* (London, 1963).

ERB, JAMES, *Orlando di Lasso: A Guide to Research* (New York, 1990).

EVENNETT, H. OUTRAM (ed. JOHN BOSSY), *The Spirit of the Counter-Reformation* (Cambridge, 1968).

FENLON, IAIN (ed.), *Music in Medieval and Early Modern Europe* (Cambridge, 1981).

——, *The Renaissance* (London, 1989).

Fernandez-Moreira, D., *The Lyre and the Oaten Flute: Garcilaso and the Pastoral* (London, 1982).

Finnis, John, *Natural Law and Natural Rights* (Oxford, 1980).

Forcione, Alban K., *Cervantes and the Humanist Vision* (Princeton, 1982).

Ford, Philip and Jondorf, Gillian (eds), *The Age of François Ier* (Cambridge French Colloquia, Cambridge 1996).

Forster, Leonard, *The Icy Fire: A Study in European Petrarchism* (Cambridge, 196?).

Foucault, M., *The Order of Things: An Archaeology of the Human Sciences* (trans. Alan Sheridan) (New York, 1970).

Gadamer, H-G., *Truth and Method* (trans. and revised Joel Weinsheimer and Donald G. Marshall (London, 1989).

Gage, John, *Colour and Culture* (London, 1993).

Genaille, Robert, *Flemish Painting from Van Eyck to Breughel* (trans. Leslie Schenk) (Paris, 1954).

Gibson, Walter S., *Breughel* (London, 1977).

Gilbert, Felix, *Machiavelli and Guicciardini* (London, 1984).

Goldthwaite, R., *Wealth and Demand for Art in Italy 1300–1600* (Baltimore, 1993).

Gombrich, Ernst, *Norm and Form: Studies in the Art of the Renaissance* (London, 1966).

—— , *Art and Illusion* (Oxford, 1974).

Grafton, Antony, *Leon Battista Alberti* (London, 2001).

—— , *Cardano's Cosmos* (London, 1999).

—— , 'Humanism, Magic and Science', *The Impact of Humanism on Western Europe*, ed. Anthony Goodman and Angus Mackay (Harlow, 1990), pp. 99–117.

Greenblatt, Stephen, *Renaissance Self-Fashioning* (Chicago, 1980).

—— , *Marvellous Possessions* (Oxford, 1992).

Greene, Thomas M., *The Light in Troy* (New Haven, 1982).

Grell, Ole Peter and Scribner, Bob (eds), *Tolerance and Intolerance in the European Reformation* (Cambridge, 1996).

Haar, James, *Essays on Italian Poetry and Music in the Renaissance* (Berkeley, 1986).

Haile, H.G., *Luther An Experiment in Biography* (Princeton, 1980).

Hainsworth, Peter, *Petrarch the Poet* (London, 1988).

Hale, J.R., *Renaissance Europe 1480–1520* (London, 1971).

—— , *The Civilization of Europe in the Renaissance* (London, 1993).

—— , (ed.), *A Concise Encyclopedia of the Italian Renaissance* (London, 1981).

—— , *Florence and the Medici: The Pattern of Control* (London, 1977).

Hall, Kathleen, M. and Wells, Margaret B. (eds), *Joachim du Bellay, Poems* (London, 1985).

Hallman, B., *Italian Cardinals: Reform and the Church as Property* (Berkeley, 1985).

Hart, Vaughan and Hicks, Peter (trans.), *Sebastiano Serlio: On Architecture* (New Haven & London, 1996).

Hartt, Frederick H., *A History of Italian Renaissance Art* (London, 1970).

HAY, DENYS, *The Church in 15th century Italy* (Cambridge, 1977).

HELGERSON, RICHARD, *Self-Crowned Laureates* (Berkeley, 1983).

HEXTER, J.H., *The Vision of Politics on the Eve of the Renaissance: More Machiavelli and Seyssel* (London, 1973).

HIMELICK, RAYMOND (trans.), *The Enchiridion of Erasmus* (Bloomington, 1963).

HOLMES, GEORGE, *Renaissance* (London, 1996).

HOPE, C., *Titian* (London, 1980).

HUIZINGA, J., *Erasmus of Rotterdam* (London, 1952).

—— , *Homo Ludens: A study of the Play Element in Culture* (London, 1998).

HUMFREY, PETER, *Painting in Renaissance Venice* (London, 1994).

HUSE, NORBERT and WALTERS, WOLFGANG, *The Art of Renaissance Venice: Architecture, Sculpture and Painting (1460–1590)* (London, 1990).

HUTCHISON, JANE CAMPBELL, *Albrecht Dürer*: A Biography (Princeton, 1990).

JARDINE, LISA, *Erasmus, Man of Letters* (Princeton, 1993).

—— , *Worldly Goods* (London, 1997).

JONES, R. and PENNY, N., *Raphael* (London, 1983).

JOSIPOVICI, G., *The world and the book: a study of modern fiction* (Basingstoke, 1994).

KAISER, WALTER, *Praisers of Folly* (London, 1964).

KEMP, MARTIN, *Leonardo da Vinci: The Marvellous Works of Nature and of Man* (London, 1981).

—— , (ed.), *Leonardo on Painting* (translations of writings) (London, 1989).

KENNEDY, W.J., *Sannazaro and The Uses of the Pastoral* (Hanover, NH, 1983).

KERR, HUGH T. (ed.), *A Compend of the Instititutes of Christan Religion by John Calvin* (London, 1965).

KIDWELL, CAROL, *Sannazaro's Arcadia* (London, 1993).

KINSMAN, R., *The Darker Vision of the Renaissance* (Berkeley, 1974).

KIRKPATRICK, R., *English and Italian Literature from Dante to Shakespeare* (London, 1995).

KNECHT, R.J., *Francis* (Cambridge, 1982).

KOYRÉ, A., *Galileo Studies* (trans. John Mepham) (Hassocks, 1978).

KRAILSHEIMER, A. (ed.), *The Continental Renaissance 1500–1600* (London, 1971).

KRAUTHEIMER, R., *Lorenzo Ghiberti* (Princeton, 1970).

KUSUKAWA, S., *The Transformations of Natural Philosophy* (Cambridge, 1995).

LEFF, GORDON, *The Dissolution of the Medieval Outlook* (New York, 1976).

LE GOFF, J., *Time, Work and Culture in the Middle Ages* (Chicago, 1980).

LÉVÊQUE, J.-J., *L'Ecole de Fontainebleau* (Ides et Calendes, Neuchâtel, 1984).

LINDBERG, CARTER, *The European Reformation* (Oxford & Cambridge MA, 1996).

McGOWAN, M., *Ideal Forms in the Age of Ronsard* (Berkeley, 1985).

McGRATH, A., *Luther's Theology of the Cross* (Oxford, 1985).

—— , *Reformation Thought* (Oxford, 1993).

MACLEHOSE, LOUISA S. (trans.), *Vasari on Technique* (New York, 1960).

McMAHON, A.P. (ed. and trans.), *Leonardo da Vinci, Treatises on Painting*, 2 vols (Princeton, 1956).

MACEY, P., 'Savanarola and the sixteenth-century motet', *Journal of the American Music Society* 36 (1983) 422–52.

MANN, NICHOLAS, *Petrarch* (Oxford, 1984).

MANN PHILLIPS, MARGARET (trans. and ed.), *The Adages of Erasmus* (Cambridge, 1964).

MARSH, CHARLES R., *Pienza: The Creation of a Renaissance City* (Ithaca, NY & London, 1987).

MARTIN, A. LYNN, *The Jesuit Mind* (Ithaca, NY & London, 1988).

MARTINES, LAURO, *Power and Imagination* (London, 1984).

MONTEIRO, G., *The Presence of Camões: His Influence in the Literature of England, America and Southern Africa* (Lexington, KY, 1996).

MORELL, A. GALEGO (ed.), *F. de Herrera: Annotaciones a Garcilaso* in *Garcilaso de la Vega* (Granada, 1966).

MURRAY, LINDA, *The Late Renaissance and Mannerism* (London, 1967).

NAVARRETE, IGNACIO, *Orphans of Petrarch* (Berkeley/Los Angeles/London, 1994).

NEBELSICK, HAROLD P., *The Renaissance, The Reformation and the Rise of Science* (Edinburgh, 1992).

NEWTON, ERIC, *Tintoretto* (London, 1952).

NUTTALL, A.D., *The New Mimesis* (London & New York, 1983).

OBERMANN, HEIKO A., *Forerunners of the Renaissance* (New York, 1966).

O'MALLEY, C.D., *Vesalius of Brussels* (Berkeley, 1964).

ORE, OYSTEIN, *Cardano, The Gambling Scholar* (with a trans. of Cardano's Latin *Book of Games of Chance*) (Princeton, 1953).

PALISCA, CLAUDE V., *Humanism in Italian Renaissance Musical Thought* (New Haven & London, 1985).

PANOFSKY, ERWIN, *Early Netherlandish Painting* (London, 1953).

—— , *The Life and Art of Albrecht Dürer* (Princeton, 1943).

—— , *Renaissance and Renascences* (London, 1965).

PARFITT, GEORGE, *John Donne: A Literary Life* (Basingstoke, 1989).

PARRY, J.H., *The Spanish Theory of Empire in the Sixteenth Century* (Cambridge, 1940).

PARTRIDGE, LOREN, *The Renaissance in Rome* (London, 1996).

PAUCK, WILHELM (trans. and ed.), *Luther: Lectures on the Romans*, The Library of Christian Classics vol. XV (London, 1961).

PERKINS, LEEMAN L., *Music in the Age of the Renaissance* (New York, 1998).

PETTEGREE, ANDREW *et al.*, *Calvinism in Europe 1540–1620* (Cambridge, 1994).

PHILLIPS, JANE E., (trans. and annotated) *Paraphrase on John* (Toronto/Buffalo/London, 1991).

PIGNATTI, TERISIO, *Giorgione* (trans. Clovis Whitfield) (London, 1971).

POESCHKE, JOACHIM, *Michelangelo and his World* (trans. Russell Stockman) (Munich, 1992 & New York, 1996).

POST, R.R., *The Modern Devotion: Confrontation with Reformation and Humanism* (Leiden, 1968).

POUJOL, J. (ed.), *The Monarchy of France* (Paris, 1961).

PUTNAM, HILARY, 'Fact and Value', in *Reason, Truth and History* (Cambridge, 1981).

——, ('The Craving for Objectivity', in *Realism with a Human Face*, ed. and introduced James Conant (Cambridge, MA & London, 1990).

QUINONES, RICHARD, *The Renaissance Discovery of Time* (Cambridge, MA, 1972).

RABIL, ALBERT, JR, *Erasmus and the New Testament: The Mind of a Christian Humanist* (San Antonio, 1972).

RADICE, BETTY (trans.), *Praise of Folly* (London, 1971).

RAITT, J., *Christian Spirituality* (London, 1982).

REBHORNE, WAYNE C., *Courtly Performances* (Detroit, 1978).

RICE, EUGENE (with Antony Grafton), *The Foundations of Early Modern Europe 1460–1559* (New York, 1994).

RIVERS, ELIAS L. *Garcilaso: Poems, A Critical Guide* (London, 1980).

ROBERTSON, ALEC, *Music of Mourning and Consolation* (London, 1967).

ROBINSON, FRANKLIN W. and NICHOLS, STEPHEN G. JR (eds), *The Meaning of Mannerism* (Hanover, NH, 1972).

ROSAND, DAVID, *Painting in Sixteenth-Century Venice* (Cambridge, 1997).

ROSSI, PAOLO, *Francis Bacon. From Magic to Science* (trans. S. Rabinovitch) (London, 1968).

ROWLANDS, JOHN, *Holbein: the Paintings of Hans Holbein the Younger* (London, 1985).

RUBIN, PATRICIA LEE, *Giorgio Vasari: Art and History* (London & New Haven, 1995).

RUSSELL, P.E., *Cervantes* (London, 1985).

RYAN, CHRISTOPHER (trans.), *Michelangelo, The Poems* (London, 1996).

—— , *The Poetry of Michelangelo* (London, 1998).

RYKWERT, JOSEPH *et al.* (trans. and intro.), *Alberti: On the Art of Building in Ten Books* (Cambridge, MA & London, 1988).

SALINGAR, LEO, *Shakespeare and the Traditions of Comedy* (Cambridge, 1974).

SANDERS, WILBUR, *John Donne's Poetry* (London, 1971).

SAUNDERS, J.B. DE C.M. and O'MALLEY, CHARLES D. (eds), *The Illustrations from the works of Andreas Vesalius* with annotations and translations (London, 1950).

SAYCE, RICHARD, *The Essays of Montaigne: A Critical Exploration* (London, 1972).

SCHMITT, CHARLES B. and SKINNER, QUENTIN, *The Cambridge History of Renaissance Philosophy* (Cambridge, 1988).

SCREECH, MICHAEL A., *Ecstasy and the Praise of Folly* (London, 1980).

—— , *Marot évangélique* (Geneva, 1967).

——— , (trans.), *Michel de Montaigne: The Complete Essays* (London, 1991).

SCRIBNER, R.W., *The German Reformation* (London, 1986).

SETTIS, SALVATORE, *Giorgione's Tempest: Interpreting the hidden subject* (trans. Ellen Bianchin) (London, 1991).

SHEARMAN, JOHN, *Mannerism* (London, 1977).

SHERMAN, WILLIAM H., 'Trade and Travel', in *Blackwell Companion to Renaissance Drama*, ed. Arthur F. Kinney (forthcoming).

SIDER, ROBERT D. (ed.), *The Collected Works of Erasmus, New Testament Scholarship* (Toronto/ Buffalo/London, 1984).

SKINNER, QUENTIN, *The Foundations of Modern Political Thought* (Cambridge, 1978).

——— , *Machiavelli* (Oxford, 1981).

SMITH, PAUL JULIAN, *Writing in the Margins* (Oxford, 1988).

SMITH, P.M., *Clément Marot: Poet of the French Renaissance* (London, 1970).

SNYDER, JAMES, *Northern Renaissance Art from 1350 to 1575* (New York, 1985).

SPEARING, A.C., *Medieval to Renaissance in English Poetry* (Cambridge, 1985).

SPENCER, JOHN R. (trans. and intro.), *Leon Battista: On Painting* (New Haven & London, 1956).

STAROBINSKI, J., *Montaigne in Motion* (trans. A. Goldhammer) (Chicago, 1985).

STRAUSS, WALTER L. (ed.), *The Complete Engravings, Etchings and Drypoints of Albrecht Dürer* (Toronto, 1972).

STRIEDER, PETER, *Albrecht Dürer: Paintings, Prints and Drawings* (trans. Nancy M. Gordon and Walter L. Strauss) (New York, 1982).

STROHM, REINHARD, *The Rise of European Music 1380–1500* (Cambridge, 1993).

SUBRANYAM, SANJAY, *The Career and Life of Vasco da Gama* (Cambridge, 1997).

SUMMERS, DAVID, *Michelangelo and the Language of Art* (Princeton, 1981).

——— , *The Judgement of Sense* (Cambridge, 1987).

TAMBIAH, S.J., *Magic, Science, Religion and the Scope of Rationality* (Cambridge, 1990).

TAFURI, M. (ed.), *Giulio Romano* (Cambridge, 1998).

TAYLOR, CHARLES, *The Sources of Self: The Making of Modern Identity* (Cambridge, 1989).

THOMSON, PATRICIA, *Sir Thomas Wyatt and his Background* (London, 1964).

TINAGLI, P., *Women in Italian Renaissance Art* (Manchester, 1997).

TOCCI, LUIGI MICHELINI (ed.), *Giovanni Santi: La vita e gesta di Federigo di Montefeltro* (Vatican, 1985).

TODD, JOHN M., *Luther: A Life* (London, 1982).

TODD, MARGOT, *Reformation to Revolution: Politics and Religion in Early Modern England* (Cambridge, 1995).

TOMLINSON, GARY, *Monteverdi and the End of the Renaissance* (Oxford, 1990).

——— , *Music in Renaissance Magic* (Chicago & London, 1993).

——— , (ed.), *Strunk's The Renaissance* (new ed., New York & London, 1998).

TUCKER, HUGO, *The Poet's Odyssey and Joachim du Bellay and the Antiquitez de Rome* (Oxford, 1990).

TURBET, RICHARD, *William Byrd: A Guide to Research* (New York, 1987).

TURNER, PAUL (trans.), *Thomas More: Utopia* (London, 1965).

UNGAR, PETER D., 'Pienza under the sign of the hour-glass: A study in observation and perception' (unpub. diss., Cambridge University, 1995).

VAUGHAN, RICHARD, *Philip the Bold* (London, 1979).

—— , *John the Fearless* (London, 1979).

—— , *Charles the Bold* (London, 1979).

VICKERS, BRIAN, *English Science, Bacon to Newton* (Cambridge, 1987).

WADE, CLAIRE LYNCH (trans. and ed.), *Marguerite of Navarre: Les Prisons* (New York, 1989).

WALLACE, D., *Boccaccio* (Cambridge, 1991).

WATKINS, GLENN, *Gesualdo: The Man and his Music*, with Preface by Stravinsky (Oxford, 1991).

WHITE, JOHN, *The Birth and Rebirth of Pictorial Space* (London, 1957).

WILDE, JOHANNES, *Venetian Art from Bellini to Titian* (Oxford, 1974).

WILLIAMSON, EDWIN, *The Half-Way House of Fiction: Don Quixote and Arthurian Romance* (Oxford, 1984).

WIND, E., *Pagan Mysteries in the Renaissance* (Oxford, 1980).

WOHL, H. (ed.), *A. Condivi: The Life of Michelangelo* (Baton Rouge, 1976).

WOODHOUSE, J.R., *Castiglione* (Edinburgh, 1978).

YATES, FRANCES, *Giordano Bruno and the Hermetic Tradition* (London, 1999).

—— , *The French Academies of the Sixteenth Century* (London, 1947).

INDEX